INSTITUTE OF MODERN LANGUAGES RESEARCH
UNIVERSITY OF LONDON

BITHELL SERIES OF DISSERTATIONS
VOLUME 49

Arthur Schnitzler in Great Britain
An Examination of Power and Translation

INSTITUTE OF MODERN LANGUAGES RESEARCH

BITHELL SERIES OF DISSERTATIONS

Launched in 1978 by the then Institute of Germanic Studies, the Bithell Series of Dissertations is designed to help young scholars publish recent work of high quality which has been accepted for the award of a research degree by a University in the United Kingdom or the Republic of Ireland. Volumes 14 to 41 were published in conjunction with the Modern Humanities Research Association. From 2015 onwards, publication has been resumed by the Institute of Modern Languages Research (IMLR). For a list of previous volumes in the series, see https://modernlanguages.sas.ac.uk/publications/bithell-series-dissertations.

Theses for possible inclusion in the series are considered by the Bithell Editorial Board twice annually, in May and November. Recommendations for theses to be considered should be made by the supervisor and/or examiner(s), should be accompanied by a copy of the Examiners' Report and Abstract, and sent to Dr Godela Weiss-Sussex at the Institute of Modern Languages Research, School of Advanced Study, University of London, Senate House, Malet Street, London WC1E 7HU (email: godela.weiss-sussex@sas.ac.uk).

Arthur Schnitzler in Great Britain

An Examination of Power and Translation

by
Nicole Robertson

Institute of Modern Languages Research

2022

Published by the
Institute of Modern Languages Research
School of Advanced Study, University of London
Senate House, Malet Street, London WC1E 7HU
https://modernlanguages.sas.ac.uk

The Institute of Modern Languages Research is an imprint of University of London Press

Cover image: Detail from the poster for the National Theatre's 1979 production of *Undiscovered Country* in a version by Tom Stoppard at the Olivier Theatre, London. Image courtesy of the National Theatre Archive.

First published 2022

ISBN 978-0-85457-281-6

ISSN 0266-7932

CONTENTS

ACKNOWLEDGMENTS

I could not have written this book without the sustained, sympathetic and generous support of my primary thesis supervisor, Dr Judith Beniston. Her knowledge and insight guided me throughout; and her encouragement and understanding were invaluable as I explored my own ideas. I have also been very fortunate in receiving help from Dr Geraldine Horan, my secondary supervisor, at crucial moments in the planning, researching and writing of the thesis. Thanks are owed to Dr Geraldine Brodie and Dr Mererid Puw Davies for their enormously helpful advice after reading and examining my upgrade submission in 2016. I am indebted to the Arts and Humanities Research Council for their generous funding; and to the UK Team for *Arthur Schnitzler digital. Digitale historisch-kritische Edition (Werke 1905–1931)* for granting me the three-year studentship. It was immensely rewarding to carry out my research in association with the UK Team and to know that, even in the midst of what could have been a lonely endeavour, I was part of a close community of academics grappling with Schnitzler in Cambridge, London and Bristol. Additional funding was provided by the Deutscher Akademischer Austauschdienst, SELCS UCL, the Institute of Modern Languages Research and the AHRC for research and conferences abroad. I cannot overstate how profitable I found these trips.

The staff at the Harry Ransom Center, University of Texas at Austin, the Theatermuseum in Vienna, the Deutsches Literaturarchiv in Marbach and the BBC Written Archives Centre in Reading, alongside those at innumerable other libraries and archives, gave me vital help in negotiating the wealth of material consulted during this project. My thanks also go to Pam Ferris and Richard De Lisle for permission to cite personal correspondence. Content from the Arthur Schnitzler Papers at Cambridge University Library is reproduced by kind permission of the Syndics of Cambridge University Library. BBC copyright content is reproduced courtesy of the British Broadcasting Corporation. All rights reserved. Reviews from the Schnitzler Press-Cuttings Archive, EUL MS 214, are cited courtesy of Special Collections, University of Exeter. Heinrich Schnitzler's papers are cited by kind permission of Michael Schnitzler; the correspondence between Heinrich Schnitzler and Charles Marowitz by permission of Jane Windsor Marowitz; Frank Marcus's papers by permission of the Frank Marcus Estate. Tom Stoppard kindly granted permission to quote from unpublished drafts of *Dalliance* and *Undiscovered Country*. April de Angelis's *Cashcows* is similarly cited by kind permission of the author.

Friends in London, Dorset and Cambridge have listened (and read) with patience and good humour as I have thought aloud about translation and power and reflected *ad tedium* on the life of the researcher. I am especially grateful to Ellen, Thea and Kate. My thanks also go to my parents, who have frequently cared for and fed me and my growing family, given endless encouragement over the years and ultimately managed to read a whole draft of the thesis when I could no longer bear to look at it.

Finally, JES, AIS, HHS and MJHS: words fail me.

NOTE ON REFERENCING

The following abbreviations are used in the text:

Briefe I	Arthur Schnitzler, *Briefe*, 2 vols, I: *1875–1912*, ed. by Therese Nickl and Heinrich Schnitzler (Frankfurt a. M.: Fischer, 1981)
Briefe II	Arthur Schnitzler, *Briefe*, 2 vols, II: *1913–1931*, ed. by Peter Michael Braunwarth and others (Frankfurt a. M.: Fischer, 1984)
CUL	Cambridge University Library
DLA	Deutsches Literaturarchiv, Marbach
ICB	International Copyright Bureau
LCP	Lord Chamberlain's Archive
Schn	Nachlass Heinrich Schnitzler, Korrespondenz, Theatermuseum, Vienna
Tagebuch	Arthur Schnitzler, *Tagebuch*, ed. by Peter Michael Braunwarth and others, 10 vols (Vienna: Verlag der Österreichischen Akademie der Wissenschaften, 1981–2000)

INTRODUCTION

Arthur Schnitzler's position as one of the major figures in European Modernist literature is well established. He has been feted in Austria and abroad, both during his lifetime (1862–1931) and in the seventy-five years since the end of the Second World War, for his extensive corpus of prose and dramatic works. Today he is regarded as part of the Western canon: his works appear on university reading lists; his plays are performed in major theatres in Vienna and beyond; and he deservedly attracts significant scholarly attention. However, his popularity has waxed and waned over the decades, with varying responses to his Jewish identity, the shifting politics of Central Europe in the twentieth century and the sometimes uneasy, if not belligerent, relations between German-speaking countries and the rest of the world. Not only are Schnitzler's works of interest for their intrinsic value, therefore, but also, through consideration of their reception, as reflections of the cultural and political undulations of the receiving contexts. There has accordingly been a wealth of energy dedicated to examining Schnitzler's writing and its dissemination. Very little of that attention, however, has concerned itself with Schnitzler's works in English translation. A quick glance at the tables of English translations in Appendices 1–3 should explain why that anomaly could not continue. Schnitzler very clearly had, and continues to have, a presence in the English language on both sides of the Atlantic. Moreover, whereas there have been monographs addressing Schnitzler's reception in France, the Netherlands, Sweden, Japan and Russia, the scholarship on Schnitzler's works in Britain has generally been limited to shorter discussions of particular texts or particular periods of time. Against that background, this study attempts a more extended synthesis, providing a broader picture of the processes involved in transferring Schnitzler's works to Britain.

Whenever a text is translated from one language into another that text changes. Such change is inevitable; the days of thinking that a translated text can in any way replicate the source are long gone.[1] Questions then arise

1 David Johnston, an important advocate for moving away from ideas of 'translation as second-order reproduction', demonstrates the continuing need to explain and justify that position: 'Sister Act: Reflection, Refraction, and Performance in the Translation of *La Dama Boba*', *Bulletin of the Comediantes*, 67 (2015), 79–98.

as to how a translation relates to its source text and why. This study takes up the second of those enquiries. It asks about the factors determining textual production: who are the key agents in the processes of selecting, rewriting and producing foreign texts for new readers or audiences? Is it passion or financial need that drives a translator to pursue a translation project? What role do domestic and international laws play in determining the presentation of a text in another language? Why are some texts translated almost immediately after initial production in the source culture while others require decades before they are presented abroad? All these questions might be gathered under a more general statement of enquiry: how is power exercised over processes of textual production and dissemination? By investigating power and translation in the context of Schnitzler's works in Britain, this study answers the above and related questions through a concrete case study informed by detailed archival research. The findings and analysis presented below emphasize the contingent nature of translation, whilst elucidating the varied forces affecting that contingency.

This Introduction provides a brief portrait of Arthur Schnitzler, as well as describing the early international dissemination of his work and subsequent scholarly reception abroad. Using existing academic approaches to Schnitzler reception as a springboard, it sets out how this study differs from its predecessors in terms of the material explored and the methodologies applied. It then expands on and refines the definitions of power and control, collaboration and agency, adaptation and translation to be adopted in the rest of the book. Finally, this Introduction assesses processes of archiving and archival research as further interpretative layers (alongside translation and theatre production) affecting our understanding of any text and as further instances of the exercise of power. An explanation of the corpus selected for analysis and the structure of the book is provided at the end of the chapter.

Schnitzler's Biography

Arthur Schnitzler was born on 15 May 1862 to upper-middle-class Jewish parents in Vienna; he was the first of three children.[2] His father was a

2 The following biographical précis and subsequent biographical detail derive from a number of primary and secondary sources. The former include, most notably, Schnitzler's diary (Arthur Schnitzler, *Tagebuch*, ed. by Peter Michael Braunwarth and others, 10 vols (Vienna: Verlag der Österreichischen Akademie der Wissenschaften, 1981–2000)); his autobiography (Arthur Schnitzler, *Jugend in Wien. Eine Autobiographie*, ed. by Therese Nickl and Heinrich Schnitzler (Vienna: Molden, 1968)); and his published letters (Arthur Schnitzler, *Briefe*, 2 vols, I: *1875–1912*, ed. by Therese Nickl and Heinrich Schnitzler (Frankfurt a. M.: Fischer, 1981); Arthur Schnitzler, *Briefe*, 2 vols, II: *1913–1931*, ed. by Peter Michael Braunwarth and others (Frankfurt a. M.: Fischer, 1984)). The volumes of the diaries are arranged chronologically. Hereinafter references to the diaries will be identified by

successful and well-respected laryngologist who treated many of the city's singers and actors and thus brought his son into contact with both the medical and the theatrical worlds. Schnitzler was expected to train as a doctor and he duly studied and qualified to practise in medicine. Nevertheless, his real passion was writing; and his earlier diary entries and autobiography are the testimony of a young man determinedly producing short stories and plays alongside his formal study.[3] When his father died in May 1893 Schnitzler left the Allgemeine Poliklinik, where he had worked as his father's assistant, and set up his own private practice. This marked the beginning of an even more energetic dedication to his writing.[4] In the same year two of his works were performed for the first time: *Abschiedssouper*, a one-act play from the *Anatol* cycle, was produced at the Stadttheater Bad Ischl; and *Das Märchen*, a three-act play, at the Deutsches Volkstheater in Vienna. It was also during these years that Schnitzler began to associate with the group which would subsequently come to be known as Jung Wien and counted among its members Hugo von Hofmannsthal, Richard Beer-Hofmann, Hermann Bahr, Peter Altenberg and Felix Salten.[5]

Over the following four decades Schnitzler maintained a prolific level of writing and enjoyed a high degree of success at home in Austria, in Germany and further afield. During his lifetime seventeen of his full-length plays were produced, as well as four cycles of one-act plays and six shorter dramatic works.[6] A number of the plays were initially staged at Vienna's Royal-Imperial Burgtheater, the 'jewel in the crown' of the Viennese theatre world:[7] *Liebelei* in 1895, *Zwischenspiel* in 1905 and *Das weite Land* in 1911, for example. Schnitzler also wrote and published two novels and almost fifty short stories and novellas. He was celebrated by his peers and the public and repeatedly courted controversy with stories and plays which picked at the hypocrisies and

'*Tagebuch*' followed by the relevant date; correspondence from the *Briefe* will be identified by '*Briefe* I' or '*Briefe* II' followed by the relevant date; page references from *Jugend in Wien* will be given in the text. Beyond those secondary sources expressly cited, the following have been immensely helpful: Konstanze Fliedl, *Arthur Schnitzler* (Stuttgart: Reclam, 2005), pp. 14–72; Dagmar C. G. Lorenz, 'Introduction', in *A Companion to the Works of Arthur Schnitzler*, ed. by Dagmar C. G. Lorenz (Rochester, NY: Camden House, 2003), pp. 1–24; and W. E. Yates, *Schnitzler, Hofmannsthal, and the Austrian Theatre* (New Haven, CT and London: Yale University Press, 1992), pp. 28–42.

3 See, for example, *Tagebuch*, 27.10.1879 and *Tagebuch*, 3.6.1882; and, more generally, on the conflict Schnitzler felt between medicine and writing see Fliedl, *Arthur Schnitzler*, pp. 19–22.

4 Fliedl, *Arthur Schnitzler*, p. 25.

5 Fliedl, *Arthur Schnitzler*, p. 22.

6 See 'Werke', in *Schnitzler-Handbuch. Leben – Werk – Wirkung*, ed. by Christoph Jürgensen, Wolfgang Lukas and Michael Scheffel (Stuttgart and Weimar: Metzler, 2014), pp. 57–142.

7 W. E. Yates, 'Continuity and Discontinuity in Viennese Theatrical Life from the 1860s to the Turn of the Century', *Austrian Studies*, 16 (2008), 51–68 (p. 53).

insecurities of contemporary Austrian society. The novella *Lieutenant Gustl* (1900) was viewed by the military authorities as an insult to the reputation of the Austro-Hungarian army, resulting in Schnitzler being stripped of his commission as an officer in the reserve. A critically acclaimed set of three one-act plays (*Paracelsus*, *Die Gefährtin* and *Der grüne Kakadu*) was withdrawn from the Burgtheater in December 1899 as a result of 'pressure from Court circles'.[8] The play for which he is perhaps now best known, *Reigen*, although first published in 1900, was only performed publicly twenty years later, when it was the subject first of litigation (Berlin, 1920–21) and subsequently of prohibition on the grounds of public disorder (Vienna, 1921).[9] Finally, his five-act comedy *Professor Bernhardi*, a behind-the-scenes hospital drama exploring end-of-life medical ethics and anti-Semitism in clerical politics, was completed in 1912 but censored in Vienna until after the collapse of the Monarchy in 1918.[10]

Notwithstanding the varied, provocative and explicitly political themes explored in his works (as evident in the controversies surrounding them), from very early in his writing career Schnitzler was pigeonholed by the domestic press as a decadent aesthete: death, love and destiny (or, as he himself ruefully observed, 'Lieb und Tod und Spiel')[11] were the thematic parameters imposed on him and they continued to plague his reputation, even

8 Yates, *Schnitzler, Hofmannsthal and the Austrian Theatre*, p. 32. *Der grüne Kakadu* was the trouble-maker amongst the three one-act plays, rich as it was 'in implications for the society of 1899, especially in the depiction of self-centred aristocrats' of the French Ancien Régime; it had been banned by the Berlin censor a year earlier, in 1898.

9 The private print run of two hundred copies in 1900 was followed by wider publication in 1903 (Wiener Verlag). Schnitzler himself blocked later attempts to produce the play; his son, Heinrich Schnitzler, adopted the same stance as trustee of his father's estate, so that it was not performed again in German (or indeed in any language in those countries where copyright law allowed Schnitzler, or subsequently Heinrich Schnitzler, to refuse permission) until 1982 (*Schnitzlers 'Reigen'. Zehn Dialoge und ihre Skandalgeschichte. Analysen und Dokumente*, ed. by Alfred Pfoser, Kristina Pfoser-Schewig and Gerhard Renner, 2 vols (Frankfurt a. M.: Fischer, 1993), I, 44–45, 140–51 and II, 40–75). For a general introduction to the 'erotic revolution' in Vienna at the time, see Edward Timms, *Karl Kraus: Apocalyptic Satirist*, 2 vols (New Haven, CT and London: Yale University Press, 1986–2005), II: *The Post-War Crisis and the Rise of the Swastika* (2005), pp. 116–20. A history of the reception of *Reigen* at the beginning of the twentieth century and its re-emergence on the expiry of copyright toward the end of the twentieth century is included in Chapter 4 of this book.

10 For detailed consideration of the censorship and reception of *Professor Bernhardi* see W. E. Yates, 'The Tendentious Reception of Professor Bernhardi: Documentation in Schnitzler's Collection of Press-Cuttings', in *Vienna 1900: From Altenberg to Wittgenstein*, ed. by Edward Timms and Ritchie Robertson (= *Austrian Studies*, 1 (1990)), pp. 108–25. See also Jacques Le Rider, 'Warum *Professor Bernhardi* von der Wiener Zensur verboten wurde', in *Textschicksale. Das Werk Arthur Schnitzlers im Kontext der Moderne*, ed. by Wolfgang Lukas and Michael Scheffel (Berlin and Boston, MA: de Gruyter, 2017), pp. 231–50.

11 Arthur Schnitzler, *Aphorismen und Betrachtungen* (Frankfurt a. M.: Fischer, 1967), p. 295.

posthumously, at home and abroad. The popularity of three early dramatic works, discussed individually in Chapters 1, 2 and 4, fed into the image thus created by Viennese critics. The three works were *Anatol* (1893), *Liebelei* (1895) and *Reigen* (1900). Although quite different in terms of form and tone, the three plays share as subject matter their characters' pursuit of romantic relations. Together they illustrate the prevalence of the aforementioned themes in Schnitzler's international representation, at both the beginning and the end of the twentieth century, which took a particularly tenacious hold on Anglophone reception.

Schnitzler in Translation: International Reception

Schnitzler's works began to be translated and published abroad very early in his writing career. It seems likely that the first translation published was a Polish version of the short story 'Mein Freund Ypsilon' in the Warsaw newspaper *Życie* in 1889, i.e., four years before the death of Schnitzler's father and the moment when his own commitment to writing experienced a change of gear. The production of *Liebelei* at the Burgtheater in 1895 represented his launch onto the international theatre scene. It was reviewed abroad and was quickly to be found in performance in a number of cities across Europe.[12] Notwithstanding the interest thereby prompted, however, it would take some time before the play was produced in translation in any of the major theatre cities. Indeed, it was not produced in French in Paris until after Schnitzler's death.[13] The fate of *Liebelei* is symptomatic of Schnitzler's early reception abroad more generally, marked as it was by inconsistencies. Judith Beniston's recent comparative assessment highlights the historical tendency for different countries to regard Schnitzler as either a dramatist or a writer of prose fiction, but rarely as both.[14] In the same study Beniston illustrates the impact which unconnected global copyright legislation had on both production patterns and remuneration. Even with those discrepancies, however, and the caesura brought on by the First World War, Schnitzler was sufficiently celebrated in 1923 to be received by a film crew on his arrival in Sweden for a lecturing tour.[15] By the time of his death a large part of his published corpus had been translated into multiple other languages and, indeed, some works translated several times within one foreign language.

12 See Chapter 1 for further details.

13 Judith Beniston, 'Schnitzler und die "Uebersetzungs-Miseren"', in *Textschicksale*, ed. by Lukas and Scheffel, pp. 251–66 (p. 252).

14 Beniston, 'Schnitzler und die "Uebersetzungs-Miseren"', esp. pp. 252–53.

15 *Tagebuch*, 17.5.1923.

Posthumous dissemination was similarly distinguished by inconsistencies across time, place and language. Heterogeneous copyright laws continued to carve up the globe into discrete areas of differing cultural transferability. The position was further complicated by Schnitzler's own testimonial decisions: although his estate was largely left to be managed by his son, Heinrich Schnitzler, the French translation rights were given to agent and translator Suzanne Clauser, leading to a different approach to Francophone dissemination. The rise of Nazi power in Central Europe and the Anschluss in 1938 resulted in an interruption to domestic consumption, while the Second World War inevitably reduced international interest. Nevertheless, two film adaptations, which enjoyed huge commercial and critical success, reflect Schnitzler's longevity and global appeal in the face of macro-political obstacles: in 1950 Max Ophüls directed a film adaptation of *Reigen* in French (*La Ronde*); and in 1999 Stanley Kubrick directed an English-language adaptation of the *Traumnovelle* starring Tom Cruise and Nicole Kidman (*Eyes Wide Shut*).

Reception of Schnitzler's corpus has been buoyed by scholarly attention to the works, beginning during Schnitzler's lifetime and gaining new momentum from the 1960s onwards.[16] That interest has extended, subsequently, to a consideration of his international reception. The individual studies produced have tended to focus on one particular country and have generally adopted a target-oriented approach, assessing how Schnitzler fits into the home context. Margot Elfving Vogel's monograph on Schnitzler in Sweden, for example, charts the discernible patterns of reviewing performances and publications and pays special attention to the political leanings of the individual reviewers and the newspapers and journals for which they wrote.[17] Vogel takes as her theoretical framework Felix Vodička's Structuralist ideas about the role of the critic; there is relatively little commentary, therefore, on the translated texts themselves. Yukio Ozawa's study of Japanese reception also starts with texts performed and published during Schnitzler's lifetime, but frustratingly goes no further.[18] Ozawa limits his remit to the forty-odd references to Japan or Japanese culture in Schnitzler's diaries, presenting in catalogue form the biographical details of the people mentioned and reciting letters and reviews often already published elsewhere. In this respect Ozawa's study is not wholly dissimilar to other, earlier studies, providing documents and lists from the perspective of the target culture. Beatrice Schrumpf's Master's thesis from 1931

16 A brief analysis of the renaissance in Schnitzler studies in the 1960s can be found in Chapter 2.

17 Margot Elfving Vogel, *Schnitzler in Schweden. Zur Rezeption seiner Werke* (Uppsala and Stockholm: Almqvist & Wiksell International, 1979).

18 Yukio Ozawa, *Japanisches bei Arthur Schnitzler. Japanische Einflüsse auf Schnitzler und die Rezeption Schnitzlers in Japan* (Frankfurt a. M.: Lang, 1995).

on American reception is a case in point;[19] while Elisabeth Heresch's study of Schnitzler in Russia is similarly concerned with newspaper and journal reviews, albeit with a limited analysis of some translated texts: the prospect is undeniably Russo-centric, with very little consideration of Schnitzler's side of the relationship.[20]

Only later studies have properly been able to take advantage of biographical resources published or made more readily available in recent decades; the landscape continues to improve in this regard, with the launch in May 2019 of *Arthur Schnitzler Tagebuch* online. Karl Zieger's monograph on reception in France focuses on the period between the first French translation in 1894 (*Les Emplettes de Noël*) and 1938 by reason of the abundance of unpublished correspondence concerning those earlier years of transmission.[21] Zieger succeeds in incorporating the material to paint a vivid picture of Schnitzler's interactions with his French intermediaries, agents and translators. Part of the fascination with Schnitzler, however, is his longevity, i.e., his ongoing interest to today's directors, filmmakers, theatre practitioners and audiences. That aspect of French reception Zieger leaves for another study.[22]

Donald G. Daviau's review of American reception considers the peak periods before 1931 (incorporating much of the work done by Schrumpf) and after 1961.[23] His approach is predominantly quantitative rather than

19 Beatrice Schrumpf, 'The Perception of Arthur Schnitzler in the United States' (unpublished Master's thesis, Columbia University, 1931). Schrumpf's survey of the reception of both dramatic and prose works in America is only available in the UK in typescript among the Arthur Schnitzler Papers at Cambridge University Library, A239,2. Content from that collection is reproduced by kind permission of the Syndics of Cambridge University Library.

20 Elisabeth Heresch, *Schnitzler und Russland. Aufnahme – Wirkung – Kritik* (Vienna: Braumüller, 1982). See also Mariana Virginia Lăzărescu, 'Zur Rezeption Schnitzlers in Rumänien. Schnitzlers Beziehungen zur rumänischen Literatur', in *Arthur Schnitzler: Zeitgenossenschaften/Contemporaneities*, ed. by Ian Foster and Florian Krobb (Bern: Lang, 2002), pp. 143–53. In addition to this article on the Romanian reception, there have been shorter studies relating to Schnitzler's reception in Belgium (Leopold R. G. Decloedt, 'Eine mühsame Reise ins Unbekannte. Arthur Schnitzler und Belgien', in *Zeitgenossenschaften*, ed. by Foster and Krobb, pp. 55–70); China (Xiaoqiao Wu, 'Die Rezeption Arthur Schnitzlers in China', in *Textschicksale*, ed. by Lukas and Scheffel, pp. 267–80); and Italy (Konstanze Fliedl, 'Arthur Schnitzler und Italien', in *Ferne Heimat – Nahe Fremde. Bei Dichtern und Nachdenkern*, ed. by Eduard Beutner und Karlheinz Rossbacher (Würzburg: Königshausen & Neumann, 2008), pp. 132–47).

21 Karl Zieger, *Arthur Schnitzler et la France, 1894–1938. Enquête sur une réception* (Villeneuve d'Ascq: Presses Universitaires du Septentrion, 2012), p. 25.

22 Zieger, *Arthur Schnitzler et la France*, p. 307. Zieger cites three doctoral theses which address later French reception but are limited to only short periods or a narrow set of works (p. 18).

23 Donald G. Daviau, 'The Reception of Arthur Schnitzler in the United States', in *The Fortunes of German Writers in America: Studies in Literary Reception*, ed. by Wolfgang Elfe, James Hardin and Gunther Holst (Columbia, SC: University of South Carolina Press, 1992), pp. 145–65.

qualitative: he assesses reception on the basis of the number and spread of publications and productions across the States rather than examining individual translation or presentation choices. Daviau finds that, as in Europe, a 'standard' image of Schnitzler 'as a decadent aesthete with a limited artistic range' had been created at the beginning of the twentieth century, courtesy of the frequency with which *Anatol* was performed and published.[24] Even in the second half of the last century that view has prevailed, as the same three works have continued to dominate American reception: *Anatol*, *Liebelei* and *Reigen*.[25] The findings set out in the following chapters demonstrate that this repertoire of three works repeatedly performed in America enjoyed popular success in Britain as well.

Prior to Beniston's analysis, only Hans Roelofs had considered international reception from Schnitzler's perspective or paid attention to the role of copyright legislation in the dissemination of Schnitzler's works. Like Zieger, Roelofs makes substantial use of the *Nachlass*, employing the documents which have been preserved to trace Schnitzler's relationships with his translators and agents, most notably with Alice van Nahuys, who was responsible for a significant part of the dissemination of Schnitzler's works in the Netherlands.[26] Roelofs also considers the undocumented dissemination of Schnitzler's works, pointing to the unhelpful state of copyright law at the beginning of the twentieth century to explain why Schnitzler's recorded income from the Netherlands very probably reflected only a small proportion of his works translated and published in that part of the world.

Britain has not been entirely neglected by academia; and a summary of the work already done in this field is now provided. Such a summary, whilst setting out the research on which this book builds, also demonstrates the need for the broader study provided here. Margit Dirscherl's brief but dense survey of reception in England represents the first attempt to give an overview of Schnitzler's reception in (part of) Britain, but is necessarily confined by the strictures of writing for a handbook.[27] Katja Krebs makes an invaluable contribution to the scholarship on the early decades of transmission in her *Cultural Dissemination and Translational Communities: German Drama in English Translation, 1900–1914*. Krebs stresses the significant role that German

24 Daviau, 'The Reception of Arthur Schnitzler', p. 150.

25 Daviau, 'The Reception of Arthur Schnitzler', p. 159.

26 Hans Roelofs, *'Man weiss eigentlich wenig von einander'. Arthur Schnitzler und die Niederlande, 1895–1940* (Amsterdam: Rodopi, 1989), p. 95.

27 Margit Dirscherl, 'England', in *Schnitzler-Handbuch*, ed. by Jürgensen, Lukas and Scheffel, pp. 369–71.

theatre, largely in translation, played in the transformation of the London stage during the Edwardian years.[28] She provides a wide-ranging assessment of the major contemporary German and Austrian dramatists translated and performed during those years, drawing on posters, programmes and reviews to support her analysis of contemporaneous reception. A doctoral thesis by Nicholas John Dekker covering a similar period includes Schnitzler among the 'German' influences on the British stage.[29] Krebs has co-authored with Kevin Bartholomew an entry on English-language translations of Schnitzler's works in the *Encyclopaedia of Literary Translation into English* which reviews a small selection of the plays and prose translations but without mention of their reception. Schnitzler's two visits to London, in 1888 and 1897, form the subject of an essay by Charmian Brinson and Marian Malet in which the authors contextualize the archival material that has survived from the period by reference to both Schnitzler's own life in Austria and the German émigré scene in London at the time.[30]

A few studies on particular plays or individual translations also warrant mention here. Catherine Spencer's essay 'Translating Schnitzler for the Stage: Losing *Liebelei*?' takes two English translations of *Liebelei* (Tom Stoppard's *Dalliance*, performed in 1986; and *Flirtations*, translated by Arthur S. Wensinger and Clinton Atkinson and published in New York in 1992) as a basis for re-examination of the topical theoretical debates in theatre translation studies; and a Master's thesis by Julia-Stefanie Maier compares London productions of Stoppard's two translations of Schnitzler (*Dalliance* and *Undiscovered Country*) with German-language productions in Vienna of Stoppard's plays *Rosencrantz and Guildenstern are Dead* and *Travesties*.[31] The popularity of *Reigen* as a source for English rewriting, in particular after the ban on performance was effectively lifted in 1982, has also given rise to critical analysis: the productions staged in 1982 itself are considered by Gerd K. Schneider in his expansive treatment of *Reigen* reception; and a textual

28 Katja Krebs, *Cultural Dissemination and Translational Communities: German Drama in English Translation, 1900–1914* (Manchester: St Jerome, 2007), pp. 32–51.

29 Nicholas John Dekker, 'The Modern Catalyst: German Influences on the British Stage, 1890–1918' (unpublished doctoral thesis, Ohio State Universtiy, 2007). Both Krebs and Dekker produce a chronology of productions at the end of their respective studies.

30 Charmian Brinson and Marian Malet, '"Die sonderbarste Stadt, die man sich denken kann"? Arthur Schnitzler in London', in *Zeitgenossenschaften*, ed. by Foster and Krobb, pp. 71–87.

31 Catherine Spencer, 'Translating Schnitzler for the Stage: Losing *Liebelei*?', in *Zeitgenossenschaften*, ed. by Foster and Krobb, pp. 273–90; Julia-Stefanie Maier, 'Cannibalizing Cultures: Schnitzler in London, Stoppard in Vienna. The Influence of Socio-Cultural, Literary, and Power-Related Norms on Drama Translation' (unpublished Master's thesis, University of Vienna, 2010).

analysis comparing some of those translations was carried out by Konstanze Fliedl.[32] David Hare's 'freely adapted' version of the play, *The Blue Room* (1998), forms the subject of articles by Ana Fernandez-Capparros Turina (2013) and Heidi Zojer (2009).[33] Apart from Zojer, however, who includes in her comparison an academic translation produced by J. M. Q. Davies in 2004, there has not been any work on translations of *Reigen* from the twenty-first century and certainly no scholarship regarding performances of the work after 2000.

New Departures

Notwithstanding these contributions, therefore, there remains a clear gap in the literature where a full survey of Schnitzler's reception in Britain should stand. This book addresses that gap in a number of ways. First, on a fundamental level, it covers over a century of transmission and, although focused on only a few plays, includes tables displaying all translations of drama published, performed or broadcast in Britain from 1903 to the present day (Appendices 1, 2 and 3). These tables provide what was not discoverable elsewhere, namely an overall picture of Schnitzler production in English in Britain. Second, this book considers the influential role that Heinrich Schnitzler, Arthur Schnitzler's son, played as trustee of his father's estate between his father's death in 1931 and his own in 1982. The correspondence between Heinrich Schnitzler and the estate's British literary agent, Eric Glass, sheds new light, for example, on the radio and television productions undertaken by the BBC in the 1950s, 1960s and 1970s. Finally, this study looks at the most recent publications and productions from the last forty years, a period in Schnitzler reception which has received less attention than the first half of the century, and thereby makes a contribution to wider scholarship on the international reception of Schnitzler in the last few decades.

32 Gerd K. Schneider, *Die Rezeption von Arthur Schnitzlers Reigen. 1897–1994. Text, Aufführungen, Verfilmungen. Pressespiegel und andere zeitgenössische Kommentare* (Riverside, CA: Ariadne Press, 1995); Konstanze Fliedl, 'Love's Labour's Lost: Translations of Schnitzler's Reigen', in *Theatre and Performance in Austria. From Mozart to Jelinek*, ed. by Ritchie Robertson and Edward Timms (= *Austrian Studies*, 4 (1993)), pp. 61–72.

33 Ana Fernandez-Capparros Turina, '"A swirling, brilliant, cloudy mass of blues": David Hare's Adaptation of Arthur Schnitzler's *La Ronde*', in *Adaptations, Versions and Perversions in Modern British Drama*, ed. by Iganacio Ramos Gay (Newcastle: Cambridge Scholars, 2013), pp. 57–70; Heidi Zojer, 'Vienna-London-Belfast: Schnitzler's *Reigen* on the Translation Roundabout', *New Theatre Quarterly*, 25 (2009), 88–98. See also Heidi Zojer, *Kulturelle Dimensionen in der literarischen Übersetzung. Eine übersetzungstheoretische Untersuchung mit exemplarischer Analyse von Arthur Schnitzlers 'Reigen'* (Stuttgart: Heinz, 2000). In it she compares seven published English translations of *Reigen* as part of a larger investigation of cultural transfer in translation.

This book departs from prior scholarship in the field in its reach and in its cross-disciplinary approach. It moves away from a target-oriented model of reception which relies heavily on published reviews and instead exploits extensively the full range of archival resources currently available, exposing a view of international transmission which incorporates both Schnitzler's position and that of his agents and translators abroad. It also includes within its scope the play texts themselves, providing comparative readings of translations as a means of revealing the decision-making process on its most detailed level. In this respect, among others, it represents a theoretical and methodological departure from much of the previous work on international Schnitzler production. By paying heed to such a varied collection of material, this study presents a comprehensive view of British Schnitzler production. The quid pro quo for that breadth of source material, however, has been a restriction on the works themselves: unlike many of the earlier studies referred to above, this one looks only at the dramatic works. Electing to restrict the subject by genre in turn allows a more closely focused consideration of theatre translation, a discipline with its own particular methodologies and theories.

This book also advances the work of prior scholarship in its accommodation of a long time frame. Whereas other studies have (most often necessarily) been limited to shorter, earlier, periods of transmission and reception, this study covers over a century of that intercultural movement in Great Britain. By doing so, it can afford to draw broader conclusions about the patterns of dissemination which appear over decades. One of those patterns charts the changing nature of control over the text: it will be shown in the following chapters that whereas Schnitzler himself exercised relatively little control over the presentation of his works in English, his son and legatee Heinrich Schnitzler wielded a far firmer grip during his fifty years at the helm; and when the corpus fell out of copyright in 1982 authorial control of any kind dropped away altogether, with the result that other factors came to bear more heavily on the translated texts. This study attempts to provide two perspectives on Schnitzler in Britain by giving an overview of the 120 years of anglophone dissemination of his dramatic works whilst also effectively focusing in greater detail on particular moments of that dissemination to expose the sometimes collaborative, sometimes combative mechanics of theatre translation.

The research presented here is more particularly framed by an attempt to explore and explain the power dynamics at play in international transmission: it seeks to discern, among other things, the nature of the translator's control over the text and thereby to test popular assumptions about authorship in translation. What emerges from that exploration is abundant evidence of unstable texts with multiple and changing authors. Power is legible in these texts, but it is often shared, challenged and sometimes reasserted. By searching for traces of the translator's voice in the 'final' text, this study reveals the layered and shifting agencies, operating on innumerable contingent and haunted texts.[34] Examination of Schnitzler's papers, of published translations and of the archived correspondence, drafts and notes of those involved in the British dissemination of Schnitzler's works demonstrates that, although an individual translator may be invisible to the public eye, he or she is not entirely without power when it comes to determining which source texts are translated and how they are translated.

Power and Translation

'Power' is used in this book to refer to the various forces affecting textual production. These might be individual or institutional, official or unofficial, conscious or unconscious. Primarily, in this context 'power' refers to the degree of control authors have over their texts once the latter are no longer physically in their hands. Accordingly, it also designates the ability of those other than the author to influence the text before it is presented to the public. As soon as an author sends a new work to a publisher or theatre director, other pressures are brought to bear on it; those recipients invariably have their own thoughts on the text, which thoughts are made manifest via attempts to alter the text itself or influence the way in which it is presented to the public (from editorial interventions and marketing strategies to directors' cuts and casting decisions). The author must, generally speaking, cede some control if the text is to reach the public at all. This loss of power is arguably accentuated in the case of writing dramatic works for theatre performance, a field in which the written text has been considered incomplete and one of multiple sign systems operating on the *mise-en-scène*.[35] The institutional power which is bound up in established theatre practices provides a structure within which textual meaning is pushed and pulled about by innumerable forces.

34 The term 'haunted' is used in the sense employed by Marvin Carlson in *The Haunted Stage: The Theatre as Memory Machine* (Ann Arbor, MI: University of Michigan Press, 2003). There it refers to the unavoidably recycled nature of dramatic texts (p. 17). See, for example: 'The present experience is always ghosted by previous experiences and associations while these ghosts are simultaneously shifted and modified by the processes of recycling and recollection' (p. 2). Jacques Derrida's 'hauntology' is more loaded: see Jacques Derrida, *Spectres de Marx: l'état de la dette, le travail du deuil et la nouvelle Internationale* (Paris: Galilée, 1993).

35 For a summary of some of the competing perspectives on script vs. performance see Marvin Carlson, 'Theatrical Performance: Illustration, Translation, Fulfillment, or Supplement?', *Theatre Journal*, 37 (1985), 5–11. Anne Ubersfeld provides one of the founding statements on the dramatic script as '*troué*', i.e., necessarily containing gaps (Anne Ubersfeld, *Reading Theatre*, trans. by Frank Collins (Toronto: University of Toronto Press, 1999), p. 10) (orig.: *Lire le théâtre* (Paris: Éditions sociales, 1977)).

In a monolingual context, the delivery of a play script by its author marks only the beginning of its journey to live performance. Between that initial script and the last performance in a run there can be hundreds of revisions: to individual words, lines of dialogue or whole scenes. These might or might not be made by the playwright him- or herself. Often playwrights attend rehearsals and so can respond to concerns raised by the director or cast by re-drafting on the spot or shortly thereafter. Schnitzler frequently attended rehearsals for the first performances of his plays in Vienna and Berlin; and he was not unfamiliar with the need to alter and cut according to the particular theatre's requirements or his own dissatisfaction with the existing draft.[36] Sometimes directors or producers insist on cuts to accommodate expected performance times, which in turn are determined by the cultural norms of the performance location.[37] Other practical problems lead to a sort of *Realtheater* in which such banalities as a venue's fire regulations can require a script to be altered in numerous places.[38] However, the decision to alter is not always run past the author. An actor on stage leaves out a word or phrase during the performance; a stage manager's decision to allow a spontaneously made revision stands for the remainder of the play's run. The result of such fluctuations is that meaning is determined afresh with every new performance.

The power an author can exercise over his or her own work is further diminished when the text is disseminated in another language and another place. Schnitzler was not a confident reader in English. When his works were translated into that language, therefore, he was obliged to accept what others ostensibly more competent in the target language reported back to him about the quality of the translation. A relatively bleak picture of Schnitzler's English skills emerges from his autobiography. His 'mäßiges Englisch', although sufficient to allow conversation with other guests at the London boarding house in which he lived in 1888, was insufficient to allow much

36 For examples of Schnitzler's attendance at rehearsals for *Professor Bernhardi* in Berlin see *Tagebuch*, 12.11.1912, 13.11.1912, 25.11.1912, 26.11.1912 and 27.11.1912; in Vienna see *Tagebuch*, 18.11.1918, 19.11.1918, 20.11.1918, 21.11.1918, 22.11.1918 and 23.11.1918; and for references to cuts made for the later production see *Tagebuch*, 2.11.1917 and 27.3.1918.

37 For examples of target-culture theatre norms affecting translation strategies, see Marta Mateo, 'Translation Strategies and the Reception of Drama Performances: A Mutual Influence', in *Translation as Intercultural Communication*, ed. by Mary Snell-Hornby, Zuzana Jettmarová and Klaus Kaindl (Amsterdam & Philadelphia, PA: Benjamins, 1995), pp. 99–110.

38 See Tom Stoppard, 'The Event and the Text', from The Whidden Lectures, McMaster University in Hamilton, Ontario, 24 October 1988, transcribed and edited by Doreen DelVechchio for *Ta Panta* (McMaster University Faculty Association), 6.1 (1988), in *Tom Stoppard in Conversation*, ed. by Paul Delaney (Ann Arbor, MI: University of Michigan Press, 1995), pp. 199–211 (pp. 208–09).

communication with his English girlfriend, Claire.[39] This self-assessment arguably reflects Schnitzler's historically imposed and self-serving modesty more than a keen sense of his own language ability and is in any event limited to Schnitzler's spoken (i.e., productive) English at an early stage in his writing career. The later documentary evidence suggests a higher level of (receptive) understanding of English than Schnitzler himself might have been willing to admit. His British correspondents, for example, occasionally wrote to him in English and there is no suggestion in the diaries that Schnitzler required help with reading or deciphering those letters.[40]

We also know from the diaries that Schnitzler received, read and engaged with reviews of his work written in the English-language press.[41] He likewise felt able to read English translations of his own works and even comment on them. In 1915, for example, he read English translations of *Der einsame Weg*, *Zwischenspiel* and *Komtesse Mizzi oder Der Familientag*, on the first of which he commented: 'Gar nicht übel – und doch mancher Unsinn (Sala zu Julian am Schluss: "Grüss Sie der Himmel" – "Send your regards to heaven!")'.[42] Of course, an important difference exists between the level of skill required to engage with the ideas discussed in a text and the level required to write or carry out full linguistic analysis.[43] Schnitzler's son Heinrich was, by contrast to his father, both a proficient reader and writer in English, to which his extensive correspondence with Eric Glass is testimony. Heinrich Schnitzler was evidently only too willing to put his English skills to the service of his father's reputation in Britain and America, insisting on previewing any new translation and returning the same with reams of annotations and comments.

39 Schnitzler, *Jugend in Wien*, pp. 300 and 304.

40 See, for example, letters to Schnitzler from Helen Macdonell (DLA, HS.NZ85.0001.03960,1–5) and Frederick Whelen (CUL, B1030). In all quoted transcriptions from the CUL and DLA archives the orthography and punctuation are as in the originals. However, umlauts have been added where it is clear that these have inadvertently been omitted. Any uncertainties, apparently omitted letters, or illegibility are marked as such and enclosed within square brackets.

41 A prime example of Schnitzler's engagement with English-language reviews is legible in his response to an article by Ashley Dukes, 'Modern Dramatists. v. Arthur Schnitzler', *The New Age*, 7 (27 October 1910), pp. 611–12. Schnitzler's initial thoughts (*Tagebuch*, 8.11.1910) were incorporated into a draft letter (*Tagebuch*, 11.11.1910) since preserved among his papers (CUL, A20,5). Both the article and Schnitzler's response are considered more fully in Chapter 2.

42 *Tagebuch*, 12.7.1915. See also *Tagebuch*, 9.4.1908; *Tagebuch*, 7.2.1911; *Tagebuch*, 28.9.1915; *Tagebuch*, 10.2.1920; letter to P. Morton Shand, 14.10.1920 (DLA, HS.NZ85.0001.01919); letter from Arthur Schnitzler to G. Valentine Williams, 29.4.1909 (DLA, HS.NZ85.0001.02224).

43 The only evidence found of Schnitzler writing in English appears in a telegram sent to Harley Granville Barker on 31.12.1930, which, although very short, contains three linguistic mistakes (DLA, HS.NZ85.0001.00881).

His engagement with the English translations only highlights further his father's apparent incapacity or unwillingness to evaluate in any depth the translations which were sent to him from Britain.[44]

In parallel with the ebbing of power from the author which results from translation are the contrapuntal growth in the influence an author enjoys when his or her works become available in another language and, when compared to the translator, the significant recognition he or she often receives in the target culture. In this respect the translator is comparatively powerless: the translator's name, if it appears at all in a publication, may appear only once or twice and, more often than not, in smaller typescript; generally the work is still referred to by readers, reviewers and theatre advertisers as being the creation of the original author alone; the translator is seen as dispensable and exchangeable, a mere service-provider in the grand scheme of cultural production. The translator's invisibility, as established in Lawrence Venuti's seminal work on the subject, is reflected in the relative lack of economic or legal recognition for his or her labour; the translated text is likewise devalued 'as derivative, simulacral, [and] false.'[45]

In the British theatre tradition the translator's invisibility is often doubled when a recognized playwright without any substantial competence in the source language is given the job of rewriting a previously commissioned 'literal' or interlinear translation. The translator of the 'literal' sometimes disappears altogether from the record of production. His or her name simply does not appear on the public documentation which accompanies and survives a performance. This practice is frequently (although certainly not exclusively) employed when the author of the source text is not yet established in the target culture, or when the target-language playwright involved has a crowd-drawing reputation. Sirkku Aaltonen refers to target-culture playwrights thus employed as 'surrogate translators who contribute primarily their name and status to the translation.'[46] By attaching the name of a well-known British playwright to a translation, a theatre can reduce the commercial risk it takes in staging a new play. As will be shown in Chapters 3 and 4, this was a practice used in respect of Schnitzler's plays on a number of occasions. Most notably, the actor, dramatist and theatre manager Harley Granville Barker was assisted by

44 Schnitzler was aware of his own failings in this regard. In his diary he wrote: 'Thayer sendet mir englische Romane, ich beginne zu lesen von James Joyce, a portrait of the artist as a young man, und ärgre mich, dass ich so wenig englisch gelesen. Überhaupt zu wenig Sprachen geübt' (*Tagebuch*, 25.1.1922).

45 Lawrence Venuti, *The Translator's Invisibility: A History of Translation*, 2nd edn (London & New York: Routledge, 2008 [1995]), p. 251. See also pp. 7–9.

46 Sirkku Aaltonen, *Time-Sharing on Stage: Drama Translation in Theatre and Society* (Clevedon: Multilingual Matters, 2000), p. 32.

a literal translator in producing his English 'paraphrase' of *Anatol* (1912); and Tom Stoppard based his adaptations of two plays by Schnitzler, *Undiscovered Country* (1979) and *Dalliance* (1986), on a combination of pre-existing translations and especially commissioned 'literal' translations. In these circumstances, questions concerning 'power' quickly expand to encompass investigations of the translator's agency.

By paying attention to power dynamics in translation this study pursues a line of enquiry in translation theory established over the last few decades in edited collections such as *The Manipulation of Literature* (1985), *Translation, Power, Subversion* (1996), *Translation and Power* (2002) and *Translation and the Reconfiguration of Power Relations* (2012).[47] The editors of *Translation and Power*, Gentzler and Tymoczko, ask at the outset what is meant by the word 'power' in this context. Rather than attempting to give one single definition, they provide examples from the four pages of entries for the word in the *Oxford English Dictionary*, picking out those that might have particular relevance to discourses on translation.[48] Revealingly, they finally nail their colours to the mast when they conclude that through 'a deliberate and conscious act of selection, assemblage, structuration, and fabrication [...] translators, as much as creative writers and politicians, participate in the powerful acts that create knowledge and shape culture'.[49] 'Power', then, is the ability to create knowledge and shape culture. It refers to the capacity for translators to 'reorder and disturb' global relations and for translations to function as both 'critique and intervention'.[50] Each choice of word, selection of accompanying image or institutional imposition of a performance window, for example, has an effect on the reception of the text in its new host culture; through it they each change the host culture, even if in almost imperceptible ways.

In accordance with their definition, Gentzler and Tymoczko advocate a methodology which recognizes 'the process of translation as heterogeneous, with different issues addressed by different translations and different translators at different times and different places, depending on the specific historical and

47. *The Manipulation of Literature: Studies in Literary Translation*, ed. by Theo Hermans (London: Croom Helm, 1985); *Translation, Power, Subversion*, ed. by Roman Alvarez and M. Carmen-Africa Vidal (Clevedon: Multilingual Matters, 1996); *Translation and Power*, ed. by Maria Tymoczko and Edwin Gentzler (Amherst, MA and Boston, MA: University of Massachusetts Press, 2002); *Translation and the Reconfiguration of Power Relations. Revisiting Role and Context of Translation and Interpreting*, ed. by Beatrice Fischer and Matilde Nisbeth Jensen (Münster: Lit, 2012).

48 Maria Tymoczko and Edwin Gentzler, 'Introduction', in *Translation and Power*, ed. by Tymoczko and Gentzler, pp. xi–xxviii (p. xvii).

49 Tymoczko and Gentzler, 'Introduction', p. xxi.

50 Sherry Simon, 'Germaine de Staël and Gayatri Spivak: Culture Brokers', in *Translation and Power*, ed. by Tymoczko and Gentzler, pp. 122–40 (p. 137).

material moment', an approach which involves analysis not just of 'the parts of the source text and source culture that are present in translated texts, but also the parts that are left out'.[51] This conceptualization of power and its consequent methodology are taken up in this book. They informed the research carried out, which in turn reveals evidence of the 'deliberate and conscious' decisions made – by Schnitzler, by his legatee, his translators and his agents – about what to translate, how to translate, what to include and what to avoid. These are just a few of the myriad decisions that represent the exercise of power to determine textual meaning.

Mona Baker's conceptualization of 'narrative' is a useful complement to Gentzler's and Tymoczko's understanding of power, providing a more nuanced vocabulary for describing the exercise of power in producing a translation. Baker challenges the historically popular view of the translator as the peace-making enabler and communicator; and instead describes translators as participating 'in very decisive ways in promoting and circulating narratives and discourses of various types'.[52] Translators are not the neutral conduits of information they are commonly held to be: rather, they bring their own histories into their work, knowingly or otherwise, so that every decision made by a translator in the process of translating a text, whether it be overtly political reportage or comic drama, is inflected by the translator's personal context.

In modelling her own narrative theory of translation Baker looks to the work of social theorists Margaret Somers and Gloria Gibson, who present narrative as being '*the* principal and inescapable mode by which we experience the world' and narratives as the 'public and personal "stories" that we subscribe to and that guide our behaviour'.[53] In order to 'query our own discourses on translation', Baker adopts the four-part categorization of narrative developed by Somers and Gibson, distinguishing between ontological, public, conceptual and meta- or master narratives:[54]

> **Ontological narratives** are personal stories we tell ourselves about our place in the world and about our own personal history. They are interpersonal and social in nature [...]. **Public narratives** are [...] stories elaborated by and circulating among social and institutional formations

51 Tymoczko and Gentzler, 'Introduction', p. xx.

52 Mona Baker, 'Narratives in and of Translation', *SKASE Journal of Translation and Interpretation*, 1 (2005), 4–13 (p. 12).

53 Margaret R. Somers and Gloria D. Gibson, 'Reclaiming the Epistemological "Other": Narrative and the Social Constitution of Identity', in *Social Theory and the Politics of Identity*, ed. by Craig Calhoun (Oxford and Cambridge, MA: Blackwell, 1994), pp. 37–99; Baker, 'Narratives in and of Translation', p. 5.

54 Baker, 'Narratives in and of Translation', p. 5.

> larger than the individual, such as the family, religious or educational institution, political or activist group, the media, and the nation. [...] [C]**onceptual narratives** [... are] the stories and explanations that scholars in any field elaborate for themselves and others about their object of inquiry. Some of these stories or conceptual narratives can have considerable impact on the world at large, while others remain limited in scope to the immediate community of scholars in the relevant field. [55]

Finally, meta- (or master) narratives are those in which we are 'embedded as contemporary actors in history', such as 'Progress, Decadence, Industrialization [and] Enlightenment'.[56] Thus Baker's assessment of the narrative drive accounts for both private and public forms of story-telling and for the dynamic, constantly changing nature of the ways in which we frame our experiences. Although Baker's theory arises out of her need to analyse political, non-fictive texts, her ideas about the narrative drive can be applied with equal force to the translation of dramatic works. No translator is immune to the influence of his or her own history, or to the wider institutional, national or global contexts in which he or she is situated. At every turn these different narratives bear down on the translator, whether consciously acknowledged or not, and inform his or her textual choices.

In the introduction to her monograph, in which she expands upon the same subject, Baker makes explicit the predicament in which the translator unavoidably finds herself: 'Narrative theory recognizes that at any moment in time we can be located within a variety of divergent, criss-crossing, often vacillating narratives'.[57] This book argues that such a moment is crystallized and made legible in the translated text, in which choices of word and presentation reflect the entangled narratives which have shaped the translator's or editor's identity at a given point in time. Indeed, as seen in Chapter 2, the legatee's narrative can also prove crucial – primarily to the management of the literary estate, but thereby also to the selection of works to be translated, the choice of translator and the final approval of a translator's efforts. Baker's recognition of the fluidity and abundance of potential narratives informing a translation coincides with an observation made by Cordingley and Montini when considering the genesis of translations: '[T]he degree to which a translator exercises his/her creativity in translation, not to mention his/her engaging in domesticating or foreignizing strategies when translating, shifts during the translation's genesis'.[58] Accordingly, there is no attempt in this study to identify any single strategy

55 Baker, 'Narratives in and of Translation', pp. 5–7.

56 Somers and Gibson, 'Reclaiming the Epistemological "Other"', p. 61.

57 Mona Baker, *Translation and Conflict: A Narrative Account* (London & New York: Routledge, 2006), p. 3.

58 Anthony Cordingley and Chiara Montini, 'Genetic Translation Studies: An Emerging Discipline', *Linguistica Antverpiensia*, 14 (2015), 1–18 (p. 4).

attributable to an individual translator (or indeed any other agent involved in generating the English-language text). Rather, it has been a priority to remain alive to the multiple evolving, shifting, recurring as well as anomalous narratives that can inform a particular choice of word, phrase or metaphor.

Manifestations of Power

As already touched on briefly above, power is made manifest in varying forms. In its most subtle appearance, power pervades the ontological, public, conceptual and master narratives which determine our behaviour. However, there are more concrete, more easily legible, displays of power over the writer, the translator and the text. Power is perhaps most easily recognizable in the legal frameworks within which translations are made and produced, in laws concerning copyright, censorship and obscenity, for example. Until the establishment of the Berne Convention for the Protection of Literary and Artistic Works, agreed and signed in 1886, there were no multi-lateral international agreements in place to protect the intellectual property rights of writers beyond their own domestic jurisdiction (although bilateral agreements provided some protection). The original signatories to the Convention included Germany and Great Britain but excluded Austria-Hungary and many of the countries into which Schnitzler was to export his work (most notably Russia and the United States of America).[59] The Convention, which still governs much international copyright law today, albeit in a modified form, only bites when either the author is a national of, or the work is first published in, one of the signatory countries.[60] Thus even when negotiating rights for publication in Britain, one of the few early signatories to the Convention, Schnitzler would have been entirely at the mercy of the purchaser were it not for the fact that until the 1920s he published a large proportion of his work with the Fischer Verlag in Berlin.[61] Even the protection thereby won was only effective for ten years after publication. What this meant, in practice, was that Schnitzler was often powerless to lay claim to his own work outside Austria.

59 See Robert Spoo for a discussion of the 'transatlantic bifurcation' resulting from America's isolationist stance on copyright (Robert Spoo, *Modernism and the Law* (London: Bloomsbury, 2018), p. 85).

60 Catherine Seville, *The Internationalisation of Copyright Law: Books, Buccaneers and the Black Flag in the Nineteenth Century* (Cambridge: Cambridge University Press, 2006), p. 73; and see Article 3 of the Berne Convention for the Protection of Literary and Artistic Works, http://www.wipo.int/treaties/en/text.jsp?file_id=283698 [accessed 3 March 2016]. For an introduction to some of the implications for translation and ideas of originality, in particular in the context of theatre translation, see Venuti, *The Translator's Invisibility*, p. 251.

61 Important exceptions to this general practice were *Fräulein Else* (Berlin; Leipzig; Vienna: Paul Zsolnay, 1924) and *Reigen* (Vienna & Leipzig: Wiener Verlag, 1903).

Plays were frequently performed abroad without Schnitzler even being notified, let alone asked for permission, consulted or remunerated. The Netherlands, for example, were not initially signatories to the Berne Convention and Schnitzler's works were accordingly unprotected for much of the period covered by Roelofs in his study, i.e., 1895 to 1940. Roelofs picks out from the correspondence the many instances of Schnitzler expressing frustration at the economic reality of his situation: 'Für Schnitzler gilt nur das zeitlich und geographisch uneingeschränkte Recht auf seinen Besitz, auf die Frucht seiner Arbeit'.[62] The same conclusion, it will be shown, can be drawn from consideration of Schnitzler's correspondence with British translators and agents. Time and time again, Schnitzler expresses regret at the absence of a proper legal remedy and hope that those who benefitted from publishing or performing his works in translation would nevertheless feel a moral obligation to pay him some sort of fee.[63]

The new Austrian Republic signed up to the Convention in 1920 as a condition of peace.[64] By this time, the length of protection had been extended, by an amendment to the Convention in 1908, to fifty calendar years after the author's death. Copyright protection for Schnitzler's works accordingly expired at midnight on 31 December 1981. Ironically, Schnitzler's son and legatee, Heinrich Schnitzler, was in many respects better placed to take advantage of this copyright protection than his father had been. His active and passive competence in English was far superior to that of the author as a result of almost two decades in exile in the United States of America (1938–57), where he worked as a drama scholar at the University of California. Consequently, Heinrich Schnitzler was able to monitor more closely the translations which were proposed and produced during his stewardship of the literary estate; and he was quick to call on the protection provided by the international legislation when he felt the estate's rights had been infringed. The following assessment of the power exercised over translations of Schnitzler's works accordingly pays heed to the discrete periods in which legal power significantly aided or undermined the efforts by the author and, after the author's death, by his son to control the text. Furthermore, this study takes into consideration the role copyright law plays in permitting and even promoting claims to authorial succession by the legatee.

Whereas international copyright legislation provided Schnitzler and later his son with some degree of positive protection, institutional censorship was to

62 Roelofs, '*Man weiss eigentlich wenig von einander*', p. 111.

63 For a comparative view of Schnitzler's position in respect to copyright protection, see Beniston, 'Schnitzler und die "Uebersetzungs-Miseren"'.

64 Article 239, Treaty of St. Germain-en-Laye (1919), in *The Treaties of Peace, 1919–1923*, 2 vols (New York: Carnegie Endowment for International Peace, 1924), I: *Containing the Treaty of Versailles, the Treaty of St. Germain-en-Laye and the Treaty of Trianon*, pp. 267–456 (p. 381).

exercise restrictive power over the writer's freedom to create and disseminate his works. For most of his lifetime Schnitzler's dramatic works fell under the domestic scrutiny of the relevant federal state or the court censor (depending on the location and ownership of the particular theatre): generally excluded from theatre performance, until the collapse of the Monarchy in 1918, was 'anything directed against the ruling house, anything that might threaten law and order or that offended public decency, anything that intruded into the private lives of individuals, and anything offensive to religion or morality'.[65] Plays had to be submitted for prior approval; and from 1911 the authorities were supposed to be represented at dress rehearsals.[66] Not only did these laws have the obvious impact of leading to the outright prohibition on some of Schnitzler's plays being performed (such as *Professor Bernhardi*), but they also resulted in marked discrepancies between the performed and published versions of drama texts, as well as contributing to the self-censorship which takes place during the writing period.

Theatre censorship in Great Britain continued for a far longer period than in Austria. The writer Arnold Bennett summed up the problem as it existed for British playwrights in his written testimony before the 1909 Joint Select Committee in the UK: 'Immediately you begin to get near the things that really matter in a play, you begin to think about the censor, and it is all over with your play'.[67] The problem affected any work proposed for performance in Britain, not only those by British writers. Thus, while published translations of Schnitzler's works have only ever been subjected to the censorial scrutiny of the criminal law in England and Wales, theatre productions of translated dramas were obliged, until 1968, to jump through the additional hoop of submission to the Lord Chamberlain's Office. Statute and common law prevented (and continue to prevent) the publication of any work that is libellous, blasphemous or obscene;[68] by contrast, prior to 1909 the Lord Chamberlain's discretion in respect of theatre plays was unrestricted. He was, according to the last Comptroller in office, John Johnston, 'expected to use his own judgement'

65 W. E. Yates, *Theatre in Vienna: A Critical History 1776–1995* (Cambridge: Cambridge University Press, 1996), pp. 43 and 47. Theatre censorship was not formally declared illegal by the Constitutional Court until 1926; the censors adopted a far more liberal approach from 1918 onwards, however, so that productions of numerous works not previously staged (including Schnitzler's *Professor Bernhardi* and *Reigen*) could be planned and executed within the following years.

66 Yates, *Theatre in Vienna*, p. 46.

67 Quoted, without a bibliographical reference, in John Johnston, *The Lord Chamberlain's Blue Pencil* (London: Hodder & Stoughton, 1990), pp. 62–63.

68 The independent existence of censorial checks formed part of the evidence in support of abolishing the Lord Chamberlain's censorship powers (L. W. Conolly, 'The Abolition of Theatre Censorship', *Queen's Quarterly*, 75 (1968), 569–84 (pp. 575–76)).

and as a matter of course 'treated all plays on their merits and judged them according to the social and moral conditions of the time'.[69] After 1909 the Lord Chamberlain had an obligation to take note of the recommendations of the Joint Select Committee, which tried to articulate the criteria to be applied. Nevertheless, his discretion was without real limit; and disgruntled recipients of a refusal found themselves without any route to appeal.

The effect of the Lord Chamberlain's blue pencil, as with censorship in Austria, fed into the self-censorship practised by writers (or translators) at the point of first writing (or translating) a play. Pierre Bourdieu sees self-censorship as a wider phenomenon than merely a response to anticipated legal proscription. We are all, according to Bourdieu, censored by the structure of the field in which we operate; censorship is effectively exercised through 'the medium of the sanctions of the field' and can be productive as well as repressive, internally as well as externally located.[70] Thus even though this examination of the various efforts to bring Schnitzler's works to British stages has brought to light few express references to the power of the Lord Chamberlain or criminal law, it is worth remaining alert to the structures within which both the source drama is written and the translated plays are produced and to the latent censorial power lurking therein. The economic circumstances of the writer/translator and individual theatre, the established reputation of the writer/translator, the theatrical conventions of the target culture and local audience expectations – all are factors which might affect the choices made at the point of writing or translating, whether consciously or unconsciously.

There is one further, discrete element of structural power worth considering at this stage, namely the power exercised through paratexts. Adopting the terminology developed by Genette, paratexts are those 'verbal or other productions' that 'surround' and 'extend' a text and so guide us in how to read that text.[71] They include both 'peritexts' (located with or in close proximity to the text) and 'epitexts', 'located outside the book, generally with the help of the media (interviews, conversations) or under cover of private communications (letters, diaries, and others)'.[72] Although Genette is concerned largely with

69 Johnston, *The Lord Chamberlain's Blue Pencil*, p. 30.

70 Pierre Bourdieu, 'Censorship and the Imposition of Form', in *Language and Symbolic Power*, ed. by John B. Thompson, trans. by Gino Raymond and Matthew Adamson (Cambridge: Polity Press, 1991), pp. 137–61 (p. 138) (orig.: 'Censure et mise en forme', in *Ce que parler veut dire: l'économie des échanges linguistiques* (Paris: Librairie Arthème Fayard, 1982), pp. 167–205).

71 Gérard Genette, *Paratexts: Thresholds of Interpretation*, trans. by Jane E. Lewin (Cambridge: Cambridge University Press, 1997), pp. 1–2 (orig.: *Seuils* (Paris: Seuil, 1987)).

72 Genette, *Paratexts*, pp. 4–5.

books, his analysis can be applied with equal force to dramatic texts more broadly, i.e., in both print and performance. Hence, for example, paratexts to a performed play might include poster design, newspaper advertisements, programmes and playbills, decisions about which might lie outside the direct control of the author and instead be taken by marketing directors or theatre managers. Each of these paratexts shapes an audience's response to the performance itself by creating expectations about the play and providing biographical detail, which in turn informs interpretation. Genette includes within his definition of the paratext such details as the name of the author and title of a text, as well as prefaces, footnotes and interviews with the author. For example, the name 'Arthur Schnitzler' might play different roles in guiding the reader of a translated text or the audience at a performance according to the reputation which Schnitzler has already established in the English-speaking world.

Paratexts are, for Genette, 'characterized by an authorial intention and assumption of responsibility' and might include both those texts explicitly intended for publication, which he labels 'public' paratexts, and those initially intended only for private consumption (such as private correspondence and diary entries), accordingly labelled 'private' paratexts.[73] However, a 'paratext' might also be a fact: for example, the author's gender or the century in which the text was written.[74] These are, for Genette, the 'implicit contexts that surround a work and, to a greater or lesser degree, clarify or modify its significance'.[75] The limitation apparently imposed by Genette on his analysis by his purporting to exclude texts produced without the author's consent is, therefore, not borne out by the range of texts and facts included in his definition (Schnitzler could not control the century in which he wrote). In any event, and regardless of their lying outside the control of the author or translator, newspaper and journal reviews often play a vital role in guiding the reader or audience-member in his reception of a given work. The critical review is also a demonstration of power ceded to others by the author. By allowing a work to be published or performed, the author opens it up for interpretation and (whether willingly or not) invites others to publish their interpretations of the work and so influence its reception.[76] In this study, 'paratext' is accordingly applied to all

73 Genette, *Paratexts*, pp. 3 and 9. 'Authorial' is subsequently defined more precisely as referring to the author 'or one of his associates' (p. 9). Paratexts produced by an 'associate' of the author might subsequently be disclaimed (p. 10).

74 Genette, *Paratexts*, p. 7.

75 Genette, *Paratexts*, p. 7.

76 Cf. Paul Prescott, 'Inheriting the Globe: The Reception of Shakespearean Space and Audience in Contemporary Reviewing', in *A Companion to Shakespeare and Performance*, ed. by Barbara Hodgdon and W. B. Worthen (Oxford: Blackwell, 2005), pp. 359–75 (p. 360).

those texts or facts which provide an immediate or more remote context for interpretation, regardless of authorship.

It goes without saying that the distance between playwright and performed script, visible in the intervening paratexts explored above, acquires new magnitude when the playwright's text is translated into another language and performed in another place. Power can become very thinly spread between the various agents involved when the additional processes of translation and re-location are introduced. In Schnitzler's case there were practical and economic obstacles to his attending the rehearsals and performances of his plays outside Austria. Although he managed, during a reading tour of Denmark and Sweden, to see *Komödie der Worte* at the Royal Theatre in Copenhagen (*Tagebuch*, 15.5.1923) and *Liebelei* at the Royal Dramatic Theatre in Stockholm (*Tagebuch*, 22.5.1923), Schnitzler never saw any of his plays performed in English translation. Even if he had been able to sit in on rehearsals in London, his relatively limited capacity to speak and understand spoken English would probably have prevented any easy, effective intervention in a production. The result, in such circumstances, is a twice-removed status for the writer of the original text; the exercise of any authorial power over the performed text becomes nigh on impossible.

Collaboration and Agency

This study provides ideal material for revisiting poststructuralist ideas pertaining to authorship and for testing application of the same to translated texts. Michel Foucault's work on the author-function, for example, highlights the fiction, or construction, of the single author within the reception of a text. This study picks apart the minutiae of that construction by setting out the evidence of multiple authors for each production or publication of a translated play. The accounts which follow in Chapters 1 to 4 chart the significant involvement of literal (or 'interlinear') translators, of English-speaking playwrights and of theatre directors in rewriting the German-language text for a British audience. Foucault argues that the illusion of singular authorship was necessary to 'literary' discourse in order to render the end product 'acceptable'.[77] Indeed, '[t]he meaning and value attributed to the text depended on this information' (i.e., the author's name).[78] Only by being referred to as

77 Michel Foucault, 'What Is an Author?', in *Language, Counter-Memory, Practice*, ed. by Donald F. Bouchard, trans. by Donald E. Bouchard and Sherry Simon (Oxford: Blackwell, 1977), pp. 113–38 (p. 126) (orig.: 'Qu'est-ce qu'un auteur?', *Bulletin de la Société française de philosophie*, 3 (1969), 73–104).

78 Foucault, 'What Is an Author?', p. 126.

'by Schnitzler' or 'by Stoppard' can a work take on sufficient cultural capital to be deemed 'literary'. If the reality were too readily apparent, if the audience or reader were aware that the play before them was the result of simultaneous or sequential collaboration, its status *as literary work* would fall.

Cordingley and Manning locate the rationale for the illusion in Romantic mythologizing of the solitary genius. The tenacity of the myth 'very likely derives from the way its apotheosis of the author emulates a prevailing theological model of monotheism and singular salvation'.[79] It is an illusion well illustrated in the widespread theatre practice of employing a literal translator, examples of which have been given above. The literal translator works as an anonymous service provider, contracted to produce a line-by-line direct translation (if indeed such a thing can be done) of the source play, so that a more renowned target-language playwright can produce a final script for rehearsal and performance.[80] Public acknowledgment of the role played by the literal translator (or, indeed, authors of prior, published, translations) in generating a performed text is rare. Rather, the name of either the source-text author or the established playwright is presented to the audience as the progenitor of the text. The other author (i.e., of the two aforementioned, the writer who is not billed as creator) is often recognized on posters, published scripts and programmes in a smaller font. Equal billing for source-text author and target-language playwright is scarce – apparently too great a challenge to the ideal, unique voice expected.[81]

Anthea Bell, the prolific translator of works by W. G. Sebald, Stefan Zweig and Arthur Schnitzler (among many others), has spoken out for the necessity of this illusion of single authorship, for the very 'invisibility' deplored by Venuti, arguing that it is crucial to the effective labour of the translator. The reader should not, according to Bell, be even remotely conscious of the translator between source-text author and target-text recipient. Translators are 'in the business of spinning an illusion: the illusion is that the reader is reading not a

79 Anthony Cordingley and Céline Frigau Manning, 'What Is Collaborative Translation?', in *Collaborative Translation: From the Renaissance to the Digital Age*, ed. byAnthony Cordingley and Céline Frigau Manning (London: Bloomsbury Academic, 2017), pp. 1–30 (p. 10).

80 Gunilla Anderman attacks the very concept of a 'literal' translation on the basis that '[e]ven conjunctions such as "and" and "but" cannot always be replaced simply by their "opposite numbers" in another language' (Gunilla Anderman, *Europe on Stage* (London: Oberon, 2005), p. 27).

81 For a rare, but complex, exception to the rule concerning apparent single-parenthood, see the later discussion of Harley Granville Barker's 'paraphrase' of *Anatol* in Chapter 2. Beniston points out that the hyphenated authors on the cover of the volume ('Schnitzler-Barker') make it very clear that the material contained therein is the 'Kind zweier Väter' (Beniston, 'Schnitzler und die "Uebersetzungs-Miseren"', p. 254).

translation but the real thing.'[82] Bell's unusual self-effacement stands in stark contrast to the views of critics such as Venuti and Geraldine Brodie, who argue that the traditionally hidden nature of the translator has very serious ethical implications in terms of recognition and remuneration.[83] They call on scholars across disciplines to recognize the vital role of the translator in the dissemination of cultural products and to make him or her present, with the aim of legitimizing the power of the translator and recognizing his or her role in the creative process. Alongside the ethical considerations, the historical hiddenness of translators also operates to obscure the real processes of making meaning.

Cordingley and Manning observe that, just as in literary studies the central figure of the author has been questioned and the myths and ideological underpinnings of single authorship deconstructed, in Translation Studies scholars have started to enquire into the 'conditions of textual production' and to examine the 'nexus at which the power and influence of different networks and agents intersect'.[84] The picture that emerges is one of frequent and complex collaboration, which is relational (rather than binary) in nature and derives from the 'conflicting sensibilities of collaborators, both friendly and adversarial'.[85] Cordingley and Manning advocate an approach which focuses 'on how collaboration or co-translating affects the subjectivity, identity and agency of the text'.[86] Theirs is an ambition adopted in this study.

Just as the deconstruction of the author subsequently led Foucault to question the ontological unity of the text, in considering translated plays we are compelled to examine the identity of and relationship between 'source text' and 'target text'. The experience is akin to nailing jelly to the wall, in particular after a thorough consideration of the papers of Tom Stoppard, an important adapter of Schnitzler's work. As draft after draft appears from Stoppard's archive, pre- and post-dating performance, pre-held concepts of finality and fixedness necessarily break down, requiring a revised view of 'text' as fluid, dynamic and ontologically independent of its creators. In the genetic exegesis of text in translation we see

82 Anthea Bell, 'Translation as Illusion', transcription of the opening talk at the conference *Shelving Translation*, London, 2004, https://www.brunel.ac.uk/creative-writing/research/entertext/documents/entertext0431-supplement/Anthea-Bell-pdf-Translation-as-Illusion.pdf [accessed 8 June 2021].

83 See Venuti, *The Translator's Invisibility*; Geraldine Brodie, 'Indirect Translation on the London Stage: Terminology and (In)visibility', *Translation Studies*, 11 (2018), 333–48; Geraldine Brodie, *The Translator on Stage* (London: Bloomsbury, 2018).

84 Cordingley and Manning, 'What Is Collaborative Translation?', p. 14.

85 John Bryant, *The Fluid Text: A Theory of Revision and Editing for Book and Screen* (Ann Arbor, MI: University of Michigan Press, 2002), p. 7.

86 Cordingley and Manning, 'What Is Collaborative Translation?', p. 21.

what Roland Barthes calls its '*irreducible* [...] plural[ity]' in concrete form.[87] Tracing a translation from the published script in German to the performed play in English, via innumerable drafts rewritten by multiple authors, it becomes impossible to speak of one being the 'same' text as the other. Nonetheless, we do, and arguably must, in order to make sense of the continuities and threads of sameness which run through the various iterations from beginning to end.

The debate concerning the nature of text and work has received new impetus from such scholars as Jerome J. McGann and N. Katherine Hayles, adding to the discussion on the challenge of incorporating digital text into our understanding of the term. Hayles's consideration of the nature of work, text and document follows from her initial questions about the digitization of printed literature. She asks: '[I]s this electronic version the same work?'. She then wonders whether we are better served by regarding the transformation from print into electronic 'as a form of translation'.[88] If 'even small differences in materiality potentially affect meaning', how is it possible to describe the performed play in English as the same 'work' as the published volume in German?[89] Such a line of enquiry enables a view of the translators' archive materials as part of a continuum that includes not only the performances of those translations, but also Schnitzler's drafts, which for much of his oeuvre are held at Cambridge University Library. Indeed, they might also be seen as an extension of *Arthur Schnitzler digital. Historische-kritische Edition (Werke 1905–1931)*, an ongoing digitization enterprise being carried out by Schnitzler scholars at the Bergische Universität Wuppertal, Trier University, University College London and the University of Cambridge.[90]

The variously mediated, located and recorded iterations of words once written by Schnitzler exemplify perfectly the reasons for Hayles's dissatisfaction with traditional conceptions of 'work' and 'text': 'our notions of textuality are shot through with assumptions specific to print'.[91] The focus on print is misplaced and ultimately unhelpful, Hayles argues: 'Concentrating only on how the material differences of *print* texts affect meaning is like feeling slight texture differences on an elephant's tail while ignoring the ways in which the tail differs from the rest of the elephant'.[92] An analogy can be drawn with the

87 Roland Barthes, 'From Work to Text', in *Image Music Text*, ed. and trans. by Stephen Heath (London: Fontana, 1977), pp. 155–64 (p. 159) (orig.: 'De l'oeuvre au texte', *Revue d'esthetique*, 3 (1971), 225–32).

88 N. Katherine Hayles, 'Translating Media: Why We Should Rethink Textuality', *The Yale Journal of Criticism*, 16 (2003), 263–90 (p. 263).

89 Hayles, 'Translating Media', p. 264.

90 *Arthur Schnitzler digital. Historische-kritische Edition (Werke 1905–1931)* (2018–), https://www.arthur-schnitzler.org [accessed 21 June 2019].

91 Hayles, 'Translating Media', p. 263.

92 Hayles, 'Translating Media', p. 265.

at times restrictive imposition of the binary terminology 'source text' and 'target text' on historical discussions about translation (a vocabulary adopted more generally in this book for its neatness and convenience). As soon as the landscape for research is opened up to include the translators' notes, drafts and revisions, on paper, in performance and in digital presentation, one quickly sees that a model for translation limited to '(final text) A into (final text) B' simply cannot account for the back, forth and sideways legible in the archive and on stage. Rather, the scholar, like the reader and audience, is faced with single instantiations of textual meaning.

These palimpsests are haunted both by past and future iterations.[93] The privilege of looking into the archive is the privilege of tracing the otherwise unseen transition from one textual manifestation to another (or at least, some part of that transition). The continuous rewritings are evidence of individual agents exercising power by putting their stamp on the chronologically prior text, momentarily bringing out a new interpretation and taking ownership of the story that is told. The pencil that deletes and scribbles over, queries and replaces could be said to represent a continuation of Schnitzler's own practice of sketching out, drafting and rewriting.[94] Moreover, Schnitzler's own practice is itself a manifestation of that writer's very modern notion of authorship: there is no pretence of the Romantic genius in Schnitzler's labours. Rather, his meticulous preservation of notes and drafts indicates an appreciation of the non-finality of his own creations and their openness to further re-working by others. According to Edwin Gentzler these iterations without beginning or end locate the translator/writer in a *mise en abîme* 'that erases any sense of access to an "original"'.[95] Research into the multiple authors and multiple texts involved in translating drama not only allows threads to be drawn between the working practices of Schnitzler and his Anglophone translators, but also upsets the constraining and superficially binary hierarchy of primary, superior, original text and secondary, inferior translation.

93 Cf. Linda Hutcheon's 'palimpsestic intertextuality' (Linda Hutcheon, *A Theory of Adaptation*, 2nd edn, with an epilogue by Siobhan O'Flynn (London & New York: Routledge, 2012 [2006]), p. 22). This adopts the terminology of Michael Alexander, who wrote of the 'palimpsestuous' nature of Ezra Pound's *Cantos* (Michael Alexander, *The Poetic Achievement of Ezra Pound* (Berkeley, CA and Los Angeles, CA: University of California Press, 1981), p. 144).

94 Schnitzler's writing practice has emerged from the editorial work carried out for *Arthur Schnitzler digital* and *Arthur Schnitzler. Werke in historisch-kritischen Ausgaben*, ed. by Konstanze Fliedl, 14 vols (Berlin and Boston, MA: de Gruyter, 2011–). It is discussed in greater detail in Chapter 3.

95 Edwin Gentzler, 'Translation, Poststructuralism, and Power', in *Translation and Power*, ed. by Tymoczko and Gentzler, pp. 195–218 (p. 196).

Adaptation and Translation: Defining the Terms of the Enquiry

This study includes within its remit any text in English which claims to be a translation, adaptation or version of a play by Schnitzler, taking each of these terms or categories to be subsets of the more general field of rewriting. The employment of the different terms by a translator or playwright signals the broad approach adopted in rewriting the source text in a new language. A writer who claims to produce an adaptation rather than a translation, for example, indicates the greater level of freedom (i.e., from authorial or other control) that he or she purports to exercise in the process.[96] The writer asserts a degree of ownership over an earlier work which arguably reflects a tip in the balance of control between source-text producer and target-text writer. The labels also help the reader or audience to anticipate where on the continuum of (inevitable) change the text sits in relation to its acknowledged source text.[97] However it can be difficult to identify substantive differences between what is called a 'translation', a 'version' or an 'adaptation'. Indeed, it might be argued that because the act of rewriting always takes place on a continuum of possibilities it is impossible to draw a line between one type of rewriting and another.

In the abstract, we might go further and depart even from Lefevere in his seemingly fundamental but unexplained distinction between 'writing' and 'rewriting'.[98] We might argue that 're-writers' are no more or less than writers who acknowledge their sources explicitly. If we accept that all texts are informed by prior texts, that all involve some element of copying and that there is no 'original', just as there is no 'final' text, then we must also accept that there is no 'pure' writing and that all writing is, in fact, rewriting. This is a point implicitly acknowledged by Linda Hutcheon when she expresses her preference for the term 'adapted text' over 'source' or 'original'.[99] In practice,

96 Manuela Perteghella, 'Adaptation: "Bastard Child" or Critique? Putting Terminology Centre Stage', *Journal of Romance Studies*, 8.3 (2008), 51–65 (p. 51).

97 For an alternative, reception-led approach to text categorization, see Dennis Cutchins and Kathryn Meeks, 'Adaptation, Fidelity and Reception', in *The Routledge Companion to Adaptation*, ed. by Dennis Cutchins, Katja Krebs and Eckhart Voigts (London & New York: Routledge, 2018), pp. 301–13.

98 André Lefevere, *Translation, Rewriting and the Manipulation of Literary Fame* (London & New York: Routledge, 1992), pp. 1–10.

99 Hutcheon, *A Theory of Adaptation*, p. xv. More explicit reasoning for this preference is provided later by Hutcheon: 'By stressing the relation of individual works to other works and to an entire cultural system, French semiotic and post-structuralist theorizing of intertextuality [...] has been important in its challenges to dominant post-Romantic notions of originality, uniqueness, and autonomy. Instead, texts are said to be mosaics of citations that are visible and invisible, heard and silent; they are always already written and read. So, too, are adaptations, but with the added proviso that they are also acknowledged as adaptations *of specific texts*' (p. 21).

however, the more conventional terminology of 'source' and 'original' is useful insofar as it allows us to identify the process that is chronologically prior and hence to trace more easily the conditions of production. This study examines rewritings (as Hutcheon examines adaptations) 'as deliberate, announced, and extended revisitations of prior works'.[100] It accordingly uses the terms 'translation', 'version' and 'adaptation' interchangeably, except where context dictates otherwise: where the re-writer uses one label in preference to the others, that label is acknowledged and adopted.

The terminology comes under additional scrutiny in the field of theatre translation, when the overlap between Translation Studies and Adaptation Studies comes to the fore. Here, Roman Jakobson's intersemiotic and interlingual translation models coincide; and matters are often further complicated by the presence of a literal translation (leading necessarily to the third of Jakobson's categories: the intralingual translation).[101] It is with respect to this last practice that Brodie has highlighted the camouflaging nature of the labels applied to theatre productions, which effectively hide the labours of the literal translator. She concludes that rather than necessarily reflecting a methodical criterion for rewritten texts, the 'shifting vocabulary reminds the receiving audience to question the genesis of what they are seeing, prompting them to recall that they are witnessing an act of interpretation'.[102] Elsewhere, Brodie has argued that the varying nomenclature 'serves more as a reminder that translation is a site of contention than providing a precise description of the creative processes involved'.[103] The terms do not permit or map onto a precise taxonomy of rewriting, but instead act as markers of a perceived hierarchy.[104] This summary coincides with the findings of this study: the labels applied to the English rewritings of Schnitzler's dramas do not in any obvious way reflect back on or describe the relationship between the English-language text and the source text. Rather they tend to be directed outwards, to the receiving audience, as a means of establishing the status of the new text in the

100 Hutcheon, *A Theory of Adaptation*, p. xvi.

101 Roman Jakobson, 'On Linguistic Aspects of Translation', in *The Translation Studies Reader*, ed. by Lawrence Venuti, 3rd edn (Abingdon: Routledge, 2012), pp. 126–31. Jakobson identifies three kinds of translation: *interlingual* (between languages), *intralingual* (rewording within the same language) and *intersemiotic* (the transposition from one medium to another) (p. 128). Cf. Brodie for a more detailed application of these three models to theatre translation (Brodie, 'Indirect Translation', p. 336).

102 Brodie, 'Indirect Translation', p. 346.

103 Brodie, *The Translator on Stage*, p. 5.

104 For an illuminating discussion of the distinction between 'translation' and 'adaptation', the function of the terminology and the particular case of literal translators, see Katja Krebs, 'Translation and Adaptation – Two Sides of an Ideological Coin', in *Translation, Adaptation and Transformation*, ed. by Lawrence Raw (London & New York: Bloomsbury, 2012), pp. 42–53.

receiving culture. Three very different plays claim to be 'adapted' from *Reigen*, for example: *La Ronde* (adapted by John Barton, 1982), *The Blue Room* ('freely' adapted by David Hare, 1998) and *Fucking Men* (adapted by Joe DiPietro, 2008). No two of the three are alike in their approach to the source material, as shown in more detail in Chapter 4.

Here, as above, this study advocates an approach that recognizes the indiscrete nature of the categories of rewriting. The editors of *Adapting Translation for the Stage* develop Hutcheon's idea – of a continuum of adaptation, with literary translation at one end and at the other spin-offs, fanzines, sequels and prequels – and propose 'that instead of an either/or dichotomy, translation and adaptation are understood as spectrum or continuum, that is forever in flux and embodies the potential to loop back on itself'.[105] Similarly, Margherita Laera suggests:

> Rather than talking about translation in terms of duality or purity, it is more helpful to describe its multiple practices as a spectrum of hybridity. Translation practice, and especially theatre translation, involves the constant negotiation and renegotiation of choices which always end up in the blending of target- and source-oriented strategies within the same text.[106]

Such an understanding of rewritten texts as being located on a continuum or spectrum of hybridity corresponds with the above assessment of collaborative and multiple authorship and, as will be seen below, is supported by the genetic and micro-historical methodologies subsequently applied in this study, which reveal through their detailed findings the shifting policies and approaches to decision-making which inform the process of rewriting.

Using the Archive: Developing Methodologies and De-Stabilizing Texts

In three of the four chapters in this book substantial use is made of archive materials held at Cambridge University Library, the Deutsches Literaturarchiv in Marbach, the Theatermuseum in Vienna and the Harry Ransom Center at the University of Texas at Austin. To a lesser degree, but of equal importance to the research, use was also made of the BBC Written Archives Centre in Reading, the National Theatre Archive in London, the Schnitzler

105 Geraldine Brodie and Emma Cole, 'Introduction', in *Adapting Translation for the Stage*, ed. by Geraldine Brodie and Emma Cole (London: Routledge, 2017), pp. 1–18 (p. 7).

106 Margherita Laera, 'Theatre Translation as Collaboration: Aleks Sierz, Martin Crimp, Nathalie Abrahami, Colin Teevan, Zoë Svendsen and Michael Walton Discuss Translation for the Stage', *Contemporary Theatre Review*, 21 (2011), 213–25 (p. 214).

Press-Cuttings Archive at the University of Exeter and the Lord Chamberlain's Archive in the British Library. The work carried out in the archives takes this project beyond the more traditional realms of translation research, that is to say, beyond consideration of the 'primary text product' as per Gideon Toury's Descriptive Translation Studies, and in some respects necessarily so.[107] This study engages with performed as well as printed drama, straddling the disciplines of Translation Studies and Theatre Studies; and hence it requires an exercise in reconstruction in order to re-create as far as possible the live production. It therefore looks behind the published remnants of translated texts in performance to investigate the preceding written correspondence, the drafts, the corrections, the prompt scripts and the post-performance revisions. Research of this nature also contributes to the overall picture of the paratexts surrounding a play, the significance of which has been set out above. However, there is a more fundamental reason for the dive into the archives. This study examines the process, as well as the product, of translation and, in particular, the ways in which individual agents exercise power over that process. This could only be guessed at if its survey were limited to published texts. By looking at manuscripts and personal papers, as well as post-production notes and revisions, it is possible to start solving the puzzle of how and by whom meaning is made in any given textual iteration. The flipside of this situation, however, is that it can be difficult to assess the exercise of power in more recent productions for which no archive yet exists. Chapter 4, which is concerned with post-2002 adaptations of *Reigen*, is accordingly an anomaly: power is located in places not so easily identified or investigated. As a result, the more public manifestations of power, those discernible in the texts and performances themselves and in the published paratextual material, provide the focus, rather than any private negotiations.

Support for the general approach adopted is found in the scholarship of Jeremy Munday, who promotes a micro-historical study of translations and their producers. With 'microhistory' Munday describes the project of looking through 'the personal papers, manuscripts and related archives and other testimony' of translators, placing it in opposition to 'quantitative macro-social history'.[108] By looking in this way, the micro-historian 'excavate[s] and recover[s] details of lives past' and so provides a means of understanding the individual relationships between actors' beliefs, values

107 Gideon Toury, *Descriptive Translation Studies – and Beyond* (Amsterdam & Philadelphia, PA: Benjamins, 1995), p. 65.

108 Jeremy Munday, 'Using Primary Sources to Produce a Microhistory of Translation and Translators: Theoretical and Methodological Concerns', *The Translator*, 20 (2014), 64–80 (pp. 64 and 75).

and social affiliations.[109] This in turn 'uncover[s] the power relations at work in the production of the literary text'.[110] Thus 'drafts of the translation are crucial for revealing some of the translator's decision-making' and can help to 'identify the changes made at different stages and those points in a text that are particularly problematic or "critical"'.[111] A similar approach is described by Cordingley and Montini under the title of 'genetic translation studies'. They identify the roots of their new discipline in the French school of *critique génétique*, which methodology maintains that 'the published text is but one phase in the text's evolution, and that this process of textual transformation continues well *after* the work's publication through its re-editions, its retranslations and its different reception by heterogeneous communities of readers'.[112] This is a methodology which chimes with the above conceptualization of text and meaning as unstable and unfixed. Indeed, Cordingley and Montini explicitly state that it is the purpose of the collection of essays they introduce to 'stimulate [...] research into the contingencies of the translated text'.[113] The following assessment of Schnitzler's dramas in translation picks up the gauntlet thus thrown down and takes as its object of study not merely the published or 'finished' text (elsewhere described as the 'last state in a continuum of textual becoming') but the 'work in progress'.[114] By paying attention to each scrap available in relation to the process of creating a text in translation, these efforts also 'problematize the much-debated "agency" of the translator'.[115] With both 'genetic' and 'micro-historical' approaches to examining the process of translating, therefore, the concepts of 'author' and 'text' are productively destabilized and revised.

No discussion of archival research is complete without reference to the pioneering work of Foucault and Derrida in challenging traditional ideas about the archive as a neutral preserver of truth and knowledge. This is particularly the case in a study concerned, as this one is, with the exercise of power. Archivists, like translators, have conventionally been regarded as transparent, unbiased conveyors of a source product: 'Traditional belief states that archives as institutions are guardians of truth; archives as records contain the pristine evidence of past acts and historical fact'.[116] Postmodern reflections on this

109 Munday, 'Using Primary Sources', p. 64.

110 Munday, 'Using Primary Sources', p. 67.

111 Munday, 'Using Primary Sources', p. 72.

112 Cordingley and Montini, 'Genetic Translation Studies', p. 2.

113 Cordingley and Montini, 'Genetic Translation Studies', p. 2.

114 Cordingley and Montini, 'Genetic Translation Studies', p. 3.

115 Cordingley and Montini, 'Genetic Translation Studies', p. 4.

116 Joan M. Schwartz and Terry Cook, 'Archives, Records, and Power: The Making of Modern Memory', *Archival Science*, 2 (2002), 1–19 (p. 11).

topic have, however, made it 'manifestly clear' that archives and archivists (like translators) wield power in shaping our national identity, our memories and our self-knowledge – or, to put it in Mona Baker's language, in directing our ontological, public, conceptual and meta-narratives.[117] Only by interrogating the root policies which inform or motivate the archivists' collection, categorization and presentation of material can we begin to dismantle some of that power and render more transparent the stories we tell about ourselves.

Derrida's oft-quoted footnote continues to act as a beacon to scholars in this regard: 'There is no political power without control of the archive, if not memory. Effective democratization can always be measured by this essential criterion: the participation in and access to the archive, its constitution, and its interpretation'.[118] It is accordingly imperative for the researcher to be aware of the underlying principles and politics of an archival institution and its employees, which result in the selection and preservation of some materials and the rejection and disposal of others. With each election made by the archivist, status is attributed or denied to the individual object. Foucault puts the point rather more poetically:

> [T]he archive is [...] that which determines that all these things said do not accumulate endlessly in an amorphous mass, nor are they inscribed in an unbroken linearity, nor do they disappear at the mercy of chance external accidents; but they are grouped together in distinct figures, composed together in accordance with multiple relations, maintained or blurred in accordance with specific regularities; that which determines that they do not withdraw at the same pace in time, but shine, as it were, like stars, some that seem close to us shining brightly from afar off [*sic*], while others that are in fact close to us are already growing pale.[119]

The translation 'star', to continue Foucault's metaphor, has been allowed to fade all too quickly.

Munday observes that '[w]hen it comes to the study of translation, until recently exclusion seems to have been the norm[;] [t]races of the translator are generally hard to find in many collections and require some excavation'.[120]

117 Schwartz and Cook, 'Archives, Records, and Power', p. 2.

118 Jacques Derrida, 'Archive Fever: A Freudian Impression', *Diacritics*, 25.2 (1995), 9–63 (p. 11 n. 1) (orig.: *Mal d'archive: une impression freudienne* (Paris: Galilée, 1995)).

119 Michel Foucault, *The Archaeology of Knowledge*, trans. by A. M. Sheridan Smith (London & New York: Routledge, 2002), pp. 145–46 (orig.: *L'archéologie du savoir* (Paris: Gallimard, 1969)).

120 Munday, 'Using Primary Sources', p. 71.

Rachel Foss, a curator of modern literary transcripts at the British Library, recognized the problem as it still existed in 2011:

> [T]his material is generally not held in a discrete, signposted way, but absorbed within larger collections of writers who were not necessarily known primarily for their work as translators. [...] At the present time, there are very few collections that have been built around the work of a translator *as translator*.[121]

This historical treatment of the traces of the translating process and the papers of the translator coincides with the wider trends of dismissing translation as a derivative practice. Translators' manuscripts lack sufficient 'authorial capital' and have been considered 'ephemeral and historically contingent'.[122] Thus '[o]nly when the translator had acquired independent "symbolic power" [...] could some traction be gained for the idea that translators' avant-textes were worthy objects of study'.[123] Even Foss, who seeks to explain the situation from the perspective of the archive, accepts that collecting has, historically, centred 'on the idea of the pre-eminent individual writer' so that 'translators problematize notions of single territories and of the single author and [...] pose a challenge to traditional collecting models'.[124] The situation is changing. In 2013 the British Library acquired the archives of Michael Hamburger, who translated Celan, Rilke and Hölderlin among others, and of Michael Meyer, who translated Ibsen and Strindberg; and in 2018 the Bodleian Libraries at the University of Oxford acquired the papers of Ilsa Barea, an Austrian writer and translator who lived as an exile in Britain from 1939 and was involved in translating Schnitzler's works. It is hoped that this recognition of the value of translators' archives will become the norm.

How should a researcher proceed in the meantime, when faced with very apparent gaps in the archive? As Munday points out, '[i]n the absence of a central catalogue of archives searchable by keyword or theme, it is often difficult to locate collections that are relevant for translation studies research'.[125] However, in the digital age today's researchers have a distinct advantage over colleagues working even only a decade ago. From the static desk one can search archive catalogues around the world; and the more archives digitize their catalogues and collections, the easier life becomes for those researching marginalized groups of any kind. In the absence of translators' drafts clues have been drawn from other areas of the archive. For example, references to draft translations

121 Rachel Foss, 'Collecting Translators' Papers', *In Other Words*, 38 (2011), 30–32.
122 Cordingley and Montini, 'Genetic Translation Studies', p. 6.
123 Cordingley and Montini, 'Genetic Translation Studies', p. 6.
124 Foss, 'Collecting Translators' Papers'.
125 Munday, 'Using Primary Sources', p. 71.

could be discovered in the correspondence between Heinrich Schnitzler and individual translators. In another case, a translator has corresponded with Arthur Schnitzler, responding in detail to a third party's criticism of her translation work. These scraps of detail assist enormously in building up the bigger picture of the translator's practice and go some way towards counteracting that erasure of memory effected by the failure of the archive to preserve and record. They represent what Munday has called a '[t]riangulation of findings': by cross-referring between public statements, published translations, private correspondence and the rare example of a translator's draft, it becomes possible to reconstruct a detailed picture of the evolution of Schnitzler's plays in Britain over the course of more than a century.[126]

Due to its exploration of the papers of the text producers – the translators, the author himself, the agents, publishers and theatre-managers – this study might be accused of trying to reintroduce a biographically oriented hermeneutics. Ever since Barthes declared the death of the author in 1967 the trend within literary criticism has been to follow suit and, at the very least, to question the relevance of any writer's identity or biography to an understanding or interpretation of his or her work: the text is everything, the author's intentions irrelevant.[127] That shift has not taken place in Translation Studies. Indeed, the opposite has occurred. The title of Venuti's work – *The Translator's Invisibility* – sums it up neatly: Venuti calls on scholars across disciplines to recognize the vital role of the translator in the dissemination of cultural products and to make him or her present. Far from wishing to kill off the translator, the most recent tranche of translation theorists apparently want to bring him or her *as a person* to the forefront of our imaginations. To this end there have already been various studies which have focused to some degree on the biographical details of particular translators.[128] The possible inconsistency between approaches, that is to say, between our post-Barthesian treatment of the author and our Venuti-inspired naming of the translator, becomes even more apparent when author and translator are viewed as collaborators: as the translator's status grows in terms of creative responsibility and recognition for the published or performed text, we must

126 Munday, 'Using Primary Sources', p. 74.

127 Roland Barthes, 'The Death of the Author', in Roland Barthes, *Image Music Text*, pp. 142–48 (orig.: 'La mort de l'auteur', *Manteia*, 5 (1968), 12–17). For a recent riposte to the status of Barthes' essay and its key argument, see Joshua Landy, 'The Most Overrated Article of All Time?', *Philosophy and Literature*, 41 (2017), 465–70.

128 See, for example, Susanne Stark, *'Behind Inverted Commas': Translation and Anglo-German Cultural Relations in the Nineteenth Century* (Clevedon: Multilingual Matters, 1999); Krebs, *Cultural Dissemination*.

ask ourselves why he or she should not be dropped from the picture, like the author, when analysing that text.

There are two responses to that challenge. First, an approach to the study of translation which seeks to make the translator visible is justified by the aim of legitimizing the power of the translator and recognizing his or her role in the creative process. An investigation of power, in all its manifestations, in the relationship between translator and author is an ethically determined project that necessarily draws us outside the narrow confines of the text and its interpretation and into the socio-political context in which it was produced. Indeed, for this very reason biographical research is not only justified but required in the proper execution of this study. Second, the biographical-genetic approach remains a legitimate lens through which one might read a text's meaning, as long as it is not the only interpretative lens applied. Seen in a different (Foucauldian) way:

> the subject should not be entirely abandoned. It should be reconsidered, not to restore the theme of the originating subject, but to seize its functions, its intervention in discourse, and its system of dependencies. [...] In short, the subject (and its substitutes) must be stripped of its creative role and analysed as a complex and variable function of discourse.[129]

Both Rosemary Arrojo (in respect of translation) and Linda Hutcheon (in respect of adaptation) have sought to re-assess the position of the interpreter (i.e., translator or adapter) after the death of 'traditional authorship'.[130] For Arrojo, the accompanying birth of the reader signals 'the acceptance of the interpreter's inevitable visibility', so that 'translator-function', like 'author-function', is treated as a 'a key factor in the necessary repression of meaning proliferation that takes place in any act of interpretation'.[131] In a more explicitly radical vein, Hutcheon argues that we 'need to rethink the function of adapter intention *for the audience*', consciously re-engaging with the historically asserted fallacy of deploying intentionality as 'the *sole* arbiter and guarantee of the meaning and value of a work of art'.[132] Knowledge about the maker's mind, Hutcheon continues, can 'affect the audience members' interpretation: what they know

129 Foucault, 'What Is an Author?', pp. 137–38.

130 Rosemary Arrojo, 'The "Death" of the Author and the Limits of the Translator's Visibility', in *Translation as Intercultural Communication*, ed. by Snell-Hornby, Jettmarová and Kaindl, pp. 21–32 (p. 30); Hutcheon, *A Theory of Adaptation*, pp. 106–11.

131 Arrojo, 'The "Death" of the Author', p. 30.

132 Hutcheon, *A Theory of Adaptation*, pp. 109 and 106–07; and generally on 'Intentionality in Adaptations', see pp. 105–11.

about artists' desires and motivations, even about their life situations when they are creating, can influence the interpretation of any work's meaning, as well as the response to it'.[133] The audience, like the adapter, interprets in a context. Furthermore, both adapter and audience can be informed by 'journalistic curiosity and scholarly digging'.[134] A study such as this, therefore, which digs up the whys and wherefores of rewriting Schnitzler by investigating the individuals involved, affords new perspectives on the rewritten text. It does not set out to prescribe or delimit possible interpretations, but to expand our means of understanding the translated play.

The methodologies applied here provide practical resources for engaging with questions concerning the ontology of the text. The discovery and analysis of translation-related archive material interrogate popular conceptualizations of the hierarchy of texts, which posit certain texts as final and authoritative while others are contingent and subservient. As the archives bear witness to the multiple agents who influence or author any given textual iteration, we are led to see all texts as unfinished and meaning likewise as unfixed. The idea that any individual actor might forever determine a text's meaning becomes a farce. Cordingley and Montini draw a pertinent comparison between translation as a practice and genetic criticism as a method of research: like translation itself, 'it is in the very nature of genetic criticism to unfinish that which seemed to be finished, to destabilize textual authority by submitting a text to its multiple witnesses and incarnations'.[135]

Susan Howe takes the point further when she writes about the materiality of the in-person encounter with the archived object, such that meaning for Howe is generated in that moment: 'Each collected object or manuscript is a pre-articulate empty theater where a thought may surprise itself at the instant of seeing'.[136] The power to determine textual meaning, then, is rarely, if ever, located in just one person. Rather, it is diffuse and fluid. Indeed, the researcher him- or herself holds some of that power: '[T]he new narratives we construe based on these "little facts" [i.e., our findings in the archives] have the potential to challenge dominant historical discourses of text production'.[137] When researchers explore the processes of rewriting texts, they, too, exercise power over those texts and thereby contribute to the rewriting of public and conceptual narratives.

133 Hutcheon, *A Theory of Adaptation*, p. 109.
134 Hutcheon, *A Theory of Adaptation*, p. 111.
135 Cordingley and Montini, 'Genetic Translation Studies', p. 15.
136 Susan Howe, *Spontaneous Particulars: The Telepathy of Archives* (New York: Christine Burgin/New Directions, 2014), p. 24.
137 Munday, 'Using Primary Sources', p. 77.

Corpus and Structure

Only Schnitzler's dramatic works are considered in this book and of those the focus is on just four. Schnitzler's corpus is substantial in volume, varied in genre and covers an extensive range of subjects. The thinking behind this project would be spread too thinly and the opportunities to demonstrate its hypotheses too rare if the whole corpus were assessed. The dramatic works are the more obvious candidates when it comes to considering collaborative authorship, unstable texts and contingent meaning. Production for and performance in a theatre accentuate and extend all these features of literary creation and they often do so in a more transparent way. It is easier to see that a play text does not have a fixed ontology – that it might be altered by any given director, producer or actor, from one performance to the next. It is not the argument of this book that prose texts are not similarly unfixed, merely that the evidence is more legible in the world of theatre and live performance.

The four dramatic works which form the subject of this book are *Anatol* (1893), *Liebelei* (1895), *Reigen* (1900) and *Das weite Land* (1911). This selection, whilst made after reasoned reflection, is not unproblematic: it excludes all the later plays and includes the three dramatic works whose over-representation in overseas productions and ensuing impact on his reception abroad were lamented by Schnitzler. However, it is precisely because *Anatol*, *Liebelei* and *Reigen* have been taken up with such enthusiasm in anglophone literary circles that their translations merit special attention. It is these three works which have generated the most translations, theatre productions and publications. Examination of these three therefore allows comparison across multiple interpretations, so that patterns can be discerned with greater confidence. On balance, the spoils to be won by studying these three plays outweigh the risks of further promoting a selection that is by no means representative of Schnitzler's full corpus. The fourth play, *Das weite Land*, is included for a number of reasons, but primarily because it was the first of Schnitzler's plays to be produced at the National Theatre in London; it therefore marks a moment of canonization in the history of Schnitzler's reception in Britain.

Over the course of four chapters this book charts the arc of the British reception of Schnitzler's works as it unfolded over 115 years. Generally excluded from the study are American production and reception, notwithstanding the obvious overlap which results from the (largely) shared language. Not only would inclusion of America extend the project beyond what is practically manageable within such a volume, but it would also complicate the analysis carried out below by reason of the very different legal histories (copyright and censorship) and further federal differentiation. The approach here is chronological, beginning with translations proposed and produced in the early years of the last century and concluding with British interpretations made in the first decades of this century. Thus Chapter 1 looks at the process of transporting *Liebelei* to London as it happened during the writer's lifetime. This is a period for which it makes sense to think about direct authorial control. It has been possible, in writing this chapter, to draw on letters between the author and his various agents in Britain and so to re-create, to some degree, the delicate negotiations which led first to failure but ultimately to a small success for Schnitzler's play on the London stage. The correspondence reveals how various parties vied to determine the presentation of *Liebelei* in English, thereby exposing clashing interests among Schnitzler's agents.

Chapter 2 considers the period immediately following the writer's death. For fifty years the trustee of the literary estate, Heinrich Schnitzler, controlled the dissemination of his father's works. It is accordingly argued that we can speak of a diminished, secondary or indirect authorial control during this period. The source texts, Schnitzler's plays, were still owned by an identifiable proprietor, an individual with a claim to privileged knowledge of the author's intentions and the legal power to prevent any interpretation that contradicted those presumed intentions. The degree to which Heinrich Schnitzler succeeded in controlling the posthumous estate is interrogated through consideration of the *Anatol* cycle of playlets in their various English-language manifestations over the half-century. Of significance during this period is the role played by the BBC, which provided one of the major outlets for the production of Schnitzler's works in Britain. At the opposite end of the scale, fringe or off-West-End theatres maintained a steady interest in performing Schnitzler in translation, with major theatres like the new National Theatre remaining, frustratingly, largely uninterested.

Chapter 3 can be read as a bridging chapter, marking the point at which Schnitzler's works moved out of copyright and further into the mainstream. It looks at two translations, both nominally written by Tom Stoppard and both produced at the National Theatre. The first, *Undiscovered Country*, was produced in 1979, a clear two years before the expiry of copyright. The second, *Dalliance*, was produced in 1986, after Heinrich Schnitzler's death and when Arthur Schnitzler's works had entered the public domain. Examination of the two translated texts and their genesis shows us what changes when copyright ends and those with a claim to authorial knowledge (whether directly or due to a close father-son relationship) are no longer able to determine or guide interpretation. Stoppard's and Schnitzler's overlapping practices of the seemingly constant drafting, revising and testing of their work also highlight a shared conception of the text as contingent and unfinished.

Chapter 4 considers productions of one play, *Reigen*, in the post-copyright period. As might be expected, this is a time when interpretations run fast and loose with the original text. This particular play, for so long the most stringently controlled of Schnitzler's works, has generated a spectacularly large corpus of spin-offs on the anglophone stage and, indeed, in radio, television and cinema. In this study the formal and substantive continuities and discontinuities have been sought in an effort to explain the extraordinary malleability of Schnitzler's most infamous play. The brief conclusion draws together the threads of the previous chapters and suggests how these findings inform the wider fields of Schnitzler research, Theatre Studies and Translation Studies.

CHAPTER 1

Liebelei in London

This chapter analyses the British transmission of Schnitzler's play *Liebelei* from 1896 to 1920 through scrutiny of the correspondence between Schnitzler and his British agents and translators; consideration of reviews of the various German and English productions of the play in London; and a comparative reading of three English translations written during the period in question. Integral to the enquiry is an understanding of the complex web of negotiations leading up to the English-language première in 1909, as well as the unusual circumstances that gave rise to an unauthorized book publication in 1914.

The chapter starts with an account of the play itself and its initial domestic reception, before touching on its swift dissemination further afield. The subsequent examination of attempts to produce *Liebelei* in London provides a chronologically ordered case study of the challenges encountered when bringing the works of an as yet unknown foreign writer into Britain. By probing the play's relatively dilatory transmission in Britain, light is simultaneously cast on the reasons for its success elsewhere. Attention is directed to the interaction between particular individuals involved in the transference and reception of this single work, thereby enabling broader reflection on how Schnitzler came to be represented in the English-speaking world. What follows, then, is a 'micro-history' (to use Munday's term) of *Liebelei* in London; it is an attempt to identify, through minutely detailed research, the contingencies of textual production at the beginning of the twentieth century.

The years in question overlap with what was soon afterwards called the 'period of the greatest dramatic energy [in English theatre] since the Elizabethans',[1] that of the 'New Drama' and the 'New Theatre',[2] elements of which were '[r]ichly important [...] to the future of the stage'.[3] This survey of the entrance of one play onto the Edwardian stage in London therefore illuminates further a particularly dynamic era in British theatre history.

1 James Agate, *A Short View of the English Stage, 1900–1926* (London: Jenkins, 1926), p. 68.

2 Cary M. Mazer, 'New Theatres for a New Drama', in *The Cambridge Companion to Victorian and Edwardian Theatre*, ed. by Kerry Powell (Cambridge: Cambridge University Press, 2004), pp. 207–21 (p. 208).

3 J. C. Trewin, *The Edwardian Theatre* (Oxford: Blackwell, 1976), p. 4.

The chapter concludes with a comparative reading of the translations from 1909 and 1914 alongside fragments of an earlier, unpublished translation by Schnitzler's first known English translator, Helen Macdonell. At each stage the documentary material is assessed for evidence of the power dynamics between Schnitzler and those working to introduce the play to a London audience and readership. It becomes clear through such analysis that power can be read: (1) in the translated text itself (for example, in the target culture's norms imposed at the expense of those of the source culture); (2) in the meta-language of the paratexts describing both the act of translation and the ultimate product; and (3) in the nuts and bolts of the negotiation process, in which agent and translator battle for recognition and remuneration.

The Play and its Initial Reception

The three-act drama *Liebelei* is arguably one of the most important works in Schnitzler's oeuvre, not least for the part it played in establishing his reputation as a writer, both at home and abroad. It was the first play by Schnitzler to be performed at the Burgtheater and it coincided with a significant moment of transition, of 'contrasts and tensions [...] between tradition and novelty, conservatism and change', in Viennese theatre.[4] The play concerns a love affair in Vienna around 1895 between a young petty-bourgeois woman, Christine, and an affluent middle-class student, Fritz. The two have been introduced by their respective friends, Mizi and Theodor, who are themselves engaged in a light romance. Theodor seeks, via the introduction, to steer Fritz away from a more dangerous ongoing liaison with a married woman. In the opening act Fritz hosts Theodor, Christine and Mizi for an evening of food, drink and song. The general frivolity of the evening is interrupted by the arrival of the cuckolded husband and Fritz is challenged to a duel. Both the concurrent love interest and the proposed duel remain unknown to Christine, who declares herself Fritz's in the sincerest, if sentimental, terms. In Act 2 Fritz visits Christine in her own home. The shadow of the imminent duel and the possibility of death hang over him and he meditates with a similar mix of sincerity and sentimentality on the alternative life he might have enjoyed with Christine had he not felt bound to accept the cuckolded husband's challenge. Christine remains oblivious. Finally, in the third act the multiple tragedies of Christine's situation unfold: Fritz has died for another woman and Christine has been told of neither the affair nor the death until after his funeral. Her insignificance to the dead man becomes clear to her; she rushes off to his grave

4 Yates, 'Continuity and Discontinuity', p. 53.

and, if her father's melodramatic curtain line ('Sie kommt nicht wieder – sie kommt nicht wieder') is believed, to her own death.

The drama displays many features soon considered typical of Schnitzler's work. Indeed, Schnitzler would complain only a few years later: '[I]ch bin in das Kastl mit der Aufschrift "Liebelei" hineingethan; die Kritiker haben das nicht gern, wenn die Taferln gewechselt werden' (*Briefe* I, 438–39, 4.7.1901). Christine can be seen as the archetypal suburban *süßes Mädel*; she seems innocently available for romantic dalliance, subject to the double-standards which governed at the time and allowed wealthy young men to have their fun and walk away without any consequences.[5] Similarly, Fritz might be viewed, in certain respects, as a successor to Schnitzler's earlier creation Anatol (from the *Anatol* cycle) and a forerunner to numerous further lost souls struggling at the threshold between decadent self-indulgence (confined by societal convention) and disruptive self-examination. On fuller consideration, however, the differences between Christine and Fritz are revealed to be even more complex. Their relationship is doomed, not because of class discrepancies or differing expectations, but because of fundamental divergences in their respective sense of self and their relations with the outside world. Whereas Christine is someone unwilling to compromise where her own feelings are concerned, a woman in possession of a 'beinahe schon anachronistisch anmutendem absoluten Ich',[6] Fritz appears vulnerable to change at the slightest breeze and frequently expresses scepticism at the possibility of consistency or permanence in anyone's feelings.

The première of *Liebelei* on 9 October 1895 came almost a year after Schnitzler first presented the play to the director of the Burgtheater, Max Burckhard. The lapse between Burckhard reading the play and its première resulted not from any lack of enthusiasm on the director's part, but from two other, related factors. First, Burckhard was concerned about the potential for scandal. In Act 2 two unmarried women socialize with men in the privacy of a bachelor's rooms and in Act 3 Fritz visits Christine at home without the protection of a chaperone. Either scene would have been sufficient to provoke moral indignation in contemporary Viennese society; and the performance

5 Yates makes the connection between Schnitzler's own first encounter with a *süßes Mädel*, his familiarity with Johann Nestroy's *Das Mädl aus der Vorstadt* and the first plans for what would eventually come to be called *Liebelei* (Yates, *Schnitzler, Hofmannsthal, and the Austrian Theatre*, p. 130). Arguably Mizi is the character in *Liebelei* most easily described by reference to the *süßes Mädel* mould; by contrast, Christine's tragedy is that she is cast by those around her as a *süßes Mädel* when her own encounter with the world far exceeds such limitations.

6 Vivien Friedrich, '*Liebelei. Schauspiel in drei Akten* (1895)', in *Schnitzler-Handbuch*, ed. by Jürgensen, Lukas and Scheffel, pp. 60–64 (p. 63). This chapter is indebted to this entry on *Liebelei* for its summary of the initial performance history of the play in Vienna.

of such scenes in the Royal-Imperial, and therefore historically conservative, Burgtheater would have been even riskier.[7] Second, as a consequence of that potential scandal, the only Burgtheater actress suitable for the role of Christine, Stella von Hohenfels, refused to play it. Instead, the popular Adele Sandrock from the Volkstheater was engaged.[8] When the play was finally produced, the critical response was mixed (as had been expected) but, perhaps more importantly, the popular response was hugely positive. In the 1895–96 season the play was performed sixteen times, rendering it the most played piece in the repertoire of the Burgtheater (*Tagebuch*, 28.6.1896). Schnitzler records that his own wish to attend the ninth performance was frustrated by the fact that the theatre was sold out (*Tagebuch*, 6.11.1895). The production remained in the Burgtheater's repertoire until 15 September 1910, by which time it had achieved forty-two performances.[9] Schnitzler's wife Olga recalled attending one of these performances as a young girl and her reminiscences sum up the play's popular appeal:

> Da standen sie nicht wie sonst auf der Bühne in einer heroischen Dekoration, in farbigem Kostüm, große Verse rollend, nein, ein junges Mädchen aus dem Volk klagte im wienerischen Dialekt ihre Liebe und ihre Verzweiflung, einfache Menschen, nah und vertraut, waren in die Sphäre der Dichtung gehoben worden.[10]

Liebelei was undoubtedly the play which marked Schnitzler's breakthrough as a playwright, as well as signalling the 'breakthrough of indigenous modern drama' in Vienna.[11] It also set the tone for Schnitzler's subsequent reception in Austria and abroad, painting him forever after, and much to his chagrin, as creator of the figure of the *süßes Mädel*.

The play quickly proved itself a 'Schwerpunkt der weiteren Rezeption':[12] it had its première in Berlin on 4 February 1896; in Frankfurt on 11 January 1896; and in Cologne in April 1896; on 26 March 1896 it enjoyed huge success in

7 Burckhard was still concerned, five months after having accepted the play, that it would be seen as 'dangerous' (*Tagebuch*, 16.6.1895).

8 Stella von Hohenfels was born in 1857, so would in any event have made rather an old Christine. Adele Sandrock was Schnitzler's mistress until March 1895, having first met him when she played the lead in the first production of *Das Märchen* in the Deutsches Volkstheater (Yates, *Schnitzler, Hofmannsthal, and the Austrian Theatre*, pp. 29–30).

9 Minna von Alth, *Burgtheater von 1776–1976. Aufführungen und Besetzungen von zweihundert Jahren*, 2 vols (Vienna: Ueberreuter, 1979), I, 381.

10 Olga Schnitzler, *Spiegelbild der Freundschaft* (Salzburg: Residenz-Verlag, 1962), p. 17. This was one of the first times that Viennese dialect was heard on the stage of the Burgtheater (Yates, *Theatre in Vienna*, p. 180).

11 Yates, *Theatre in Vienna*, p. 180.

12 Hans-Peter Bayerdörfer, 'Weitere Rezeption und Wirkung', in *Schnitzler-Handbuch*, ed. by Jürgensen, Lukas and Scheffel, pp. 380–87 (p. 380).

St Petersburg in its original German (*Tagebuch*, 26.3.1896); and Russian-language premières were eventually staged in Moscow and St Petersburg in 1899.[13] In 1896 there were foreign-language productions in Copenhagen (*Tagebuch*, 24.9.1896 and 28.3.1897), Stockholm,[14] Milan and Prague (both *Tagebuch*, 15.10.1896) and Verona (*Tagebuch*, 2.7.1896). It is difficult to speculate in general terms as to the attractions *Liebelei* presented to its turn-of-the-century, international audiences. Schnitzler's reception abroad will have been helped or hindered in differing measure according to the particular legal, social, political and cultural circumstances obtaining in each different location. For example, the important part played by duelling and honour in the (off-stage) action of *Liebelei* would have been more difficult to grasp in places where duelling was scarcely more than a romantic cultural memory, if even that. In the case of Britain, it seems likely that the duel still held some sentimental appeal; certainly, George Bernard Shaw did not shy away from employing it as a dramatic device.[15]

At best one might argue that a Europe-wide Naturalist movement in modern theatre, with Ibsen and Strindberg in the vanguard, had carved a way for Schnitzler and his peers and given rise to an audience open to a new type of drama. Schnitzler's works captured a moment of change in Europe, a point of living on the brink between old and new worlds; and he treated the manifestations of this change in an unromantic way that presumably spoke to many across the Continent and even further afield. Counterbalancing such attractions was the above-mentioned potential for the play to prompt scandal and even provoke censorship: Viennese discomfort at the idea of two unmarried women spending an evening un-chaperoned in the private rooms of a bachelor would have been shared in many quarters of late-nineteenth-century Europe. Nevertheless, Schnitzler had sufficiently vocal and influential supporters outside Austria-Hungary to ensure that his play found a public abroad.

The Edwardian Theatre

Five key dates provide a structure to the story of *Liebelei* in London, among them those marking the work of three different translators:

1895 German-language première in Vienna
1897 Schnitzler reads first English translation, by **Helen Macdonell**

13 Alexander Belobratow, 'Russland und Osteuropa', in *Schnitzler-Handbuch*, ed. by Jürgensen, Lukas and Scheffel, pp. 358–63 (p. 359).

14 Ernst-Ullrich Pinkert, 'Skandinavien', in *Schnitzler-Handbuch*, ed. by Jürgensen, Lukas and Scheffel, pp. 372–74 (p. 372).

15 See, for example, Act 3 of *Arms and the Man* (1894).

1900	German-language première in London
1909	English-language première in London, translated by **G. Valentine Williams**
1914	First English-language publication by a London publishing house, translated by **P. Morton Shand**

These dates draw attention to the chronotopical context of Schnitzler's reception: they cover a twenty-year period of radical change in British theatre, when the dramatist George Bernard Shaw (1856–1950), the actor, dramatist and theatre manager Harley Granville Barker (1877–1946), the critic and Ibsen translator William Archer (1856–1924) and the Dutch-born theatre critic and impresario Jacob Thomas Grein (1862–1935) led the move away from a theatreland dominated by actor-managers running commercially driven outfits into an era in which a national repertory theatre was not merely conceivable but in development.[16] These and other protagonists of the 'Theatre of Ideas' (a serious, intellectualizing, 'writer's theatre')[17] made slow but steady incursions into the established theatre culture until the outbreak of war in 1914.[18] Although an unquestioned narrative of 'philistines versus impossibilists', i.e., of commercial versus non-commercial theatres, can no longer be upheld, the division between theatrical and idea-driven drama remains a helpful model when assessing the reception of a new foreign dramatist.[19]

Two major projects undertaken in the London theatre world were to have a direct bearing on Schnitzler's success in Britain, as well as more broadly on British theatre of the day: the Deutsches Theater in London (January 1900 to May 1908) and the John Eugene Vedrenne-Harley Granville Barker management of the Court Theatre (from October 1904 to June 1907).[20] Both had the effect of opening up London to new foreign drama. Although the West End had welcomed influence from France for much of the nineteenth century, this tended to be in the realm of light comedies and operettas rather than

16 William Archer and Harley Granville Barker, *Scheme & Estimates for a National Theatre* (London: Duckworth, 1907).

17 Jeffrey Richards, 'Henry Irving: The Actor-Manager as Auteur', *Nineteenth Century Theatre and Film*, 32 (2005), 20–35 (p. 21).

18 Trewin, *The Edwardian Theatre*, p. 24.

19 Thomas Postlewait describes the complex nature of developments during the period, including the not-infrequent collaboration between commercial theatre and non-commercial company or dramatist (Thomas Postlewait, 'The London Stage, 1895–1918', in *The Cambridge History of British Theatre*, ed. by Joseph Donohue and others, 3 vols (Cambridge: Cambridge University Press, 2004), III: *Since 1895*, ed. by Baz Kershaw, pp. 34–59 (p. 43)).

20 The Court Theatre was later named the Royal Court, becoming home to the English Stage Company in 1956.

the more literary drama that began to emerge at the turn of the century.[21] The two above-mentioned enterprises provided otherwise unheard-of foreign playwrights with performance space at the heart of the capital city, thereby exposing such playwrights and their work to an influential group of intellectuals. It was arguably the fortunate coincidence of Schnitzler's foray onto British territory with the two ventures in question that resulted in his (eventual) success in Britain.

When first produced in London, at the Deutsches Theater in 1900, *Liebelei* was performed in German and so was still relatively (if not completely) inaccessible to the everyday playgoer.[22] Krebs has highlighted that the aims of the Deutsches Theater were to reach both English and German audiences, notwithstanding the potential language barrier: this was not an enterprise designed solely to keep the German expatriate community happy, but was marketed to attract the British cosmopolitan as well.[23] The audience quite possibly included weighty figures like Barker, Archer and Shaw, all of whom were known to attend performances by the new company and to take a keen interest in drama coming out of Germany and Austria.[24] Support also came from the British Royal Family and the German Ambassador.[25] The networks of influence flowing from the venture lead Krebs to conclude: '[I]f one were to map Anglo-German relations forged and subsequent translations performed because of the European project that was the *Deutsches Theater in London*, it would be a busy map'.[26] The theatre company was founded by Jacob Thomas Grein and ultimately employed the skills of German actor-managers Max Behrend and Hans Andresen. Grein first built his reputation on the foundation of the Independent Theatre Society in London in 1891 and so was responsible for introducing plays by both Ibsen and Shaw to the (subscribing) London

21 Postlewait reports William Archer's observation that in 1898 'about 20 per cent of the productions in the West End [...] were adaptations from the French theatre – mainly comedies, farces and musicals' ('The London Stage', p. 41). See also W. E. Yates, 'Internationalization of European Theatre: French Influence in Vienna between 1830 and 1860', *Austrian Studies*, 13 (2005), 37–54 (pp. 38 and 43).

22 It has been suggested that a further German-language production was performed at the Deutsches Theater in 1903 'with Hans Andresen and Else Gademann' (Dekker, 'The Modern Catalyst', p. 187). No references are given, however, and no corroborative evidence has been found.

23 Katja Krebs, 'A Portrait of a European Cultural Exchange: The Deutsches Theater in London at the Turn of the Twentieth Century', *Angermion*, 5 (2012), 119–34.

24 Krebs, 'A Portrait of a European Cultural Exchange', p. 120.

25 Edward VII, a German-speaker and great advocate for German culture, attended two performances in 1902 and apparently 'laughed heartily'; and in 1905 the German Ambassador supported the project by way of a £100 guarantee (Michael Orme, *J. T. Grein: The Story of a Pioneer 1862–1935* (London: Murray, 1936), pp. 176 and 177).

26 Krebs, 'A Portrait of a European Cultural Exchange', p. 133.

public.[27] The native Dutchman became a naturalized British citizen in 1895 and thereafter continued to play a vital role in British theatrical life as a drama critic and producer.

According to his biography, written by his actress-translator wife Alix Augusta Greeven under the pseudonym 'Michael Orme':

> The [Deutsches Theater] scheme fell into line with [Grein's] cherished dreams of tightening the bonds between nations by the interchange of dramatic art and of widening the outlook of our English dramatists and managers by throwing open the gates of theatrical enterprise.[28]

By contrast, the motives informing Harley Granville Barker's translation, production and theoretical work were arguably inward-looking and distinctly patriotic in nature; his use of foreign theatre texts formed part of a strategy to create the tradition of a national theatre, i.e., a domestic tradition designed for domestic audiences.[29] Schnitzler's works accordingly benefitted from the two-fold support of those keen to use his work as part of a larger promotion of German culture and those wanting to put his works to the service of an expanding domestic scene, divorced from what was considered excessive French influence.[30]

The Vedrenne-Barker management of the Court Theatre between 1904 and 1907 was an important part of the expanding domestic scene. Unlike the Deutsches Theater and its scions, the Vedrenne-Barker years have received significant scholarly attention, not least because of the important role played by the Court Theatre in bringing George Bernard Shaw to a wider public.[31] In addition, however, Vedrenne and Barker gave much-needed new energy to the seeds of a movement which had already been sown by such groups as the New Century Theatre Company, the Independent Theatre Society and the Stage Society.[32] The managers replaced the usual long production runs with a

27 For some of the socio-political consequences of the Independent Theatre Society venture, see Tracy C. Davis, 'The Independent Theatre Society's Revolutionary Scheme for an Uncommercial Theater', *Theatre Journal*, 42 (1990), 447–54.

28 Orme, *J. T. Grein*, p. 167.

29 Cf. Krebs, *Cultural Dissemination*, p. 45.

30 Krebs, *Cultural Dissemination*, pp. 14–15.

31 See, for example, Sos Eltis, 'The Court Theatre', in *George Bernard Shaw in Context*, ed. by Brad Kent (Cambridge: Cambridge University Press, 2015), pp. 68–75; Dennis Kennedy, *Granville Barker and the Dream of the Theatre* (Cambridge: Cambridge University Press, 1985); Jan MacDonald, 'Shaw and the Court Theatre', in *The Cambridge Companion to George Bernard Shaw*, ed. by Christopher Innes (Cambridge: Cambridge University Press, 1998), pp. 261–82; James Woodfield, *English Theatre in Transition: 1881–1914* (London and Sydney: Croom Helm; Totowa, NJ: Barnes & Noble, 1984).

32 Desmond MacCarthy, *The Court Theatre, 1904–1907: A Commentary and Criticism* (London: Bullen, 1907), p. xiii.

regularly changing bill of plays and the dominant 'star' system with a style of direction which emphasized ensemble acting and promoted the appreciation of even the most minor roles.[33] Moreover, perhaps most importantly, they produced plays that no other theatre would touch: plays 'which have been attacks on current ideas [...], plays so unconventional in form and construction that no other manager in London would look at them'.[34] Among the thirty-two plays produced during their management were eleven by Shaw, two by Ibsen, plays by Gerhart Hauptmann, Maurice Maeterlinck, Barker and John Galsworthy and one by Schnitzler.

The Court Theatre was the first London theatre to produce a Schnitzler play in English. In 1905 a translation of *Die letzten Masken* was performed on nine occasions under the title *In the Hospital* as part of a triple bill, alongside W. B. Yeats's *The Pot of Broth* and Shaw's *How He Lied to Her Husband*. The production represents a marker in the story of the arrival of *Liebelei* in London and further highlights the role of the Vedrenne-Barker theatre as the nucleus for a web of radical theatrical activity, building on and overlapping in some respects with the Deutsches Theater project. The majority of theatre-goers might still have flocked to the farces and musicals of the West End, but there was a growing receptivity among English audiences to the type of Naturalist drama emerging from the German-speaking countries, Scandinavia and Russia at the turn of the century.

In light of that receptivity, together with the enormous success of *Liebelei* in Austria and Germany at the end of the nineteenth century, the question arises as to why it should be a further fourteen years before the play's English-language première in London. That delay is perhaps all the more unexpected when one considers that Schnitzler had young relatives, his uncle and aunt Felix Markbreiter (1855–1914) and Julie Markbreiter (1862–1938), on the ground in London and keen to act on his behalf. These were relatives with whom Schnitzler got on well. Julie was very close to Schnitzler in age and the two had shared a 'warmen Kuß' when teenagers, remembered in Schnitzler's autobiography, *Jugend in Wien* (p. 58). From subsequent references to her in the same volume we might legitimately conclude that Schnitzler admired and cared about his uncle's wife in adult life as well (pp. 54 and 59). Felix, on the other hand, is described in slightly less complementary terms (p. 54), at one point as a 'liebenswürdiger Philister' (*Tagebuch*, 25.5.1897). Schnitzler had visited the couple in London for a number of months in 1888 and maintained a stream of correspondence with them for several decades, as well as visiting a second time in the summer of 1897 and seeing them during the couple's own

33 MacCarthy, *The Court Theatre*, pp. 4–5.
34 MacCarthy, *The Court Theatre*, pp. 16–17.

visits to Austria before the First World War. In many of Julie Markbreiter's letters in particular she expresses her keen desire to see her nephew's works translated into English and performed and published in Britain. In explaining the puzzling lapse prior to the première of *Liebelei* in 1909 the extensive correspondence between Schnitzler and these London relatives is particularly fruitful.

Liebelei in English: The Early Years

In this and the following section a detailed account is provided of the earliest attempts to stage an English translation of *Liebelei* in Britain, including an assessment of Helen Macdonell's efforts to maintain control over her English text in the face of determined resistance. By adopting an approach which seeks to incorporate the full array of available primary sources, this book aims to reveal something of the 'conditions, working practices and identity' of Schnitzler's translators and agents, in their interactions with one another and with the translation process.[35] In so doing, it applies Munday's appraisal of social and cultural micro-history as a means of 'shed[ding] light on the bigger picture of the history of translation in specific socio-historical and cultural contexts'.[36] The following record and analysis of the surviving documents pertaining to Schnitzler's earliest forays into English-language productions of his works also assist us in grasping more broadly how his plays eventually arrived in British theatres.

The rather slow start *Liebelei* had in Britain is partly attributable to the amateur nature of its promotion and the lack of relevant experience of some of its greatest advocates. Felix Markbreiter is a good example: a full-time banker in the City of London, and in many respects a pioneer in the early enthusiasm he brought to his nephew's work, he was embarking upon largely unknown territory when he decided to take the British dissemination of *Liebelei* into his own hands. As early as 7 February 1896 Felix wrote to his sister Louise, Schnitzler's mother, congratulating her and her son on the success of the German première of *Liebelei* in the Deutsches Theater in Berlin on 4 February 1896. Felix suggested Schnitzler send him a copy of the playscript as soon as it was published so that he could present it to Herbert Beerbohm Tree, then director of the Haymarket Theatre.[37] A copy was duly sent and on 21 February Felix advised Arthur Schnitzler that as soon as he had received the promised reviews he would visit Tree. He had also tried to obtain an introduction to

35 Munday, 'Using Primary Sources', p. 64.

36 Munday, 'Using Primary Sources', p. 65

37 Felix Markbreiter to Louise Schnitzler, 7.2.1896 (DLA, HS.NZ85.0001.03999).

Charles Wyndham, the director of the Criterion Theatre, where in Felix's opinion *Liebelei* might best be placed. However, subsequent silence on the subject suggests the approach to Wyndham had come to nothing. By 29 February Felix was able to report to Schnitzler that he had spoken to Tree (on 28 February) and delivered both script and reviews. Tree apparently received Felix very warmly, promised to look at everything immediately and to let him know what he thought of the performability of the play in an English theatre.[38] The last letter from Felix on the subject is dated 19 March 1896: Tree had gone quiet, perhaps busy with his own preparations for *Henry VI* [*sic*].[39] Although *Liebelei* was eventually performed in Tree's His Majesty's Theatre in 1909, it is evidence of Felix's lack of familiarity with the late-Victorian theatre scene that he approached these two particular actor-managers on Schnitzler's behalf.

Tree and Wyndham were at the time archetypal West End commercial actor-managers, known for 'generally resist[ing] the kinds of play that Shaw, Barker and others championed'.[40] Although both Tree and Wyndham were probably able to read some German, the chances of them accepting an as yet untranslated play from an as yet unknown Austrian writer would have been close to nil.[41] Felix demonstrated some appreciation of British conservatism (or, as he put it, the ostensibly 'virtuous' nature of the English) when he wrote to Schnitzler of his concern that the play's subject could prevent its performance in London.[42] Nonetheless, his attempt to have *Liebelei* produced in early 1896 was quite possibly premature (in terms of general English receptivity to the themes of the play) and misdirected (in terms of the appropriate theatre); and Felix himself was ill-prepared. When his wife Julie subsequently took over as the member of the family responsible for helping Schnitzler in London, she was equipped with an English translation of the play and access to more sympathetic and experimental theatre practitioners. She would lean heavily, for example, on the advice and services of Jacob Thomas Grein when promoting Schnitzler's interests only a few years later.

38 Felix Markbreiter to Arthur Schnitzler, 29.3.1896 (DLA, HS.NZ85.0001.03999). 'Performability' is used here and subsequently in a sense akin to 'fluency' and without reference to the ongoing debate concerning 'performability' as a criterion for theatre translation.

39 Felix Markbreiter to Arthur Schnitzler, 19.3.1896 (DLA, HS.NZ85.0001.03999). Tree played Falstaff in Shakespeare's *Henry IV* at the Haymarket Theatre in 1896. Schnitzler replied on 23.3.1896, admitting: 'Meine Hoffnungen für London sind ziemlich gering' (DLA, HS.NZ85.0001.01377).

40 Postlewait, 'The London Stage', p. 44.

41 Both Tree and Wyndham had spent some of their educational years in Germany.

42 Felix Markbreiter to Arthur Schnitzler, 21.2.1896: 'die äußerlich so tugendhaften Engländer' (DLA, HS.NZ85.0001.03999).

Following the initial burst of curiosity sparked by Felix's ventures in the West End came a brief period for which there is little indication of any move to publish or produce *Liebelei* in England, whether in German or in English; but publications and productions of the play in the German-speaking world did not go unnoticed by the English-language press. On 15 February 1896, for example, the Berlin production had been very favourably reviewed in the London theatre trade journal *The Era*, so Schnitzler's name began the long journey to recognition and establishment in the public sphere.[43] The author of the review had to explain the otherwise unknown writer as 'an Austrian, [whose] present work has already been produced successfully at Vienna'.[44] Six months later John G. Robertson, then a lecturer at the University of Strasburg,[45] wrote an admittedly less favourable review in *Cosmopolis*,[46] a journal with an international circulation of 24,000 (in Amsterdam, Berlin, London, Paris, Vienna, St Petersburg and New York).[47] Given that the journal counted among its contributors Archer and Shaw and that its subject matter included the London theatre scene, we might legitimately speculate that members of the late-Victorian, theatregoing intelligentsia would have read the review and that Schnitzler's name thereby continued to acquire cultural capital, as its familiarity to British consumers grew.

After Felix Markbreiter's efforts in 1896 the next surge of interest in promoting *Liebelei* in Britain came from another amateur agent and, this time, translator, Helen Macdonell. Relatively little is known about Macdonell's life, although some biographical detail can be gleaned from the small amount of scholarship on her mother, the German-Jewish migrant and feminist educationist, Fanny Hertz (1830–1908).[48] Macdonell was born Helen Augusta Hertz in 1854, the middle child of three born to Fanny and her husband and cousin, William David Hertz, a yarn merchant. Helen was the only child to survive into adulthood; it has not been possible to establish her date of death. She would have spent her early years in Bradford surrounded by her parents' friends, a collection of writers, artists and politically radical thinkers; and it can safely be assumed that she would have benefitted from the progressive views on education espoused by her mother. When Macdonell was three

43 By 'Our Own Correspondent', *The Era*, 15 February 1896, p. 9, col. 3.

44 By 'Our Own Correspondent', *The Era*, 15 February 1896, p. 9, col. 3.

45 John L. Flood, 'John G. Robertson', in *Oxford Dictionary of National Biography*, 61 vols (Oxford: Oxford University Press, 2004), XLVII: *Rippon–Rowe*, pp. 247–48.

46 John G. Robertson, 'Current German Literature', *Cosmopolis* (August 1896), 357–73 (p. 371).

47 'Cosmopolis', in *Waterloo Directory of English Newspapers and Periodicals 1800–1900*, ed. by John S. North, 10 vols (Waterloo: North Waterloo Academic Press, 1997), II: *C-D*, p. 1274.

48 Meg Gomersall, 'Fanny Hertz', in *Oxford Dictionary of National Biography*, XXVI: *Haycock–Hichens*, pp. 843–44.

her mother helped to establish the Bradford Female Educational Institute; and in 1868, when Macdonell was fourteen years old, Fanny was involved in the establishment of the Bradford Ladies' Educational Association, which would later lead to the establishment of Bradford Girls' Grammar School. It is likely, in the circumstances, that Macdonell would have received a broad and progressive education, incorporating the physical sciences, physiology, history, geography, poetry, choral singing and drawing recommended by her mother for all women, regardless of class. She would also have been encouraged to strengthen her reasoning powers, not simply to learn facts for regurgitation; and she might have been inspired by her mother's own translation work, which resulted in at least one publication (part of Auguste Comte's *Système de politique positive* in 1876).

In the early 1870s, when Macdonell was still a young adult, the family moved to Harley Street in London. Their habit of entertaining writers continued, with visitors such as Robert Browning, Walter Pater, Henry James and James Scully. In January 1880 Macdonell married George Paul Macdonell, a barrister and member of Lincoln's Inn,[49] but she was widowed in June 1895, i.e., a few months before the Viennese première of *Liebelei*.[50] The couple had a daughter and the family lived at 40 Lansdowne Crescent, Notting Hill. By 1897, when Schnitzler visited Macdonell, she was still in Notting Hill and her mother was living with her. The evidence suggests that she, like her mother, was politically active. In 1900, for example, she was listed as a member of the General Committee of the South Africa Conciliation Committee. When Fanny died in 1908, Macdonell and her daughter were the only surviving members of the immediate family. It is likely that Macdonell would have been the main, if not sole, beneficiary of Fanny's estate of £33,527, enabling her to pursue her literary and translating interests relatively free of financial concerns. Her publications included translations of two works by the contemporary German feminist writer Ilse Frapan (*God's Will and Other Stories* (London: Fisher Unwin, 1893); and *Heavy Laden and Oldfashioned Folk* (London: Fisher Unwin, 1892), both published under her married name); and an edited collection of English poems (*Short Readings from English Poetry, Chosen and Arranged with Notes by Helen A. Hertz* (London: Rivingtons, 1879)).

From the surviving correspondence between Macdonell and Schnitzler we can begin to build up a picture of the power dynamics at play between the two writers. What emerges resists easy categorization along the lines of 'master

49 Henry James, *The Complete Letters of Henry James, 1878–1880*, ed. by Pierre A. Walker and Greg W. Zacharias, 2 vols (Lincoln, NE and London: University of Nebraska Press, 2014), I, 123, footnote to ll. 17–18.

50 Obituary, *The Times*, 12 June 1895, p. 10, col. B.

author' and 'servant translator', a model described and historically prescribed in numerous accounts of the author-translator relationship.[51] However, neither could the Macdonell-Schnitzler exchange be understood by reference to models that see translation as an act of appropriation, a paradigm rendered explicit in its violent connotations by George Steiner and a key to understanding some post-colonial readings of translation.[52] Rather, in the meta-language used to describe the work-in-progress there is a focus on collaboration, on mutual give-and-take and on reciprocal claims and counterclaims.

Author and translator were initially introduced by Macdonell's mother, who wrote to Schnitzler on 17 December 1896 seeking permission for her daughter (who was unused to writing in German) to translate *Liebelei*.[53] On 19 April 1897, in the earliest available letter between Macdonell and Schnitzler, the former describes herself as Schnitzler's 'admiring translator' whilst simultaneously giving reasons why she could not comply with Schnitzler's reported request that a copy of 'our play' be sent to him: the typed copy was being read by Miss Robbins [*sic*], an actress and member of the managing committee of the XXth Century Theatre.[54] Clearly author and translator had been in touch previously and, we might assume, reached some sort of agreement by which Macdonell would translate and try to find a theatre to produce *Liebelei*.[55] Macdonell went on:

51 On metaphors applied to translators from Antiquity to the present day, see Theo Hermans, 'Metaphor and Image in the Discourse on Translation: A Historical Survey', in *Übersetzung. Translation. Traduction. Ein internationals Handbuch zur Übersetzungsforschung. An International Encyclopedia of Translation Studies. Encyclopédie Internationale de la recherche sur la traduction*, ed. by Harald Kittel and others, 3 vols (Berlin; New York: de Gruyter, 2004), I, 118–28. The dominant–subservient relationship is a necessary counterpart to the idea that translations should be faithful to the original text, hence the proliferation of metaphors of translation which feminize the translator (Lori Chamberlain, 'Gender and the Metaphorics of Translation', *Signs*, 13 (1988), 454–72).

52 See, for example, Douglas Robinson, *Translation and Empire: Postcolonial Theories Explained* (Manchester: St Jerome, 1997).

53 Fanny Hertz to Arthur Schnitzler, 17 December 1897 (DLA, HS.NZ85.0001.03427). The letter cited is the first of fifteen from Fanny Hertz to Schnitzler, dated between 1896 and 1899.

54 Macdonell appears to have misquoted the name of the new theatre and misspelt the name of her contact: in 1897 Elizabeth Robins founded the New Century Theatre Company with William Archer, H. W. Massingham and Alfred Sutro. The group's plans included producing English-language versions of Hauptmann's *Die Weber*, Goethe's *Iphigenie auf Tauris* and plays by Schnitzler (Dekker, 'The Modern Catalyst', p. 46). Robins was herself a playwright, a central protagonist in the revolution in Edwardian theatre and a strong supporter of the women's suffrage movement. Her play *Votes for Women!* was produced during the Vedrenne-Barker years at the Court Theatre.

55 Helen Macdonell to Arthur Schnitzler, 19.4.1897 (DLA, HS.NZ85.0001.03960). All subsequently cited letters from Helen Macdonell to Schnitzler can be found in the same DLA file.

> Failing an equivalent for *Liebelei*, I have taken the title 'Playing with fire'. I should have preferred 'On ne badine pas avec l'amour', but it's a little late in the day for that unfortunately.[56] You will see that I have changed the name *Mizi* into *Mimi*, as no one here would have known how to pronounce the former. Other departures from your text are simply such as are rendered necessary to preserve the author's real intention.

Macdonell might ultimately allow Schnitzler to exert some authority, but it seems to be a question of her permission, not his imposition. In a subsequent letter she writes:

> By all means let it be 'Playing with love', if you like that better. To my English ears I confess it reads tame, & in no way renders the unrenderable charm of 'Liebelei', scarcely even its meaning. But having said this much, I am prepared to be docile: you must decide the point.[57]

This correspondence very probably represents the first interaction between Schnitzler and one of his English translators. Macdonell's tone throughout is at once confident and reverential. She does not hesitate in claiming shared ownership of the translated play ('our play'), nor does she withdraw from expressing in clear terms her views on Schnitzler's chosen title, even if ultimately, on this occasion, she is willing to bow to his authority. It is intriguing to note in the first excerpt above her apparently overriding aim in the translation, namely to 'preserve the author's real intention', whilst in the second excerpt she positions herself as a superior arbiter of the meaning of the word 'Liebelei'. She takes as a given her capacity both to discern authorial intention from and to read objectively available meaning in the original text – arguably contradictory tasks – but what is more important in this context is the power she appears to draw from that capacity, real or otherwise, in her negotiations with Schnitzler.[58]

Macdonell is the only English translator of Schnitzler's works whom the author is known to have met and hers was quite possibly the only English translation of *Liebelei* he read before 1920.[59] Although the final text did not reach publication,

56 Presumably Macdonell was thinking of the French play of the same name by Alfred de Musset, published in 1834. Giving the translation a French title would have suggested risqué content to a British audience, so that arguably this comment indicates something of Macdonell's own view of the play.

57 Helen Macdonell to Arthur Schnitzler, 28.5.1897 (DLA, HS.NZ85.0001.03960).

58 See, for example, M. C. Beardsley and W. K. Wimsatt, 'The Intentional Fallacy', *The Sewanee Review*, 54 (1946), 468–88; Barthes, *Image Music Text*, pp. 142–48.

59 In a letter to P. Morton Shand of 14.10.1920 Schnitzler wrote that he had finally received a copy of Shand's translation of *Liebelei*, notwithstanding the fact that it had been published six years earlier in 1914 (DLA, HS.NZ85.0001.01919).

the interaction between author and translator provides a valuable illustration of the way in which Schnitzler actively engaged with and viewed the translation and dissemination of his works in the English-speaking world. He visited London in May 1897 for just over a week; and although nowhere stated explicitly, it appears from his diaries for that period that his primary objective in going to London was to meet Macdonell. He arrived on 24 May 1897 and on 27 May tried, in vain, to visit the translator. On 28 May Schnitzler recorded in his diary 'Mscrpt. engl. Übers. Liebelei', suggesting that he read the translation on this occasion, if not also earlier. A second, successful, visit was made on 31 May: 'N[ach]m[ittag]. Besuch Landsdowne Crescent bei Mrs. Hertz und Macdonell (Übersetzer). Alte kluge Dame, weiss; Mrs. Macd. häßlicher traurig sympath. Blaustrumpf.– Mrs. Liebreich.– Man sagte mir viel freundliches.– '.[60] The diary entry is notable for the absence of business language used; indeed, Schnitzler's observations might almost be described as those of a curious sociologist: he takes the opportunity to record his first impressions of Macdonell in the flesh, whilst taking care to note also the friendliness with which he was met. Far from treating Macdonell as an employee or even a business associate, Schnitzler seems to regard her as an intriguing social acquaintance with whom he is embarking upon a joint project.[61]

Macdonell had voiced concerns to Schnitzler as early as April 1897 that the English stage might not be ready for a production of *Liebelei*:

> [T]he adequate rendering of your play on an English stage is scarcely thinkable. On many sides we are very strong, but in the region of dramatic art our claims cannot be rated high. Many circumstances are against us. In real life we speak with uninflected voices, & seldom gesticulate; it is therefore far from easy for us to produce [ourselves?] affectively for the public divertion [*sic*]. Then, alas! in this land of Shakespeare the standard of dramatic art has sunk sorrowfully low, & work of a delicate quality does not always call forth enthusiasm.[62]

It is tempting, when trying to explain why Macdonell's translation was never produced, to note that the initial interest shown by Elizabeth Robins was never borne out and so to blame the poor state of English theatre identified by Macdonell in her letter. The subsequent correspondence between Schnitzler and his various British supporters paints a slightly different picture.

60 *Tagebuch*, 31.5.1897. The word 'Übersetzer' and the subsequent descriptions of Mrs Hertz and Helen Macdonell suggest Schnitzler was referring to both mother and daughter as translators.

61 Schnitzler's lack of business astuteness comes in for criticism from a later translator, Bertha Pogson, who feels the need to instruct him, in quite precise terms, on how to deal with London literary agents (Bertha Pogson to Arthur Schnitzler, 26.8.1908, 27.9.1908, 13.1.1909 (DLA, HS.NZ85.0001.04209)).

62 Helen Macdonell to Arthur Schnitzler, 27.4.1897 (DLA, HS.NZ85.0001.03960).

On 4 June 1897, five days after Schnitzler's visit to the Hertz-Macdonell home, Macdonell wrote to the playwright in response to a commentary on her translation produced by a friend of Schnitzler's, which had reached her the previous day and included comments on some sixty-two words or phrases from her work. This 'friend' was Hermann Oelsner (1871–1923), a close acquaintance of the Markbreiters in London and a companion of Schnitzler's during his second visit to London.[63] Oelsner was a native of Berlin, largely educated in England and later, in 1905, the first holder of the Taylorian Lectureship of the Romance Languages in the University of Oxford.[64] Macdonell was thoroughly unimpressed by his comments on her work:

> While recognizing that he has for all practical purposes an enviable mastery of a foreign language, I cannot admit him to be in the present instance a competent critic. He is evidently unfamiliar with the sort of shorthand that Englishmen make use of in talking to one another. I learned something of it during the fifteen years of my married life; several of my dear husband's habitual expressions are embalmed in Theodor's & Fritz's translated talk.

This attempt to 'improve' Macdonell's translation is the first sign of what might be described as a concerted effort on the part of Julie Markbreiter and J. T. Grein to wrest power from Macdonell.

Although there follows a two-year gap before the subject is taken up in the surviving correspondence between Markbreiter and Schnitzler, the subsequent letters give an indication of the impasse that had been reached in the meantime. In January 1899 Julie Markbreiter writes to her nephew in Vienna:

> Was die Übersetzung der Mrs. M.D. betrifft, so hält [Grein] sie für unmöglich und wollte mit Dr Oelsner's Beistand eine selbst machen. Seiner Ansicht nach könntest Du mit benannter Dame Unbequemlichkeiten haben, wenn sie einfach übergangen würde. Man müßte sie sehr zart

63 *Tagebuch*, 25.5.1897: 'Mit Oelsner Hermann in die Stadt'; see also entries for 28, 29 and 30.5.1897; and possibly the first meeting on 3.6.1888. A further reference is made to an *Ölsner* family in Schnitzler, *Jugend in Wien*, pp. 302–03; members of the family were guests of the Markbreiters and accompanied Schnitzler on walks and outings. A copy of the Oelsner corrections in the DLA includes corrections corresponding exactly to the three cited in Macdonell's letter (DLA, HS.NZ85.0001.03999).

64 According to John Venn, Hermann Oelsner was educated at Dulwich College and was then admitted for the Modern and Mediaeval Languages Tripos at Cambridge in 1892 (John Venn, *Biographical History of Gonville and Caius College 1349–1897*, 2 vols (Cambridge: Cambridge University Press, 1897–98), II (1898), 509). He obtained his PhD from the University of Berlin and went on to be Taylorian Professor of Romance Languages at Oxford from 1909 to 1913 (*The Palgrave Dictionary of Anglo-Jewish History*, ed. by William D. Rubinstein, Michael A. Jolles and Hilary L. Rubinstein (Basingstoke: Macmillan, 2011), p. 730).

> u. fein behandeln um ihre Einwilligung zu Veränderungen zu erlangen, o. ihr den Standpunkt zu erklären[.] G[rein] behauptet von ihr zu wissen, dass sie das alleinige Recht von Dir ertheilt erhielt. Dr Oelsner ist der Ansicht dass die Übersetzung verbessert, o. ausgebessert, sehr gut verwendbar wäre. Vielleicht kommst Du im Frühlinge nach London und kannst Du die ganze Geschichte selbst am besten in Ordnung bringen.[65]

We quickly see the important and influential role Grein has come to play in Markbreiter's activities on behalf of her nephew. In another, undated, letter from Markbreiter to an unknown recipient (possibly Louise Schnitzler) and apparently filed by Schnitzler together with the above letter from January 1899, she writes:[66]

> Weiß Arthur schon dass Grein gerne seine 'Liebelei' aufführen möchte? Mrs Mc.Donald [*sic*] weigert sich irgend etwas an ihrer Übersetzung zu ändern, diese ist aber so schwach dass sie dem Stücke nur Schaden bringen könnte. Hat Arthur ihr alleinziges Übersetzungsrecht gegeben? [...] Mrs M.D. ist durchaus keine erfahrene Schrif[t]stellerin u. gar nur Übersetzerin, und es wäre doch wirklich zu stark, wenn wegen ihres Eigendünkels das Stück hier nicht aufgeführt werden könnte. Grein kennt sogar schon seine Besetzung, die sehr gut ist, wird aber Mrs Mc. D. Stück nicht aufführen.[67]

The last line of the above might suggest that Macdonell's translation was the only obstacle to Grein's agreement to produce the play; in fact, Schnitzler was unwilling to satisfy another of Grein's conditions for involvement, namely provision of the funds for production.[68]

Markbreiter was keen to move matters on from the work done by a 'mere translator', i.e., Macdonell, if that was what was required in order to have Schnitzler's play performed. Arguably she adopted an approach which was quite close to Schnitzler's, regarding the native language of the translator as a low priority. Markbreiter was unconcerned by the prospect of a Dutchman

65 Julie Markbreiter to Arthur Schnitzler, possibly January 1899 (DLA, HS.NZ85.0001.03999).

66 Presumably the order in which the correspondence is currently held at the DLA reflects the order in which it was received by that archive; and the staff at the DLA count the number of pages in each file as these are released to researchers and then recovered. However, at present the Schnitzler papers remain unfoliated. This means that in practice it is almost impossible to trace how those papers have been re-arranged since removal from source. Nevertheless, the content of the undated letter supports an assumption that it was written shortly before the letter of January 1899.

67 Julie Markbrieter to Anon. [Louise Schnitzler?] (DLA, HS.NZ85.0001.03999).

68 Arthur Schnitzler to Julie Markbreiter, 4.2.1899 (DLA, HS.NZ85.0001.01377). All subsequently cited correspondence from Arthur Schnitzler to Julie Markbreiter can be found in this DLA file.

(Grein) translating into English with the assistance of a native German (Oelsner). This contrasts with the views of both Macdonell herself and another of the translators of Schnitzler's early dramas, a homeopath called Charles E. Wheeler.[69] Macdonell had discreetly warned Schnitzler against accepting Grein as a translator in her final letter to him on 17 June 1897:

> Mr Grein [...] expressed a wish to see the English version of 'Liebelei'. He had [...] purposed translating it himself, as he admires it exceedingly, & cherishes some hope of getting it acted later in the year. Lest you do not know Mr Grein's name – he is quite young – I may mention that he started the Théatre Libre [*sic*] in Paris, & the Independent Theatre here.[70] He is a Dutchman, but more than at home in the French language.

Six years later, Wheeler was to write in less ambiguous terms when justifying his wish that his own translations of *Die Gefährtin*, *Der grüne Kakadu*, *Die letzten Masken* and *Das Märchen* be used by Jacob Thomas Grein and Harley Granville Barker:

> [Grein] has done good work in bringing before English audiences masterpieces of Continental writers, but if I may say so – it has always seemed to me that the actual translations he has used have been very bad. You see, as he is not an Englishman, he is naturally less sensitive on the point.[71]

Discernible in both Macdonell and Wheeler's withholding of support for the 'non-native' speaker is an assertion of the power to determine the rights and wrongs of translating into English and a protectionist attitude to work that is seen as belonging solely to the native English speaker. This assumption of authority might be considered curious in Macdonell's case, given her exclusively German parentage. Indeed, Macdonell exemplifies the ambiguity surrounding the terminology 'native speaker' and 'mother tongue': her mother's dominant or first-learnt language was, we must assume, German, but it is possible that both parents chose to speak a foreign language, English, in their English family home.[72] Macdonell herself, though born in England, seemingly relies

69 Beniston, 'Schnitzler und die "Uebersetzungs-Miseren"', p. 256.

70 Macdonell is very likely mistaken about Grein's involvement with the Théâtre Libre. According to his wife's biography, Grein was in Paris for six months in 1887, where he witnessed the beginnings of André Antoine's influential theatre, and '[i]deas were [...] put into his head'; but there is nothing to suggest that Grein ever worked there (Orme, *J. T. Grein*, p. 52).

71 Charles E. Wheeler to Arthur Schnitzler, 20 or 28.7.1903 (CUL, B550).

72 The terminology 'mother tongue' and 'native speaker', otherwise uncritically adopted by Translation Studies, is interrogated in Nike K. Pokorn, 'In Defence of Fuzziness', in *The Metalanguage of Translation*, ed. by Luc van Doorslaer and Yves Gambier (Amsterdam: Benjamins, 2009), pp. 135–44.

on her husband's fluency to support her position when challenged by Oelsner. However, given her reluctance to write to Schnitzler in German, this reliance might itself be a response to the possible, implicit allegation in Oelsner's criticism that Macdonell, as a woman, cannot know how men speak when in exclusively male company.

It is also worth questioning the contrast between Wheeler and Macdonell on the one hand and Markbreiter and Schnitzler on the other: should a distinction be made between Austrians and Britons when assessing attitudes to translation competence and native speaker status? Nike K. Pokorn suggests that native-speaker fluency is attributed a higher priority in single-language countries than in multi-lingual areas, where competence is measured according to acquired linguistic skills; and Beniston argues that this might explain the difference between the approach to translating taken by Schnitzler's British translators and that taken by Schnitzler himself.[73] However, in this particular case the differences of opinion are more probably attributable to loyalty, respect, egotism and practicality. Markbreiter is loyal to and respects Dr Oelsner (a family friend and a scholar of some distinction); similarly, she respects J. T. Grein for his position in the theatre world. By contrast, Macdonell, a relative stranger, has only the status of a translator. Wheeler's concern that Grein not be left in charge of translating Schnitzler's plays can be seen as an effort to ensure that his own hard work does not go unrecognized and that his translations are saved from redundancy and obscurity. Similarly, Macdonell's defensiveness might be best understood as precisely that: a desire to defend her own translation choices in the face of third-party criticism. The deployment of 'native speaker' superiority might thus be interpreted, in both cases, as a means of asserting power and, indeed, of grasping at straws from a position of impotence, rather than a genuinely felt claim to authority.

Schnitzler's response to the squabbling was, effectively, to throw up his hands in despair: 'Zu diesem Fall bitte ich alle Betheiligten, Dich, Dr Oelsner, Grein sich absolut nicht mehr zu bemühen'.[74] This plea reflects, in line with the hypothesis suggested above, a general pragmatism on Schnitzler's part which, when applied to translation strategies, manifests itself in a disregard for questions of native language status. He explains in the same letter that he has no time to visit London in the near future, as had been suggested by Markbreiter: 'An Mrs Macdonell habe ich unter den anliegenden Umständen natürlich nicht geschrieben'. Britain was perhaps not as significant to Schnitzler as other

73 Pokorn, 'In Defence of Fuzziness'; Beniston, 'Schnitzler und die "Uebersetzungs-Miseren"', p. 256.

74 Arthur Schnitzler to Julie Markbreiter, 4.2.1899 (DLA, HS.NZ85.0001.01377).

importers of his work.[75] Certainly he was not persuaded, despite repeated efforts by Markbreiter and various other directors and agents, to visit Britain for business purposes.[76] Whether he had failed to recognize the potential size of the market, or was still influenced by his earlier unfavourable impressions of the capital city, is unknown.[77] In any event, and notwithstanding Schnitzler's express request to let matters lie, a final attempt was made by Markbreiter and Grein to bring an alternative translation of *Liebelei* to the stage. Markbreiter reported to her nephew on 6 March 1899: 'Herr Grein kommt nächstens zu uns, dann werden wir hören was er jetzt beschloßen hat. Er wird sich wahrscheinlich mit Mrs MacDonald [*sic*] schon wieder besprochen haben. Ich bin sehr froh daß die gute Dame zur Besinnung gekommen ist'.[78] Clearly some progress had been made with Macdonell, but the nature of that progress remains a mystery: the trail of correspondence concerning the efforts between 1896 and 1899 to produce an English-language *Liebelei* in London ends with that letter of 6 March.

There follows in the correspondence with Schnitzler no further discussion of producing the Macdonell version of his play on a London stage and Macdonell herself appears to fall out of the picture altogether. The powerful stance she had occupied at the outset had slowly been undermined by Markbreiter, Oelsner and Grein. Moreover, Schnitzler's own loyalty to his first English translator was not such that he would stand by her work in the face of such constant criticism, especially given that the translation had not yet been published or performed.[79] Here we see one of the many strengths

75 Schnitzler was possibly also preoccupied by the pregnancy of his girlfriend, Marie Reinhard, who had already suffered a stillbirth in 1897 (*Tagebuch*, 2.2.1899 and 12.2.1899). It has been suggested that Reinhardt's death on 18 March 1899 was the result of sepsis caused by an abortion (Rolf-Peter Lacher, *'Der Mensch ist eine Bestie': Anna Heeger, Maria Chlum, Maria Reinhard und Arthur Schnitzler* (Würzburg: Königshausen & Neumann, 2014), pp. 238–41).

76 Although Schnitzler was a frequent traveller abroad when the purpose of the journey was leisure (which itself often included drafting and even proof-reading work), he was not particularly willing to travel for his own self-promotion. Apart from reading tours of Germany, the occasions on which he travelled further afield were relatively rare and only came later in life: in April and May 1922 he undertook a reading tour of the Netherlands (Roelofs, '*Man weiss eigentlich wenig von einander*', pp. 123–56); in October and November of the same year he went on a reading tour of the new Czechoslovak Republic (*Tagebuch*, 25.10.1922–5.11.1922); and in 1923 he read to audiences in Copenhagen and Stockholm (Pinkert, 'Skandinavien', p. 372).

77 For Schnitzler's thoughts on London, see *Briefe* I, 39–42, 25.6.1888.

78 Julie Markbreiter to Arthur Schnitzler, 6 March 1899 (DLA, HS.NZ85.0001.03999).

79 A fruitful contrast might be drawn between Schnitzler's apparent disloyalty and the admittedly success-fuelled, but at times blind loyalty of George Bernard Shaw to his Austrian translator, Siegfried Trebitsch (*Bernard Shaw's Letters to Siegfried Trebitsch*, ed. by Samuel A. Weiss (Stanford, CA: Stanford University Press, 1986); Siegfried Trebitsch, *Chronik eines Lebens* (Zurich: Artemis, 1951); Judith Woodsworth, 'Bernard Shaw on and in Translation', in *Translation, Translation*, ed. by Susan Petrelli (Amsterdam; New York: Rodopi, 2003), pp. 531–52).

of Munday's micro-historical methodology: it shows up the silences as well as the sounds, telling us about failure in translation as well as the successes which usually provide the subject of study. Even without any full record of Macdonell's translation, we are able to re-construct some of the ontological narratives determining the earliest attempt to bring *Liebelei* to London.

Investigating Failure: 1899–1909

The ten years following the end of Macdonell's direct involvement failed to give rise to either a publication or a theatre production of the play in English.[80] At first glance, then, this is a period from which we should learn little about the dissemination of the play in Britain. Once more, however, examination of the correspondence reveals a significant amount of activity. The following section briefly surveys the printed press for the appearance of Schnitzler's name in this otherwise quiet decade, before re-constructing, through the documentary evidence, the role of Macdonell's translation in continuing to generate interest in *Liebelei*, thereby exposing its otherwise hidden power to influence the London theatre scene. Such a re-construction also functions to bring to light the ongoing importance of Julie Markbreiter and Jacob Thomas Grein as Schnitzler's (largely unofficial) agents in Britain.

The German-language première of *Liebelei* at the Deutsches Theater in London took place a year after Markbreiter's last letter to Schnitzler regarding the Macdonell translation. The performance was in the very central St George's Hall, on Langham Place, under the general direction of Karl Junkermann, but was doubtless informed by Grein's by now well-established interest in the play. Schnitzler's name also continued to appear in a number of British-published journals and periodicals. In January 1900 the *Era Almanack* listed the major plays running in Berlin at the time and included among them work by Schnitzler;[81] in April 1900 the *Outlook* (a weekly political and literary review) celebrated the anticipated move by the Deutsches Theater from St George's Hall to a 'regular West End playhouse' and referred to the past success of *Liebelei*, 'with its Viennese lightness and verve';[82] in December 1900 the *Outlook* called for more modern German plays and cited the works of Schnitzler by way

80 Unauthorized translations of the play were produced in America in 1905 and 1907: *Flirtation* (Anon.) and *The Reckoning* (Grace Isobel Colbron) (*Briefe* I, 555–59, 17.4.1907 (p. 556)); and note 4 to that letter.

81 'New Plays and Important Revivals Presented at the Principal Berlin Theatres from December 1898 to November 1899', *Era Almanack*, January 1900, pp. 80–83 (p. 81).

82 'Notes', *Outlook*, 21 April 1900, pp. 357–59 (p. 358).

of example.[83] In July 1901 Ernst Heilbron included a critical review of *Frau Berta Garlan* in his annual survey of contemporary German literature for the *Athenaeum*; and in July 1902, in the same publication, his survey included more favourable references to Schnitzler's latest cycle of one-act plays, *Lebendige Stunden*.[84] In October 1903 Walter Sichel published a thirty-two-page article in the *Quarterly Review* in which, following a wide-ranging analysis of German thought through the ages, he praised German drama, including the 'genial Schnitzler's "Lebendige Stunden"'.[85] Although these reviews and commentaries necessarily relied on publications or performances of Schnitzler's works in the original German, they added force to Schnitzler's name as a paratext for future translations. The English-speaking audience was being prepared for a closer acquaintance.

In 1903 Britain witnessed the first published translation of a work by Schnitzler. One of the *Anatol* playlets, *Die Frage an das Schicksal*, appeared as *Questioning the Irrevocable*, translated by W. H. H. Chambers, in Volume 12 of Alfred Bates's *The Drama: Its History, Literature and Influence on Civilization*.[86] The translation is at best a curiosity in the story of Schnitzler translation. It did not come to the attention of the press or the theatre set and hence is highly unlikely to have made any, or at least any significant, impact on the general reception of Schnitzler in Britain. By contrast, Macdonell's unpublished translation was relatively influential during this period. From the piecing together of various documentary sources it is possible to build up a picture of the processes of cultural exchange operating between 1899 and 1909, when the play was finally performed in English in a translation by G. Valentine Williams (1883–1946).

In June 1903 Grein expressed an interest in translating all of Schnitzler's works; the first he wanted to attempt was *Liebelei*. Schnitzler responded positively, replying on 23 June 1903 with proposed contractual terms and on 10 July 1903 writing: 'Alles, was ich von Ihnen weiss, [...] berechtigt mich zu der Hoffnung, dass Ihre freundlichen Bemühungen mir und meinen Arbeiten in England zum grössten Vorteil gereichen werden, und ich versichere Sie,

83 'In Passing', *Outlook*, 22 December 1900, pp. 660–61 (p. 661).

84 Ernst Heilborn, 'Germany', *Athenaeum*, 6 July 1901, pp. 16–19 (p. 18); and 5 July 1902, pp. 13–18 (p. 16).

85 Walter Sichel, 'The "Time-Spirit" in German Literature', *Quarterly Review* (October 1903), 404–35 (p. 431).

86 Arthur Schnitzler, 'Questioning the Irrevocable', trans. by W. H. H. Chambers, in *The Drama: Its History, Literature and Influence on Civilization*, ed. by Alfred Bates, 22 vols (London: The Athenian Society, 1903), XII, 329–44. There is no evidence that Schnitzler was aware of this publication, let alone that he had authorized the translation. W. H. H. Chambers does not appear anywhere else as a translator of Schnitzler's work and it has not proved possible to find any biographical details concerning him or her.

dass Ihr liebenswürdiges Interesse mich aufrichtig erfreut.'[87] By this time Schnitzler had given apparently broad and temporally unlimited English translation rights in *Das Märchen*, *Die Gefährtin*, *Die letzten Masken* and *Der grüne Kakadu* to the above-mentioned Charles E. Wheeler, a translator who had been introduced to him by the Austrian journalist Johannes Horowitz.[88] Wheeler subsequently surrendered his rights, on request from Schnitzler, after having failed to secure the interests of a manager to stage the plays.[89] In doing so he stressed his hope that his translations would nevertheless be used by Grein or Barker (the anticipated recipients of the rights) in any future production.[90] Grein eventually acted on behalf of Ernst Meyer, the managing director of a literary agency called the International Copyright Bureau, in acquiring rights over Schnitzler's works. Schnitzler entered into a contractual relationship with the ICB on 1 September 1903, effectively giving Meyer English-language rights in respect of *Liebelei*, *Das Vermächtnis* and *Freiwild*.[91] Correspondence with Grein then seems to dry up and certainly any talk of him carrying out the translations himself disappears.[92]

On 20 February 1904 Schnitzler wrote directly to Ernst Meyer to explain the position in respect to, among other works, *Liebelei*:

> Mrs. Macdonall [*sic*] hat die "Liebelei" etwa im Jahre 1896 ins Englische übersetzt; im Jahre 1897 hatte ich das Vergnügen, sie persönlich in London zu sprechen; seit dem Jahre 99 habe ich überhaupt nichts mehr von ihr gehört, und obwohl ich seinerzeit bei der Erteilung der Autorisation einen bestimmten Termin nicht fixiert hatte, so scheint es mir doch keineswegs im Sinne einer solchen Autorisation zu liegen, dass ein Uebersetzungsrecht für ewige Zeiten in den Händen eines Uebersetzers verbleibt, der von diesem Recht keinen weitern Gebrauch machen will oder kann.[93]

This letter highlights the steep learning curve travelled by Schnitzler since his first contact with Macdonell in 1896 or 1897. Whereas his initial foray into the

87 Arthur Schnitzler to Jacob Thomas Grein, 23 June 1903 (DLA, HS.NZ85.0001.00889).

88 See *Tagebuch*, 10.6.1902; and letters from Johannes Horowitz to Arthur Schnitzler, 10.6.1902 and 13.7.1902 (DLA, HS.NZ85.0001.03519a).

89 Charles E. Wheeler to Arthur Schnitzler, 12.7.1903 (CUL, B550).

90 Charles E. Wheeler to Arthur Schnitzler, 28.7.1903 (CUL, B550).

91 Arthur Schnitzler to Ernst Meyer, 3.4.1907 (DLA, HS.NZ85.0001.01419). In this letter he also explains that the contract ended on 1 January 1906. Records from Companies House show that the ICB was incorporated on 27 June 1903 and dissolved on 11 November 2003, i.e., the ICB was, at the time it was engaged by Schnitzler, a newly limited company.

92 His wife, Alix Grein, would later co-translate Schnitzler's *Abschiedssouper* and *Literatur* with Edith A. Browne for a production by the New Stage Club at the Bijou Theatre (now the Twentieth Century Theatre) in Bayswater, London, on 11 March 1908.

93 Arthur Schnitzler to Ernst Meyer, 20.2.1904 (DLA, HS.NZ85.0001.01419).

export of his work demonstrated a clear naivety regarding the particularity that might be required to reach an effective and legally binding agreement (for example, the need for an express term for the duration of the contract), by the time that Schnitzler came to engage Meyer his attitude was somewhat more cautious and his ability to dictate terms more pronounced. The loose arrangements made with both Macdonell and Wheeler had left him in the awkward position of not being absolutely certain of his own rights over his works. Schnitzler's attitude to the sale of foreign rights has evolved, therefore, since 1897, but not to such an extent that he can be said to exercise full control over his international presence. There remains, in the correspondence with Meyer among others, an overriding sense of uncertainty and ambiguity as to Schnitzler's legal position, albeit one that was combined with a consistently held but largely ineffectual reliance on his moral position.

Very little was achieved by the ICB in the following three years, but by late April 1907 Meyer appears to have at last made some progress: he had piqued the interest of well-established actor Norman McKinnel and actor-manager Lena Ashwell. Schnitzler explained to his German publisher Samuel Fischer that Ashwell wanted to use a pre-existing translation of *Liebelei* which she had first seen and admired some two years earlier, when she had been prevented from pursuing it by reason of her own diary being full (*Briefe* I, 555–59, 17.4.1907 (p. 557)). Confirmation that the pre-existing translation was in fact Macdonell's is provided by a letter from Hermann Oelsner to Julie Markbreiter: McKinnel 'was trying to attempt Liebelei for Lena Ashwell', having read 'the MacDonald [*sic*] version' of the play and 'greatly admire[d]' it.[94] Both McKinnel and Ashwell, important figures in the changing landscape of British theatre, had gained access to and been impressed by Schnitzler's works as a result of Macdonell's by then ten-year-old translation.

Matters must have progressed sufficiently for money to be discussed: during a visit to the Markbreiters in May 1907, McKinnel explained to Julie Markbreiter that the otherwise expected first cheque from Ashwell had been delayed by the actress being unwell but the matter would soon be brought into order. According to Markbreiter's report of the visit, McKinnel planned to translate the title simply as 'Christine'.[95] A week later Markbreiter clarified: McKinnel and Ashwell had a common interest in *Liebelei* and were in negotiations with the ICB.[96] McKinnel was due to take over the Court Theatre from Vedrenne and Barker in the autumn; *Liebelei*, it was implied, would be performed

94 Hermann Oelsner to Julie Markbreiter, [May?] 1907 (DLA, HS.NZ85.0001.01377).

95 Julie Markbreiter to Arthur Schnitzler, 13.5.1907 (date according to Schnitzler's subsequent annotation) (DLA, HS.NZ85.0001.04000). All letters from Julie Markbreiter to Arthur Schnitzler falling in or between 1901 and 1909 can be found in this DLA file.

96 Julie Markbreiter to Arthur Schnitzler, 21.5.1907 (DLA, HS.NZ85.0001.04000).

there.[97] On 21 October 1907 Markbreiter reported the cause of further delay to Schnitzler:

> Dass Miss Ashwell das Court Theater nicht nahm wirst du wohl wissen, sie hat es vorgezogen ein Haus zu nehmen das durch seine Lage im Centrum, ihr bessere Chancen bot. 'Irene Wycherley' scheint wahre Zugkraft zu haben. (Vorläufig immerhin wahrscheinlich bekommen wir Liebelei etwas später[)].[98]

In March 1908 Schnitzler explained to another of his English translators, Edith A. Browne, that Miss Ashwell was supposed to perform *Liebelei* that season, but that he had not heard anything further about the plan for some time.[99]

On 26 August 1908 Schnitzler was approached by yet another interested party, Bertha Pogson, a Berlin-based translator, who wrote that she was keen to translate *Liebelei* herself but could not get past Ernst Meyer. She understood that Ashwell had claims on the play, but also knew from a reliable source that Ashwell's diary for the following two seasons was full and that there was no mention of a *Liebelei* performance.[100] Schnitzler chased Meyer, who apparently assured Schnitzler that Ashwell remained interested in the play and would pay some of the fee by 7 January 1909 or lose her existing rights.[101] In the meantime, Markbreiter continued to provide agent-like services to Schnitzler, reporting on 17 November 1908:

> Lena Ashwell hat durch ihren ersten Erfolg mit einem Stück von einem ganz unbekannten Autor, sich ermuthigt gefühlt weiter unbekannte heimische Größen zu produzieren.[102] Das letzte Stück 'The Sway Boat' hat nur ein kurzes Leben, trotzdem kündigt sie wieder ein *home made* Werk an. Ich muß einmal indirect heraus bekommen wie es mit 'Liebelei' steht.[103]

97 The Court Theatre, since renamed the Royal Court, is in Sloane Square, i.e., some distance from the West End. Lena Ashwell took a ninety-nine-year lease on the more central Great Queen Street Theatre, renamed the Kingsway, in the summer of 1907 (Margaret Leask, *Lena Ashwell: Actress, Patriot, Pioneer* (Hatfield: University of Hertfordshire Press, 2012), p. 57).

98 *Irene Wycherley*, by Anthony Wharton, opened on 9 October 1907 as the first play to be produced in the theatre since it had been taken over by Ashwell earlier in the year (Leask, *Lena Ashwell*, p. 57).

99 Arthur Schnitzler to Edith A. Browne, 21.3.1908 (DLA, HS.NZ85.0001.00469).

100 Bertha Pogson to Arthur Schnitzler, 26.8.1908 (DLA, HS.NZ85.0001.04209).

101 Arthur Schnitzler to Ernst Meyer, 29.9.1908 (DLA, HS.NZ85.0001.01419).

102 This 'first success' most probably refers to Wharton's *Irene Wycherley*, which opened on 9 October 1907, the first play produced in the theatre since its takeover by Ashwell earlier in the year (Leask, *Lena Ashwell*, p. 57).

103 Julie Markbreiter to Arthur Schnitzler, 17.11.1908 (DLA, HS.NZ85.0001.04000).

Schnitzler was not over-concerned by the news:

> Von Miss Ashwell hab ich in der letzten Zeit nichts gehört, doch bekam ich einen Ausschnitt aus irgend einem englischen Blatt [...], enthaltend eine reclamehafte Inhaltsangabe der 'Liebelei' sowie die Mitteilung, dass Miss Ashwell das Stück nächstens aufführen und wahrscheinlich grossen Erfolg damit haben würde. Ich nehme an, dies ging vom Copyright-Bureau aus, dem ich mitgeteilt hatte, dass ich, wenn der Termin nicht eingehalten werde, das Stück zurückzufordern und einer andern Bewerberin (das ist Frau Berta Pogson) zu übergeben gedächte. Der Termin läuft am ersten Jänner ab, doch steht Miss Ashwell gegen Erlag einer gewissen Summe das Recht zu bis zum ersten Juli 1909 zu prolongieren. Du siehst, liebe Tante, man kann es in England noch erwarten.[104]

In fact, Ashwell failed to make the due payment and Schnitzler refused to extend her performance rights further.[105]

Lena Ashwell's withdrawal of interest was understood by Oelsner as a concern about the role of Christine: '[Ashwell] feels she is scarc[e]ly youthful enough for the part'.[106] Markbreiter concluded the same: 'Miss Ashwell sah ein dass sie für die Rolle nicht paßte'.[107] Nevertheless, it is also quite possible that *Liebelei* simply suffered from bad timing on this occasion: *The Sway Boat* by Wilfred T. Coleby had opened on 9 October only a year after Ashwell had opened her new theatre, the Kingsway, and had fallen far short of expectations, closing after only six weeks. The failure was accounted for by reference to its chief concern with psychological problems. Under ever-present financial pressure, Ashwell quickly opted for a series of lighter, more popular plays for the remainder of the season.[108] *Liebelei* would not have fitted into such a programme. With Ashwell and McKinnel out of the picture, Schnitzler turned his attention to Bertha Pogson, but he did not entirely give up on his earlier business relationships in London.

Notwithstanding Meyer's failure (and therewith Grein's) to secure a production of *Liebelei* in English, Schnitzler decided to persevere with Grein, now acting alone, as his London agent. On 18 February 1909 Schnitzler wrote to Grein to clarify the terms of their new arrangement, whilst making it plain that he was not free to negotiate with regard to *Liebelei* as the play was by then subject to negotiations with Pogson.[109] Correspondingly, in a

104 Arthur Schnitzler to Julie Markbreiter, 23.11.1908 (DLA, HS.NZ85.0001.01377).

105 Arthur Schnitzler to Ernst Meyer, 15.1.1909 (DLA, HS.NZ85.0001.01419).

106 Hermann Oelsner to Julie Markbreiter, 18.1.1909 (DLA HS.NZ85.0001.01377).

107 Julie Markbreiter to Arthur Schnitzler, May 1909 (DLA, HS.NZ85.0001.04000).

108 Leask, *Lena Ashwell*, pp. 81–82.

109 Arthur Schnitzler to Jacob Thomas Grein, 18.2.1909 (DLA, HS.NZ85.0001.00889). Proposals for the contract were initially made through Julie Markbreiter.

document from 9 February 1909 detailing the English translation status of all Schnitzler's works, it was noted under 'Liebelei': 'Miss Ashwell hat verzichtet. Verhandlungen mit Frau Bertha Pogson Hamburg schweben.'[110] Indeed, only a day earlier, on 8 February, Schnitzler had sent Pogson a copy of the play in response to her request of 3 February; she intended to send him a contract shortly thereafter.[111] However, on 12 March Pogson wrote to Schnitzler with serious concerns: she had heard from her London representative that the situation regarding *Liebelei* remained complicated; Ashwell had taken *Liebelei* as far as a final rehearsal before dropping it, but it was nevertheless due to be performed at the Afternoon Theatre (a matinee series at His Majesty's Theatre) in the near future.[112] Pogson demanded to know whether Schnitzler was aware of this.

In a letter to his aunt (dated 29 April 1909) Schnitzler explained that he had in fact had some notice of the Afternoon Theatre production from the translator himself:

> Ein Herr Williams, englischer Korrespondent in Berlin, teilte mir vor etwa sechs Wochen mit, er habe das Stück übersetzt, ich wies ihn darauf an, seine Uebersetzung an Grein zu senden, der sie offenbar gutgefunden und die Annahme an His Majesty's Theater durchgesetzt hat.[113]

Contrary to the position conveyed to Pogson, and indeed that initially conveyed to Grein, Schnitzler was, in fact, happy to play two translators off against each other. Whilst allowing Pogson to assume that she was the sole contender for the position of translator of *Liebelei*, Schnitzler simultaneously encouraged a second translator, Valentine Williams, to send his work to Grein for consideration. The first approach made by Williams to Schnitzler has not survived, but we can hazard a guess at its contents by reference to Williams's own account of the affair. According to his autobiography, *The World of Action* (1938), Williams had the opportunity to show his translation to Herbert Beerbohm Tree, who by this time owned His Majesty's Theatre and was sponsoring a new series of matinee performances known as the Afternoon Theatre; Tree approved of the translation.[114] Given this information, Schnitzler

110 This document is included with the correspondence from Schnitzler to Julie Markbreiter in the DLA (DLA, HS.NZ85.0001.01377); according to the catalogue it was produced by Olga Schnitzler.

111 Bertha Pogson to Arthur Schnitzler, 3.2.1909 (DLA, HS.NZ85.0001.04209); and Arthur Schnitzler to Bertha Pogson, 8.2.1909 (DLA, HS.NZ85.0001.01611).

112 Bertha Pogson to Arthur Schnitzler, 12.3.1909 (DLA, HS.NZ85.0001.04209).

113 This earlier letter from Valentine Williams does not seem to have survived.

114 G. Valentine Williams, *The World of Action* (London: Hamish Hamilton, 1938), p. 132. Page references will henceforth be given in the text.

seems to have adopted a ruthlessly pragmatic approach to the matter, disregarding what he might otherwise have considered a moral commitment to his prior translator and thereby finally securing a production of his play in English on a London stage.[115]

A degree of ethical flexibility thus emerges in Schnitzler's relationships with his translators, publishers and agents. Whereas he expected honourable behaviour from his business associates, unbounded by legal niceties, he did not himself feel obliged to operate according to the same moral compass. This incongruity perhaps results from the confused identity of Schnitzler as writer and businessman in an age when artists increasingly viewed their works as commodities from which to profit. Schnitzler was a writer who, in many respects, embraced the realities of this practical, commercial age; he scarcely had any choice if he were to support himself and later his wife and children. However, he also appears to have clung on to the possibly romantic idea that his very personal investment in his works gave rise to some sort of superior moral claim on them, a claim quite inconsistent with legal reality. Perhaps unsurprisingly, Schnitzler tends to wear his commercial hat when it serves him best and reserves his moral outrage for occasions on which the law cannot help him.

Liebelei on the Stage: The Williams Translation, 1909

The following two sections examine more closely the circumstances in which *Liebelei* was first performed in English in a London theatre and the critical response to that production. The first sets out a brief biography of the translator, G. Valentine Williams, in order to highlight factors informing his approach to translating and placing the play: in Baker's terminology, the biography provides a route to understanding the ontological narratives driving Williams's efforts. This section goes on to consider the available correspondence regarding the production, which reveals the interests of some of the parties involved and, notably, Schnitzler's relative lack of interest in the substance of the translation or the press response, by contrast to his desire for financial remuneration. Williams's translation was never published and was quite possibly not even seen by Schnitzler. The only surviving copy resides in the Lord Chamberlain's Archive in the British Library as a typed document with some pencil revisions in manuscript (LCP 1909/11). It forms the basis of a close reading at the end of this chapter, alongside remnants from the text of Macdonell's work and the published translation by P. Morton Shand.

115 See Beniston for an account of Schnitzler's 'Darwinistic' justification for allowing competition between translators ('Schnitzler und die "Uebersetzungs-Miseren"', pp. 258–59).

Valentine Williams's autobiography provides some interesting clues with regards to his translating history and philosophy, as well as opening up avenues for interpreting his version of *Liebelei*. From the start he is keen to set out his linguistic and editorial inheritance from both his father and his paternal grandfather. One of his grandfather's 'recreations was to turn the Gospels into Greek or render the Latin and Greek classics into English verse'; and his father's Sunday task as a boy was 'to translate the Lesson into French, or Italian, or Spanish' (p. 18). Williams's father went on to work as one of the earliest Chief Editors employed by the Reuters Office in London and his son followed in his footsteps a year after leaving school. The interim twelve months (*c.* 1901) were spent living with a family in Cleves to learn German (p. 42), a language whose 'prestige was at its zenith' (p. 63). Williams's editorial training had begun even earlier: as a child he was made to 'summarize the leading articles of *The Times*, and reversing the process, expand into newspaper form the Reuter message in "cablese" that arrived at home in the daily batch' (p. 61). Williams spent three years in Reuters London editorial department (1902–05) before being sent away as the Berlin correspondent for the following five (1905–10). He describes the 'fine training for journalism' he received in the early days: one of his tasks while in London was 'to edit for the newspapers the messages coming in from abroad, many of which arrived in French or German' (p. 82); '[a]ccuracy in all things was insisted upon, and while translations might be literary, they had always to be faithful. Sloppy or even colloquial English was frowned on' (p. 83). The degree to which these early instilled translation norms of diligently tested accuracy, faithfulness to the original and appropriate economy of words were to inform his subsequent translation of *Liebelei* will be explored at the end of this chapter.

Williams's years in Berlin coincided not only with much Anglo-German political drama, exacerbated by fractious relations between the British King and his nephew the German Emperor, but also with Herbert Beerbohm Tree bringing his company to play a season of Shakespeare in the spring of 1907. The young Berlin correspondent went to Friedrichstraße train station to greet them on their arrival, only to meet and fall in love with one of the rising actresses of the period, Alice Crawford. The couple would later marry and in the meantime the romance 'thrilled' the entire company, 'from Tree downwards', and kept Williams in regular contact with the director of His Majesty's Theatre (p. 132). This relationship ultimately led to Valentine Williams becoming the first successful translator of *Liebelei*: '[Tree] liked an English version I made of Arthur Schnitzler's well-known play *Liebelei* and put it on at the Afternoon Theatre [...] under the title of *Light o' Love*' (p. 132). Years later Williams returned to literary pursuits in the form of writing his own detective and spy novels. Peculiarly, however, *Liebelei* was his only serious, or at least successful, effort at literary translation and arguably the only point at which the languages of his first career were brought to bear on the creative output of his later calling.

On 22 April 1909 Schnitzler received details of the forthcoming première from Williams: 'Wie Sie wahrscheinlich bereits von Herrn Grein gehört haben, geht "Liebelei" am 14 Mai im Afternoon Theatre in meiner Uebersetzung in Szene unter dem Titel "Light o' Love".'[116] Schnitzler replied that he would be interested in seeing the translation and asked whether Williams intended to have it published.[117] There is no indication in the subsequent correspondence or in Schnitzler's diaries to suggest, however, that his wish was ever fulfilled or his query answered. We do learn from a letter to Markbreiter that Schnitzler did not approve of the title, finding it simply 'nicht sehr gut'.[118] As well as providing Shakespeare with the name of a dance tune (in *Much Ado About Nothing* and *Two Gentleman of Verona*), a 'light o' love' can refer to a woman who is inconstant or capricious in love, even a harlot (*Oxford English Dictionary*). As a paratext to the translation, therefore, it set a very particular tone for the play, undermining, or perhaps ironizing, Christine's experience of love and focusing attention on female charms in a way that 'Liebelei' does not. It seems unlikely that Schnitzler would have been informed about these nuances of meaning; the choice of title accordingly reflects an exercise of power by Williams (in the face of Schnitzler's assumed ignorance) in defining how Schnitzler's then most popular work would first be presented to British, English-speaking audiences. As an indication of the significance of that title it is worth noting that it was recorded, in brackets, in an account of a German-language production of *Liebelei* in London in 1913. The parentheses presumably represented a nod to the prior existence and performance of the English translation and, perhaps more interestingly, an assumption that audiences would be familiar with the translation.[119]

The two letters from Valentine Williams that have survived (22 April and 9 May 1909) provide further evidence of a translator keen to make his own mark on Schnitzler's text and on the final theatre production in English. He advises Schnitzler of the strategic decisions he has made both in executing his translation and in guiding the direction of the play; of his desire to see the Viennese atmosphere of the original maintained; of his view that idiomatic English should be employed but any sort of 'adaptation' avoided; of his recommendation that a German director with a familiarity with the London theatre scene be

116 G. Valentine Williams to Arthur Schnitzler, 22.4.1909 (CUL, B1038).

117 Arthur Schnitzler to G. Valentine Williams, 29.4.1909 (DLA, HS.NZ85.00001.02224).

118 Arthur Schnitzler to Julie Markbreiter, 29.4.1909 (DLA, HS.NZ85.0001.01377).

119 *'The Stage' Year Book 1913*, ed. by L. Carson (London: Carson & Comerford, 1913), p. 108.

appointed; and of his various casting suggestions.[120] He even goes so far as to try to manipulate the constitution of the audience, asking the management of the theatre to invite the Austrian and German Ambassadors to attend the première in the hope that they might attract the attention of the foreign press.

This is an unexpected level of involvement for a one-off theatre translator, suggesting that Williams was driven more by his own personal interest in the play and the company than by any potential remuneration or reputation to be earned. In general, his ambitions might be described as steering a careful course between determinedly 'foreignizing' or 'domesticizing' agendas; hence the desire to maintain a Viennese atmosphere (i.e., keep the 'foreign' feeling of being abroad) whilst employing English idioms (i.e., a fluent, or domesticated, target language). Venuti discusses how these well-established binaries ('foreignization/domestication'; 'fluent/resistant') 'demarcate a spectrum of textual and cultural effects that depend for their description and evaluation on the relation between a translation project and the hierarchical arrangement of values in the receiving situation at a particular historical moment'.[121] An analysis of Williams's playscript at the end of this chapter tests how far his text reveals and further refines the values prevalent in Edwardian London, as well as probing how those values reflect a particular part of the London theatre scene and the norms of Edwardian-era literary translation.

According to the manager of the Afternoon Theatre, Frederick Whelen, who wrote to Schnitzler directly (12 May 1909), 'a good deal of interest is being taken in the forthcoming production, and I am hoping that this may be the first of many opportunities of seeing your works in London'.[122] The première took place on the afternoon of 14 May 1909 and the production ran for a further two afternoons.[123] Julie Markbreiter immediately wrote to Schnitzler to report on the performance and on its general reception, referring to both the audience's reaction and two newspaper articles, copies of which she enclosed.[124] Although the performance was not perfect, she wrote, 'das Publicum [hat] sehr großen Gefallen daran gefunden'. She had strained her ears to detect what was being said around her and heard only favourable responses; all had found the play

120 Both letters can be found in CUL, B1038. Although Williams had suggested, according to his earlier letter, that his future wife, Alice Crawford, play Christine, the role was in fact given to Margaret Halstan, the daughter of H. A. Hertz. Hertz translated *Komtesse Mizzi* for a Stage Society production at the Aldwych Theatre in 1913 and was an important financial supporter of the Deutsches Theater in London (Orme, *J. T. Grein*, p. 168).

121 Venuti, *The Translator's Invisibility*, p. 19.

122 Frederick Whelen to Arthur Schnitzler, 12 May 1909 (CUL, B1030).

123 J. P. Wearing, *The London Stage 1900–1909: A Calendar of Productions, Performers and Personnel*, 2nd edn (Lanham, MD: Scarecrow Press, 2014 [1976]), entry 09.137.

124 Julie Markbreiter to Arthur Schnitzler, May 1909. Neither of the two newspaper articles has been preserved.

'clever' and moving. Moreover, there was a good turnout from other actors and writers: Markbreiter demonstrates an impressive familiarity with the London theatre scene by listing Norman McKinnel, Harley Granville Barker and his wife (the well-known actress Lillah McCarthy), Constance Collier (the actress), Johnston Forbes Robertson (the actor-manager), Lena Ashwell and Ellen Terry, all of whom had attended the première.

Commenting on the two newspaper cuttings, Markbreiter wrote:

> Bei jedem Erscheinen eines Fremden schreien die Zeitungen dass heimische Talente vorgeführt werden müßten u[nd] schon deshalb lassen sie den Ausländer nicht gerne gelten. [...] Es ist ein Unsinn zu sagen dass das engl.[ische] Publicum für diese Situation kein Verständnis hat. Das Duell natürlich ist [ihnen?] fremd, aber sonst ist es hier nicht anders als sonst wo.

Clearly the newspaper reviews had not been over-complimentary. There appears to have been a concern (arguably revealing more about the protectionist policies of the newspapers than anything else) regarding the foreignness of the play, both in the sense that its original author was not a native (and, so the argument followed, support had necessarily been denied to local talent) and in the sense that the content of the play, and specifically the inescapable nature of the duel, were incomprehensible to the English audience. Markbreiter perhaps recognized what was most important to Schnitzler, however, when she touched upon the production's lack of financial merit: 'Natürlich ist financial [*sic*] nicht viel dabei zu gewinnen, [aber] ein Anfang ist gemacht und Dein Name ist nun allgemein bekannt'.[125] This was not the only occasion when she would stress to Schnitzler the advantages of his dramas appearing before an influential, theatrically literate audience. Markbreiter recognized, probably more than her husband in his earlier efforts to help Schnitzler, that the Austrian's works could only succeed if accepted by the small but dynamic group of theatre radicals who were out to shake to its core the commercial theatre status quo.

Reviews of *Light o' Love*

Newspaper and periodical reviews of literary or dramatic works are explicitly excluded from Genette's scheme of paratexts by virtue of the fact that they lack

125 The letter from Julie Markbreiter to Arthur Schnitzler is not fully dated. Markbreiter has written 'Samstag' at the top; Schnitzler has added 'Mai 09' (DLA, HS.NZ85.0001.04000). Schnitzler also received a report on the production from the Markbreiters in person. According to his diary he saw them both in Vienna on 8 June 1909, when they told him about the London performance of *Light o' Love*.

any pretence to authorial intention or assumption of responsibility.[126] Indeed reviews can often function in a manner contrary to the author's wishes by criticizing the text, highlighting its weaknesses and undermining its authority. Nevertheless, they operate as an auxiliary to the main text in a similar way to paratexts proper: reviews, like book covers, theatre programmes, prefaces and author interviews instruct the reader or prospective audience-member on how to receive and interpret the text. Furthermore, they play a peculiarly important role in the field of historical Theatre Studies, for which alternative contemporaneous accounts of individual productions and performances are rare. In the absence of camera footage, still photographs or other materials produced and preserved by the theatre company itself (prompt books and stage models, for example), the theatre review can often provide the best, if not the only, record of such features as casting, lighting, scenery, sound and stage design. With that in mind, the surviving reviews of *Light o' Love* are considered here and provide a clearer portrait of the production at the Afternoon Theatre.

The *Observer's* review was particularly damning of both play and production: 'No very useful purpose was served' by the play except 'in its indication of the rather elementary taste of the Viennese playgoer of to-day'.[127] There proved to be:

> really very little in it, and what little there is bears the process of exportation no better than those typical wines of the country which are so refreshing on a Rhine [...] steamboat, but seem so disappointingly thin if we are tempted to try them at home.

On the subject of the production, the reviewer wrote: 'The whole performance [...] was taken much too slowly, especially in the first act, where we caught neither the tripping movement of the Viennese waltz nor the bright crispness of Viennese air'. The casting was apparently equally disappointing, the acting 'a record of good intentions and little more'. The geographical origin and location of the drama provide a constant thread in this criticism, both as a source of potentially refreshing exoticism sadly neglected in the production (the 'tripping' waltz, the crisp air) and as an indicator of inferiority. However, the reference to the waltz might also suggest a reviewer whose expectations have been coloured by exposure to operetta or sentimental comedies.[128] Thus

126 Genette, *Paratexts*, p. 3.

127 'At the Play', *Observer*, 16 May 1909, p. 6. Reviews referred to in this section can be found in the Schnitzler Press-Cuttings Archive, EUL MS 214, courtesy of Special Collections, University of Exeter.

128 As well as such international hits as Meyer-Förster's *Alt-Heidelberg*, London saw the première of the English-language adaptation of Franz Lehár's *Die lustige Witwe* at Daly's Theatre in 1907, which ran for an astonishing 778 performances.

Vienna comes to represent both the inferior other as well as the kitsch epitome of the Southern German lands. This double-view, in which the foreign is both attractive and repulsive to the domestic critic, is not wholly dissimilar to that model of the exotic, inferior other described in Edward Said's *Orientalism*.[129] This reviewer certainly aspires to position himself, and with him his readers, above the Austrians (and Germans) somehow attributed collective responsibility for *Liebelei*.

By contrast, the reviewer for the *Daily Mail* appears to have been altogether more familiar with Vienna and so better able to judge the play's relationship to its place of origin. The 'inherent realism and sentimental handling of the eternal theme' made sure of a 'very interesting afternoon', notwithstanding the fact that 'the atmosphere, as the thing itself, is somewhat alien to our national life'.[130] The review from the *Athenaeum*, like that from the *Observer*, pays close attention to the geographical setting of the text. The production was 'curiously Viennese in setting', but 'to such playgoers as can recognize that there are other types, other manners, and ways of love-making than those of the English, the picture of the lighter side of life in Vienna must have seemed most interesting'. Again there is a celebration of the exotic. Vienna itself is mentioned three times in the central paragraph of the review (by its own name, adjectivally and then as 'the gay city'); Schnitzler is identified using the German 'Herr'; and the contrast between the English 'types, [...] manners, and ways' and those of the 'other' expressly drawn to the reader's attention.[131] This is theatre that must succeed or fail, in the eyes of the English-press reviewer, precisely *because of* its foreignness.[132]

The Times's reviewer explained by way of opening that the play 'is very successful in Austria and Germany, [and] has a simple story'.[133] No reference is made, beyond the headnote, to the author, Schnitzler, or any of his other works. A synopsis is provided which mentions the duel without further comment and describes the four 'friends [...] drinking *Bruderschaft*'. The assumption, then, is that the reader will understand both cultural phenomena without difficulty, perhaps indicating that the reviewer had a particularly well-educated readership in mind. Although unconvinced by Christine's final outburst in Act 3, deeming it an unlikely moment of eloquence from her mouth and sounding more like Schnitzler's words than Christine's own, the judgment is generally positive: '[T]he play is a sincere, artfully-constructed, and occasionally moving

129 Edward Said, *Orientalism* (New York: Vintage Books, 1979).

130 A. H., '"Light O' Love"', *Daily Mail*, 15 May 1909, p. 3.

131 See Chapter 2 for full consideration of the anglophone tendency to view Vienna as the 'gay' city.

132 'Drama. The Week', *Athenaeum*, 22 May 1909, pp. 627–28.

133 *The Times*, 15 May 1909, p. 12.

piece of work'. Notwithstanding the largely approving tone adopted, the writer cannot resist a small dig at the foreigners represented in the play – in Act 1 the friends are described as doing 'all sorts of amusing Austrian things' – so that again the reader is elevated by comparison with the inferior other. The same point is made more forcefully by the reviewer for the *Daily Telegraph*, who refers to the play's 'distinctly German air' and actions that were hard to reconcile with 'our own ideas of the fitness of things'.[134]

Schnitzler himself was not over-concerned by the criticism he received in reviews from the English press. By contrast to his domestic critical reception, responses to *Light o' Love* seemed positively pleasant:

> Es scheint mir auch, daß ich im ganzen mit dem Ausfall der Sache nicht unzufrieden sein darf; und was speziell die sogen.[annten] 'schlechten Kritiken' angelangt, so ist ihr Ton gegenüber dem, den ich in der lieben Heimat von 'schlechten' Kritikern gewohnt bin, ein wahrhaft wohlthuender. Die endgiltige 'Eroberung' Englands werd ich aber wohl auf ein andres Mal verschieben müssen. Die Aufführung scheint ja ein mäßiger Genuß gewesen zu sein – Und *wie* ist man davon abhängig.[135]

None of the reviews quoted was coloured by any obvious anti-Semitism, marking a significant difference from many of the reviews Schnitzler received in the German-language, and especially Viennese, press. It is possibly for this reason that Schnitzler was unworried by what might otherwise have been regarded as negative criticism.

Given the language of superiority and projected exoticism in the reviews, it is interesting to note Schnitzler's own use of 'Eroberung'. Should it be interpreted as a manifestation of the employment, much discussed in post-colonial translation theories, of language and text in a manner akin to the empire-builder's violent tools? The quotation marks suggest that Schnitzler intended for the word to be read ironically, possibly as an implicit reference to the reviewers' own imperialist stance; but even if Schnitzler was understood to have slipped inadvertently into such language, it is an anomaly in his correspondence and scarcely appears in his diaries. Rather Schnitzler's two main concerns, in respect of the translation and export of his works, were financial and moral accountability to the author.

There is little, if any, discussion in Schnitzler's letters to his English correspondents regarding *how* his work should be translated or presented to the English-speaking public and relatively little concern as to whether

134 *Daily Telegraph*, 15 May 1909.

135 Arthur Schnitzler to Julie and Felix Markbreiter (*Briefe* I, 590–91, 19.5.1909).

the press had, in Schnitzler's view, correctly understood the play.[136] Instead the correspondence largely comprises fee negotiations and demands for all-too-often elusive royalties. Schnitzler frequently complained of the lack of moral fibre evident in theatre managers and publishers, as made manifest by their taking advantage of the lax copyright position to publish translations with hardly a nod of recognition to the author. He longed for financial stability (through appropriate remuneration for his work) and acknowledgment for his achievements. The point is highlighted by an entry in Schnitzler's diary on 24 August 1906 that he was:

> über eine Notiz (aus der Times) geärgert, in der Hauptmann das einzige originale dramat.[ische] Talent der Deutschen genannt wird [...]. – In jener Notiz übrigens auch, dass von Sudermann 6 Stücke in dieser Saison im Londoner Dtsch. Theater aufgeführt wurden . . . Eins von beiden sollte Einem doch blühn. Der große Ruhm oder das viele Geld. Meine Position ist ganz lächerlich.[137]

As discussed above, Schnitzler in fact had to be a realist where his finances were concerned. He appreciated that the age of patronage had passed and that he had to sell his work if he were to remain financially buoyant. Although fame could be an aspiration, remuneration had to be a priority.

These dominant concerns on the part of Schnitzler are borne out in the particular circumstances of the *Liebelei* story, the details of payment for the translation and performance rights providing a neat illustration of Schnitzler's need and capacity to turn his mind to business matters in the midst of his writing life. In a letter to Grein on 2 December 1909, some six months after the performances, Schnitzler had to remind his agent that he had still not received any payment for the Afternoon Theatre production of *Light o' Love*; another reminder was sent nine months later, on 10 August 1910. Finally, a 'kleines Honorar' was eventually sent to Schnitzler by the close of 1910, eighteen months

136 Schnitzler's repeatedly expressed frustration with regard to both his domestic and his international reception was that interpretations of his work consistently reiterated his origins as the writer of *Anatol*. See, for example, the entry in the *Tagebuch* for 29 September 1911 regarding a German-press review of *Der Schleier der Beatrice* and Schnitzler's riposte to Ashley Dukes, 'Modern Dramatists' (CUL, A20,5). Chapter 2 explores the assumption of that frustration by Heinrich Schnitzler.

137 This entry most probably refers to a review of a German-language production of Ibsen's *Rosmersholm* at the Great Queen Street Theatre in *The Times* (14 May 1906, p. 15). The reviewer noted that this was the last production in the present German season, referred to a cycle of six Sudermann dramas that had preceded the Ibsen and bemoaned the lack of any Hauptmann, 'the one great and original figure among modern German dramatists'.

after the performances had taken place.[138] Schnitzler comes out of this exchange appearing almost powerless in his pursuit, in Britain, of the rewards for his labour.

Liebelei on the Page: The Shand Translation, 1914

Schnitzler's impotence is once more visible in the next episode of the *Liebelei* story. On this occasion not only did Schnitzler fail to secure any payment to reflect his contribution to the work (a published translation), but he remained unaware even of its existence until six years after publication. From the following account, which includes an analysis of the delayed communications between author and translator, we see that, retrospectively, Schnitzler nevertheless retains some power in the relationship by virtue of the translator's interest in future translation opportunities. Ultimately, however, the publication which came to define *Liebelei* in Britain for decades to follow was produced entirely outside of Schnitzler's knowledge or control and without his receiving any remuneration: a glance through the *Radio Times* shows that Morton Shand's translation was broadcast by the BBC in the 1930s, 1940s, 1950s and 1960s.[139]

Liebelei was first printed in Britain in a translation by Philip Morton Shand (1888–1960), published by Gay & Hancock in May 1914 under the title *Playing with Love* and advertised at a price of 2s 6d.[140] It is noteworthy, although perhaps only coincidental, that the title echoes precisely that suggested to Macdonell by Schnitzler in 1897.[141] Nothing in the surviving papers shows that there was any correspondence between Schnitzler and Shand or Schnitzler and the publisher at the time of the publication. Indeed, Schnitzler gives the impression of having been wholly surprised when the fact of its existence came to his attention six years later on the occasion of a 'Herr Campbell' making enquiries on behalf of the Birmingham Repertory Theatre.[142]

138 See Arthur Schnitzler to P. Morton Shand, 26.9.1920 (DLA, HS.NZ85.0001.01920). The figure ('112') for *Liebelei* in England recorded in the 'Verzeichnis der Einnahmen aus fremdsprachigen Drucken' (including performances) is difficult to decipher because the currency is not indicated (CUL, A237,5).

139 See http://genome.ch.bbc.co.uk [accessed 16 February 2016] and Appendix 3.

140 Page references to this edition will be given in the text.

141 Cf. Macdonell's letter to Schnitzler, 28.5.1897 (DLA, HS.NZ85.0001.03960).

142 Arthur Schnitzler to Morton Shand, 14.10.1920 (DLA, HS.NZ85.0001.01919). Both Schnitzler and Shand refer to that correspondent as 'Herr Campbell'. It has not proved possible to find any record to suggest that this could, in fact, have been a mistake on their part or that the 'Herr Campbell' was actually the well-known female actor-manager, Mrs Patrick Campbell. Hence it seems most likely that the 'Herr Campbell' referred to in the correspondence was simply a local theatre agent (perhaps Grantham-based impresario John Arthur Campbell (1878–1947)) acting on behalf of the Birmingham Repertory Theatre.

In subsequent correspondence between author and translator, the latter sought to explain the circumstances in which he had come to translate the play. He had, at that time, worked as an apprentice in the offices of Gay & Hancock, who in 1913 had published a translation of Schnitzler's *Der grüne Kakadu* by Horace Samuel. Shand had been asked to edit Samuel's translation but found himself instead largely rewriting the same, affronted as he was by the appalling job Samuel had done. On learning that Samuel then intended to do the same damage to *Liebelei*, Shand offered to give his own services to the publisher free of charge and accordingly set about translating the second play. He was assured by his employers that Schnitzler's authorization was not required to publish the translation as the latter's rights under the Berne Convention had by then expired.

Insight into Shand's thoughts at the time of publication, rather than in retrospective apology, can be gained by turning to the published Foreword, signed P. M. S. and dated March 1914. There Morton Shand first sets out a brief history of *Liebelei* and its reception among German and Austrian critics, as well as mentioning that the play had been performed 'several times during the run of Sir Herbert Beerbohm Tree's Afternoon Repertoire Season at His Majesty's Theatre'. Although aware of the earlier translation, there is no suggestion that Shand took it as a model; indeed, he does not even mention its title in English or its translator's name. Apropos his chosen title he comments:

> Many suggestions for an English rendering of the German word *Liebelei* have been made from time to time – *Light o' Love, Love-Longing, Philandering*, and even *Flirtation*. None of these can be pronounced entirely happy, or even approximate or appropriate equivalents. As an adequate English translation of the German title has seemed little short of impossible to the translator, he has preferred to avoid any attempt to provide one, and to rest content with giving the play in its English dress a name which at least gives the key to the *Leitmotif* of the drama as comprehensively as anything short of the original. (p. viii)

Shand, like Macdonell before him, recognized what Genette would later claim to be the power of the paratext, in this case the title, to guide the reader or audience as to *how* to read, watch or receive the text. Shand's stated aim in this regard – to find a 'happy', 'approximate', 'adequate' or 'appropriate' equivalent to the original title – was discarded as a hopeless pursuit and replaced by an attempt to 'give[..] the key to the *Leitmotif* of the drama'. Macdonell likewise felt unable to find 'an equivalent for *Liebelei*' and with 'Playing with fire' possibly revealed something of her own moral stance in respect of the events of the play.[143]

143 Helen Macdonell to Arthur Schnitzler, 19.4.1897 (DLA, HS.NZ85.0001.03960).

Shand employs a popular translation metaphor to describe the desired product of his labours, i.e., 'the play in its English dress'.[144] Macdonell, by comparison, aimed to render the 'charm' and 'meaning' of the original and to 'preserve the author's real intention'; and Williams aspired to make the play 'dem englischen Theaterpublikum zugänglich' whilst maintaining the dramatic effect and the Viennese atmosphere of the original. The comparative reading below shows the degree to which these stated aims are made manifest in the translations themselves. Shand certainly leads his reader to expect a relatively loose translation when he concludes his Foreword thus:

> To anyone familiar with the German text the insuperable difficulties of providing a literal translation will at once be obvious. The play is written throughout in the Viennese dialect; it is not merely *Wiener*, it is *Weaner*. Nothing is claimed for the present version save that a conscientious attempt has been made to render colloquialism by colloquialism and idiom by corresponding idiom. 'To have attempted more,' in the words of Mr Granville Barker, 'one would need to be another Schnitzler – which is impossible'. (pp. viii–ix)

The phrase 'colloquialism by colloquialism' maps onto the centuries-old debate between 'word-for-word' and 'sense-for-sense' translation. Here Shand is quite clearly invoking the latter approach and so coincides with Williams's attempt at idiomatic English in his translation. Shand also demonstrates his familiarity with the most important published translation of Schnitzler's dramatic works at that time, namely Barker's *Anatol* (London: Sidgwick and Jackson, 1911). By quoting Barker's own prefatory words, Morton Shand the publisher's apprentice rides on the coat tails of the well-known actor, director and dramatist whose version of *Anatol* had already proved very successful. He thereby subtly places himself and his work in a young but dynamic and critically acclaimed tradition of introducing modern European drama to the London public. The reference to the renowned theatre practitioner might also suggest an aspiration on Shand's part for his own translation to be performed and not simply read. A careful reading of the script reveals this aspiration as most probably imagined retrospectively. Certainly it does not appear to have informed Shand's translation strategy at the time of writing.

Shand would go on, like Williams, to enjoy far greater celebrity than his earliest translating predecessor, Macdonell. He was educated at Eton, where he won prizes for German and Divinity, and Cambridge, as well as the Sorbonne

144 Cf. Hermans, 'Metaphor and Image', p. 121.

and Heidelberg.[145] After beginning the First World War in the Royal Fusiliers, he was appointed a Superintendent of prisoner-of-war camps owing to his recognized skills in French and German. He went on to become a journalist and author of numerous books on wine, food and architecture. He was a friend of Walter Gropius, whose *Die neue Architektur und das Bauhaus* he translated (1935), and of the poet John Betjeman,[146] who wrote an addendum to his obituary in *The Times*.[147] His two translations of Schnitzler (i.e., *Playing with Love* and *The Green Cockatoo* under Horace Samuel's name) are his only other known forays into translation.

The admittedly only brief correspondence between Schnitzler and Shand in 1920 is illuminating in a number of ways. It includes, for example, further evidence of where Schnitzler's priorities lie in respect of the transmission of his work. He is relatively ambivalent as to which of the two available translations should be used by the Birmingham Repertory Theatre – as long as it is 'eine möglichst gute' – thereby suggesting that quality, although important in the abstract, is not something that Schnitzler is concerned to assess or pin down.[148] His primary interest remains the pursuit of any possible remuneration:

> Könnten Sie nicht doch den Verleger veranlassen, dass er mir ein Honorar zusendet? Mag er auch juridisch heute nicht mehr dazu verpflichtet sein;- es sollte zwischen Verlegern und Autoren von Rang doch wohl noch andere Verpflichtungen geben, denk ich, als solche rein juridischer Natur.[149]

Schnitzler's language in this correspondence is essentially practical and professional, albeit full of false hopes. He can again be seen performing the role of the businessman, while (arguably inconsistently) holding his partners to an ethical code more romantic in nature than reflective of legal and commercial realities.

By contrast, Shand's language in the correspondence is full of poetic reverence and even adoration, whilst also revealing the limits of his active

145 Alan Windsor, 'Letters from Peter Behrens to P. Morton Shand, 1932–1938', *Architectural History*, 37 (1994), 165–87; Jonathan Glancey, 'Townscape and the AR: Humane Urbanism and the 20th Century', *The Architectural Review*, 7 June 2013, http://www.architectural-review.com/rethink/viewpoints/townscape-and-the-ar-humane-urbanism-in-the-20th-century/8648215.fullarticle [accessed 10 December 2015].

146 See Gyles Brandreth, *Camilla and Charles. Portrait of a Love Affair* (London: Random House, 2006), p. 77.

147 John Betjeman, 'Mr P. Morton Shand', *The Times*, 6 May 1960, p. 19.

148 Arthur Schnitzler to P. Morton Shand, 26.9.1920 (DLA, HS.NZ85.0001.01920).

149 Arthur Schnitzler to P. Morton Shand, 14.10.1920 (DLA, HS.NZ85.0001.01919).

command of German. He calls Schnitzler 'geehrteste[n] Meister'; regrets the 'Mangel an die [...] Verehrung Ihrer Genie meinerseits'; describes himself as 'eine[n] tiefe[n] Verehrer Ihrer Genie', 'Ihr[en] stete[n] Verehrer'; and writes of his desire to do 'meine Pflicht [...] Ihnen [...] in irgend welcher Weise [zu] dienen'. However, he also sees himself as elevated by his role as translator. He is somebody with 'literarische[m] Gewissen' who must produce something 'würdig des Originals'. Whereas Schnitzler writes of royalties, negotiations, authorization and agents, Shand's language is littered with evaluative vocabulary by which he carefully positions himself *in relation to* the master and genius, Schnitzler. What mention he makes of money is kept to a minimum: although he volunteered to carry out the translation free of charge, his employers offered him a five per cent royalty after the first one thousand sales; this, he assures Schnitzler, amounted to no more than £5.[150]

Shand's retrospectively reverential behaviour towards Schnitzler is not mere hero-worship. The closing lines from Schnitzler's last surviving letter to Shand provide perhaps the best clue as to Shand's true motivation: 'Auf Ihren freundlichen Wunsch noch andere Sachen von mir zu übersetzen möchte ich erst eingehen, wenn Sie mir über Ihre Verbindungen mit englischen Verlegern, Theaterdirektionen, Zeitschriften und über Ihre bisherigen Arbeiten nähere Mitteilungen gemacht haben'.[151] Shand, we must assume, has offered to translate more of Schnitzler's works; Schnitzler, the increasingly astute businessman, demands information about the production or publication potential before taking matters any further. There has been a further subtle shift in the author's stance towards his translators. As he emerges from a world war, suffering the financial consequences shared by other citizens of the new Austrian Republic, he now carries with him twenty-five years' experience of exporting and living from his art. His final words to Shand demonstrate a wariness borne of previously burnt fingers.

Following the publication of *Playing with Love*, there was an apparent hiatus in new British *Liebelei* translations: in 1954 Frank and Jacqueline Marcus provided a translation for a one-hour BBC television dramatization, but it was not until 1982 that Charles Osborne included the play (as *Love Games*) in his printed collection of Schnitzler translations and 1986 that Tom Stoppard's version, *Dalliance*, was published to coincide with its production at the Lyttelton Theatre.[152] For a period of almost seventy years Shand's

150 P. Morton Shand to Arthur Schnitzler, 9.10.[1920] (DLA, HS.NZ85.0001.04586).

151 Arthur Schnitzler to P. Morton Shand, 14.10.1920 (DLA, HS.NZ85.0001.01919).

152 Arthur Schnitzler, *The Round Dance and Other Plays*, trans. by Charles Osborne (Manchester: Carcanet New Press, 1982); Tom Stoppard, *Dalliance*, in *Dalliance and Undiscovered Country* (London: Faber & Faber, 1986), pp. 1–53.

unauthorized translation stood as the only British publication of the play in English and was accordingly used (in an adaptation by Marianne Helweg) for various BBC radio productions over the intervening decades. The result was that Shand's interpretation dominated British appreciation of the play for much of the twentieth century. Reading his text alongside the playscript produced by Williams and the fragments that have survived from Macdonell's version discloses some of the strategies employed by the three translators and sheds light on the socio-cultural norms which informed their decision-making, norms which, in the case of *Playing with Love*, would become a long-term fixture in British reception of Schnitzler's play.

Comparative Reading

Given that only small parts of Macdonell's translation have been preserved, any comparison with Shand's and Williams's work is necessarily limited and an imperfect exercise. Unlike the two fully preserved translations, Macdonell's can only be judged in a vacuum, with individual lines or words read alone rather than against the breadth of her rendering. Furthermore, the examples which have survived do so only as a result of their having been criticized by Oelsner.[153] Macdonell's importance as Schnitzler's first English translator outweighs those particular concerns, but with the obvious caveat that caution be exercised before drawing concrete conclusions about her approach. Some of the textual passages for which direct comparison is possible are set out in the table below, with relevant words highlighted in bold in the source material. All are from the first act of the play.

Even from this restricted set, it is possible to identify instances of more widely established patterns which emerge from reading *Liebelei* and its fuller translations by Shand and Williams and hence to hazard a guess at Macdonell's approach more broadly. Schnitzler's frequent use of 'Kind' and 'Kinder' as an ostensibly affectionate sobriquet, for example, is largely mirrored by Shand, as it is in the example below. Of the twenty-one instances of either 'Kind' or 'Kinder' appearing in Act 1, Shand keeps all as 'child' or 'children', with the result that, to the modern ear at least, the repetition grates. By contrast, Williams tends to vary his translation ('girls and boys', 'beloved', 'baby', 'dear') or omits an equivalent altogether. Macdonell, in the example below, opts for an alternative, 'Dear people', for which Oelsner suggests 'Good people' or 'my good friends'. Elsewhere she keeps 'child', substitutes 'dear youth' or, like

153 Letter from Julie Markbreiter to Arthur Schnitzler, *c.* January 1899, which includes Oelsner's corrections to Macdonell's translation (DLA, HS.NZ85.0001.03999).

Original[154]	**MacDonell**	**Williams**[155]	**Shand**[156]
THEODOR. Was schreibt denn der Papa? (p. 927)	What's the Governor upon?	Well, what does the Guv'nor say? (p. 2)	What does your father say then? (p. 10)
THEODOR. Du weißt nämlich gar nicht, wie **fidel** Du da draußen gewesen bist. (p. 927)	larky	good sport (p. 3)	You have no idea how jovial you were out there. (p. 11)
FRITZ. **Herrgott**, bist Du energisch! (p. 928)	Bless us and save us!	Good Lord. How determined you are! (p. 3)	My word – you're energetic! (p. 11)
THEODOR: Besser ich als ein anderer. Denn der Andere ist unausbleiblich wie das Schicksal. (p. 933)	As soon I as another.	If I don't, some other fellow will. For the other fellow is bound to come as sure as fate. (p. 7)	Better I than another – for the other is as unfailing as fate. (p. 17)
MIZI: **Kinder**, dunkel wird's! (p. 941)	Dear people	I say, it's getting dark. (p. 15)	Children, it's getting dark. (p. 24)
FRITZ: […] **die großen Worte**, die hab' ich nicht gern. (p. 943)	Big language	I don't care for fine phrases. (p. 18)	I do not like vows and protestations. (p. 27)
MIZI *lachend.* Alleweil macht er Dummheiten. (p. 951)	He's forever doing nonsensical things	He fools the whole time. (p. 25)	He plays the fool the whole time. (p. 36)

Williams, omits any equivalent. In *Liebelei* the majority of the 'Kind/Kinder' are spoken by Fritz or Theodor when addressing either one or both of the two young women in the play, or by Weiring addressing his daughter Christine. It

154 Page references are to Arthur Schnitzler, *Liebelei*, ed. by Peter Michael Braunwarth, Gerhard Hubmann and Isabella Schwentner, 2 vols, in *Werke in historisch-kritischen Ausgaben*, 12 vols (Berlin and Boston, MA: de Gruyter, 2011–), IV (2014).

155 Page references are from the Lord Chamberlain's Archive, British Library, LCP, 1909/11.

156 Page references are from P. Morton Shand, *Playing with Love* (London: Hancock & Gay, 1914).

is undoubtedly a signal of power, equating women with infants in relation to the 'adults', men.[157] The effect of both Williams's and Macdonell's variations and omissions, therefore, is to reduce that particular (critical) expression of the gender dynamic portrayed by Schnitzler and smooth the way for easier public reception.

Williams's stated overall aim is performability, an approach which is all the more noticeable when compared to Shand's text. Whereas the tone of *Playing with Love* is relatively flat and the differences between speakers non-existent, Williams writes an Edwardian vernacular marked according to the speaker's position in the social hierarchy. Thus Williams's Katherina (the 'Frau eines Strumpfwirkers') is given such lines as 'You was just going out?' (*Light o' Love*, p. 44) and 'Go on with you, I says to him, you can't have seen straight' (*Light o' Love*, p. 46). Shand's Katharina, on the other hand, says more blandly: 'You're just going out' (*Playing with Love*, p. 56) and '"Oh," I said to him, "you have made a mistake"' (*Playing with Love*, p. 58). *Light o' Love* is full of abbreviated, informal and even playful expressions: 'Man alive' (*Light o' Love*, p. 2); 'Fritz, old man' (*Light o' Love*, p. 3); 'Fact!' (*Light o' Love*, p. 17); and 'Ripping' (*Light o' Love*, p. 27). Williams has also been quicker than Shand to cut text, often for the sake of avoiding unfamiliar cultural references (to the novelist and poet, Wilhelm Hauff, for example, cut from Act 2), sometimes for less apparent reasons (*Light o' Love*, p. 41: no translation for Mizi's 'Ja, das ist fesch!' etc. and Theodor's following line); and further cuts have been made by hand to the already translated (typed) text by Williams or possibly somebody else (*Light o' Love*, p. 5). The economizing he learnt in his newspaper days has clearly been put to use once more.

Macdonell's approach seems to fall somewhere between Williams's and Shand's. Whilst sometimes more adventurous in the idioms and words she chooses (for example, 'larky', 'she's simply a treasure' and 'Governor' instead of the tamer 'father' used by Shand), on other occasions her language stumbles rather than flows. For Weiring's question in Act 3 'Aber was fällt Dir denn ein ...' (*Liebelei*, p. 1007), Macdonell suggests 'What in the world are you meaning'. Earlier, Christine's disarmingly prescient statement to Fritz, 'Du bist ja frei – du kannst mich ja sitzen lassen' (*Liebelei*, p. 994), is rendered as 'You can leave me planted there wherever you choose'. On at least two occasions Macdonell adopts obsolete or archaic words reminiscent of a real or imagined German original: 'be-think' for Theodor's 'Bedenken Sie' (*Liebelei*, p. 1013); and 'got belated' for Fritz's 'Ich bin aufgehalten worden' (*Liebelei*, p. 986). The comparative exercise starts to come unstuck here. Both Shand and Williams make at least as many mistakes, or write as many

157 For an alternative reading of the significance of 'Kind' in Fritz's mouth, see Martin Swales, *Arthur Schnitzler: A Critical Study* (Oxford: Clarendon Press, 1971), p. 185.

inelegant phrases, as are listed by Oelsner in his criticisms of Macdonell. For Macdonell, however, we cannot set those unfortunate choices in a context of possibly much more appropriate, speakable translations. Nevertheless, a tentative assessment is legitimate: even the few fragments Oelsner has selected for correction demonstrate a translator with a live audience rather than a reader in mind and an awareness of the sound of her words spoken out loud.

Shand can (and does) rely on the slower and independently determined pace of a reader, providing time to digest his sometimes awkward-sounding syntax and to absorb the additional information given in the preface and footnotes. This in turn allows him to keep certain German and French phrases which might otherwise exclude members of a live audience or prove confusing. For example, Schnitzler apparently trusted that visitors to the Burgtheater would understand 'So, und jetzt *à place!*' (*Liebelei*, p. 953). Williams initially includes the French in his typed script, but those two words have subsequently been struck through with a pencil line and replaced with 'and now back to our places' (*Light o' Love*, p. 27). Shand apparently felt no need to make such adjustments (*Playing with Love*, p. 37). However, Williams does not exclude the foreign altogether. At the end of Act 1 he introduces a French word which was not in the source and which is not cut by the editorial pencil responsible for the earlier excision: when Theodor hurries Mizi out of the door with 'Geh, geh, geh, geh' (*Liebelei*, p. 969), Williams substitutes 'Outside vite!' (*Light o' Love*, p. 42). (Shand translates the same line as 'Come–come!' (*Playing with Love*, p. 54).)

Certain alien ideas could also be elucidated via stage directions and so kept in the text for performance. When the four companions drink 'Bruderschaft' in *Liebelei* (*Liebelei*, p. 953) both Shand and Williams retain the German word. Williams adds to the stage directions to ensure British actors perform the ritual properly: for example, 'Each drinks out of his own glass' (*Light o' Love*, p. 26). Shand instead provides a footnote: 'The custom is essentially a Teutonic one, for which there is no English equivalent. [...] after it has taken place the familiar second person singular is employed instead of the more formal plural' (*Playing with Love*, p. 19). Both translators include, at different times, German titles for characters, so that reader and audience are exposed to 'Herr Weiring', 'Fräulein Christine', 'Frau Binder' and 'Fräulein Mizi'. However, whereas Shand tends to keep unfamiliar names like the 'Orpheum' (*Playing with Love*, p. 28) or 'Lehnergarten' (*Playing with Love*, pp. 56 and 62), Williams reduces the particular to a generic alternative ('the circus' (*Light o' Love*, p. 19) and 'the garden' (*Light o' Love*, p. 44)). More confidence in the audience is visible in Williams's retention of 'Voeslauer Ausstich' for the wine drunk in the first act and the accompanying toast

'Prosit!' (*Light o' Love*, p. 25). Shand also sticks with 'Prosit' but, curiously, replaces the originally named wine with 'Vöslauer Auslese', adding in an extended footnote:

> *Auslese* has here been substituted for the Austrian term *Ausstich* as being more intelligible to English readers to whom Hock and Moselle vintages are familiar, while Austrian wines are all but unknown. The meaning is in both cases identical, and implies that the vintage is of a selected growth. (*Playing with Love*, p. 35)

It is tempting, given Shand's subsequent publishing history in viniculture, to put this anomalous alteration down to his burgeoning interest. The reference to 'English readers' makes clear the target consumer of the text; a reference to 'English audiences' might have indicated an anticipated performance. In any event, as a general rule Shand is more willing than Williams to preserve unfamiliar or foreign names for a readership assumed ready to embrace alterity.

Shand, Williams and (to the very limited degree legible from Oelsner's corrections) Macdonell coincide in at least one respect, namely their circumspect treatment of the words 'Gott' and 'Herrgott' in the source text. Schnitzler's characters (more often than not, the women) are unafraid of exclaiming in what might conventionally be considered blasphemous language. In Act 1 alone Christine utters 'Gott' or 'Oh Gott' on four occasions; in Act 2 she says 'O Gott' once more; and in Act 3 'Oh Gott' expresses Christine's desperation when she realizes how little she meant to Fritz. As seen in the table above, only Macdonell's response to a single 'Herrgott' survives (Oelsner preferred 'Heavens'). On this occasion Shand opted for 'My word' and Williams braved a 'Good Lord'. More generally, neither Shand nor Williams tends to meet the frequency with which Schnitzler incorporated the potentially provocative words. The word 'God' appears only four times in Shand's translation and only two of those occurrences are exclamatory (*Playing with Love*, pp. 82 and 97). Williams, like Shand, either omits 'God' altogether (*Light o' Love*, p. 22) or finds a gentler alternative such as 'Good heavens!' (*Light o' Love*, p. 23). Both translators, however, keep the 'Oh God' of Christine's climactic speech in Act 3 (beginning 'Auch von mir hat er gesprochen!' (*Liebelei*, p. 1010)), apparently warranted by the depth of her despair. Undoubtedly these cuts and substitutions represent conscious or unconscious censorship by the translators and/or their editors or directors. Although the word 'God' on its own cannot have been sufficient to attract the prosecutor's wrath or the Lord Chamberlain's blue pencil, there was perhaps an appreciation that excessive references to the Christian deity risked upsetting the audience, the reader, or anyone who had invested in the publication or production, including the director, the theatre-owner and the editor. Whereas a young woman in Vienna did not shock excessively with her 'O Gott', the English equivalent must have seemed too much to Schnitzler's early British translators.

It is evident from reading the three translations in parallel that Williams and Macdonell employ strategies which anticipate performance, while Shand steers a course for publication. Both Shand and Williams use German titles and refer to 'Bruderschaft', so that neither audience nor reader is allowed to forget that the play tells a Germanic story. However, apart from setting the play in Vienna, Williams drops other cultural references which might locate the play more specifically. Two factors could have informed that approach. First, a live theatre performance is a challenging space in which to introduce wholly foreign names or concepts, even when aided by supporting signs (e.g., gesture, costume, prop) to assist the audience in deciphering meaning. Second, in a context in which Schnitzler was hardly known in Britain, Williams perhaps sought to smooth the path of this early play by rendering it as familiar as possible whilst never denying its roots elsewhere. Shand could afford to be bolder: every line is translated; every geographical or cultural name incorporated. Shand holds tenaciously to the source material, at the cost of his dialogue sounding like naturally spoken English. Neither of these strategies is particularly surprising given the target markets (i.e., theatre for Williams's and Macdonell's translations and publication for Shand's). What is surprising, however, is that it was Shand's script which was, in fact, produced for decades afterwards (in BBC broadcasts).[158] Thus in the case of *Liebelei* the chance punt taken by a publishing house on one of its employees evolved to determine the play's English-language presence in the UK for years to come. Neither the translator who met Schnitzler in person nor the translator whose script was performed in the première could make such a claim.

158 The script was 'adapted for broadcast' by a BBC scriptwriter, Marianne Helweg, in or around 1935. The surviving script, for broadcast in 1962, shows that although significant cuts were made (most probably to fit in with programme times) the remaining text is easily traceable to Shand's work (BBC Written Archives Centre, *Playing with Love*, tx 19/12/62, TP). BBC copyright content is reproduced courtesy of the British Broadcasting Corporation. All rights reserved. There was only one English-language theatre performance of *Liebelei* in London between 1909 and 1986, *viz.* a matinee performance at the Kingsway Theatre on 7 December 1925 in aid of the Royal Free Hospital. According to J. P. Wearing, it was called *Light o' Love*, was translated by Williams and 'revised by Moreton Shand [*sic*]' (J. P. Wearing, *The London Stage 1920–1929: A Calendar of Productions, Performers, and Personnel*, 2nd edn (Lanham: Rowman & Littlefield, 2014 [1984]), p. 405, entry 25.372).

CHAPTER 2

Controlling the Posthumous Legacy

After Schnitzler's death on 21 October 1931 his only surviving child, Heinrich Schnitzler (1902–1982), became sole executor of the literary estate.[1] For the following fifty years Heinrich controlled the global dissemination of his father's works, except and insofar as such rights had been sold or given away during the writer's lifetime. In practice, this meant that Heinrich could grant or withhold permission for the translation, publication or performance of any of Schnitzler's plays in Britain until 31 December 1981, when copyright protection under the Berne Convention expired. This chapter is a case study of the shifts that occur when the primary power to determine textual meaning moves from author to executor. Mona Baker's categorization of 'narratives' in translation is particularly helpful in charting Heinrich's attempt to re-direct the dominant narratives driving the presentation of Schnitzler's works outside Austria. Heinrich seeks to undo the public narratives of both Vienna as the city of waltzes and joviality and Schnitzler as a writer limited to frivolous themes.[2] His attempt to shape his father's legacy accordingly goes hand in hand with considerations of how to represent Austria in the post-war world, in both the public and academic spheres.

Heinrich Schnitzler's exploits as executor of the estate were undeniably informed by his own ontological narrative, elements of which begin to emerge from the brief biographical section immediately below. This chapter goes on to provide evidence of his wider approach to managing Arthur Schnitzler's estate, before locating his agenda in the context of post-war historiographies of turn-of-the-century Vienna as well as that of the reception of his father's works in the anglophone world. The two collide for Heinrich Schnitzler in what he terms the 'myth of Gay Vienna'.[3] The impact of these concerns on his operations relating to his father's estate are explored through the lens of one play cycle, *Anatol*, and the translations of it by Harley Granville Barker

1 To avoid confusion, Heinrich Schnitzler is referred to mainly by his first name in the remainder of this chapter.

2 Baker, *Translation and Conflict*, p. 44.

3 Henry Schnitzler, '"Gay Vienna" – Myth and Reality', *Journal of the History of Ideas*, 15 (1954), 94–118 (p. 94).

and Frank Marcus. As in the previous chapter, a micro-historical approach involving a detailed reading of correspondence between Heinrich Schnitzler, his agent and others uncovers the complex negotiations regarding ownership of, and control over, the two translations. A comparison of the two texts, as well as a survey of their reception by British audiences, completes the picture and allows an assessment of the success with which Heinrich Schnitzler pursued his goals.

Heinrich Schnitzler: A Short Biography

Heinrich Schnitzler began his career as a student of the University of Vienna and as an actor.[4] Over the course of eleven years, from 1921 to 1932, he played 182 roles in more than 2,500 performances. These included roles in plays by his father. From acting he moved into directing, occupying positions before the war at the Raimundtheater and the Deutsches Volkstheater in Vienna and the Staatstheater Berlin. He also held a guest directorship at the Embassy Theatre in London in 1936, where he directed the first English-language production of *Professor Bernhardi*. In 1938 he took his family via Switzerland to America, where they were granted citizenship and remained until 1957. During those years of exile, Heinrich Schnitzler found full-time employment as an academic, teaching theatre history, acting and directing at the University of California in Berkeley (1942–48) and later at UCLA (1948–56).[5] His return to Vienna was intended to launch a renewed career as a director, thus in 1959 Heinrich began as director at the Theater in der Josefstadt, whilst also taking up guest directorships in Zürich, Düsseldorf, Stuttgart, Hamburg, Berlin, Munich, Rotterdam, Graz and Helsinki. His wide repertoire included numerous works by his father, both in German and translated into English. Heinrich was also active as a theatre translator, adapting English-language dramas for his own productions in German-speaking contexts. He was as well equipped as anyone could be to manage his father's literary estate.

His professional familiarity with the corpus was further bolstered by the editorial work in which he engaged as executor, a task almost frustrated by the geographical and political distance between himself (in America) and the

4 According to Reinhard Urbach, Heinrich studied Philosophie, Kunstgeschichte and Literaturgeschichte at the University between 1920 and 1922 (Reinhard Urbach, 'Heinrich Schnitzler – 75 Jahre', *Modern Austrian Literature*, 10.3 (1977), 1–18 (p. 1)).

5 For more detailed consideration of Heinrich's years in America and his role during that period as a facilitator of intercultural exchange and understanding, see Wolfgang Sabler, 'Heinrich Schnitzler, passeur entre les cultures et les héritages', *Études Germaniques*, 252 (2008), 737–48.

holders of significant parts of the *Nachlass* at Cambridge University Library.[6] Not only was Heinrich Schnitzler eventually able to oversee the publication (and in one case – *Anatols Größenwahn* – production) of various previously unpublished (and unperformed) literary works from the *Nachlass*, he also co-edited his father's autobiography, *Jugend in Wien*, as well as a number of volumes of letters; and he was responsible for the new collected editions of prose and dramatic works (two volumes of each) published by the Fischer Verlag in 1961 and 1962.[7] Heinrich's engagement with the British dissemination of his father's dramas, as well as being informed by the personal and private nature of their familial relationship, was infused with the professional experience of an actor, director, scholar and editor concerned with all aspects of the writer's output.

Management of the Estate

Two features of Heinrich Schnitzler's management of the literary estate stand out when compared with Arthur Schnitzler's own grasp of his affairs in Britain: first, the constancy of Heinrich's relationship with one single agent, Eric Glass, for almost fifty years; and, second, his fluency in English relative to that of his father. In addition, Heinrich's years at the helm were informed by his overriding concern with the myth of 'Gay Vienna'. This chapter now explores each of those three factors before taking British productions of the play cycle *Anatol* as a concrete example of Heinrich Schnitzler's approach to the posthumous control of his father's works.

Eric Glass was an Austrian émigré in London whose interest in promoting Schnitzler's works in the anglophone world began as early as December 1928, when he approached the writer in Vienna about 'Engl[ish] press representation'.[8] The earliest record of any contact between Glass and

6 Cf. Wilhelm Hemecker and David Österle, '"… so grundfalsch war alles Weitere". Zur Geschichte des Nachlasses von Arthur Schnitzler', *Jahrbuch der deutschen Schillergesellschaft*, 58 (2018), 3–40.

7 *Anatols Größenwahn* was first performed at the Deutsches Volkstheater in Vienna in 1932. It was the first play by his father that Heinrich Schnitzler directed in Vienna (Urbach, 'Heinrich Schnitzler', p. 6).

8 See *Tagebuch*, 17.12.1928: 'Früh Hr. Erich Glass, "Engl. press representation" – wegen Interview;– ich erklärte warum ich keines gäbe – woraus er eines machen wird'. The only other relevant entry in the diaries is *Tagebuch*, 22.4.1931: 'Erich Glass (Corresp. etc.) läßt sich die Anatol Angelegenheit Amerika, zu ev. journal. Verwendung erzählen'. In a letter dated 22.5.1970 from Glass to Heinrich Schnitzler, the former refers to 'a very old understanding first reached with your father and subsequently with you' (Theatermuseum, Wien, Nachlass Heinrich Schnitzler; Korrespondenz, Schn 21/8/60). Hereinafter references to this collection are marked by 'Schn', followed by the document number and, where available, the date. Erich Glass most probably changed his name to 'Eric' on his migration to the UK. He is possibly

Heinrich dates from 11 March 1934, the last from 20 January 1982.[9] More than nine hundred letters from the intervening years survive, providing a dense documentary trail of Heinrich Schnitzler's efforts to present his father's works in Britain. Although most of these are copies of letters from Heinrich to Glass, reflecting the former's policy of destroying business correspondence every ten years, it is nevertheless possible to build up a detailed picture of the exchange between literary executor and agent and thereby gain an understanding of how Arthur Schnitzler's posthumous reputation in Britain was steered remotely by his son.[10] Although largely formal in tone, the letters between the men display an increasing familiarity and even fondness for each other. They exchanged news from their family lives and met in London on a number of occasions.[11] A relationship of trust undoubtedly arose, although Heinrich would not hesitate to breach that trust and seek alternative representation when Glass temporarily fell out of contact.[12] It was first and foremost a business relationship.

For the first four years of their correspondence, Heinrich wrote to Glass in German, the mother tongue for both men. From 1938, the year in which Heinrich moved to America, he began to write in English as well;[13] and after

---

the same 'Erich Glass' credited with a translation of St John Ervine's *The First Mrs Fraser* for a production at the Raimundtheater (*Die Erste Mrs. Selby*) (St John Ervine, 'At the Play', *Observer*, 2 November 1930, p. 15). Heinrich similarly adopted an anglicized name during his years in America, 'Henry' (Sabler, 'Heinrich Schnitzler, passeur', pp. 738–42), only to re-assume his birth name after his return to Austria in 1957. For an illustration of the shift, see two letters to Ilsa Barea (Schn 6/24/1, 18.6.1953 and Schn 6/24/2, 12.3.1960), the earlier of which is written in English and signed 'Henry Schnitzler'; the later one is written in German and signed 'Heinrich Schnitzler'.

9 Heinrich Schnitzler to Eric Glass, 11.3.1934 (Schn 21/4/1); and Heinrich Schnitzler to Eric Glass, 20.1.1982 (Schn 21/13/29).

10 The first preserved letter from Eric Glass is dated 6.1.1970 (Schn 21/8/38).

11 See, for example, the letter dated 13.8.1937 (Schn 21/4/23). It was around this time that acquaintance with Glass was of increasing personal value to Heinrich, acting as a possible conduit to enable Heinrich's escape from the Continent to the USA.

12 Cf. Heinrich Schnitzler's letter to Gerda Niedieck (his Swiss agent) on 18.9.1977: 'An [*sic*] meine Existenz hat Glass übrigens völlig vergessen und ich existiere überhaupt nicht mehr für ihn' (Schn 40/5/30). See also the letter dated 10.11.1977: 'Bitte überleg' Dir, was wir mit Glass tun sollen? So hat diese Verbindung keinen Sinn mehr' (Schn 40/5/39). Heinrich was in the process of transferring the UK business to S. Fischer (see letter dated 26.11.77 (Schn 40/5/43)) when direct communication with Glass started again (letter of 6.2.1978 (Schn 21/12/2)). A misunderstanding concerning Heinrich's association with the literary agents Niedieck-Linder AG was identified as the cause of Glass's silence. See Heinrich's letter to Glass of 11.2.1978: 'Our friendship, not to mention our professional association goes back over a period of several decades and I could not understand what caused your complete silence' (Schn 21/12/3).

13 The first evidence of this is a letter dated 25.6.1938 (Schn 21/4/37).

a four-and-a-half-year gap in the correspondence between March 1939 and August 1943 Heinrich's letters were written only in English. By this stage Heinrich had been living in America for five years and his confidence had evidently grown. By 1951 his English competence was such that he thought of it as 'now almost a second mother-tongue'.[14] His increasing capacity to work in English sharpened his ability to control anglophone dissemination. He could communicate directly with translators, directors and publishers and understand reviews in the English-language press concerning the latest productions.[15] Heinrich's fluency also enabled him to examine and assess translations of his father's works with a far greater degree of thoroughness and conviction than the author himself could have done. Before allowing a new translation to go into production he insisted on reading it closely, comparing translation with source line by line and requiring those amendments to be made which he found necessary. Inevitably this slowed down the generation of new interpretations of Schnitzler's works quite considerably. It also meant that any translator in search of approval would have his or her text subjected to Heinrich's critical eye and his sometimes bafflingly incoherent criteria (examined below). Certainly, Heinrich's method of reading and assessing translations revealed his unspoken but transparent belief that a translation could only be judged by explicit reference to the source text.

The boundaries of Heinrich's evaluative agenda were marked by the poles of 'literal' and 'free' translation, both of which were, according to him, to be avoided. Whereas a literal translation was 'in most instances [...] an impossibility' leading 'only to a stilted text',[16] the alternatives, variously labelled 'adaptation', 'modernizing' and 'rewriting', were equally unappealing and generally unacceptable. Indeed, such was Heinrich's disdain for more liberal approaches to translation that he would distance himself from the relevant word by placing it in quotation marks.[17] Heinrich's navigation of the land between those poles would, however, shift from case to case. Perhaps this

14 Heinrich Schnitzler to Eric Glass, 4.8.1951 (Schn 21/5).

15 The Heinrich Schnitzler *Nachlass* at the Theatermuseum in Vienna includes Heinrich's direct correspondence with, among others, Terry Hands and Michael Kustow (at the National Theatre), Ronald Adam (playwright and translator), Ned Sherrin (playwright) and Charles Dyer (playwright and translator).

16 Heinrich Schnitzler to Eric Glass, 23.10.1953 (Schn 21/5/35).

17 See, for example, a letter dated 21.5.1953 from Heinrich to the translator Frank Marcus: 'I feel that the play can stand as it is – [...] nothing would be gained by "modernizing" it' (Schn 34/18/15). Also, in a letter to Glass dated 18.1.1964 he writes: 'I still hold strong reservations as to the necessity of "adapting" a work which hardly needs any adaptation' (Schn 21/7/81). Heinrich admittedly also used quotation marks around 'literalness', but this practice was rare.

is unsurprising, given that for Heinrich the primary objective of a translation, whether merely an *interlingual* translation from German to English or simultaneously *intersemiotic* (e.g., from short story to film), was that it should recapture, or iterate, the 'spirit', 'essence', 'tone', 'basic idea' or 'characteristic aspects' of the source text.[18] These ontological indefinables inevitably differed from one work to the next and so required a different approach on each occasion.

Proposed temporal, geographical and genre shifts, for example, met with arguably contradictory responses, depending on the text in question. Heinrich did not think in 1962 that *Lieutenant Gustl* could be adapted for film because '[i]n this particular instance, the form of the story represents its very essence and any attempt to change that form will inevitably lead to distortions of, and additions to, the story'.[19] The 'form' referred to is, in this novella, quite distinct from most other works in the corpus insofar as it is dominated by interior monologue. In other instances, i.e., in respect of other texts, Heinrich was perfectly willing to entertain translations which transported a work through time or space or across media. When considering how a story ('Ein Erfolg') might be dramatized for a British audience, Heinrich suggested:

> The 'locale' should be either London, or some other city in Great Britain. [...] What is now Viennese, would have to be changed to Cockney; instead of the horsedrawn carriages, there would have to be automobiles, motorcycles, etc. It would be quite simple to provide a modern environment, since time and place are rather irrelevant to the comic possibilities of the basic idea.[20]

He clarified: the plan would be to 'transplant [...] it right away into a contemporary British environment'. In this case, apparently, form was not an essential element of the text. Furthermore, neither Vienna nor the *fin de siècle* was so important as to render a major chronotopical shift impossible. Rather, Heinrich almost considered the transplantation a necessity in order for the dramatization to work.

Evident in the examples from Heinrich's correspondence is an underlying subscription to a concept of the author's subjectivity as 'a metaphysical essence which is present in his text and all its copies';[21] of meaning as a constant, fixed and identifiable entity; and of translation as an ideally transparent means of communicating the author's intentions as expressed in one language into another. Paradoxically, Heinrich seeks fluency and performability *without* the loss of any authorial originality and *without* muddying the

18 Jakobson, 'On Linguistic Aspects of Translation', p. 128.

19 Heinrich Schnitzler to Eric Glass, 21.6.1962 (Schn 21/7/29).

20 Heinrich Schnitzler to Eric Glass, 14.6.1956 (Schn 21/5/96).

21 Venuti, *The Translator's Invisibility*, pp. 136–37.

waters of Schnitzler's self-representation as reflected in the source texts.[22] Heinrich's apparent acquiescence in the intentional fallacy, combined with his attachment to naturalized dialogue, resulted in a reluctant pragmatism. He was more than familiar with the commercial and practical contingencies involved in publishing or producing literary works. Although very attentive to the translations themselves and at times quite stubborn about such details as a proposed new title, the casting of a play, the length of a broadcast, or minor alterations to a story's plot, he was also often ready to step back from the broader production decisions needing to be made and to submit to those operating in closer proximity to the action.[23] In one respect, however, Heinrich remained unremittingly determined: namely, in his resolve to debunk certain damaging myths surrounding Schnitzler's works.

Disentangling Schnitzler from the Myth of 'Gay Vienna'

One of the key themes running through Heinrich Schnitzler's correspondence is his determination to re-cast his father's works outside what he considered to be false representations of Vienna at the turn of the century. His concern can be read against the post-war historiography of Vienna, as well as the popular and academic reception of Arthur Schnitzler in the second half of the twentieth century. After setting out that historical context below, this section presents evidence for interpreting Schnitzler's corpus as inextricably linked to Vienna, followed by an analysis of how Heinrich's mission to disentangle the author from a particular image of the city was made manifest in his attempts to control British dissemination. A summary of an essay entitled

22 See the letter from Heinrich Schnitzler to Eric Glass dated 11.3.1947: 'I am usually struck by the lack of feeling for the author's intentions' (Schn 21/4/64). An example of Heinrich's sensitivity to the realities of theatrical performance is to be found in a later letter to Glass dated 23.10.1953: '[T]he main consideration seems to me whether the general tone of the original is recaptured and – in a dramatic translation – whether it can be spoken by modern actors and listened to by modern audiences' (Schn 21/5/35).

23 Heinrich's willingness to defer to the views of others was most obviously the case where the BBC was concerned, especially during Martin Esslin's tenure as Head of Radio Drama between 1963 and 1977. Heinrich's amicable relationship with Esslin, another émigré from Vienna, is evident from their direct correspondence (Schn 7/7): the two men met on at least one occasion (Heinrich Schnitzler to Martin Esslin, 8.12.1963 (Schn 7/7/4)) and Heinrich expressed personal trust in Esslin (Heinrich Schnitzler to Martin Esslin, 5.10.1970 (Schn 7/7/7)). Heinrich's trust in the institution only faltered when the six-part television series *Vienna 1900: Games with Love and Death*, an adaptation of five of Arthur Schnitzler's stories, was broadcast in December 1973. Heinrich's huge disappointment with the outcome, a 'distortion' of Schnitzler's texts, is documented in his correspondence with Glass from November 1973. See, for example, the letter of 27.1.1974 (Schn 21/10/35).

'"Gay Vienna" – Myth and Reality' published by Heinrich Schnitzler in 1954 provides further illumination of the motives driving Heinrich's decisions as legatee.

Schnitzler's reputation has, from his initial domestic reception, been enmeshed with Viennese Impressionism, a school of thought which 'envisage[d] the self as an extensionless point, a perspectival standpoint, or a mere fiction'.[24] From a critical perspective, Impressionism encouraged decadence, moral relativism and nihilism in the writings of its proponents. These externally imposed characteristics continued to inform even academic reception of Schnitzler in the 1920s, 1930s and beyond.[25] Thus when Heinrich took on the management of his father's estate, he also inherited a legacy of misrepresentative interpretations of the literary corpus. His subsequent efforts to undo the early pigeon-holing coincided with, and hence contributed to, the wider 'attempt to rescue Schnitzler criticism from the encroaching folkloric obsession with Schnitzler the decadent satyr'.[26] Andrew C. Wisely maps the changing landscape of the academic reception of Arthur Schnitzler over the century, including the paradigm shift which occurred in the 1960s when Schnitzler scholars began to explore the themes of freedom and ethics in the works.[27] These years represent, for Wisely, a period of resuscitation for 'author, text and milieu after years of neglect'.[28]

Wisely's reference to 'milieu' recognizes a parallel shift taking place in the historiography of turn-of-the-century Vienna. Just as Schnitzler was being reinterpreted in the post-war decades, so the city in which he had lived was being re-evaluated as scholars sought to understand Austria's role in the Second World War more broadly. The relationship between author and city found its apogee in the surviving trend among scholars in 1950 to regard Schnitzler as 'the troubadour of an eternally "gay Vienna"'.[29] As Wisely notes, new scholarship on both the cultural history of Austria and Schnitzler's position within that context was beginning to forge counternarratives to such persistent

24 Ritchie Robertson, 'Modernism and the Self, 1890–1924', in *Philosophy and German Literature, 1700–1990*, ed. by Nicholas Saul (Cambridge: Cambridge University Press, 2002), pp. 150–96 (p. 162). Viennese Impressionism is explored in greater detail in Chapter 4.

25 Andrew C. Wisely, *Arthur Schnitzler and Twentieth-Century Criticism* (Rochester, NY: Camden House, 2004), pp. 48–68.

26 Robertson, 'Modernism and the Self', p. 171.

27 Wisely, *Arthur Schnitzler*, p. 73.

28 Wisely, *Arthur Schnitzler*, p. 74. As an indication of the neglect suffered within Schnitzler scholarship, Wisely notes that Martin Swales's volume *Arthur Schnitzler* (1971) was the first English-language monograph on Schnitzler since Sol Liptzin, *Arthur Schnitzler* (New York: Prentice Hall, 1932) (Wisely, *Arthur Schnitzler*, p. 79).

29 Richard Plant, 'Notes on Arthur Schnitzler's Literary Technique', *The Germanic Review*, 25 (1950), 13–25 (p. 14).

mythological readings. Alongside the sometimes anecdotal, but nevertheless wide-ranging assessment of Viennese cultural and social history provided by, for example, Ilsa Barea in 1966 (*Vienna: Legend and Reality*) there were further pioneering English-language examinations of the subject in the late 1960s and 1970s, culminating in Carl E. Schorske's *Fin-de-Siècle Vienna* in 1980, the field-defining publication.[30] Schorske's model of Vienna as the birthplace of European Modernism has since been supplemented, and challenged, by further scholarship, but at the time of its emergence it represented, with Martin Swales's ground-breaking work on Schnitzler (published in 1971), a significant move away from the 'glitter' generated by more folkloric accounts of both the city and the writer.[31] Heinrich was far from alone in his concerns about the myth of 'Gay Vienna' and his own efforts can thus be seen as part of a broader (admittedly intellectual) movement to re-narrate the dying decades of Habsburg rule. Controlling the foreign presentation of Schnitzler's works was, accordingly, far more to Heinrich than simply a question of agreeing rights and fees: it was about promoting and preserving a particular image of Arthur Schnitzler and of *fin-de-siècle* Vienna.

The tie between city and author as a focus for popular and scholarly attention, although problematic, is at least in some respects legitimate.[32] Vienna is the locus of much of the action in Arthur Schnitzler's writing; and even in those plays for which Vienna does not provide the setting the city's presence is felt through the orientation of the drama from peripheral town or countryside villa towards the metropolitan centre. Neither does Vienna simply play the role of neutral, flat or featureless backdrop to Schnitzler's plays. Rather, we

30 Carl E. Schorske, *Fin-de-Siècle Vienna: Politics and Culture* (London: Weidenfeld and Nicholson, 1980). The essays collected in Schorske's *Fin-de-Siècle Vienna* had been published individually over the course of the previous twenty years. See also Arthur J. May, *Vienna in the Age of Franz Joseph* (Norman, OK: University of Oklahoma Press, 1966); Frank Field, *The Last Days of Mankind: Karl Kraus and his Vienna* (London: MacMillan, 1967). Although there is no record among Heinrich's papers of his having written to Ilsa Barea after the publication of her book, we know that he approved of her approach (Heinrich Schnitzler to Ilsa Barea, 18.6.1953 (Schn 6/24/1)).

31 Swales, *Arthur Schnitzler*. Heinrich Schnitzler read Swales's book and considered it to be 'the first really comprehensive and important book on my father in English' (Heinrich Schnitzler to Eric Glass, 9.2.1972 (Schn 21/9/57)). For challenges to Schorske's model see *Rethinking Vienna 1900*, ed. by Steven Beller (Oxford: Berghahn, 2001).

32 Vienna provides an explicit frame of reference in a number of cases. See, for example, Rolf-Peter Janz and Klaus Laermann, *Arthur Schnitzler. Zur Diagnose des Wiener Bürgertums im Fin de Siècle* (Stuttgart: Metzler, 1977); Bruce Thompson, *Schnitzler's Vienna: Image of a Society* (New York & London: Routledge, 1990). Long before these, however, Hugo von Hofmannsthal suggested that Vienna between 1890 and the First World War might one day 'be called simply Schnitzler's Vienna' (Hugo von Hofmannsthal, 'Vienna Letter, July 1922', *The Dial*, August 1922, pp. 206–14 (p. 210)).

hear the language of her inhabitants and recognize the names of her streets, bridges, restaurants, even a hospital; and the Prater appears with frequency. As Yates has shown in respect of *Reigen*, that drama is 'firmly rooted in Viennese reality' through its use of local dialect and 'a physical placing of the action in the city'.[33] It is thus possible to trace the action of *Reigen* from one city district to another, from the Augartenbrücke over the Danube to the Prater, on to the Porzellangasse, the Schwindgasse on the other side of the city and the Riedhof Restaurant near the Allgemeines Krankenhaus.[34] Similar mappings are possible with respect to a number of Schnitzler's other works; and even where the topography so traced is not entirely consistent with that of Vienna, Schnitzler provides a fictionalized, yet still recognizable version of the city.[35]

Heinrich Schnitzler worried, understandably, that the relationship between his father and his home city was actively reciprocal in nature, so that not only could Schnitzler's texts inform public perception of Vienna, but Vienna's reputation could colour the author's legacy. The reverberations of this reciprocity could be discerned, Heinrich thought, in the way Schnitzler's corpus was presented in Britain. He complained repeatedly in his correspondence with Eric Glass that the myth of 'Gay Vienna' dictated British reception of his father's works. The early plays in particular were too often 'misunderstood according to popular clichés of that "Gay Vienna" which is mainly a product of insipid Hollywood movies and infantile Viennese operettas'.[36] Implicit in Heinrich's frequent use of 'Lehár' in his letters as shorthand for the myth is a fear that Arthur Schnitzler and his city would be absorbed into that of the operetta-writer.[37]

Heinrich's disquiet was fuelled by his recognition of the power of 'narratives of the past [to] define and determine the narrative present'.[38] His discourse here bears a striking resemblance to that later developed by Mona

33 Yates, *Schnitzler, Hofmannsthal, and the Austrian Theatre*, p. 135. Elsewhere Yates expands his claim to cover the corpus as a whole: 'Both the charm and the limitation of Schnitzler's work, whatever its subject [...], are that it is tied to the physical world and the attitudes of turn-of-the-century Vienna' (p. 24).

34 Yates, *Schnitzler, Hofmannsthal, and the Austrian Theatre*, p. 136.

35 Perhaps the most obvious example is *Lieutenant Gustl* (cf. commentary in Fliedl, *Arthur Schnitzler*, pp. 119–22, which includes a map of Gustl's route through the city). Further examples of Vienna as particularized, geographical centre can be found in Schnitzler's *Der Weg ins Freie* (for which see Janz and Laermann, *Arthur Schnitzler*, pp. 155–62 and accompanying maps); *Die Toten schweigen*, *Liebelei* and *Fink und Fliederbusch*.

36 Heinrich Schnitzler to Eric Glass, 17.10.1953 (Schn 21/5/34). For further examples see Heinrich Schnitzler to Eric Glass, 14.9.1963 (Schn 21/7/66) and 23.4.1975 (Schn 21/11/24); and Heinrich Schnitzler to Charles Marowitz, 16.6.1974 (Schn 34/29/3).

37 Heinrich Schnitzler to Eric Glass, 17.10.1953 (Schn 21/5/34). In this letter Heinrich refers to the 'spirit [...] of Lehár's Vienna [rather] than that of Arthur Schnitzler's'.

38 Henry Schnitzler, '"Gay Vienna"', p. 99.

Baker when describing the same gathering of momentum as 'narrative accrual'.[39] Interpretative canons are established through repetition; Heinrich appreciated how an arguably misguided production in one theatre could set an undesirable precedent for subsequent interpretations. According to Baker, 'public narratives', when adopted by scholars to become 'conceptual' or 'disciplinary' narratives, can 'have considerable impact beyond their disciplinary boundaries' and so become 'pernicious'.[40] The flipside of that danger is that positive changes at the level of conceptual narratives (as, for example, those charted by Wisely in respect of Schnitzler scholarship) can be slow, first to cross-fertilize within academia and then to filter back into public and ontological narratives. An illustration is provided by William M. Johnston's vast and impressive work on Austrian intellectual history, *The Austrian Mind* (1972), which still labels Schnitzler 'the typical impressionist',[41] even though written at a time when Schnitzler scholars such as Offermanns were reading Schnitzler as a *critic* of Impressionism.[42] Notably, it was Johnston's summary of Viennese attitudes to death and duelling that was used in the programme notes for the National Theatre's production of *Undiscovered Country* in 1979, so that the paratext guiding audience interpretation was informed by a conceptual narrative regarding Schnitzler which lagged behind contemporary critical thinking on the topic.

By understanding the grand narrative of 'Gay Vienna' as perceived by Heinrich Schnitzler, it becomes easier to decipher his management of Arthur Schnitzler's literary legacy. Heinrich set out his argument in a substantial essay published in 1954 (while he was still living in America) under the title '"Gay Vienna" – Myth and Reality'.[43] At the time Austria was still divided and occupied by the victorious Allies, so that the future of the country remained very uncertain. Heinrich's declared aim in the essay was, in short, to rescue Vienna from the popular saccharine image of waltzes, operetta and sentimental nostalgia; and to emphasize by way of contrast the politically and culturally significant role the city had played in the history of Western civilization. In Baker's language, Heinrich's project amounted to an attack on what he perceived to be the 'public narrative' of 'Gay Vienna', a reading

39 Baker, 'Narratives in and of Translation', p. 9.

40 Baker, 'Narratives in and of Translation', p. 6.

41 William Johnston, *The Austrian Mind: An Intellectual and Social History, 1848–1938* (Berkeley, CA and Los Angeles, CA: University of California Press, 1972), p. 171.

42 Ernst L. Offermanns, *Arthur Schnitzler. Das Komödienwerk als Kritik des Impressionismus* (Munich: Fink, 1973).

43 Schnitzler, '"Gay Vienna"'. Further references to this essay are given in the text. The germ of his concerns is evident in an earlier article, 'Some Remarks on Austrian Literature', *Books Abroad*, 17 (Summer 1943), 215–21 (p. 220).

of the city which had been 'elaborated by and circulat[ed] among social and institutional formations'.[44] Heinrich sought to 'recover values which have been lost in a welter of sentimental and superficial generalizations and to arrive at an interpretation which should make Vienna appear infinitely more provocative than the naïve image created by a hackneyed cliché' (p. 94). In tracing the roots of this myth in music, literature and popular theatre, Heinrich sought to reveal the darker, more complex reality to be found beneath the kitsch, shiny surface.

One of the causes for the prevalent cliché was, according to Heinrich, a widespread failure to appreciate the distinction between the Austrian and the German literary traditions: 'The Viennese is an Austrian, not a German, even if his popular idiom is a German dialect' (p. 96).[45] Heinrich argued that it was only by understanding the peculiarly Austrian and 'highly problematical relation to reality' that one could understand how gaiety was used 'as an escape from reality, an escape encouraged and facilitated by a sceptical relation to reality' (p. 96). It was also this problematic relation to reality that gave rise to the concern in Austrian literature with death, the transience of life and mortality (p. 98); Heinrich here seems to advance an idea of Austrian culture as still coloured by its Catholic, Baroque heritage. Austrians, and the Viennese in particular, learnt to laugh at life, to satirize and parody, but paradoxically also to glorify their Imperial city when presenting it to outsiders. Maintaining and promoting the illusion of gay Vienna defined the city-dwellers' *modus operandi*.[46]

As Heinrich's analysis of nineteenth-century Austria's myth-creation drew to its chronological end, he touched briefly on the response of the group of young writers active at the turn of the century which included his father. 'They did not conform to the myth' (p. 116), he wrote, there being 'not much gaiety in their writings' (p. 109); accordingly, 'a large portion of their works has remained untranslated and therefore unknown to the general public in other countries' (p. 116). The consequences, then, for Schnitzler and his peers were either misinterpretation or obscurity:

44 Baker, 'Narratives in and of Translation', p. 5.

45 Cf. Sabler, 'Heinrich Schnitzler, passeur', for a reading of the essay that asks whether Heinrich Schnitzler's efforts to distinguish between German and Austrian culture (and therewith to support an assessment of Austria as the first victim of Nazi Germany) were part of a plan for his own re-integration into the Second Austrian Republic. Disagreements as to how Austrian culture does or does not differ from German culture remain alive today. See Richard J. Evans, 'A New Vision of Germany', in which Evans reviews Neil MacGregor, *Germany: Memories of a Nation* (London: Penguin, 2016) (Richard J. Evans, 'A New Vision of Germany', *The New York Review of Books*, 14 January 2016, https://www.nybooks.com/articles/2016/01/14/new-vision-of-germany [accessed 5 February 2016]).

46 Arthur Schnitzler's own exploration of the threshold between illusion and reality has become a popular focus for postmodern scholarship on the writer.

> Many writers have remained practically unknown abroad because they did not fit into the pattern of 'Gay Vienna,' while others became known, as it were, for the wrong reasons. That is, their works have frequently been interpreted in a way that coincided with the familiar pattern, which implied that what did not fit into that pattern was conveniently ignored. (p. 94)

Heinrich spelt out more explicitly in the essay what was only hinted at elsewhere in his letters: his father's image was intricately bound up with that of the city. To rescue Vienna from her myth of gaiety, therefore, was also to rescue Schnitzler from obscurity or, alternatively and perhaps worse, from eternal misinterpretation.[47]

In the face of such long-standing and well-established preconceptions, Heinrich Schnitzler sought to harness proposed new translations as instruments with which to legitimize *his* version of place and person, Vienna and Arthur Schnitzler, and to provide an antidote to the pervasive myth. Through new translations, publications and productions of his father's works Heinrich could expose the non-German-speaking world to new stories about Vienna and so counter the 'normalizing effect of [alternative or prior] publicly disseminated representations'.[48] Active resistance to and rewriting of the dominant narratives surrounding Vienna could in turn feed back into the narratives constructed about the literature which came from that city.

Anatol and its Creator: Symbiotic Relations

The British reception of Schnitzler's plays, for much of the period in question, could be legitimately divided into two strands: (1) *Reigen* and *Anatol*; and (2) everything else. Heinrich himself was painfully conscious of the fact that

47 A noteworthy parallel to Heinrich's thoughts on 'Gay Vienna' can be seen in the work of Ilsa Barea. Heinrich's article from 1954 preceded Barea's *Vienna: Legend and Reality* (1966) in publication, but coincided with the writing of it and followed an article Barea published on the subject of Schnitzler and Viennese legend in 1951 (Ilsa Barea, 'Viennese Mirage', *The Times Literary Supplement*, 15 June 1951, p. 365). On 18 June 1953 Heinrich wrote to Barea, complimenting her on the article and advising her that he was 'immensely interested' in the book she was writing; it 'was a theme which ha[d] haunted [him]' and he had 'frequently toyed with the idea of writing about it [him]self'. He enclosed a draft of what was to become his article of 1954 in its original format as the script for a one-hour lecture given at UCLA in 1950 and suggested Barea visit the *Nachlass* in Cambridge for further material for her book (Schn 6/24/1). Barea's sympathetic reading of Schnitzler was harnessed for Heinrich's cause when she agreed to write an introduction to Jacqueline and Frank Marcus's translation of *Reigen*, *Merry-Go-Round* (London: Weidenfeld and Nicholson, 1953).

48 Baker, *Translation and Conflict*, p. 3.

the majority of enquiries from Britain concerned only two of his father's earliest dramatic works: 'There never was and there never will be any interest in my father's plays in England, with the exception of REIGEN and perhaps also of ANATOL, and I have no illusions as to any change in that attitude'.[49] Of those two plays, *Anatol* bore a special burden in relation to the demythologizing of the corpus. Whereas the popularity of *Reigen* in Britain was explainable, according to Heinrich, 'because it was exploited for sensational purposes', the popularity of *Anatol* was expressly referable to the play's coinciding 'with the widespread, stupid, superficial, Hollywood-bred notion of "Gay Vienna"'.[50] In addition, *Anatol* was uniquely associated with the biographical Schnitzler: if Anatol the protagonist was judged to be frivolous and silly, then so was Schnitzler. The imagined identification between author and character always threatened to spill over into and confuse British reception. Before expanding on that perceived symbiosis, this section first introduces *Anatol* and its scholarly reception.

The title *Anatol* is most commonly used to refer to a cycle of seven playlets, in each of which the eponymous hero, a wealthy, philandering idler, contemplates his relations with different women. These contemplations are made possible by the presence of his friend and philosophical sparring partner Max, who appears in five of the seven playlets. Anatol is also joined on stage by seven current or former lovers – one in each act. A skeleton of the structure, with additional cast, is set out below for ease of reference:[51]

1. *Die Frage an das Schicksal*	Max and Cora[52]
2. *Weihnachtseinkäufe*	Gabriele
3. *Episode*	Max and Bianca
4. *Denksteine*	Emilie
5. *Abschiedssouper*	Max and Annie
6. *Agonie*	Max and Else
7. *Anatols Hochzeitsmorgen*	Max and Ilona

49 Heinrich Schnitzler to Eric Glass, 23.9.1961 (Schn 21/6/144).

50 Heinrich Schnitzler to Eric Glass, 14.9.1963 (Schn 21/7/66).

51 The order is taken from the first publication of *Anatol* in 1893 (Berlin: Verlag des Bibliographischen Bureaus): Arthur Schnitzler, *Anatol*, ed. by Evelyne Polt-Heinzl and Isabella Schwentner, 2 vols, in *Werke in historisch-kritischen Ausgaben*, ed. by Konstanze Fliedl, 12 vols (Berlin and Boston, MA: de Gruyter, 2011–), II (2012), 12–13. Henceforth page references will be given in the text.

52 In each of the playlets in which Max does appear, he appears before the lover, providing the two friends with the opportunity to anticipate her arrival. This is the case even in *Anatols Hochzeitsmorgen*, in which Ilona is in Anatol's rooms from the outset but does not appear on stage until after Max's arrival.

An eighth episode, entitled *Anatols Größenwahn*, was conceived as an alternative to *Anatols Hochzeitsmorgen*, but was not published or performed during Schnitzler's lifetime.[53] A cycle of five of the episodes, without *Denksteine* or *Agonie*, was first performed in a simultaneous première at the Lessingtheater in Berlin and the Deutsches Volkstheater in Vienna on 3 December 1910. Prior to this date individual playlets had been performed in isolation.[54]

Anatol, the protagonist, has been regarded as the 'österreichische Variante des europäischen Dandys', a familiar figure, therefore, but one which is nevertheless 'weniger exzentrisch als vielmehr passiv-elegisch'.[55] He has no social purpose or function, representing what, in an undated aphorism, Schnitzler terms 'de[n] kernlose[n] Mensch[en]' whose psyche 'aus einzelnen gewissermaßen flottierenden Elementen zu bestehen [scheint]'.[56] Anatol fritters away his time and energy on sometimes overlapping love affairs. The women who interest him range from the married mothers of the metropolis to the innocent young girls of the suburbs, as well as the dancers and other performers of the bohemian demi-monde. He longs for a true and wholly faithful romance, but in reality cannot bring himself to believe in the possibility of such a love and is quickly bored.

His affairs are seemingly most interesting to him when viewed, and narrated, historically: 'What Anatol sees in each young woman [...] is not so much the individual herself as a figure elaborated by his own imagination, in an atmosphere sentimentally cherished'.[57] Thus, in *Episode* Anatol's mementoes of past loves are curated not by name but by particular, memorable features. The women themselves are insignificant. What is important to Anatol is *his* way of loving them and remembering them. The point is spelt out by Anatol's recollections of a circus performer called Bianca, also in *Episode*, when Max is trying to understand what made this affair so special:

> ANATOL Du kannst das Schöne gar nicht herausempfinden. Das Geheimnis der ganzen Sache ist, daß ich's erlebt habe. [...] Das Episodenhaft der Geschichte kam mir so deutlich zum Bewußtsein. Während ich den warmen Hauch ihres Mundes auf meiner Hand fühlte, erlebte ich das Ganze schon in der Erinnerung. (pp. 918–19)

53 See Schnitzler, *Anatol*, II, 1067. Informed by his father's dislike in later years of *Anatols Hochzeitsmorgen*, Heinrich Schnitzler encouraged directors and producers to use *Anatols Größenwahn* as an alternative final scene to the cycle.

54 Cf. 'Zeittafel', in Arthur Schnitzler, *Anatol; Anatols Größenwahn; Der grüne Kakadu* (Stuttgart: Reclam, 1970), pp. 153–57.

55 Fliedl, *Arthur Schnitzler*, p. 76.

56 Schnitzler, *Aphorismen und Betrachtungen*, p. 53.

57 Yates, *Schnitzler, Hofmannsthal, and the Austrian Theatre*, p. 126.

Similarly, in *Anatols Größenwahn* Anatol explains that the women he has loved are indeed different from those loved by other men, precisely because it is he who has loved them (*Anatol*, II, 1073). A point of *reductio ad absurdum* is reached when he claims: 'Ich mache mir meine Jungfrauen selber!' (*Anatol*, II, 1073). Objective reality has lost meaning in the face of his extreme scepticism, so that only solipsism-fuelled make-believe can hope to satisfy him. Thus Anatol narrates his life for his own sake and his friend's amusement. Nevertheless, he is also an introspective hypochondriac, constantly worrying about whether or not his girlfriends are or have been faithful to him.[58] This seems, at least in part, a matter of public projection: Anatol does not want to be humiliated. His affairs provide him with his main occupation in life and therefore they need also to be a source of pride, not shame.

Although for Anatol one woman might as easily replace another, Schnitzler in fact portrays seven very different characters as the seven lovers. Cora, the first presented to the audience in *Die Frage an das Schicksal*, is the most enigmatic: she has relatively little to say and spends a good deal of the first playlet in a state of silent hypnosis. The audience is teased with the possibility of discovering whether Cora has been unfaithful to Anatol, but the pertinent question is never put to her: Anatol chooses ignorance over knowledge. In the second playlet, *Weihnachtseinkäufe*, Anatol bumps into a former love interest, married mother-of-two Gabriele, when out shopping for Christmas presents. Whilst at first irritated by Anatol's flirtatious manner, Gabriele becomes increasingly curious about the details of Anatol's new suburban lover, concluding their exchange with a rushed expression of regret at her own lack of courage in earlier encounters with Anatol (i.e., she never actually had an affair with him).

In the third playlet, *Episode*, Schnitzler presents two very different versions of Bianca: the first as recalled by Anatol and the second in the woman herself when she arrives towards the end of the scene. The second Bianca is quite at odds with the subservient, overwhelmed and enamoured creature remembered by Anatol. Bianca the circus-performer appears to treat life and love with far less seriousness and romanticism than the eponymous hero would have liked to believe. Most upsetting of all for Anatol, however, is the fact that Bianca cannot remember who he is. Their night of passion was, for her, so insignificant as to be forgettable. In *Denksteine*, it is arguably the capacity to recall which proves the undoing of another relationship. Anatol confronts his fiancée Emilie with his discovery of two precious stones from her desk drawer, survivors of a policy imposed by Anatol to throw away all souvenirs of her previous affairs. Although Emilie recollects with pleasure the

58 Anatol calls himself 'ein[en] Hypochonder der Liebe' (Schnitzler, *Anatol*, II, 973).

moment one of the stones, a ruby, fell from a medallion on the day she was made a 'wissende[s] Weibe', she discards it (*Anatol*, II, 939). By contrast, she will not part with the far more valuable (in monetary terms) black diamond, for which canniness she herself is discarded by Anatol.[59] She has become (or perhaps, remained always) for him a 'Gefallene' and a 'Dirne' (*Anatol*, II, 938 and 941). If she is unable or unwilling to forget her own sexual past completely, then neither can Anatol.

Abschiedssouper presents Anatol with his equal in matters romantic. Dancer Annie (surely a play on the hero's name) upends Anatol's plans to end the relationship by beating him to it. At the outset of their affair the two had agreed that whosoever should fall in love with another person, he or she would immediately disclose the same and so end the relationship. However, the outward appearance of equality (i.e., the recognition that both men and women can fall in love with or experience lust for multiple partners) conceals Anatol's secret assumption that only he would invoke his rights under the agreement. Else, in the penultimate playlet *Agonie*, unwittingly reveals that she is using Anatol as a diversion from the boredom of her married life. Nevertheless, Anatol does not end the relationship with one swift move, as recommended by Max, but, we are led to conclude, will allow the affair to fizzle out over many months.

Finally, in *Anatols Hochzeitsmorgen* Max is shocked to discover that Anatol has brought home a former lover on the eve of his wedding. Ilona, the woman in question, proves herself to be lively, feisty and intransigent. When she discovers that Anatol's nuptials are to take place in only a matter of hours she declares in the clearest terms her intention to disrupt the ceremony. Catastrophe is averted by Max's smooth talking, as he paints a picture of Anatol's future married life and Ilona's sustained occupation of prime position as his lover.[60] Max is once again the comic foil to Anatol's pathetic self-delusion,

59 Joseph M. Kenney considers Anatol's discovery of the two stones to amount to his discovery that Emilie's love for him is not absolute and suggests this is the reason for his ending the engagement (Joseph M. Kenney, 'The Playboy's Progress: Schnitzler's Ordering of Scenes in *Anatol*', *Modern Austrian Literature*, 27.1 (1994), 1–24 (p. 12)). Such a reading ignores the fact that the relationship survives Emilie's reminiscences about her first love; it is only Emilie's unemotional but pragmatic attachment to the valuable black diamond that spurs Anatol into walking out. The playlet is not the obvious 'Kontrapunkt zu *Episode*' as which it is sometimes presented: cf. Irène Cagneau, '*Anatol* (Einakterfolge, 1889–1893; inkl. *Anatols* Größenwahn, aus dem Nachlass 1955)', in *Schnitzler-Handbuch*, ed. by Jürgensen, Lukas and Scheffel, pp. 111–15 (p. 113).

60 There are echoes here of the last chapter of Guy de Maupassant's *Bel Ami* (1885). Maupassant not only provided contemporary critics with a popular comparison, but was also one of Schnitzler's favourite writers (Françoise Derré, 'Schnitzler und Frankreich', *Modern Austrian Literature*, 19.1 (1986), 27–48 (pp. 32 and 41)).

the 'Mephistophelean companion [...] the realist, the pragmatist, the cynic'.[61] Schnitzler was never satisfied with this last (although first-written) playlet in the sequence. In 1909 he saw it in performance for the first time and referred to it in his diary as an 'Unerträglichkeit' (*Tagebuch*, 9.1.1909); it was 'Form ohne Seele, und schwache Form dazu' (*Tagebuch*, 29.11.1910).

The order of the seven playlets as first published together, so often dismissed as arbitrary,[62] on closer examination reveals a logical progression. The atomization and discontinuity of experience perceivable in the episodic nature of *Anatol* are, of course, reflected in the themes treated in the play and, indeed, in the syntax of the text: for example, the deployment of parataxis and aposiopesis.[63] However, the episodes are far from being interchangeable or stand-alone: Joseph M. Kenney has argued convincingly for a reading of their order as meaningful and of the whole as 'greater than the sum of its parts'.[64] While recognizing the genesis of the one-acters over a number of years and in a sequence not repeated when the cycle was finally published as a whole,[65] Kenney argues that there was a rationale to the selection and ordering of the seven playlets combined by Schnitzler in 1893 and that the consequence of that selection and ordering was 'the depiction of the increasing absurdity and untenability of Anatol's philosophy and lifestyle'.[66] The sequence can also be understood by reference to genre switches. While *Anatol* is known as comedy, Kenney suggests the modified nomenclature of 'seriocomedy', recognizing the very sombre nature of *Denksteine* and *Agonie*. Tonal differences were evened out by Schnitzler's buffering of the more serious playlets between the most comedic: *Episode*, *Abschiedssouper* and *Anatols Hochzeitsmorgen*.[67] By ordering the playlets as he did, Schnitzler allowed the pendulum of his portrait of Anatol to swing back and forth, increasingly wildly, between folly and melancholy.[68]

The eponymous protagonist and his creator were easily (and often understandably) confused or conflated. The root of that perceived fusion is

61 Mark W. Roche, 'Schnitzler's "Anatol" as a Philosophical Comedy', *Modern Austrian Literature*, 22.3 (1989), 51–63 (pp. 52–53).

62 See, for example, Gerhart Baumann, 'Nachwort', in Schnitzler, *Anatol; Anatols Größenwahn; Der grüne Kakadu*, pp. 158–74 (p. 159); Ernst L. Offermanns, 'Materialien zum Verständnis der Texte', in Arthur Schnitzler, *Anatol: Anatol-Zyklus, Anatols Größenwahn, Das Abenteuer seines Lebens*, ed. by Ernst L. Offermanns, Komedia, 6 (Berlin: de Gruyter, 1964), p. 160; Roche, 'Schnitzler's "Anatol"', p. 57.

63 Roche, 'Schnitzler's "Anatol"', p. 57.

64 Kenney, 'The Playboy's Progress', p. 2.

65 See *Anatol*, II, 4.

66 Kenney, 'The Playboy's Progress', p. 10.

67 Kenney, 'The Playboy's Progress', p. 16.

68 Kenney, 'The Playboy's Progress', p. 19.

to be found in Arthur Schnitzler's own identification with the name and the character of Anatol, as well as in his use of material from his own life in writing the playlets. Schnitzler adopted the pseudonym 'Anatol' for the publication of nine poems in the magazine *An der schönen blauen Donau* before the play cycle was written.[69] The need for an alter ego when publishing dramatic or prose texts arguably disappeared with the death of Schnitzler's father in 1893 and with the author's diminishing financial dependence on his own medical practice. Nevertheless, the spectre of 'Anatol' as an autobiographical figure lingered in the playlets, fed by the fact that sources for *Anatol* were clearly traceable to Schnitzler's publicly lived (and privately recorded) experiences.[70]

Schnitzler firmly resisted the popular identification of writer with creation, stressing: 'Ich bin *nicht* Anatol. Ich hab wohl auch manches von ihm – gottlob auch manches andre, und von ihm gottlob […] nicht alles'.[71] He similarly regretted the common reduction of his oeuvre to this one cycle. In respect of his later play, *Professor Bernhardi* (1912), for example, he explained: '[G]eradeso "Schnitzlerisch" als der "Anatol" und gewissermaßen noch etwas mehr; - man wird sich eben entschließen müssen den Begriff Arthur Schnitzler etwas weiter zu fassen als es bisher vielfach, wenigstens in deutschen Landen, geschieht'.[72] Nonetheless, eight years later he had to admit that the (German-language) reviewers still struggled to imagine his later work as anything more than extensions of *Anatol* or *Reigen*:

> [M]eine andern Werke existiren gleichfalls weiter; – man kann ihr Vorhandensein nicht aus der Welt decretiren – selbst wenn die Rezensenten sich anstellen, als existire außer Reigen und Anatol überhaupt kein Buch von mir. Daß man meine Sachen (allerdings nur in deutschen Landen) beinahe ausschließlich aufs erotische hin ansieht, durchschnüffelt, beurtheilt, bin ich gewohnt; ich habe zu lesen bekommen, daß der Professor Bernhardi eigentlich ein alter Anatol sei.[73]

69 The poems were published in 1889/1890. In September 1889 the playlet *Episode*, eventually part of the *Anatol* cycle, was published in the same magazine but under Schnitzler's given name. For a detailed analysis of the Anatol-Schnitzler identification see Reinhard Urbach, 'Schnitzlers Anfänge: Was Anatol Wollen Soll', *Internationales Archiv für Sozialgeschichte der deutschen Literatur*, 33 (2008), 113–54. Urbach makes a very good case for elements of the character 'Anatol' being traceable to *Les vieux garcons* by Victorien Sardou, including the name itself (p. 130).

70 See *Anatol*, II, 1015, 1016 and 1025 for examples from Schnitzler's autobiography, diaries and letters.

71 Arthur Schnitzler to Else Singer (*Briefe* I, 241–43, 12.12.1894).

72 Arthur Schnitzler to Robert Roseeu (*Briefe* II, 34, 17.12.1913). For a fuller exploration of this subject see *Anatol*, pp. 6–7.

73 Arthur Schnitzler to Dora Michaelis, *Briefe* II, 220–22, 22.11.1920. The offending review was by Marco Brociner, 'Professor Bernhardi', *Neues Wiener Tagblatt*, 22 December 1918, p. 10.

The same grievances plagued Schnitzler abroad. When Ashley Dukes accused Schnitzler of being typically Viennese, of re-hashing the same light-hearted themes and characters through all his works, with *Anatol* the quintessential exemplar,[74] Schnitzler felt compelled to draft a lengthy response to what he considered 'ein entstelltes Bild meiner literarischen Persönlichkeit'.[75] Dukes's article provides yet another example of city, author and protagonist coinciding in British reception and once more justifies Heinrich Schnitzler's own inherited sensitivity. Schnitzler's reputation at home and abroad remained anchored in the *Anatol* cycle of playlets up to and beyond his death. Symptomatically, when he died Schnitzler was mourned in Britain as 'The Creator of "Anatol"' and the 'Austrian Doctor Who Created "Anatol"'.[76]

Ownership of the English *Anatol*

At the same time as Schnitzler sought to dissociate himself from the figure of Anatol, he undoubtedly claimed paternity for the play cycle. However, ownership in the English-speaking world was far from straightforward: confusion in this respect not only caused Schnitzler himself huge frustration and financial loss, but also complicated (yet further) the posthumous presentation of the play. The following account describes the roots of *Anatol* in English, in a translation ostensibly by Harley Granville Barker, to demonstrate the balance of power between author and named translator and to shed further light on Heinrich Schnitzler's subsequent treatment of the play in Britain.

From the moment that Arthur Schnitzler granted Barker the opportunity to produce the play in English, he found himself having to compete for the right to call the play his own. Three of the English-language *Anatol* playlets were produced and performed individually at the Palace Theatre in February 1911.[77] These three playlets, plus at least two more, were then put on together at

74 Dukes, 'Modern Dramatists'.

75 Arthur Schnitzler to Ashley Dukes, draft letter, 'Ende von [1]910' (CUL, A20,5).

76 'Death of Arthur Schnitzler: The Creator of "Anatol": The famous Austrian dramatist and novelist Dr. Arthur Schnitzler, creator of "Anatol", died in Vienna yesterday at the age of 69' (*Manchester Guardian*, 22 October 1931, p. 4); see also 'Austrian Doctor Who Created "Anatol"', *Scotsman*, 22 October 1931 (cited by Yates, *Schnitzler, Hofmannsthal, and the Austrian Theatre*, p. 29). Almost forty years after his death the reduction of Schnitzler's whole oeuvre to one work continued. See, for example, Sarah Luverne Walton, who asserts: '*Anatol* has become the symbol for Schnitzler. The work of the youth has justifiably become the token of the man' (Sarah Luverne Walton, '*Anatol* on the New York Stage', *Modern Austrian Literature*, 2.2 (1969), 30–44 (p. 30)).

77 The playlets were *Ask No Questions And You'll Hear No Stories*, *Farewell Supper* and *Wedding Morning* ('Drama: The Week', *The Athenaeum*, 18 March 1911, pp. 314–50). See also the

the Little Theatre at the beginning of Granville Barker's and Lillah McCarthy's season there, opening on 11 March 1911.[78] The production ran for fifteen performances, with *Keepsakes* added to the cycle from 18 March.[79] The script for all seven playlets was published in anticipation of the productions and submitted to the Lord Chamberlain's Office for a licence for performance.[80] According to the title on the front page, *Anatol* was 'A Sequence of Dialogues by Arthur Schnitzler; Paraphrased for the English Stage by Granville Barker'. The reference to the text as a 'paraphrase' is indicative of the claim Barker would later make on the play. The cover displayed its double paternity more explicitly in the hyphenated 'Schnitzler-Barker'.[81]

Although Barker is the only credited translator in the published edition of *Anatol*, he himself was not a German speaker and so must have relied on the skills of a literal translator.[82] It has not been possible to pin down who that translator was, but there are two strong candidates: Charles Wheeler and a young diplomat, Robert Vansittart.[83] The lack of clarity on this question and the inevitable absence of any literal translator from the remainder of this chapter reflect his or her impotence in respect of the published text. Barker was not the first to ask for the translation rights in *Anatol*. Indeed, he was initially invited to collaborate with Robert Vansittart in the latter's ongoing

---

advertisement in *The New Age: A Weekly Review of Politics, Literature, and Art*, 8.15 (1911), p. 360; and a review by Ashley Dukes in *The New Age*, 8.16 (1911), p. 379.

78 Woodfield, *English Theatre in Transition*, p. 89.

79 Cf. J. P. Wearing, *The London Stage 1910–1919: A Calendar of Productions, Performers, and Personnel*, 2nd edn (Lanham, MD: Scarecrow Press, 2013 [1982]), entries 11.54–59; and 'The Little Theatre', *The Times*, 13 March 1911, p. 10 and 20 March 1911, p. 12. At least five actresses played the roles of the different women in the play: Gertrude Robins, Katherine Pole, Dorothy Minto, Lillah McCarthy and Alice Crawford. This allowed 'Anatol's five sweethearts [to be] neatly differentiated' ('Drama: The Week', *The Athenaeum*, 18 March 1911, p. 315).

80 Lord Chamberlain's Archive, LCP 1911/7.

81 Beniston points out that the hyphenated authors on the cover make it explicit that the material contained therein is the 'Kind zweier Väter' (Beniston, 'Schnitzler und die "Uebersetzungs-Miseren"', p. 254).

82 Kennedy, *Granville Barker and the Dream of the Theatre*, p. 117.

83 Wheeler and Barker were already collaborating on translating Schnitzler's dramas in 1903 (CUL, B550). They were the co-authors of *In the Hospital*, a translation of *Die letzten Masken* publicly attributed to a pseudonymous 'Christopher Horne' when produced at the Court Theatre in 1905 (Lord Chamberlain's Archive, LCP 1905/5); and *Das Märchen* when produced at the Little Theatre in 1912. Vansittart, on the other hand, had pursued the English-language rights to *Anatol* since 1901 and involved Barker from 1903 (DLA, HS.NZ85.0001.04822), but negotiations came to a standstill in 1905 as a result of a dispute with another party claiming English-language rights (DLA, HS.NZ85.0001.02694, 1–2; HS.NZ85.0001.04822, 1–9; HS.NZ85.0001.01744; HS.NZ85.0001.05250, 1–3; and HS.NZ85.0001.02114, 1–3).

negotiations with Schnitzler.[84] Nevertheless, it was Barker who ultimately managed to secure an agreement when he made enquiries directly and was advised by the author to make contact with J. T. Grein.[85] The rights must have been granted to Granville Barker alone and a copy of the translated text sent to Schnitzler for his approval, because on 9 February 1911 the latter wrote to Barker:

> Besten Dank für [...] die Zusendung Ihrer Anatol-Übersetzung, die ich schon zum größten Teil gelesen habe und, soweit meine Kenntnis der englischen Sprache ein Urteil zuläßt, recht gelungen finde. Ich habe sehr wohl gefühlt, daß Sie an manchen Stellen dem englischen Geschmack Konzessionen machen mußten, die aber jedenfalls nicht nur Ihnen, sondern auch natürlich mir im weiteren Sinne zum Vorteil gereichen werden. Von meinem Vertreter, Herrn Grein, bekomme ich in der letzten Zeit leider keine Nachricht und so bitt ich Sie, lieber Herr Barker, um freundliche Auskunft, zu welchen Bedingungen wir eigentlich abgeschlossen haben, wie die Sache bisher in London ausgefallen ist und wie Sie sich den weiteren Verlauf der Angelegenheit vorstellen. Ich mache Sie zugleich aufmerksam, daß ich für Amerika freies Verfügungsrecht habe und daß wir dort vielleicht auch etwas gemeinsam machen könnten.[86]

Even without claims from the literal translator, ownership of the English *Anatol* was ambiguous. Schnitzler's 'naïve-enthusiastic' response to unsolicited offers to translate his works led to the sort of muddle discernible in the above letter.[87] Schnitzler did not know the terms on which Barker had translated the play cycle or, therefore, the nature of his own rights in the English text.

Relations between Schnitzler and Barker were accordingly already cooling in 1912, when Barker purported to give permission for the 'paraphrased' text to be used for an operetta and then sought to instigate a sale of the English *Anatol* to America. Schnitzler considered Barker's behaviour an 'Eingriff in

84 Some of the history of the tussle for translation rights in *Anatol* is given in Beniston, 'Schnitzler und die "Uebersetzungs-Miseren"', p. 258.

85 Arthur Schnitzler to Jacob Thomas Grein, 10.8.1910 (DLA, HS.NZ85.0001.00889). Barker's enquiry arrived through Shaw's translator, Siegfried Trebitsch, a long-standing friend of Schnitzler who, on Barker's request, translated the letter for Schnitzler. Barker wanted to know whether the English and American performance rights remained available and, if so, whether he could be entrusted with them for a year (Siegfried Trebitsch to Arthur Schnitzler, 6.8.1910 (DLA, HS.NZ85.0001.04810)).

86 Arthur Schnitzler to Harley Granville Barker (*Briefe* I, 655–56, 9.2.1911).

87 Beniston writes: '[Er] setzte den Übersetzern keine Frist, erkundigte sich kaum über ihre Befähigungen, bat nur um Teilung des eventuellen Gewinns und machte sich keine verlässlichen Aufzeichnungen über getroffene Vereinbarungen' (Beniston, 'Schnitzler und die "Uebersetzungs-Miseren"', pp. 257–58).

meine Autorrechte' and demanded that Grein take appropriate measures.[88] Whereas Schnitzler regarded the English text as a 'Schnitzler-Barker'schen Anatol', so that his own rights stood on a par with those of Barker, Barker asserted complete ownership over the text. After a hiatus in the correspondence during the First World War, Schnitzler and Barker were in contact once more from 1920, with Schnitzler chasing payments for British performances that he understood had taken place in the interim. Around the same time, Schnitzler discovered that Barker had been involved in negotiations for the making of a silent film in America (*The Affairs of Anatol*, directed by Cecil B. DeMille and released in 1921) and that he had already been remunerated for the same. Schnitzler tried to assert, as a point of principle, that payment of royalties to Barker would eventually lead to an impossible situation because of the potential for the film to be shown all over the world (i.e., in multiple different languages, with fees owed to multiple translators).[89] His retrospective attempt to argue the point only serves to demonstrate further his own powerlessness.

Schnitzler's position proved impossible to defend in any meaningful way because of the inadequate state of international copyright protection and the lack of any physical evidence of the contractual terms between author and translator.[90] Instead, Schnitzler had to resort to appealing to Barker's sense of decency ('Anstandsgefühl')[91] and collegiality ('kollegiales Gefühl').[92] Thus when it came to negotiating the sound-film rights in early 1931, he wrote to his lawyer, Karl Michaelis:

> Ich habe [...] den Eindruck, daß mein Übersetzer Granville Barker anständig genug sein wird das an mir versuchte Unrecht nicht zuzulassen. Wenn es mir auch kaum gelingen dürfte für die Tonfilmrechte des 'Anatol' die von mir verlangte Summe zu erzielen, so hoffe ich doch zumindest nicht ganz leer auszugehen.[93]

The sound film was never made and Schnitzler died later that year, but the dispute crawled on even after Barker's death in 1946, reaching a new peak in

88 Arthur Schnitzler to Jacob Thomas Grein, 16.9.1912 (DLA, HS.NZ85.0001.00889).

89 Arthur Schnitzler to Harley Granville Barker, 21.2.19[21?] (DLA, NZ85.0001.00881).

90 Cf. Arthur Schnitzler to Harley Granville Barker, 19.1.1931 (DLA, NZ85.0001.00881). Schnitzler had expressed his frustration at what he regarded to be a perverse situation in an earlier letter to Barker dated 12 January 1931: '[I]st es nicht ein geradezu grotesker Zustand, dass gerade ich, der Dichter des "Anatol", ohne den es weder Uebersetzungen, noch Aufführungen, noch Bearbeitungen, noch Verfilmungen, noch Vertonfilmungen des "Anatol" gäbe, [. . .], dass ich nicht nur so weit als möglich von jeder materiellen Verdienstmöglichkeit an meinem Werk ausgeschlossen werden kann oder soll' (DLA, NZ85.0001.00881).

91 Arthur Schnitzler to Julie Markbreiter, 16.9.1912 (DLA, HS.NZ85.0001.01377).

92 Arthur Schnitzler to Harley Granville Barker, 19.1.1931 (DLA, NZ85.0001.00881).

93 Arthur Schnitzler to Karl Michaelis (*Briefe* II, 736–38, 7.1.1931.

the late 1950s and early 1960s when hostility erupted between the Schnitzler and Barker estates.

It appears from Heinrich Schnitzler's correspondence with Eric Glass that the Barker estate claimed rights over all English-language versions of *Anatol*, regardless of the identity of the translator. Heinrich argued that Barker had only ever owned a fifty per cent stake in the 'paraphrase' and that royalties from that version only should be split equally between the two estates. The language in Heinrich's letters indicates his horror at the position adopted by the Barker estate: they 'really act as if they owned ANATOL altogether'; 'as if Granville-Barker had been the author of ANATOL, while my father wrote a German adaptation'.[94] The extensive correspondence dedicated to defending the estate's position provides evidence of the time and worry Heinrich must have invested in the cause. Matters only finally settled down in early 1964, when both sides apparently ran out of energy and funds for the fight and so decided to let 'sleeping dogs lie'.[95]

For Heinrich, the history of the dispute with Barker, coupled with the tenacity with which the playboy protagonist clung to author in the British public imagination, meant that the play cycle demanded careful treatment. Either Arthur Schnitzler needed to be disentangled from 'Anatol' by having attention drawn to his other works, or *Anatol* had to be presented in a way that (a) confirmed Schnitzler's paternity without (b) delimiting further interpretations of Schnitzler's corpus.[96] Much of Glass's time and effort was directed to the first of these projects, but without initial success. It proved difficult to persuade theatre directors and managers to take on the lesser-known plays and the accompanying artistic and commercial risks; and Heinrich refused permission to produce the well-known (and frequently requested) *Reigen* for the fifty-year copyright period out of respect for his father's ban (discussed in Chapter 4). Heinrich Schnitzler's approach to productions of *Anatol* was, for several decades, conservative in spirit, with the perhaps perverse result that the text by which the play was best known to the British public was that written by Harley Granville Barker twenty years before Heinrich even took responsibility for the literary estate.

94 Heinrich Schnitzler to Eric Glass, 16.5.1960 (Schn 21/6/66) and 21.5.1960 (Schn 21/6/69). Barker hyphenated his name in 1918. For consistency across this study the hyphen has been omitted, unless used in a quotation.

95 Heinrich Schnitzler to Eric Glass, 5.12.1963 (Schn 21/7/74) and 18.4.1964 (Schn 21/7/89).

96 This type of association between text and author is the perfect example of what Michel Foucault describes as 'the singular relationship that holds between an author and a text, the manner in which a text apparently points to this figure who is outside and precedes it' (Foucault, 'What Is an Author?', p. 115). In this case, however, it is not just that the play points outside itself to Schnitzler, but that 'Schnitzler', as author-function, appears to point only to *Anatol*.

Stagnation Feeds the Myth: Reliance on Barker's 'Paraphrase'

Ironically, the effect of Heinrich Schnitzler's conservatism was the further spread of an 'Anatol' bound up with the myth of 'Gay Vienna'. As will be seen below in a comparative reading of Barker's 'paraphrase' alongside a much later translation, the former promoted a version of 'Anatol' the figure that was anathema to Heinrich's preferred view. Nevertheless, Heinrich's prolonged rejection of applications to produce new translations of the play meant that the unhelpful, and legally contested, Barker text was allowed to dominate anglophone reception. From the correspondence with Glass, it is possible to infer that there were probably at least three distinct reasons for Heinrich's prolonged reliance on the Barker 'paraphrase'. The primary reason was his attachment to the status quo. Arthur Schnitzler himself had endorsed Barker's text; without good cause to commission a new translation, Heinrich paid heed to his father's judgment and redeployed the old one. Second, the 'paraphrase' was popular with the BBC and so provided Heinrich with a welcome source of income. Just as his father's financial situation had become all the more precarious during and after the First World War, so Heinrich's exile to America from a soon-to-be 'annexed' Austrian Republic left him more in need of international sources of income. Heinrich would have recognized Barker's status within the British theatre establishment and the weight his name therefore added to productions of *Anatol* in English. Finally, Heinrich's caution when approving new translations required the dedication of significant time on his part: he read the new English texts closely, alongside the source, line by line, and commented generously.[97] Given the success of the existing (Barker) translation of *Anatol*, together with Barker's reputation within the British theatre establishment, it is easy to see why Heinrich was in no hurry to take on seemingly unnecessary work by commissioning and then auditing a new version.

In fact, in numerous places in the correspondence Heinrich praises Barker's text, albeit often by comparison with the limited alternatives. In 1944 he wrote to Glass that, notwithstanding the accompanying obligation to pay Barker fifty per cent of the royalties, his 'version is so immensely superior to the other existing translation, that it ought to be used by all means'.[98] (It is assumed that the 'other' to which Heinrich Schnitzler refers is that by Grace Isabel Colbron, published in America in 1917.)[99] A few months later the point

97 See, for example, Heinrich Schnitzler to Eric Glass: 'As you no doubt realize, to check a translation really carefully (as I have done it on previous occasions) is a tremendously time-consuming task. I, for one, do not believe in merely "reading" the new text but have always compared it line by line with the original' (15.12.1957 (Schn 21/6/13)).

98 Heinrich Schnitzler to Eric Glass, 27.3.1944 (Schn 21/4/50).

99 Arthur Schnitzler, *Anatol; Living Hours; The Green Cockatoo*, trans. by Grace Isabel Colbron (New York: Boni & Liveright, 1917).

was reiterated: Heinrich hoped that the Barker version would be used in a proposed production, as it was 'far superior to any other existing translation'.[100] Although he was later sometimes critical of the English text, his attachment to the 'paraphrase' and his unwillingness to absorb the additional labour involved in approving a new text endured for many of his years at the helm.[101]

To understand the reception of *Anatol* in Britain for over half a century, therefore, one must know Harley Granville Barker's 'paraphrase'; his was the text to which British audiences were most frequently exposed. The brief foreword to the published text gives advance notice of the liberties Barker has taken with the source material:

> It seems that in a faithful translation the peculiar charm of these dialogues will disappear. To recreate it exactly in English one must be another Schnitzler: which is absurd. This is the only excuse I can offer for my paraphrase.[102]

Indeed, although formally based on Schnitzler's cycle (each playlet has a title corresponding to the original title; in each playlet the same combination of characters appears, albeit some with different names), Barker's text departs from the source text in innumerable places and in varying ways. As Krebs puts it, his voice is 'discernible throughout the entire text, and [is] at times quite deafening'.[103] Barker cuts, substitutes and supplements at almost every turn.

Krebs's analysis of the Barker text, the only substantial assessment to date, explores certain patterns of alteration by reference to the contemporaneous socio-political climate. Hence, for example, some of the alterations can be understood as Barker 'downplay[ing] issues relating to sexual morality and social code'.[104] Krebs provides a number of illuminating examples of the English playwright exercising sensitivity to local (i.e., British) social norms, contemporary political reverberations and the known concerns of the censor.[105] She also draws attention to the way Barker's text operated as an

100 Heinrich Schnitzler to Eric Glass, 9.5.1944 (Schn 21/4/51).

101 For examples of Heinrich's criticism, see letters dated 19.1.1956 (Schn 21/5/87); 5.3.1956 (Schn 21/5/90); 28.11.1959 (Schn 21/6/37); 11.6.1953 (Schn 34/18/16); and 8.3.1956 (Schn 34/18/31).

102 Arthur Schnitzler, *Anatol: A Sequence of Dialogues*, trans. by Harley Granville Barker (London: Sidgwick & Jackson, 1911), n. pag. Page references to Barker's translation of the play itself will henceforth be given in the text.

103 Krebs, *Cultural Dissemination*, p. 115.

104 Krebs, *Cultural Dissemination*, p. 115.

105 Krebs, *Cultural Dissemination*, pp. 118–22. For for further analysis of the censoring and censored nature of Barker's rewriting of *Anatol* see Katja Krebs, 'Anticipating Blue Lines: Translational Choices as Sites of (Self)-Censorship', in *Modes of Censorship and Translation: National Contexts and Diverse Media*, ed. by Francesca Billiani (Manchester: St Jerome, 2007), pp. 167–86.

instrument of the playwright's broader artistic aspirations, in particular by way of contributing to the cultural capital of an emerging theatrical field.[106] For the purposes of this study, however, it is most important to note the overall effect of the changes, which make the play shorter, sharper and funnier at the expense of a more nuanced portrait of Anatol. Barker executed drastic cuts whilst also embellishing dialogue with flamboyant additions, with the result that the play's more provocative aspects were neutralized or diluted and the wit of the two men at its centre heightened.

The broader consequences of such textual radicalism were twofold. First, the ground was prepared for the English playwright (and later his estate) to claim ownership of the English *Anatol*. Some of the ramifications of that claim have already been explored above. Second, insofar as the play was still identified with its Austrian author, Barker's text promoted the very same tropes of light-weight Schnitzler and gay Vienna that Heinrich Schnitzler was later so keen to dismantle. By sanctioning the Barker version as the default translation for use by the BBC, therefore, he allowed those tropes to continue to govern British reception of *Anatol* for a further thirty-five years after his father's death.[107] The following section of this chapter illustrates, through examples, how Barker's text furthered an interpretation of *Anatol* which coincided perfectly with the myth of 'Gay Vienna'. The skewed nature of Barker's 'paraphrase' is shown in sharper relief by virtue of a comparative reading with a later translation eventually authorized by Heinrich, namely that by the playwright Frank Marcus.

Marcus's translation of *Anatol* was used for a production directed by Charles Marowitz (an American director based in London) at the Open Space Theatre in 1976. Marcus had previously translated two of Arthur Schnitzler's plays, *Reigen* and *Liebelei*, in 1953 and 1954 respectively.[108] He had first sought permission to translate *Anatol* at around the same time but

106 Krebs, *Cultural Dissemination*, pp. 116–17. See also Katja Krebs, 'Theatre, Translation and the Formation of a Field of Cultural Production', in *Betwixt and Between: Place and Cultural Translation*, ed. by Stephen Kelly and David Johnston (Newcastle: Cambridge Scholars, 2007), pp. 69–82.

107 See Appendix 3. Of a total of twelve broadcasts (radio and television) of the *Anatol* playlets, at least eight and possibly ten were based on Barker's 'paraphrase'.

108 *Reigen* was published under the title *Merry-Go-Round* by Weidenfeld and Nicolson, translated by Frank and Jacqueline Marcus, with illustrations by Philip Gough and introduction by Ilse Barea (whom the publishers had wanted as the translator because of her potential influence with *The Times*). A live reading was given of the translation on 26 October1952 (Heinrich Schnitzler to Frank Marcus, 14.10.1952 (Schn 34/18/8) and 8.11.1952 (Schn 34/18/9)). Apparently the 'reading' was reviewed by Roy Walker in *Theatre* on 8 November 1952, but no further trace of the review has been found. *Liebelei* was broadcast under its original title on BBC television on 15 June 1954, directed by Rudolph Cartier and starring Jeanette Sterke as Christine. Frank and Jacqueline Marcus were credited in the *Radio Times* as the authors of the English version.

had met with resistance. Heinrich's reasons for refusing Marcus permission were various: he lacked time to read a new translation; he was disenchanted by Marcus's apparent sense of entitlement (because of his previous work translating Schnitzler, Marcus seemed to regard himself as the natural choice for *Anatol*);[109] Heinrich was already engaged in negotiations for a musical adaptation; or he feared the play would not 'appeal to London audiences right now' (i.e., the mid- to late-1950s).[110] Heinrich's attitude changed when he was approached by Marowitz and Marvin Liebman (a producer) in 1974, requesting a 'nine month option on the Frank Marcus version of [*Anatol*]'.[111] As well as the obvious commercial appeal of such an offer, Heinrich was also encouraged (at this stage) by Marcus's text itself (which he thought was 'very good indeed', the 'liberties' taken being 'in the spirit of the play')[112] and by assurances from Marcus and Marowitz that 'the customary "Old Vienna" nonsense' would not be dragged in.[113]

The correspondence reveals that Eric Glass now effectively acted as an advocate for Marowitz, about whose reputation for a certain 'type of re-writing' Heinrich Schnitzler was understandably worried.[114] Marowitz had gained notoriety in the 1960s as the '*enfant terrible*' of British theatre,[115] refusing to treat playwright or text as sacrosanct, 'mutilat[ing]' Shakespeare[116] and generally antagonizing the Lord Chamberlain in the exercise of his censorship duties.[117] Glass assured his principal that Marowitz was 'a very much liked and successful "regisseur"' who 'voiced the same sentiments as you do concerning the whole Schnitzler image'.[118] Marowitz also went to great lengths in his direct correspondence with Heinrich to assuage any concerns the latter might still have had and stressed: 'One is trying very hard to present your Father's work in the proper spirit, without the sentimental tone which frequently creeps in, attenuating the effect of much of his material'.[119] He had read Heinrich's essay from 1954 and assured the author that it 'fits exactly with my own

109 Heinrich Schnitzler to Eric Glass, 5.3.1956 (Schn 21/5/90).

110 Heinrich Schnitzler to Eric Glass, 15.12.1957 (Schn 21/6/13); Heinrich Schnitzler to Eric Glass, 5.3.1956 (Schn 21/5/90); Heinrich Schnitzler to Frank Marcus, 14.2.1955 (Schn 34/18/27); and Heinrich Schnitzler to Frank Marcus, 30.8.1959 (Schn 34/18/37).

111 Heinrich Schnitzler to Eric Glass, 19.3.1974 (Schn 21/10/44).

112 Heinrich Schnitzler to Eric Glass, 26.3.1974 (Schn 21/10/45).

113 Frank Marcus to Heinrich Schnitzler, 3.5.1974 (Schn 34/18/49).

114 Heinrich Schnitzler to Eric Glass, 12.3.1974 (Schn 21/10/41).

115 Simon Trussler, 'Charles Marowitz in London: Twenty-Five Years Hard: Marowitz in the Sixties', *New Theatre Quarterly*, 30 (2014), 203–06 (p. 204).

116 Charles Marowitz, *Burnt Bridges* (London: Hodder & Stoughton, 1990), p. 119.

117 Steve Nicholson, 'Charles Marowitz', in *Oxford Dictionary of National Biography*, https://doi.org/10.1093/odnb/9780198614128.013.108751 [accessed 7 February 2019].

118 Eric Glass to Heinrich Schnitzler, 13.3.1974 (Schn 21/10/43).

119 Charles Marowitz to Heinrich Schnitzler, 28.5.1974 (Schn 34/29/1).

views of ANATOL'; it would be 'required reading for the entire company' and would 'inform the rehearsal-period'.[120] Marowitz could not have been more explicit in communicating the alignment of his sentiments with Heinrich's. Through the efforts of Eric Glass, Charles Marowitz and Frank Marcus (with his translation) Heinrich was persuaded to grant rights to produce the new translation at the Open Space Theatre.

Comparative Reading

Marcus's translation feels, by comparison with Barker's 'paraphrase', much plainer. The language is more neutral, almost to the point of being dull, and it lacks any of the Edwardian embellishments in which Barker indulges.[121] Marcus fails to find an equivalent for the colourful vernacular used by Schnitzler: whereas Barker adopts a flamboyantly contemporary voice by way of compensation (e.g., 'fellow', 'a jot', 'damnably', 'rather!', 'awfully jolly', 'dash it' and 'you cad'), Marcus avoids any obvious chronotopical markers. None of the cuts Barker makes is evident in Marcus's writing and nor are any of the additions, whether to dialogue or stage directions. The translation maps onto Schnitzler's source text with few exceptions. When Anatol advises Max, 'Es giebt [*sic*] so räthselhafte Dinge . . .' (Schnitzler, *Anatol*, p. 123), Marcus notably introduces a *Hamlet* reference: 'There are more things in heaven and earth, Horatio . . .' (Marcus, *Anatol*, p. 11).[122] Also, in the archived typescript a line has been added in manuscript to the first playlet to raise a laugh: Anatol asks Max to imagine 'a dim dusky room', while Cora is in her state of hypnosis; the line originally given to Max ('Dim . . . dusky . . . I'm imagining it . . .') is instead given to Cora (speaking in her 'sleep'), to whom Anatol responds 'Not you!'.[123] The general approach adopted by Marcus, however, seems to have been to take one line at a time and find as unobtrusive an English equivalent as possible. The result is that the nuances of the German-language Anatol are allowed to survive in Marcus's text.

120 Charles Marowitz to Heinrich Schnitzler, 12.7.1974 (Schn 34/29/5); and date unknown (Schn 34/29/9).

121 Two versions of Marcus's translation exist. One, an undated typescript, is preserved at the Theatre and Performance Archives, Victoria and Albert Museum (hereafter 'V&A Theatre Archives') with other scripts from the Open Space Theatre (THM/271/15/1). The other was published in 1982 'to coincide with the first performance of *La Ronde* for sixty years' (Arthur Schnitzler, *Anatol* (London: Methuen, 1982), back cover). The two texts are almost identical. Page references are to the published text, except where discrepancies exist, in which case they are highlighted.

122 William Shakespeare, *Hamlet*, ed. by Harold Jenkins, The Arden Shakespeare (London: Methuen, 1982), I. 5. 174.

123 Marcus, Typescript, p. 10. This is the only manuscript revision or addition to the typescript and was not kept in the published edition (see p. 10).

The concrete differences between the Barker and Marcus texts are readily apparent (and revealing) from the very first page. Schnitzler's opening stage directions are extremely bare:

> *Anatols Zimmer*. (Schnitzler, *Anatol*, p. 870)

Whereas Marcus provides the equally minimalistic '*Anatol's room*', Barker adopts a Shavian extravagance in setting the scene:

> ANATOL, *an idle young bachelor, lives in a charming flat in Vienna. That he has taste, besides means to indulge it, may be seen by his rooms, the furniture he buys, the pictures he hangs on the walls. And if such things indicate character, one would judge, first by the material comfort of the place and then by the impatience for new ideas which his sense of what is beautiful to live with seems to show, that though a hedonist, he is sceptical of even that easy faith. Towards dusk one afternoon he comes home bringing with him his friend* MAX. *They reach the sitting-room, talking* .... (Barker, *Anatol*, p. 3)

Such significant extension of stage directions has been attributed to 'the struggle for the establishment of naturalism as the dominant theatrical mode on the English stage'.[124] Such reasoning can also explain changes made by Harley Granville Barker to maintain the illusion of realism on the stage. At the end of *Die Frage an das Schicksal*, for example, Max remarks to himself, unheard by the lovers:

> Eines ist mir klar: Daß die Weiber auch in der Hypnose lügen ... Aber sie sind glücklich – und das ist die Hauptsache. (Schnitzler, *Anatol*, p. 887)

The audience is thereby let in on the secret that Max is sceptical of Cora's veracity, but that he is not going to disrupt what he believes to be Anatol's continuing delusion. Marcus maintains the conspiracy between character and audience:

> One thing is certain: women tell lies even under hypnosis ... but they are happy ... and that's the main thing. (Marcus, *Anatol*, p. 13)

By contrast, Barker's Max beckons Anatol to him so that he can ensure his friend hears his final words:

> Perhaps you've made a scientific discovery besides. That women tell lies just as well when they're asleep. But so long as you're happy ... what's the odds? (Barker, Anatol, p. 18)

124 Krebs, *Cultural Dissemination*, p. 116.

A similar revision is made towards the end of *Episode*: what should be spoken by Max '*für sich*' – 'Ich räche dich, so gut ich kann, Freund Anatol . . .' (Schnitzler, *Anatol*, p. 928) – is addressed directly to Bianca in Barker's version ('All the revenge I can give him you see' (Barker, *Anatol*, p. 49)). Through both amendments Barker creates a greater sense of male solidarity: Max and Anatol against the women. By contrast, Marcus's Max speaks '*to himself*': 'I've avenged you as well as I could, Anatol, my friend . . .' (Marcus, *Anatol*, p. 35). Whereas Marcus's text gives the audience access to Max's interior monologue, Barker's departs from the source text in order to maintain the smooth naturalistic view of the exterior alone and to consolidate gender divisions.

Apart from the extended stage directions Barker's text tends to be more skeletal than either the German source or Frank Marcus's translation. Often the effect is to sharpen dialogue and produce quick-fire repartee between characters. In *Weihnachtseinkäufe*, for example, Gabriele enquires (with implied criticism) about Anatol's habit of taking walks:

> GABRIELE: Sie gehen wohl immerfort spazieren?
> ANATOL: Spazieren! Da legen Sie so einen verächtlichen Ton hinein! Als wenn es was Schöneres gäbe! – Es liegt so was herrlich Planloses in dem Wort! (Schnitzler, *Anatol*, p. 894)

Marcus provides the following:

> GABRIELE: I suppose you go for walks all the time?
> ANATOL: Go for walks! You say that so contemptuously! As though there were anything nicer! There is a marvellously vague sound about that phrase. (Marcus, *Anatol*, p. 15)

In Barker's version the exchange is rendered as:

> GABRIELE: (*with a touch of feeling*) You idler!
> ANATOL: Don't despise idlers. They're the last word in civilization. (Barker, *Anatol*, p. 23)

Thus a five-word question from Gabriele is turned into a two-word tease by Barker and the twenty-four-word response from Anatol is cut in half. When so much dialogue is cut away, it seems inevitable that something of the characters themselves will also be lost. In this case, Barker has turned Anatol into a civilized, fast-talking loafer and he has lost the 'Planloses', i.e., the purposeless, melancholy side to his character. Although Marcus sticks more closely to Schnitzler's words (he keeps Gabriele's line as a question, for example, and each segment of Anatol's response has its counterpart in the English text), he, too, falls short in his translation of 'Planloses'. 'Vague' suggests imprecision of meaning, rather than a reluctance to direct oneself. This example apart, however, Marcus generally succeeds in retaining the darker aspect of Anatol's character.

The protagonist's meditation on the past and his own irrecoverable youth survives intact in Marcus's text; Barker, on the other hand, allows Anatol to have a past but not acknowledge his own aging. Thus in *Episode* Anatol explains to Max:

> Hier bringe ich dir meine Vergangenheit, mein ganzes Jugendleben
> [. . .]
> Dieses Jugendleben hat in meinem Haus kein Quartier mehr! (Schnitzler, *Anatol*, p. 911)

In Marcus's version Anatol's lines become:

> I am entrusting you with my past, with my entire youth
> [. . .]
> There's not room for my youth in my house! (Marcus, *Anatol*, p. 23)

Barker's Anatol has to remain young, or at least to pretend that he is. There is no mention of irrecoverable youth:

> I have brought you my dead and buried past.
> [. . .]
> I really cannot live with my past any longer. (Barker, *Anatol*, pp. 35–36)

The introspective side of Schnitzler's Anatol is thereby lost in Barker's text. Barker's Anatol cannot contemplate his own aging (or, therefore, his mortality), so that rather than being a '[l]eichtsinniger Melancholiker' (Schnitzler, *Anatol*, p. 900) (in Marcus's hands a 'frivolous melancholic' (Marcus, *Anatol*, p. 19)) he is turned into a 'Toy Philosopher' (Barker, *Anatol*, p. 28). As a result, Barker's Anatol is often only two-dimensional where Schnitzler's protagonist is multi-dimensional, multifaceted, complex and hence more credible.

Anatol's conflicted, yet (in some respects) unconventional or even progressive politics are likewise neatly excised from Barker's portrait. This is especially evident in the treatment of women in the text. In *Die Frage an das Schicksal* Anatol tries to explain to Max why he struggles to believe in the fidelity of any of his lovers: knowing himself and his own philandering ways he assumes that his lovers behave similarly. Anatol assumes the shared incapacity of both men and women to act faithfully, even if his male ego nevertheless expects total commitment from his lovers. In this respect the playlets arguably anticipate Ernst Mach's concept of selfhood, according to which the self (regardless of gender) is merely a bundle of experiences without a stable centre and hence without continuity.[125] Max's response reflects the prevailing hypocrisies of the Viennese society with which Schnitzler was familiar: 'Nun ja! Ein Mann!'. A woman's behaviour is, according to Max, self-evidently different from a man's. Anatol does not hold back with his opprobrium of Max's old-fashioned attitude:

> Die alte dumme Phrase! Immer wollen wir uns einreden, die Weiber seien darin anders als wir! Ja, manche . . . die, welche die Mutter einsperrt, oder die, welche kein Temperament haben . . . Ganz gleich sind wir. (Schniztler, *Anatol*, p. 873)

There are no grounds for unequal treatment of the sexes where sex is concerned. We are all the same. Not according to Barker, however, who muddies the waters and leaves a question mark hanging over Anatol's real thoughts on the subject:

> Thank you . . . it only needed that! Of course . . . we are men and women are different. Some! If their mammas lock them up or if they're little fishes. Otherwise, my dear Max, women and men are very much alike . . . especially women. (Barker, *Anatol*, p. 6)

The last two words in the translation are entirely uncalled for by the source text, they are pure invention on Barker's part and they transform the sense of Anatol's (originally) more progressive stance on women's sexuality into a blurred politics.[126] Marcus's translation, by contrast, follows the source text closely and thereby leaves intact the force of Anatol's condemnation:

> The same old cliché! We are always trying to convince ourselves that women are different from us in this respect! One or two perhaps . . . those who have been locked in by their mothers or those who have no spirit . . . we are all alike. (Marcus, *Anatol*, p. 3)

125 Ernst Mach, *Die Analyse der Empfindungen und das Verhältnis des Physischen zum Psychischen* (Jena: Fischer, 1886). Mach is discussed in Chapter 4, along with Schnitzler's own ideas of the self. See Abigail Gillman for an assessment of Anatol's concerns with interpersonal fidelity as a trope for the wider dilemma regarding Impressionism and the discontinuous self (Abigail Gillman, '"Ich suche ein Asyl für meine Vergangenheit". Schnitzler's Poetics of Memory', in *Zeitgenossenschaften*, ed. by Foster and Krobb, pp. 141–56 (p. 145)).

126 Harro H. Kühnelt reads in Barker's addition to the line an anticipation of George Orwell's *Animal Farm* ('some animals are more equal than others'), thereby presenting Barker's Anatol more sympathetically than the other examples from the translation might permit (Harro H. Kühnelt, 'Harley Granville-Barker und Arthur Schnitzlers "Anatol"', in *Studien zur Literatur des 19. und 20. Jahrhunderts in Österreich. Festschrift fürAlfred Doppler zum 60. Geburtstag*, ed. by Johann Holzner, Michael Klein and Wolfgang Wiesmüller (Innsbruck: Institut für Germanistik der Universität Innsbruck, 1981), pp. 69–77 (p. 72)). See George Orwell, *Animal Farm: A Fairy Story* (London: Secker & Warburg, 1949), p. 105.

In *Episode* Barker once more casts Schnitzler and his protagonist in a damning light. Max remarks on the absence of letters in one of the packages brought to him by Anatol, to which the friend explains that the woman in question could scarcely write: 'Wo kämen wir aber hin, wenn uns alle Weiber Briefe schrieben!' (Schnitzler, *Anatol*, p. 914). Anatol is such a successful lothario, we are led to believe, that he could not possibly accommodate letters from all his lovers. Whereas Marcus once more keeps closely to Schnitzler's words ('Where would we be if all women wrote letters to us!' (Marcus, *Anatol*, p. 25)), Barker takes the line in an entirely different direction: 'Don't you sometimes wish women weren't taught to write?' (Barker, *Anatol*, p. 38). Suddenly Anatol has become a philistine in matters of female emancipation and education. The discrepancy between Barker's translation and the source text in this regard is peculiar, given the obvious affinity between the Suffragist inclinations evident in Barker's other theatre activities and Schnitzler's 'Gleichheitsthese' as presented by Anatol.[127] Krebs accounts for Barker's at times antithetical treatment of *Anatol* by reference to his employment of translation as 'a strategy of identity creation' in the service of constructing a national dramatic tradition: such a construction relies 'on the constant comparison and overlap with and at the same time differentiation from the Other'.[128] By marking Schnitzler's protagonist as politically conservative, Barker highlights his own emerging tradition of liberalism. More circumstantial causes might have also been involved: *Anatol* was the first play to be produced at the Little Theatre under its new manager-director team, Harley Granville Barker and his wife Lillah McCarthy, following what must have been a worrying nineteen months during which Barker had directed only one play.[129] The softening of Schnitzler's politically provocative message about sexual equality might well have seemed sensible at the outset of this new venture.[130]

Just as Anatol's politics and philosophy are neutered, so is his bad behaviour diluted in Barker's version: the cuckolded husband is removed from recollections in *Episode* to avoid emphasizing that Anatol's lovers

127 Urbach, 'Schnitzlers Anfänge', p. 145. For discussions of Schnitzler's stance in respect of female emancipation see Barbara Gutt, *Emanzipation bei Arthur Schnitzler* (Berlin: Spiess, 1978); for a summary of 'Emancipation Approaches' to Schnitzler scholarship see Wisely, *Arthur Schnitzler*, pp. 113–18. Barker's support of the Suffragist cause is readily apparent in his playwriting and directing, but perhaps most evident in his production of Elizabeth Robins's *Votes for Women!* in 1907 (Kennedy, *Granville Barker and the Dream of the Theatre*, pp. 57–61).

128 Krebs, *Cultural Dissemination*, pp. 65, 66 and 122.

129 Kennedy, *Granville Barker and the Dream of the Theatre*, p. 100.

130 See also Barker's evidence on self-censorship, given only a year earlier and reproduced in the *Report from the Joint Select Committee of the House of Lords and the House of Commons on the Stage Plays (Censorship)* (London: H.M. Stationery Office, 1909), pp. 70–85 (p. 72).

included married women (Barker, *Anatol*, p. 37);[131] and the protagonist goes from viewing himself as 'eine[n] von den Gewaltigen des Geistes' (Schnitzler, *Anatol*, p. 917) ('one of the giants of history' (Marcus, *Anatol*, p. 27)) to being 'one of the world's great heroes of romance' (Barker, *Anatol*, p. 41). Instead of 'trampl[ing]' (Marcus, *Anatol*, p. 27) girls and women underfoot ('ich zermalmte sie unter meinen ehernen Schritten' (Schnitzler, *Anatol*, p. 917)), Barker's Anatol imagines himself 'pluck[ing] them, crush[ing] the sweetness from them' (Barker, *Anatol*, p. 41). Reviewing the Barker translation, Krebs concludes that the 'offensive yet self-reflective Anatol of the source text is replaced by a romantic rogue in the target text'.[132] Certainly romance is preferred by Barker to Schnitzler's fairy tale and illusion. In the source text Max accuses Anatol of portraying a lover 'wie eine Märchengestalt' (Schnitzler, *Anatol*, p. 919) – in Marcus's text 'something out of a fairytale' (Marcus, *Anatol*, p. 29) – whereas for Barker's Max the lover '[s]ounds too romantic' (Barker, *Anatol*, p. 43). When advising Anatol not to re-visit an old flame, Max warns 'dann ist nichts trauriger, als ein aufgewärmter Zauber' (Schnitzler, *Anatol*, p. 923). While Marcus opts for 'warmed up magic' (Marcus, *Anatol*, p. 31), Barker once more eschews the magical or illusory for the socially safer ground of romance – 'yesterday's romance warmed up' (Barker, *Anatol*, p. 45).

With Barker's 'paraphrase' we are left with the fun and frivolous parts of Anatol, exaggerated and smartened up for a London audience. The challenging, contemplative and melancholic elements of Schnitzler's creation have been removed. The Anatol poised self-consciously at the threshold between illusion and reality is lost. The English version of *Anatol* that would survive for decades and reach hundreds of thousands of listeners and viewers through radio and television broadcasts was a pared-down, comic reiteration, with little relation to the nuanced figure originally portrayed in Schnitzler's playlets. The Marcus translation, by contrast, maps onto its source text far more closely, allowing the

131 Adultery could not be altogether avoided if the playlet *Agonie* was to be included, given its premise of Anatol as 'der Liebhaber einer verheirateten Frau' (Schnitzler, *Anatol*, p. 970). Although Barker's published 'paraphrase' included *Dying Pangs*, that playlet has only rarely been included in performances or broadcasts of Barker's text. When first performed at the Palace Theatre in 1911, only *Ask No Questions And You'll Hear No Stories*, *Farewell Supper* and *Wedding Morning* were shown. These were supplemented by *Episode* and *A Christmas Present* at the Little Theatre in March 1911. When a sixth playlet was added later in the season, it was *Keepsakes* and not *Agony* (see 'The Little Theatre', *The Times*, 20 March 1911, p. 12; and the review from *Daily Chronicle*, 20 March 1911 (Schnitzler Press-Cuttings Archive, University of Exeter, EUL MS 214)). The only record of the playlet's inclusion in later performances is for the 1973 radio broadcast (BBC Written Archives Centre, *Anatol*, tx 30/12/73, Afternoon Theatre, R4).

132 Krebs, *Cultural Dissemination*, p. 122.

nuances of 'Anatol' to emerge. It thereby succeeds in distancing the protagonist (and therewith Schnitzler) from an over-simplistic view of 'Gay Vienna'.

The Marowitz Production and its Reception

The fate of Marcus's translation provides an opportune reminder that the relationship between text and performance complicates any assessment of translation for theatre. Although the text itself met with Heinrich's approval, the decision to cast Prunella Scales in all the female roles threatened to de-rail the whole production. The ensuing dispute between Heinrich Schnitzler and Charles Marowitz was framed as a disagreement about meaning and authorial intention. For Heinrich, the casting of just one woman 'not merely distorts but contradicts the very meaning of the play';[133] it 'openly disregards the author's intentions' and 'completely distorts its very meaning'.[134] Heinrich was confident that he knew his father's mind in this regard and cited in his support letters from Arthur Schnitzler to the literary critic and theatre director Otto Brahm emphasizing the need for different women to play the different roles.[135] His perspective was, he advised Glass, 'identical with that of the author'.[136] Furthermore, he asserts: 'I don't know whether I know ANATOL better than any living person [as suggested by Marowitz] but I believe that I do know it pretty well and that I understand its essential meaning'.[137] Marowitz defended his decision by reference to his general freedom to re-interpret *Anatol* afresh and by explaining the rationale for his particular interpretation in this instance.

133 Heinrich Schnitzler to Charles Marowitz, 14.11.1975 (Schn 34/29/21).

134 Heinrich Schnitzler to Eric Glass, 11.9.1975 (Schn 21/11/46). For further reliance on the author's 'intentions' see Heinrich Schnitzler to Eric Glass, 25.11.1975, when he writes that the 'author's intentions [...] entirely manifest in the script' (Schn 21/11/56). See also the telegram from Heinrich Schnitzler to Eric Glass sent on 3 December 1975: 'CAST[ING] CLEARLY AT VARIANCE WITH AUTHORS MANIFEST INTENTIONS' (Schn 21/11/57).

135 Heinrich Schnitzler to Charles Marowitz, 14.11.1975 (Schn 34/29/21). Heinrich quoted two letters in particular (*Briefe* I, 593–94, 4.8.1909 and 594–96, 14.8.1909), both of which were published that year in *Der Briefwechsel Arthur Schnitzler – Otto Brahm*, ed. by Oskar Seidlin (Tübingen: Niemeyer, 1975), pp. 281–82 and 283–85.

136 Heinrich Schnitzler to Eric Glass, 14.1.1976 (Schn 21/11/67).

137 Heinrich Schnitzler to Eric Glass, 11.9.1975 (Schn 21/11/46). Heinrich Schnitzler was by no means alone in attributing such importance to the multiplicity of women. French director Louis-Do de Lencquesaing's primary interest in producing the play in 1995 was the variety of female characters: 'Anatol cherche la femme, il ne rencontre que les femmes, et une seule ne suffirait pas à la décrire' (extract from de Lencquesaing's collection of press-cuttings, as quoted in Florence Hetzel, 'The Reception of Arthur Schnitzler on the French Stage: Contemporary Adaptations of "Reigen"', *Austrian Studies*, 13 (2005), 191–210 (p. 193)).

He considered Anatol to be 'a man [...] locked into an obsessive pattern which he does not understand':

> By giving him a variety of affairs with what is in effect, the same woman, one underlines the fantasy element in his psychic life. [...] All the characterizations will be entirely different and there will be no attempt made to iron out the differences of class, temperament or behaviour. But by being played by one actress, the sense of 'pattern' in Anatol's life will be dramatically displayed. [...] As you must appreciate, there are men who continually get involved with the same woman – despite apparent social and physical differences.[138]

Earlier in the same letter Marowitz makes the Freudian underpinnings to his interpretation more explicit, reminding Heinrich of the mutual admiration felt by Arthur Schnitzler and Sigmund Freud for each other's work and recalling that Freud found, in Schnitzler's work, 'the demonstration of many of his psychological theories'. Charles Marowitz does not go into any more detail; he instead appears satisfied merely to invoke the name of the psychoanalyst and thereby to lend legitimacy to his reading of the play. In parallel with Heinrich Schnitzler's quasi-genetic claims to knowledge of the 'essential meaning' of the play, Marowitz also purports to quote Schnitzler in support of his differentiation between source and adaptation:

> Somewhere in your father's writing there is an epigram about the children of parents being very different from the off-springs originally conceived or anticipated. This is the case with almost every good play which survives from one generation to the next. It is a testament to the health and vigour of the work-of-art in question.[139]

Marowitz here promotes a concept of 'good' theatre as being able to speak differently, through a play's different incarnations, to each new generation. To deny a play its re-interpretations, he seems to suggest, is to deny it life.[140]

138 Charles Marowitz to Heinrich Schnitzler, 4.11.1975 (Schn 34/29/20).

139 Charles Marowitz to Heinrich Schnitzler, 4.11.1975 (Schn 34/29/20). It has not proved possible to identify the epigram to which Marowitz alludes, although a somewhat similar sentiment is expressed when Arthur Schnitzler writes about the dismay experienced by the writer when his work leaves the safety of the home and is exposed to the critic. At that point, the work no longer belongs to the writer, but to everyone else (Schnitzler, *Aphorismen und Betrachtungen*, pp. 388–89).

140 The idea advanced by Marowitz of translation as a means of extending the life of an original is reminiscent of Walter Benjamin's conception of translation as *Überleben* or *Fortleben* (Walter Benjamin, 'Die Aufgabe des Übersetzers', in Walter Benjamin, *Gesammelte Schriften*, ed. by Rolf Tiedemann and Hermann Schweppenhäuser, 7 vols (Frankfurt a. M.: Suhrkamp, 1985), IV.I, 9–21).

Notably, both Heinrich and Marowitz call on the authority of Arthur Schnitzler as an answer to their moral and artistic disagreement.[141]

Law dictated the outcome. The parties' contractual terms limited Heinrich's veto to the casting of the lead role (i.e., Anatol). Notwithstanding boldly asserted plans to 'withhold the play', Heinrich was powerless to prevent the production from going ahead.[142] He did not hesitate in blaming his agent for failing to protect Arthur Schnitzler's interests: '[T]he mere fact of a production, or a publication, is not enough and [...], in my opinion, it is the obligation of an author's representative to find out the circumstances of such a production or publication.'[143] The play ran for six weeks, from 10 February until 13 March 1976, and comprised six of the playlets (*The Crucial Question*, *Christmas Shopping*, *Farewell Supper*, *Episode*, *Agony* and *Wedding Morning*).[144] Contrary to Heinrich's assumption that the length of the run spoke to the poor quality of the production, Eric Glass assured him it was in fact a reflection of its success in the preview week. Usually, previews would be followed by a further four weeks of performance; in this instance that was extended to five.[145] The production had 'undoubtedly [been] regarded in the profession and also in the press as an outstanding success.'[146] Many reviewers commented on the 'tension between surface and substance',[147] the 'undertones of wry longing and fatalistic searching for that elusive something love pretends to satisfy',[148] or similar. They quite possibly took their lead from a programme note, which clearly took as *its* cue Heinrich Schnitzler's article from 1954 and made explicit the shift in perception which Marowitz had set out to prompt in his audience:

> Although Vienna of the turn-of-the-century is traditionally depicted as a city of Strauss, waltzes, cream cakes and rampant frivolity, like all 'swinging' cities, it had a deeply-troubled, seamier side. Although for generations, Schnitzler has been associated with Viennese fripperies, no author of the period dealt so incisively with what was smouldering beneath the social ambiance of what was perhaps the most complicated city in Europe.[149]

141 See also Heinrich Schnitzler to Eric Glass, 31.1.1976: '[I]t is my obligation to protect the heritage over which I have to watch' (Schn 21/11/70).

142 Heinrich Schnitzler to Eric Glass, 11.9.1975 (Schn 21/11/46).

143 Heinrich Schnitzler to Eric Glass, 31.1.1976 (Schn 21/11/70).

144 V&A Theatre Archives, THM/271, 'Anatol' programme, 11 February 1976. This records the order of performance and that there was an interval of fifteen minutes between the first and the last three playlets.

145 Eric Glass to Heinrich Schnitzler, 30.3.1976 (Schn 21/11/78).

146 Eric Glass to Heinrich Schnitzler, 30.3.1976 (Schn 21/11/78).

147 Michael Billington, 'Anatol', *Guardian*, 12 February 1976, p. 8. Reviews referred to in this section can be found in the V&A Theatre Archives.

148 Milton Shulman, 'A wry look at love', *Evening Standard*, 12 February 1976.

149 V&A Theatre Archives, THM/271, 'Anatol' programme, 11 February 1976.

Marowitz met his mark. According to reviews from the major newspapers, as well as several nationally distributed magazines, the production was 'serious and thoughtful',[150] the translation 'knowing',[151] 'admirable'[152] and a 'thoroughly professional job'.[153] The versatility of Prunella Scales was likewise praiseworthy. The actress had distinguished the six roles 'magnificently'.[154] Vienna, it was concluded, 'had other faces to show than sentimentality'.[155] Against Heinrich's will, and notwithstanding the controversial casting of Scales, Marowitz and Marcus had together produced an *Anatol* that undoubtedly undid some of the prejudice generated by the Barker 'paraphrase'.

According to Glass, the production gave rise to numerous requests for a transfer to the West End, but all were conditional upon Scales once more playing all the female roles.[156] Glass was well aware that Heinrich did not want to perpetuate that interpretation and, as he expected, permission was not given. Nevertheless, Heinrich stressed that wherever *Anatol* was put on in future, Frank Marcus's text should be used 'simply because of its excellence'.[157] Indeed, permission was given on at least one further occasion during Heinrich Schnitzler's reign over his father's estate. In 1979 Glass was approached by Michael Kustow, an Associate Director of the National Theatre, about directing the Marcus translation for a seven-week tour by the Cambridge Theatre Company.[158] Kustow understood that there must be different actresses playing the different female roles and permission was given on that basis. Only in the middle of the run did Heinrich learn that Kustow, with Marcus's cooperation, had added an epilogue to the cycle, as well as excerpts from Schnitzler's autobiography between playlets.[159] At one point in the production an actress even sang 'Wien, Wien nur du allein', a well-known *Wienerlied* composed by Rudolf Sieczyński in 1912 and popularized by the émigré tenor Richard Tauber as 'Vienna, City of My Dreams' in 1935; Heinrich considered it a 'piece of cheap trash'.[160] Kustow's production thus provides a conclusion to this chapter. Although Marcus's translation came to replace Barker's as

150 Harold Hobson, 'Recipe for a Revolution', *Sunday Times*, 15 February 1976, p. 37.
151 Irving Wardle, 'Anatol', *The Times*, 12 February 1976, p. 13.
152 Keith Nurse, 'Six into One', *Sunday Telegraph*, 15 February 1976, p. 18.
153 B. A. Young, 'Anatol', *Financial Times*, 12 February 1976, p. 3.
154 Robert Cushman, 'Austrian Attitudes', *Observer*, 15 February 1976, p. 26.
155 B. A. Young, 'Anatol', *Financial Times*, 12 February 1976, p. 3.
156 Eric Glass to Heinrich Schnitzler, 30.3.1976 (Schn 21/11/78).
157 Heinrich Schnitzler to Eric Glass, 7.4.1976 (Schn 21/11/78).
158 Eric Glass to Heinrich Schnitzler, 24.10.1979 (Schn 21/12/41).
159 Heinrich Schnitzler to Eric Glass, 12.11.1979 (Schn 21/12/42); and Eric Glass to Heinrich Schnitzler, 7.12.1979 (Schn 21/12/45). Unfortunately, it has not been possible to establish which excerpts of *Jugend in Wien* were used and there is no record of the epilogue performed.
160 Heinrich Schnitzler to Eric Glass, 12.11.1979 (Schn 21/12/42).

the default *Anatol* text in English, mastery over that text remained elusive in Heinrich's battle to decide Schnitzler's posthumous legacy in Britain. As both Marowitz's and Kustow's productions demonstrate, complete control is effectively unattainable: further lines can be added at the rehearsal stage, cuts can be made by the director, clichéd songs are inserted and choreographed dance interludes smuggled between scenes.[161]

Total control is not required, however, in order to effect change. Even with the slippages relayed above, Heinrich could legitimately claim success in respect of his broader aims. The Marcus/Marowitz production at the Open Space Theatre presented Britain with an *Anatol* disentangled from the myth of 'Gay Vienna' by portraying the play's protagonist in all his different shades and with all the gloomy shadows he casts. More particularly, Marcus's translation provides directors and actors with a foundation for further, differentiated interpretations; Barker's reading no longer circumscribes British reception of the play. Arthur Schnitzler's reputation in Britain would finally be stretched beyond the confines of *Anatol* and *Reigen* when Tom Stoppard's adaptation of *Das weite Land* was produced at the National Theatre in 1979. That project is considered, along with Stoppard's 1986 adaptation of *Liebelei*, in the next chapter.

161 Marowitz employed four female dancers to perform between playlets, allowing Prunella Scales to change costumes. These 'add[ed] nothing to the atmosphere' (B. A. Young, 'Anatol', *Financial Times*, 12 February 1976, p. 3).

CHAPTER 3

Performing Schnitzler through Stoppard

Tom Stoppard (b. 1937) has adapted two of Schnitzler's plays for production at the National Theatre in London. The first, a 'version' of *Das weite Land* called *Undiscovered Country* (1979), preceded the expiry of copyright protection for Schnitzler's plays in Britain on 31 December 1981.[1] The second, *Dalliance* (1986), is Stoppard's interpretation of *Liebelei* and postdates both copyright protection and Heinrich Schnitzler's death in July 1982.[2] In this respect Stoppard's engagement with Schnitzler's dramas can be viewed as marking a period of transition for Schnitzler's presence within Britain. While contextualizing *Undiscovered Country* and *Dalliance* in terms of their significance to Schnitzler's place in Britain, this chapter also considers how they fit into Stoppard's evolution and establishment as a celebrated playwright. As will be seen, both adaptations were produced at a time of transition for Stoppard as well, as he began to embrace more emotional themes in his 'original' works.

Seen side by side, *Undiscovered Country* and *Dalliance* demonstrate the shifts in the process and product of translation when a foreign-language playwright's works fall out of copyright and outside the control of the literary estate. This chapter assesses for the first time how both plays came to be produced at the National Theatre through a close examination of the documentary trail left in the papers of Heinrich Schnitzler (in Vienna) and Tom Stoppard (in Austin), as well as the production files held by the National Theatre Archive (in London). Those archives collectively reveal the layered and multiple agencies involved in producing the plays, the individual assertions of power and the competing narratives, identifying the often

1 See programme cover, *Undiscovered Country*, National Theatre, 1979, preserved at the Harry Ransom Center, The University of Texas at Austin (Tom Stoppard Papers, Container 32.8). References to these papers are hereinafter marked in the text by the Container number and, where available, page numbers or other identifying features.

2 *Dalliance* was also described as a 'version' of *Liebelei* on its programme cover (Container 79.16). For the reasons set out in the Introduction, terminology such as 'version', 'translation' and 'adaptation' is generally used in this chapter without making claims about the nature of the text, unless otherwise specified.

uncredited or forgotten contributors to the transformation of the text from German-language source to English-language performance. That multiplicity will be contrasted to the critical reception of the plays, which posits a more traditional conception of authorship and allows acknowledgment of only one or, at most, two authors of the translated play. At the same time, the archived material highlights the inherent instability of the playscripts and therewith the impossibility of legitimately referring to an 'authoritative' text.

Building on and departing from the previous scholarship, in which the published texts have been compared to their published sources, attention is given here to the substantial volume of paratextual material, both published and unpublished. Letters, drafts, interviews and reviews combine to provide a new, comprehensive picture of the process of interlingual transmission. Notably, they expose the collaborative nature of the work involved in translating Schnitzler for the stage. By doing so, they undermine Romantic conceptions of authorship, which restrict agency to a single individual, as well as laying bare the tendency for such problematic conceptions to inform and be repeated in critical reviews of foreign-language drama. This chapter shows that far from the simple relationship of author and translator historically portrayed in programme notes and on book covers, or the relationship of source text and translated text so readily imagined by the observing public, in fact what we see performed on stage is one iteration of a continuum of creative transfer between numerous individuals engaged with an autonomous text.

Breaking New Ground for Schnitzler

Das weite Land was written between 1908 and 1910 and opened on 14 October 1911 in nine German-language theatres simultaneously, including the Lessingtheater in Berlin, the Deutsches Landestheater in Prague and the Hofburgtheater in Vienna. It was a moment which marked the pinnacle of Schnitzler's fame and popularity in the German-speaking world and a play which Schnitzler himself liked enormously: '[I]ch halte es [...] so ziemlich für mein wirksamstes Theaterstück'.[3] *Das weite Land* is a tragi-comedy, comprising five acts and focusing on industrialist Friedrich Hofreiter and his wife Genia within a social network of tennis parties and casual flirtations. Friedrich is a philanderer who displays little concern for his wife's feelings; Genia's response is to fear for her husband's life at the hands of the latest cuckold.[4] Duelling

3 Arthur Schnitzler to Firmin Gémier, *Briefe* II, 515–16, 12.12.1927. See also *Tagebuch*, 14.6.1915: 'Das Stück eins der sehr wenigen zu dem ich mich bedingungslos bekenne'.

4 Arthur Schnitzler, *Das weite Land*, in *Gesammelte Werke. Die Dramatischen Werke*, 2 vols (Frankfurt a. M.: Fischer, 1962), II, 217–320 (p. 226). Henceforth references to the play

remains a central part of the code of honour observed in Austrian society pre-World War I and casts a shadow over much of the play before providing the dénouement at its conclusion. When Friedrich shares with Genia his disgust that her integrity has caused a friend's suicide (Genia rejects the advances of Russian pianist Korsakow before the curtain first goes up), Genia allows herself to enter into an affair with the young marine officer Otto von Aigner. Friedrich discovers the affair on his return from a mountaineering trip (during which he has embarked upon a new romance with Erna Wahl, the daughter of a family friend) and provokes Otto into defending his honour. Friedrich appears to be indifferent to the outcome of the duel, except at the moment when faced by his opponent: 'Wie er mir gegenübergestanden ist mit seinem frechen, jungen Blick, da hab' ich's gewußt … er oder ich' (*DwL*, p. 318). He duly kills the younger man, notwithstanding the opportunity to avoid such an outcome.[5]

Friedrich's apparently spinning moral compass and its opposite, in the consistent but nevertheless vulnerable selfhood of Genia, undoubtedly serve as the tragic touchstones of the play. However, they are accompanied by streams of comic lightness in the frivolity of the society that surrounds them. Theirs is a 'transitional world hovering between seriousness and irresponsibility', out of which tension there are innumerable opportunities for witty quips, cynicism and humorous exchange.[6] Dialogue and mood move smoothly between tragic and comic modes, thereby allowing the audience to find relief through laughter between episodes of contemplating more serious moral and psychological themes. Martin Swales has mapped out a mirroring of structure and themes in the 'careful rhythmic alternation of intimate scenes (duologues) and group scenes'.[7] The wider cast of characters represent what the character Dr Mauer calls the 'Atmosphäre' (*DwL*, p. 253), in which 'emotional abandon' mixes unchecked with prescriptive social norms and which 'constantly impinges on the more forthright attempts [in the duologues] at emotional frankness'.[8] That alternating structure is likewise fixed in the settings, which are themselves locations of inbetweenness. Three of the acts are set in the Hofreiters' garden,

in this edition are given in parentheses in the body of the text as *DwL*, followed by page number(s).

5 Reinhard Urbach, 'Arthur Schnitzler. *Das weite Land*. Genia. Lesarten und Sichtweisen. Anmerkungen zu einer spekulativen Dramaturgie', in *Überschreitungen. Dialoge zwischen Literatur- und Theaterwissenschaft, Architektur und Bildender Kunst. Festschrift für Leonhard M. Fiedler zum 60. Geburtstage*, ed. by Jörg Sader and Anette Wörner (Würzburg: Königshausen & Neumann, 2002), pp. 127–37 (p. 134).

6 Martin Swales, 'Schnitzler's Tragi-comedy: A Reading of "Das weite Land"', *Modern Austrian Literature*, 10 (1977), 233–45 (p. 236).

7 Swales, 'Schnitzler's Tragi-comedy', p. 237.

8 Swales, 'Schnitzler's Tragi-comedy', pp. 239 and 242.

with the tennis court in the background; the third act is set in the lobby of an Alpine hotel; and the fifth in a room of the Hofreiters' villa, looking onto the veranda and garden viewed in Acts 1, 2 and 4. All are liminal spaces, thresholds between private and public zones across which people and moods pass easily and sometimes swiftly.[9]

In all but the central act, Genia is the anchor steadying this otherwise constantly moving body of people: like a lynchpin, she holds the network of family and friends together, operating as its 'passive centre'.[10] Nevertheless, her affair with Otto, and Friedrich's subsequent success in killing Otto, threaten to fracture Genia's solidity.[11] It is difficult to see in what state, if any, the marriage between Genia and Friedrich can survive. To more than one reader of the play it is wholly broken – 'shattered beyond repair, even for appearances' sake'.[12] The relationship on which all others are founded collapses. It is the last 'fall' of the play and, like those which precede it (from mountain, window and pistol shot), this fall also 'schwebt [...] zwischen Unfall und wissentlichem Akt'.[13] One wonders to what degree the self-destruction evident in Friedrich's behaviour, at least, is carried out knowingly. In any event, Friedrich's execution of the public sanction due for an emotional abandon he himself pursues in private cannot withstand Genia's scrutiny. A sense of disintegration thus marks the final moments of the play, when Genia leaves Friedrich in order to break the news to Otto's mother. It is not insignificant that Genia leaves the stage with Mauer (*DwL*, p. 319), a figure Swales considers representative of an 'other' atmosphere at odds with the moral climate promoted by Friedrich.[14]

9 See Janet Stewart's analysis of Schnitzler's negotiation of space and boundaries in his dramas, particularly *Reigen* (Janet Stewart, 'Raum und Raumwahrnehmung in den dramatischen Werken Schnitzlers', in *Arthur Schnitzler im zwanzigsten Jahrhundert*, ed. by Konstanze Fliedl (Vienna: Picus, 2003), pp. 105–19).

10 J. P. Stern, 'Anyone for Tennis, Anyone for Death? The Schnitzler/Stoppard "Undiscovered Country"', *Encounter*, 53/54 (Oct. 1979), 26–31 (p. 31). For an examination of Genia's role in a constellation that incorporates two other key women in the play, Erna Wahl and Anna Meinhold-Aigner, see Alfred Doppler, 'Die Frauengestalten in Arthur Schnitzlers Schauspiel "Der einsame Weg" und in der Tragikomödie "Das weite Land"', in *Arthur Schnitzler im zwanzigsten Jahrhundert*, ed. by Fliedl, pp. 92–104.

11 For an alternative, less orthodox reading of Genia as a self-determining character, one who is 'der freieste der Menschen', see Urbach, 'Arthur Schnitzler', p. 136; Evelyne Polt-Heinzl, 'Der Genia Effekt oder Schnitzlers Umgang mit den strukturellen Lücken im Verhältnis der Geschlechter', *Internationales Archiv für Sozialgeschichte der deutschen Literatur*, 33 (2008), 101–12 (p. 106).

12 Kari Grimstad, 'The Institution of Marriage in Schnitzler's *Komtesse Mizzi oder der Familientag* and *Das weite Land*', *Modern Austrian Literature*, 25 (1992), 141–56 (p. 151). See also Urbach, 'Arthur Schnitzler', p. 133; Rudolf Denk, '*Das weite Land. Tragikomödie in fünf Akten* (1911)', in *Schnitzler-Handbuch*, ed. by Jürgensen, Lukas and Scheffel, pp. 87–92 (p. 89).

13 Andrew J. Webber, 'Namens- oder Familienähnlichkeiten. Fallgeschichte und Falldrama bei Schnitzler und Freud', in *Textschicksale*, ed. by Lukas and Scheffel, pp. 72–92 (p. 89).

14 Swales, 'Schnitzler's Tragi-comedy', p. 238.

Das weite Land is a play very much of its time and place. It is occupied by the wealthy middle classes residing or holidaying in the spa town of Baden, outside Vienna, before the First World War. The group of individuals portrayed are governed in their actions by a code of honour largely unknown outside German-speaking Europe. Dialogue, rhythm, characterization and humour all depend on an understanding of chronotopically marked conversational styles, dialects and sociolects.[15] Why should such a play speak to audiences seventy years (and two World Wars) later, in another part of Europe? The existing scholarship provides a number of possible answers. Polt-Heinzl identifies the gaps in the play which point to a shifting relationship between the sexes, a technique which renders it 'bis heute spannend'.[16] For Swales, its attraction lies in the insight Schnitzler brings to the world around him, his psychological probing, which presents us with such figures as Genia, the embodiment of 'the psychological possibility that concepts, values, principles such as fidelity function not as abstract imperatives [...] but as the existential condition of a character's being and selfhood'.[17] Certainly this is a side of the play picked up on, and appreciated, in the critical reviews of Stoppard's adaptation, as will be shown below. However, *Das weite Land* satisfies a commercial need to fill seats as well – through its humour. As Stoppard has observed, the audience must be entertained before it can be lectured: 'Theatre is first and foremost a recreation. But it is not just a children's playground; it can be recreation for people who like to stretch their minds'.[18] *Das weite Land* provides just such a service, delivered in such a way that it transcends time and location. The moral puzzles presented in *Das weite Land*, although set in a specific context, are universal in their potential application. Probing 'das weite Land', i.e., the human soul, is as worthy an exercise today as it was at the turn of the last century and Schnitzler's skill in bringing comedy to his tragic themes renders them all the more palatable to contemporary audiences.[19]

15 Maier, 'Cannibalizing Cultures', pp. 75–83.

16 Polt-Heinzl, 'Der Genia Effekt', p. 111.

17 Swales, 'Schnitzler's Tragi-comedy', p. 238.

18 Tom Stoppard in an interview by Maya Jaggi, 'You can't help being what you write', *Guardian*, 6 September 2008, https://www.theguardian.com/stage/2008/sep/06/stoppard.theatre [accessed 30 June 2021]. See also his interview with John Stead, in which he said: 'If you write a play your primary aim must be that people don't leave before the end' (*Evening Mail*, 10 June 1971, n. pag., cited by William Demastes, *The Cambridge Introduction to Tom Stoppard* (Cambridge: Cambridge University Press, 2012), p. 27).

19 *Das weite Land* has been a mainstay of the post-World War II theatre scene in Germany and Austria, but also further afield. Most notably, besides the Stoppard adaptation discussed in this chapter, Luc Bondy produced a celebrated translation, *Terre Étrangère*, at the Théâtre des Amandiers in Nanterre in 1984.

Notwithstanding the success of *Das weite Land* on the European mainland, both during Schnitzler's lifetime and in the second half of the century, the play failed to find a home in Britain until sixty years after its multi-staged launch in 1911. During that period the only access non-German speaking readers might have had to the play was through a translation by Alexander Caro and Edward Woticky, 'The Vast Domain', published in the American journal *Poet Lore* in 1923.[20] The delay in British translations was not for want of efforts made much earlier. The actor Arnold Korff, for example, who had created the role of Hofreiter at the Burgtheater, was keen to translate the play for England and America and approached Schnitzler on a number of occasions with his proposals (*Tagebuch*, 19.10.1912, 18.5.1913 and 24.1.1926). Schnitzler himself suggested that Harley Granville Barker take on the role of Hofreiter, but he also questioned whether Barker was in a position to include a five-act tragi-comedy by a German [*sic*] author in his repertoire.[21] The writer's son, Heinrich Schnitzler, also attempted to bring it to Britain and place it with a theatre from as early as 1934, i.e., at the very beginning of his stewardship of the literary estate.[22] However, Heinrich Schnitzler's approach was generally one of hesitance and caution. Some of the reasons for that have been examined in the previous chapter, but his archive provides an example pertinent to the particular case of *Das weite Land*.

In 1974, director and translator Christopher Fettes was denied permission to put on his own version of *The Vast Domain* at the Drama Centre, along with *Intermezzo* and *The Lonely Road*, on the basis that the plays were too ambitious for a mere 'school' and would require 'the most accomplished actors, capable of creating an impression of absolute maturity not only as actors but also as human beings'.[23] Heinrich Schnitzler admitted to Eric Glass that '[r]ather than having these plays done in a manner which would hardly do them full justice, I'd prefer not having them done at all'.[24] His longstanding protectionist stance represented an immovable obstacle to dissemination in this instance,

20 Alexander Caro and Edward Woticky, 'The Vast Domain', *Poet Lore*, 34 (1923), 317–407. Distribution statistics are not readily available for *Poet Lore*, but it may be inferred from the fact that the journal is only mentioned in the 'American Notes' of *The New Age* (see 29 January 1914, p. 402 and 30 April 1914, p. 817, both by 'E. A. B.') and in a similarly themed column in *The Egoist* (Richard Aldington, 'Young America', 1 November 1915, p. 176) that it was not then a regular feature on the British journal scene. Nevertheless, the journal was, and remains, a highly esteemed institution within American literary culture and so represented a promising address for the translation.

21 Arthur Schnitzler to Harley Granville Barker, 16.3.1911 (DLA, HS.NZ85.0001.00881). At that time, Barker had recently taken on the management of the Little Theatre with his wife Lillah McCarthy (Kennedy, *Granville Barker and the Dream of the Theatre*, p. 117).

22 See Heinrich Schnitzler to Eric Glass, 11.3.1934 (Schn 21/4/1).

23 Heinrich Schnitzler to Eric Glass, 19.10.1974 (Schn 21/10/73).

24 Heinrich Schnitzler to Eric Glass, 19.10.1974 (Schn 21/10/73).

as in others. The choice of institution appears to have been key to gaining Heinrich Schnitzler's approval: the first occasion on which British audiences could hear the play was in a radio adaptation, *Uncharted Sea*, commissioned and broadcast by the BBC in 1972 and written by Ronald Adam, an already approved Schnitzler adapter (notwithstanding his lack of German).[25]

The National Theatre was another such institution, inherently trusted by Heinrich Schnitzler at the beginning of negotiations, although by no means beyond reproach. Eric Glass, and through him Heinrich Schnitzler, had tried to woo the National Theatre for several years with Schnitzler's dramas. They had, however, been blocked by a stubborn interest in *Reigen* alone. In 1964 and 1976 first Laurence Olivier and subsequently his successor, Peter Hall, sought permission from the estate to stage *Reigen*;[26] Heinrich Schnitzler remained firm in upholding his father's ban. Alternatives were suggested by Heinrich Schnitzler and Glass – *Der einsame Weg* might suit the current London understanding for '"Chekhovian" mood and atmosphere';[27] or the Open Space production of *Anatol* could transfer easily[28] – but to no avail. The groundwork for a National Theatre production of Schnitzler had undoubtedly been laid by Heinrich Schnitzler and Glass and they were supported by the theatre's Literary Manager (i.e., dramaturg) Kenneth Tynan, who included in his List of Plays recommended for the National Theatre no fewer than six of Schnitzler's dramas.[29] However, the selection of *Das weite Land* itself appears to have come from director Peter Wood, who, according to Stoppard, would 'bustle [...] back from Vienna, where he occasionally direct[ed], with his latest discovery', ready to enthuse his colleagues accordingly.[30] These various factors combined

25 In his autobiography Ronald Adam concedes that he could 'not speak much German' (Ronald Adam, *Overture and Beginners* (London: Gollancz, 1938), p. 83). He also sets out his method for producing an English version of *Professor Bernhardi* in 1936 with Louis Borrell, a Dutchman, who provided the necessary German language skills (p. 161). Heinrich Schnitzler had directed Adam as Flint in the London production of the Adam/Borrell *Professor Bernhardi* (1936) and so was already familiar with both the man and his writing.

26 Heinrich Schnitzler to Eric Glass, 16.11.1964 (Schn 21/7/101); and Eric Glass to Heinrich Schnitzler, 30.3.1976 (Schn 21/11/78).

27 Heinrich Schnitzler to Eric Glass, 23.11.1964 (Schn 21/7/102).

28 Eric Glass to Heinrich Schnitzler, 30.3.1976 (Schn 21/11/78).

29 The 'List' was produced during Tynan's incumbency (1963–72) and included *Liebelei*, *Reigen*, *Anatol*, *Der Einsame Weg*, *Der Grüne Kakadu* and *Dr Bernhardi* [*sic*] ('Some Plays: A List Compiled for the National Theatre by Kenneth Tynan', https://www.nationaltheatre.org.uk/sites/default/files/kenneth-tynan_list-of-plays.pdf [accessed 16 January 2019]).

30 Clare Colvin, 'The Real Tom Stoppard', *Drama*, 3 (1986), 9–10. Stoppard first saw a translation of *Das weite Land* during the rehearsals in 1978 for his play *Night and Day*, directed by Peter Wood. It seems justifiable to infer, therefore, that Wood had seen the production of *Das weite Land* at the Akademietheater in Vienna in early 1978, which starred Helmuth Lohner as Friedrich and Gertraud Jesserer as Genia.

to give rise to arguably the most significant Schnitzler production in Britain to that date. *Undiscovered Country* was staged in the largest of the three theatres at the National, the Olivier Theatre (accommodating 1,150 people), for its run of sixty-seven performances between 15 June 1979 and 31 January 1980.[31]

Previous analyses of Stoppard's first Schnitzler adaptation have been based on a comparison of published editions of *Das weite Land* and *Undiscovered Country* (the latter of which purports to be 'a record of what was performed at the National Theatre').[32] Such an approach to the fixed published texts reveals evidence of significant cuts and re-ordering of text, as well as the compression, or sharpening, of dialogue. The effect, according to one commentator, has been to remove the conversational realism and reduce characters' psychological depth.[33] By and large, however, the dialogue which remains is a close English approximation of what Schnitzler wrote in German. Stoppard later claimed that 'the Ibsenesque undercurrents of the play made it important to establish as precisely as possible what every phrase meant, root out the allusions, find the niceties of etiquette, and so on, and generally to aim for equivalence'.[34] His 'inventions' for *Undiscovered Country*, he observed, 'were guilty secrets, almost admissions of failure, bits of non-Schnitzler trying not to look un-Schnitzler, put in because I couldn't make the thing bounce properly'.[35] In a number of places Stoppard's humour has unmistakably left its mark. Erna, for example, quips that 'Korsakow wouldn't be seen dead with a suicide note' (*UC*, p. 63) in place of Schnitzler's more naturalistic line: 'Korsakow hat nicht zu den Menschen gehört, die Abschiedsbriefe schreiben' (*DwL*, p. 222). For

31 From the available data regarding lengths of run for all performances of Schnitzler's works in Britain, this was the longest run enjoyed by any production. See Appendix 2.

32 Tom Stoppard, 'Introduction', in *Dalliance and Undiscovered Country* (London: Faber & Faber, 1986), pp. ix–x (p. x). Henceforth references to this edition are given in parentheses in the body of the text: *Dall.* for *Dalliance* and *UC* for *Undiscovered Country*, followed by page number(s). For previous scholarship on the adaptations see Anderman, *Europe on Stage*, pp. 206–12; Kurt Bergel, 'The Recent Reception of Arthur Schnitzler's "Das weite Land" on Two American Stages', *Modern Austrian Literature*, 9.3 (1986), 90–96; Beatrix Hesse, 'Rediscovered Country – Tom Stoppard's Austrian Plays', in *Austria and Austrians: Images in World Literature*, ed. by Wolfgang Görtschacher and Holger Klein (Tübingen: Stauffenberg, 2003), pp. 171–82; Maier, 'Cannibalizing Cultures'; J. G. Schippers, 'Stoppard's Nestroy, Schnitzler's Stoppard or Humpty Dumpty im Wiener Wald', *Linguistics and the Study of Literature*, 53 (1986), 245–67; Spencer, 'Translating Schnitzler for the stage'; Guy Stern, 'From Austria to America via London: Tom Stoppard's Adaptations of Nestroy and Schnitzler', in *The Fortunes of German Writers in America*, ed. by Elfe, Hardin and Holst, pp. 167–83; J. P. Stern, 'Anyone for Tennis?'.

33 Hesse, 'Rediscovered Country', p. 174.

34 Tom Stoppard, 'Across Nestroy with Map and Compass', in the programme for *On the Razzle*, National Theatre, 1981, n. pag. (Container 20.6).

35 Stoppard, 'Across Nestroy with Map and Compass'.

Kurt Bergel this verged on the farcical and did not 'sound right coming from a young Viennese upper-middle-class girl'.[36] Even more worryingly for another commentator, '[s]tupid' Mrs Wahl was given the 'clever' German-language joke about her son being a 'wanderlust *wunderkind*' (*UC*, p. 65), one of a number of 'jokes [...] distributed over the various characters with little regard for consistency of characterization'.[37] The effect is one of alienation, reminding the audience that this is not just Schnitzler's play magically transformed into English without any traces of its journey, but the product of another writer's creativity. Thus, elsewhere Stoppard's Friedrich anachronistically recommends his tennis partner take up 'some local pastime – light opera – or psychoanalysis . . .' (*UC*, p. 83) instead of the original suggestion: 'einen andern Beruf [...] . . . Advokat . . . oder Raseur . . .' (*DwL*, p. 246). Far from violating the source material, however, Stoppard's playfulness generally enhances traits already legible in Schnitzler's characterization. Stoppard has accordingly tended to be praised by his commentators for having 'reinvigorated' Schnitzler's play,[38] while at the same time demonstrating 'care and restraint' in his treatment of the source material.[39]

Genia is undeniably altered through the adaptation. Her responses are on occasion much snappier, her tongue far sharper and her tone more sarcastic. When Mauer, on learning that Genia and Friedrich might travel to America together, reflects, 'Na, das ist schön, das freut mich', Schnitzler's Genia gently reprimands him: 'Warum denn so feierlich ...?! Vielleicht, hab' ich gesagt!' (*DwL*, p. 247). In Stoppard's text, Mauer's reflection is reduced to a 'Bravo', to which Genia almost spits back: 'Spare the celebration . . . I said I might' (*UC*, p. 83). Earlier, on Friedrich's mentioning of a newspaper article he had found interesting, Stoppard provides Genia with an entirely new line: 'Why? Did they dig up a light bulb?' (*UC*, p. 72). The sometimes severe cuts executed throughout the play have the effect on Genia of diminishing her softer side. Thus, for example, we do not hear her, in *Undiscovered Country*, mention to Mrs von Aigner that she has not seen her son since Christmas and that it is, 'Kein leichtes Los, seinen Einzigen so in der Fremde haben' (*DwL*, p. 256; *UC*, p. 90). Schippers, like Hesse, observes this to be a more general trait of Stoppard's treatment of *Das weite Land*: the sometimes-radical cuts result in a play 'with characters of considerably reduced psychological depth and

36 Bergel, 'Recent Reception', p. 93.

37 Schippers, 'Stoppard's Nestroy, Schnitzler's Stoppard', pp. 262–63.

38 Guy Stern, 'From Austria to America', p. 168. See also Daviau, who considers *Das weite Land* to have 'received new life' through Stoppard's adaptation (Daviau, 'The Reception of Arthur Schnitzler', p. 147). The only substantially critical view is found in Maier, 'Cannibalizing Cultures'.

39 Schippers, 'Stoppard's Nestroy, Schnitzler's Stoppard', p. 262.

with little or no personal background left to them'.[40] Guy Stern has stressed, by contrast, the expanded (and prior) theatricalism of the adaptation effected when, for example, Friedrich's greeting to his wife and her lover from the balcony – 'meine Herrschaften' (*DwL*, p. 294) – becomes 'Friends, Romans, and countrymen!' (*UC*, p. 124), an allusion to Mark Antony's 'manipulative speech'.[41] Although the overall approach, therefore, appears to have been to respect structure and dialogue, Stoppard's flourishes of linguistic playfulness and his manifold cuts both add to and detract from the existing themes and thread of Schnitzler's drama while diminishing the particularity of his characters.

The above analysis, whilst limited to one edition of the printed text, gives a flavour of Stoppard's method when adapting others' work. The genesis of *Undiscovered Country* is explored in greater detail below and provides a fuller account of Stoppard's writing and adapting processes. In the first instance, however, it is useful to read *Dalliance* from the same printed edition, thereby allowing for the similarities and differences legible at the surface of the texts to come to light. As will be seen, even when carrying out only a skin-deep examination, it is possible to discern a far freer hand at play with the later adaptation.

Dalliance: The Post-Copyright Text

By comparison with *Undiscovered Country*, *Dalliance* demonstrates even more significant alterations to its source. As well as the linguistic compression, word games and sharpened repartee already evident in *Undiscovered Country*, which give rise to 'a heightened sense of conflict and theatricality', there are major structural changes to the play.[42] The whole of the third act is re-located from Christine's rooms to 'backstage at the Josefstadt theatre', where her father plays in the orchestra. In addition, Mizi is changed from an unemployed hat-shop assistant (*Liebelei*, p. 950) to a fully occupied seamstress, thereby allowing a *Hamlet* joke from Theodore ('Seams, madam? I know not seams') and explaining her presence in Act 3 (*Dall.*, p. 18).[43] A tenor and a soprano are added to the cast, rehearsing a duet on stage in the final act to

40 Schippers, 'Stoppard's Nestroy, Schnitzler's Stoppard', p. 266.

41 Guy Stern, 'From Austria to America', p. 172. Mark Antony's speech is found in William Shakespeare, *Julius Caesar*, ed. by David Daniell, The Arden Shakespeare (London: Thomas Nelson, 1998), III. 2. 74. Mark Antony begins his speech at Caesar's funeral with the words 'Friends, Romans, countrymen, lend me your ears'.

42 Anderman, *Europe on Stage*, p. 208.

43 See Shakespeare, *Hamlet*, I. 2. 76. In response to his mother's question as to why his father's death 'seems […] so particular' to Hamlet, he replies: 'Seems, madam? Nay, it is. I know not "seems"'.

provide commentary on the 'real' love story between Christine and Fritz. The transition from second to third act is performed on stage by the 'opera stage-hands' without an intermission, so that, as in Stoppard's *The Real Thing* (1982), the audience is left to ponder whether it is watching a play within a play. Perhaps most significantly, though, Christine's last words have been completely re-written and her fate thereby drastically revised.

Whereas Schnitzler's Christine rushes off stage to Fritz's graveside with the line 'Ich will nicht dort beten . . . nein . . .' (*Liebelei*, p. 1015), leaving all to assume she will take her own life,[44] Stoppard's Christine is given a distinctly feminist closing statement: 'What? That I loved him? You shit-bucket, Theo. You fat, ugly, ignorant, lecherous, dirty-fingered God's gift to the female race, your breath stank of stale women when you kissed me, I was nearly *sick!*' (*Dall.*, p. 53). The outbreak of uncontrolled, emotionally charged language is prefigured by a similar rant by the Gentleman in Act 1, where again Stoppard has written entirely his own lines. In the source text Fritz asks, 'Der Herr', 'Was wünschen Sie noch von mir?', to which the scornful reply comes: 'Was ich noch wünsche –?' (*Liebelei*, p. 959). Stoppard supplements his translation ('Anything more?') with 'That *you* might do for *me*? [...] You young know-it-alls . . . take-it-alls . . . My box, my table, my – You grab – brag – strut – rut like dogs in the street – and you'll be shot down like dogs' (*Dall.*, p. 23). The lines could almost have been spoken by Friedrich in *Undiscovered Country*, for whom it is the audacious face of youth, full of perceived intent to usurp the older generation of Casanovas, which drives the animosity and enables the cuckolded man to shoot to kill. Here, surely, is an example of Stoppard adding more Schnitzler to Schnitzler.[45]

The revision of Christine's final lines is not so obviously successful. Not only do the lines lack the poetic momentum of the Gentleman's lines, but they are also internally inconsistent, incorporating both criticism of and solidarity with other women. Regardless of that inconsistency (perhaps itself a reflection of the increasing agitation experienced by Christine and the disgust at her own complicity), her departure is a sign of strength.[46] She has been transported into the present day, in which 'women [no longer] passively accept [...] their fate at the hands of men'.[47] Unlike Schnitzler's heroine, Stoppard's will survive the deception acted upon her and emerge a more emotionally independent woman.

44 Fliedl, *Arthur Schnitzler*, p. 83.

45 Cf. Guy Stern, who identifies Stoppard's emphasis on theatricalism in the two adaptations as grafting 'Schnitzlerisms upon Schnitzler' (Stern, 'From Austria to America', p. 174).

46 A worthy comparison, unfortunately falling outside of the scope of this book, could be made with Luc Bondy's Young Vic production in 2010 of David Harrower's adaptation of *Liebelei* as *Sweet Nothings*, at the end of which Christine was prevented from leaving the stage by the other characters and hence denied any resolution.

47 Anderman, *Europe on Stage*, p. 212.

Christine's transformation should not come as a complete shock to reader or audience, as Stoppard has made subtle changes throughout the play in order to demonstrate a gradual development of character not represented in *Liebelei*. In Act 2, for example, the playwright takes a relatively inane question in the source text – Fritz asking Christine whether she looks at the pictures in her 'Conversationslexicon' – together with its simple response and alters and extends the exchange significantly. In *Liebelei* Christine merely agrees, 'Natürlich hab' ich mir die Bilder angeschaut' (*Liebelei*, p. 990). In *Dalliance*, however, she at first challenges Fritz's question, only then to accept his condescension wholeheartedly:

> CHRISTINE: What do you mean, Fritz?
> FRITZ: You look at the pictures. In the encyclopaedia. You like to look at the pictures.
> CHRISTINE: Well, yes, I look at the pictures too.
> FRITZ: Oh – I didn't mean – it's only because I love your pretty little head, and I don't want it bothered about . . . I've said the wrong thing.
> CHRISTINE: Oh, no Fritz – ! I love you loving my head – if you like I'll never read anything again! (*Dall.*, p. 39)

In a context in which Stoppard generally cuts text, this represents quite a substantial addition to the source material. Its effect is twofold: Christine makes clear that she is not unread, having done more than merely look at books for their pictures in the past (Anderman notes that Christine is 'in many respects culturally superior to Fritz' even in Schnitzler's text);[48] but at the same time she throws herself (and her intellect) at Fritz's feet, sacrificing all to his will. A similar ambiguity can be found in the line added to the dialogue a little earlier in the same conversation between Fritz and Christine. The couple have been looking at the drawings in Christine's home. In the source text Christine describes one in her father's room, out of sight, as depicting: 'ein Mädel, die schaut zum Fenster hinaus, und draußen [...] ist der Winter – und das heißt "Verlassen". –' (*Liebelei*, p. 989). In Stoppard's version, the couple look at the picture directly, as Fritz asks: 'And what's this? *Forsaken*! Poor girl!'. Christine's reply, without any equivalent in Schnitzler's work, is: 'It's those Dragoons, I expect' (*Dall.*, p. 39). This wry comment on the unreliability of Fritz's regimental colleagues comes only moments after Mizi has called Christine a 'cretin' for looking for a decent man 'in the Dragoons' (*Dall.*, p. 36). Again, this exchange between Mizi and Christine is completely new and has no equivalent

48 Anderman, *Europe on Stage*, p. 211.

in Schnitzler's text. It is, therefore, not only in the final speech in Act 3 that Christine is altered by virtue of Stoppard's additions. By minimalizing the less conservative elements of her character at the beginning of the play and giving freer rein to them as time passes, Stoppard can show Christine developing over the course of the three acts.

The same change is evident in Stoppard's treatment of blasphemous language in the mouths of his female characters. As already seen in Chapter 1, Schnitzler does not shy away from exclamatory references to 'Gott' and 'Herrgott'. In Act 1 the five references to 'Gott' which do not form part of the greeting 'Grüß Sie Gott' are made by the female characters, i.e., both Mizi and the otherwise more conservative Christine. This language is not reserved for male characters in male-only society. In the cases mentioned, Stoppard either cuts the word or substitutes 'heavens' (*Dall.*, p. 11; twice on p. 18), or 'honestly' (*Dall.*, p. 17). Fritz's 'Herrgott', in Act 1 (*Liebelei*, p. 928), becomes 'My God' (*Dall.*, p. 7), whereas Mizi's (*Liebelei*, p. 947) is toned down to 'Goodness' (*Dall.*, p. 17). In Act 2 Stoppard permits Christine one 'Oh God!' (*Dall.*, p. 38), corresponding to the single 'O Gott!' in the source text (*Liebelei*, p. 988). However, in Act 3 the increase in the blasphemous bursts from Christine is dramatic. Whereas in Schnitzler's text Christine says 'O Gott' only once (*Liebelei*, p. 1011), in Stoppard's version the coarseness of the language is ramped up in frequency and intensity to demonstrate Christine's heightened emotions, culminating in the much-discussed final outburst: 'For God's sake tell me, Theodore' (*Dall.*, p. 50); 'Oh, my God – ' (*Dall.*, p. 50); 'Damn you, Theo – ' (*Dall.*, p. 51); and '*Damn* you, Theo' (*Dall.*, p. 53). None of these additions has a direct equivalent in the source text. Stoppard's aim is unlikely to have been the avoidance of blasphemy; he is not overtly sensitive to the risks of censorship or apparently concerned at the prospect of offending his audience. Rather, his application of this particular type of language shows the contrast between characters more sharply and it vividly paints the unfolding of a more fully developed Christine through her experiences in the play.

Stoppard makes further modifications in his treatment of Christine. Her position in society is portrayed as more obviously universal and the circumstances of her response to it as more particular. This is achieved by the combination of two minor changes to the play. First, Christine's mother is given a role in Stoppard's version. Whereas in *Liebelei* she is never mentioned, in the adaptation the audience learns that Christine 'never knew' her mother (*Dall.*, p. 10). The maternal absence is made explicit and planted as a determining factor in Christine's fate. The second change of relevance is the introduction of new song lyrics in 'The False Hussar'. Part of this is sung in the first act by Mizi,

Christine, Theodore and Fritz. The pertinent lines are not heard until Act 3, however, when the Soprano (a new character) sings:

> Mother told me all about you
> Mother told me what I should do
> Mother said it's all Liebelei
> Daughter mine
> Daughter mine, you must reply –. (*Dall.*, p. 46)

She then continues with the earlier chorus from Act 1, effectively telling the young lover to leave her alone. Whereas 'Mother' would have known what sort of person Fritz really was and advised Christine accordingly, the young woman's father is ill-equipped to protect her. He is guided instead by feelings of guilt at having denied his late spinster sister any chance of happiness through his keenness to keep her safe. As a consequence, he allows Christine a freedom for which she is not adequately prepared.

The repetitive nature of the song lyrics drives home the point that elements of Christine's story are already well rehearsed, most obviously the young officer looking for light romance rather than marriage. Whereas Mizi represents the behaviour of the better-informed young women of the lower social classes, Christine is a typical victim of the 'conspiracy of silence' which surrounded the subject of sex for more sheltered women.[49] However, certain features of Christine's story stand out from these common threads. By highlighting the universal via his new song, Stoppard also draws attention to the particularities of Christine's experience: the absence of the mother figure, the conflicted father and Christine's peculiar naivety about romantic or sexual relations. In doing so Stoppard continues a pattern of treatment present in the source text: his modifications further 'individualize' Christine.[50]

In *Dalliance* and, to a lesser degree, *Undiscovered Country* Stoppard had to address the dominant theme of duelling, an unfamiliar practice in 1970s and 1980s Britain but key to understanding the very real threat of death that hung over the characters in Schnitzler's dramas. In *Das weite Land* Schnitzler had already done some of the legwork for Stoppard, lining up references to death and duelling (subsequently retained by Stoppard in *Undiscovered Country*) as a means of anticipating the final denouement. British audiences would nevertheless have been assisted by Stoppard's

49 Yates, *Schnitzler, Hofmannsthal, and the Austrian Theatre*, p. 116.

50 See Yates, *Schnitzler, Hofmannsthal, and the Austrian Theatre*, for Schnitzler's multi-sided female characters (p. 124).

choice of title (discussed further below) as well as the odd textual addition – Genia's ironic dismissal of the final duel as a 'deadly serious business' (*Dall.*, p. 140), for example. Of greater significance for *Undiscovered Country*, the programme notes included the following two quotations from Johnston's *The Austrian Mind* (1972), which were set out, in isolation, in white text against a black background:

> On duelling:
>
> The code of honour, which Schopenhauer called a code for fools, dogged officers . . . Although the duel had died out in England before 1850, in Austria-Hungary until 1911 a challenge by one officer to another imposed a sacred obligation. An officer who declined a challenge would lose his commission, besides being cut dead in good society. (pp. 53–54)
>
> On the Austrian attitude to death:
>
> Viennese literati who around 1900 frequented coffeehouses and wrote *feuilletons* shared a preoccupation with evanescence, especially with its definitive form – death . . . Fascinated by decay, these unemployed sons of the upper and middle classes carried Baroque reverence for death to unheard-of extremes. To them death promised release from ennui; in a world gone stale, it alone remains a mighty unknown. (p. 169)

These programme notes represent paratexts to the performed drama, assisting the audience in its reception of an otherwise alien concept. They also draw into Stoppard's adaptation Johnston's conceptual narrative of turn-of-the-century Vienna and Schnitzler's place within it, in particular by stressing Impressionism (implicitly) as the philosophy underlining the play.[51]

A similar explanation of duelling was inserted into the programme for *Dalliance* as part of a more extensive narrative introduction by Hugh Rank, a Jewish migrant to Britain from Vienna. On this occasion, however, Stoppard noticeably intensified the references to death and duelling within the adapted text itself, rendering both themes much more visible than they were in *Liebelei*. As in *Das weite Land*, death is a significant figure in *Liebelei*: a Viennese audience watching at the end of the nineteenth century would have been aware, as soon as Fritz's affair entered the discussion in the opening of the play, that a duel, with potentially fatal consequences, was on the cards. Stoppard ensures the shadow of death is cast as early as possible and in a way that is legible to the modern British audience by adding text and action to the source material and by skewing the translation of certain lines. Fritz is

51 See discussion in Chapter 2 above.

shown practising his shooting before even a word is said on stage; his poor performance, demonstrated by stage directions designed to communicate that 'he is not much of a shot', hints at his future vulnerability (*Dall.*, p. 5).[52] Not long afterwards Stoppard adds a few words to add portent to the otherwise light-hearted atmosphere: Theo explains to Mizi that he only dons his Dragoon uniform 'for funerals' (*Dall.*, p. 11). Thus the omen is delivered whilst also ensuring the audience knows how to read Theodore's appearance in Act 3 wearing his uniform (*Dall.*, p. 50).[53]

Later in Act 1 the Gentleman's arrival is announced by the doorbell ringing, which in turn interrupts Fritz's piano playing (*Liebelei*, p. 955). Stoppard again gives Theo an extra line ('Has somebody shot the piano player?' (*Dall.*, p. 21)), which, whilst riffing on the popular quip 'Don't shoot the piano player', also alerts the audience to the ominous nature of the Gentleman's visit.[54] Christine's explanation to Fritz in Act 2 of how she feels when they are apart – 'Wie verschwunden bist du da für mich, so weit weg . . .' (*Liebelei*, p. 993) – becomes in Stoppard's English: 'You seem so far away it's as if you're dead!' (*Dall.*, p. 41). Each of these otherwise relatively inconsequential additions or alterations makes clearer to a modern British audience what would already have been apparent to Schnitzler's contemporaries. The duel and its code are eventually made explicit and duly derided in a further exchange without equivalent in Schnitzler's text:

> THEODORE: He fought a duel. A matter of honour. He was killed.
> CHRISTINE: Honour? (*Dall.*, p. 51)

The absurdity of the arbitrary rules which have led to Fritz's death are left hanging in Christine's one-word question.

52 Two manuscript fragments dated '7.3.86' and '11.3.86' comprise sketches of the dialogue following on from this shooting practice (*Dalliance*, second typed draft, Container 3.8). In Container 3.9 one of two first pages of a typed draft, both of which are dated 'March '86' and entitled 'Act 1', has in pencil the additional stage direction: 'FRITZ approaches the target and looks for the bullet-hole. He holds the target up to the light. He has evidently missed the target entirely'. This solo pantomime was, therefore, apparently being sketched from the outset of Stoppard's work on *Liebelei*.

53 In the source text Theo appears in Act 3 wearing black, suggestive of mourning (*Liebelei*, p. 1008). Although an audience in Britain today would very probably appreciate this signal, the change to uniform gives a reason for the additional line in Act 1 and therewith the additional foreshadowing of death.

54 Audiences in the Burgtheater in 1895 will have recognized the 'great Viennese actor' Friedrich Mitterwurzer in the part of 'Der Herr' and so have known he was a character of some significance, even if only briefly on stage (Swales, *Arthur Schnitzler*, p. 187). Swales reads 'Der Herr' as an allegorical Death figure and the scene as a modern contextualization of the 'supremely Baroque moment' when Death visits Everyman at the feast (p. 186). It has not proved possible to trace a reliable source for 'Don't shoot the piano player'.

Consideration of the published texts for these two adaptations reveals a marked shift from Stoppard's approach in respect of *Das weite Land* to that adopted with *Liebelei*. The reasons for, and mechanics of, that shift are examined in more detail below. While it is clear that the two productions at the National Theatre represented a significant moment of arrival for Schnitzler in Britain, the timing of the adaptations was far from meaningless in terms of Stoppard's own development. The next section of this chapter assesses the role of Schnitzler's plays in Stoppard's career and in so doing sheds further light on the various forces acting on the genesis of the two adaptations.

Locating Schnitzler in Stoppard's Corpus

Stoppard's involvement in the project of presenting *Das weite Land* at the National Theatre was, at first glance, pure opportunism. Having commissioned a literal translation (a practice examined more closely in the Introduction to this book), the National Theatre initially asked Simon Gray to adapt the text for performance.[55] Gray's withdrawal coincided approximately with Stoppard picking up Peter Wood's copy of the literal translation during the latter's rehearsals of Stoppard's play *Night and Day* in 1978. (He claimed: 'I was just being nosy'.)[56] He certainly was not motivated by 'a long interest in Austria and Austrian drama in general and Schnitzler in particular'.[57] Stoppard has claimed that he writes adaptations 'to keep busy' between his 'personal plays'.[58] That claim is not borne out by any consideration of his corpus as a whole, however, and neither does it ring true when considering *Undiscovered Country* on its own.

Stoppard's practice of borrowing from other texts when writing his own plays has been commented on substantially; he is a renowned recycler and 'textual mingl[er]'.[59] Adapting whole plays by others is, therefore, arguably a

55 Eric Glass to Heinrich Schnitzler, 15.9.1978 (Schn 21/12/16).

56 Mel Gussow, 'Stoppard's Intellectual Cartwheels Now With Music', in *Tom Stoppard in Conversation*, ed. by Delaney, pp. 129–34 (p. 132); first published in the *New York Times*, 29 July 1979, sec. 2, pp. 1 and 22.

57 Gussow, 'Stoppard's Intellectual Cartwheels', p. 132.

58 Shusha Guppy, 'Tom Stoppard: The Art of Theater VII', in *Tom Stoppard in Conversation*, ed. by Delaney, pp. 177–92 (p. 189); first published in *Paris Review*, 109 (Winter 1988), 26–51; Gussow, 'Stoppard's Intellectual Cartwheels', p. 133.

59 Katherine E. Kelly, 'Introduction: Tom Stoppard in Transformation', in *The Cambridge Companion to Tom Stoppard*, ed. by Katherine E. Kelly (Cambridge: Cambridge University Press, 2006), pp. 10–22 (p. 11). See also Harold Bloom, *Dramatists and Dramas* (Philadelphia, PA: Chelsea House, 2005), pp. 273–74; Clive James, 'Count Zero Splits the Infinite: Tom Stoppard's Plays', *Encounter*, 45.5 (November 1975), 68–75 (p. 73); Kinereth Meyer, '"It Is Written": Tom Stoppard and the Drama of the Intertext', *Comparative Drama*, 22 (1989), 105–22.

mere extension of this creative pattern. He takes inspiration from, parodies, repeats and turns to his own purpose the work of others in almost all his 'original' plays. *Travesties* (1974), for example, is framed by a recollected performance of Oscar Wilde's *The Importance of Being Earnest* (1895) but also incorporates text written by the historical figures portrayed in the play and a sonnet by Shakespeare. *Rosencrantz and Guildenstern Are Dead* (1966) re-conceives Shakespeare's *Hamlet* from the perspective of two minor characters, with a large helping of Beckett's *Waiting for Godot*. *The Invention of Love* (1997) riffs on *Three Men in a Boat* (Jerome K. Jerome; 1889) in its treatment of the life and work of the poet A. E. Housman. Against this background of intertextuality it is not surprising that scholars have regarded Stoppard's adaptations as further expressions of the same method, arguing that they should accordingly be positioned 'somewhere near the heart of his oeuvre'.[60] The adaptations can be seen as a more extreme version of the postmodern project legible in his 'original' works, where Stoppard explodes authority and undermines 'modernist notions of univocality' by 'eschewing the impoverished single-voiced master narrative in favour of a more variegated text whose greatest strength lies in its plurality of authorial voices'.[61] It is this aspect of Stoppard's writing, his openness to multivocality, that is legible in concrete form when the preparatory notes and drafts for his adaptations are considered in detail, as shown later in this chapter.

Stoppard wrote his adaptation of *Das weite Land* between *Travesties* (1974) and *The Real Thing* (1982), two plays which, according to one commentator, 'best exemplify the drama of the intertext as a means of engagement'.[62] Indeed, just as *Travesties* is framed metatheatrically, *The Real Thing* takes its audience (after a deceptive first act) through 'a series of plays within plays' which include August Strindberg's *Miss Julie* (1888), John Ford's *'Tis Pity She's a Whore* (1633) and Shakespeare's *Othello* (1622).[63] *Undiscovered Country* can thus be seen as being firmly lodged within Stoppard's pattern of intertextual borrowing. The chronology of production is also significant because of the turning point marked by *The Real Thing*, which demonstrates a more openly emotional aspect to Stoppard's writing, one continued in *Arcadia* (1993), *Indian Ink* (1995) and *The Invention of Love* (1997).[64] Far from merely filling

60 Schippers, 'Stoppard's Nestroy, Schnitzler's Stoppard', p. 250; see also Meyer, 'Tom Stoppard and the Drama of the Intertext', p. 119 n. 2; Hesse, 'Rediscovered Country', p. 172.

61 Todd F. Davis and Kenneth Womack, 'Reading (and Writing) the Ethics of Authorship: "Shakespeare in Love" as Postmodern Metanarrative', *Literature/Film Quarterly*, 32 (2004), 153–62 (p. 154).

62 Meyer, 'Tom Stoppard and the Drama of the Intertext', p. 107.

63 Meyer, 'Tom Stoppard and the Drama of the Intertext', p. 113.

64 Hersh Zeifman, 'The Comedy of Eros: Stoppard in Love', in *The Cambridge Companion to Tom Stoppard*, ed. by Kelly, pp. 185–200 (p. 185); Enoch Brater, 'Tom Stoppard's Brit/lit/

the gaps in Stoppard's flow of inspiration, his adaptation of *Das weite Land*, at least, appears to play the part of a bridge, continuing and extending the textual appropriation already well established in the earlier works whilst also acting as a springboard to the play which would move the corpus in a thematically new direction.[65] Thus in Henry's pronouncements on the true nature of love (*The Real Thing*, Act 2, scenes 7 and 9) we hear echoes of Mauer's protest against Genia's attempted treatment of love as a game: 'A game? Oh yes, if that's how it was played!' (*UC*, p. 135). Similarly, the numerous infidelities of *The Real Thing* recall the never-ending cycle of marital deception in *Undiscovered Country*; and arguably in Henry's dedication to Annie (in the face of her cheating) we can sense the influence of Genia's integrity and commitment to Friedrich. *Undiscovered Country* even anticipates (or possibly informs) Stoppard's metatheatrical deployment of playwright (Henry) and actresses (Charlotte and Annie) in the figures of Albert Rhon (the writer of 'a tragedy' in Act 3) and Mrs Meinhold von Aigner (Otto's mother, an actress), although, as already noted, putting plays within plays was already a favourite Stoppard technique before *Undiscovered Country*.

Dalliance likewise fits into the new trend of Stoppard's more emotional writing, once more giving him the themes of 'real' love versus flirtation and of infidelity's ill effects to bend to his own will. In *Dalliance* Stoppard turns the material into something more self-consciously melodramatic than in its original constitution, distancing the audience from the emotion by reflecting the Christine-Fritz story through an operetta playing simultaneously in the background. In this respect, among others, the second Schnitzler adaptation is altogether more 'Stoppardian'.[66] Copyright had ended four years earlier (in 1982), so that Stoppard could act with a far freer hand and, as demonstrated above, his own voice comes through more clearly in the published text: his love of wordplay, his addition of incongruous allusions, his penchant for

---

crit', in *The Cambridge Companion to Tom Stoppard*, ed. by Kelly, pp. 203–12 (p. 207). See Anthony Jenkins for an alternative view of *The Real Thing* as presenting a 'familiar conflict [in Stoppard's work] between reason and feeling and the latter's ultimate victory' (Anthony Jenkins, *The Theatre of Tom Stoppard* (Cambridge: Cambridge University Press, 1989), p. 166).

65 Cf. Schippers, who goes further in suggesting that Schnitzler 'as an expert guide [...] had invaluable services to render on this first major reconnaissance into the undiscovered country of marital relations, which, now ready for the real thing, Stoppard then proceeded to explore on his own' (Schippers, 'Stoppard's Nestroy, Schnitzler's Stoppard', p. 267). See also Hermione Lee, who considers *The Real Thing* to be 'haunted' by *Undiscovered Country*, which play had a 'powerful after-effect' on Stoppard (Hermione Lee, *Tom Stoppard: A Life* (Faber & Faber: London, 2020), p. 413).

66 For a succinct discussion of 'Stoppardianism' see Demastes, *The Cambridge Introduction to Tom Stoppard*, pp. 1–4.

metatheatrical references and his 'proclivity for disguises and costume changes' are all indulged in *Dalliance*.[67] The noticeable shift in attitude to the source text (acknowledged by Stoppard in his confession of having taken 'bolder liberties' with *Dalliance* than with *Undiscovered Country*) is attributable also to his own scepticism about the play:[68] whereas he described *Undiscovered Country* as 'remarkable',[69] he was not 'all that keen on' *Liebelei*.[70] Finally, Stoppard was almost certainly aware of the more substantial heritage *Liebelei* already enjoyed in the UK, with existing translations having been produced on stage in 1909, aired by the BBC in the 1930s, 1940s, 1950s and 1960s and adapted for television broadcast in 1954 and a new translation by Charles Osborne having been published in 1982.[71] The combination of disenchantment, legal freedom and literary precedent meant that Stoppard and Peter Wood (once more directing) together felt able to make quite radical changes to the play.

A quick survey of the other two adaptations written by Stoppard in the same period provides further context to the production of *Undiscovered Country* and *Dalliance*. In 1981 Stoppard adapted Johann Nestroy's nineteenth-century play *Einen Jux will er sich machen* as *On the Razzle*; three years later Stoppard adapted Ferenc Molnár's *Játék a Kastélyban* (1926) as *Rough Crossings* (1984). Both plays were farces (both originally and as treated by Stoppard) and had been successfully translated and produced prior to Stoppard's interpretations (as *The Matchmaker/Hello Dolly!* and *The Play's the Thing*). Seen as a collection of four (as they were by Faber & Faber when published together in 1999), the two Schnitzler adaptations stand out as the weightier dramas.[72] By contrast to the Nestroy and Molnár plays, Schnitzler's works provide Stoppard with a testing ground for applying his skills to psychologically, morally and emotionally demanding dramas. Just as Stoppard undoubtedly played a key

67 Guy Stern, 'From Austria to America', pp. 174–81; Hesse, 'Rediscovered Country', p. 174.

68 Stoppard, 'Introduction', p. x.

69 Gussow, 'Stoppard's Intellectual Cartwheels', p. 132. See also *Peter Hall's Diaries*, in which Stoppard is quoted as saying of *Undiscovered Country*: 'Working on the play, [...] I often felt as if I were driving up the M1 in a Triumph Stag and finding myself overtaken by a 1922 Bentley' (*Peter Hall's Diaries: The Story of a Dramatic Battle*, ed. by John Goodwin (London: Hamish Hamilton, 1983), p. 446).

70 Colvin, 'The Real Tom Stoppard'.

71 The programme notes for the National Theatre production include references to the production of *Light o' Love* at His Majesty's Theatre, the staging by the Vienna Burgtheater in 1973 as part of Peter Daubeny's World Theatre Seasons at the Aldwych and the film adaptations, including that by Ophüls (1933) and 'a French version with Romy Schneider' in 1958 (*Christine*, directed by Pierre Gaspard-Huit) (Container 79.16).

72 Tom Stoppard, *Tom Stoppard: Plays 4* (London: Faber & Faber, 1999). The edition also included Stoppard's adaptation of *Chayka* [*The Seagull*] by Anton Chekhov, which had been produced in 1997 and so falls outside the relatively narrow period considered here, i.e., 1979 to 1986.

role in bringing Schnitzler to London, there is a strong case for arguing that Schnitzler was an important companion to Stoppard through a pivotal phase in his development as a writer. Moreover, Schnitzler's continued significance to Stoppard is apparent from the latter's most recent play, *Leopoldstadt* (2020), in which there are clear intertextual references to *Reigen* and *Liebelei* and, indeed, to Schnitzler himself.[73]

Traces of Collaboration and Multiplicity

The genesis of Stoppard's title 'Undiscovered Country' presents in microcosm the methods and agents involved in transforming *Das weite Land* into its English 'version'. It accordingly seems a sensible focus through which to begin substantiating the above arguments about the collaborative nature of translating Schnitzler, as well as highlighting once more the role of the title as a paratext guiding the audience through the play. The original title, *Das weite Land*, is best understood by reference to its appearance in the body of the source play. Doktor von Aigner, the director of the hotel in which Act 3 is set, reflects on the love affair which led to the end of his marriage. He tries to explain his seemingly irrational actions to the industrialist Friedrich Hofreiter by invoking the complicated nature of humankind:

> Sollt' es Ihnen noch nicht aufgefallen sein, was für komplizierte Subjekte wir Menschen im Grunde sind? So vieles hat zugleich Raum in uns – ! Liebe und Trug . . . Treue und Treulosigkeit . . . Anbetung für die eine und Verlangen nach einer andern oder nach mehreren. Wir versuchen wohl Ordnung in uns zu schaffen, so gut es geht, aber diese Ordnung ist doch nur etwas Künstliches . . . Das Natürliche . . . ist das Chaos. Ja [. . .], die Seele . . . ist ein weites Land, wie ein Dichter es einmal ausdrückte . . . Es kann übrigens auch ein Hoteldirektor gewesen sein. (*DwL*, p. 281)

Aigner's only means of explaining himself is to 'take refuge in the [. . .] idea that man has room for all manner of contradictory responses which make clarity and commitment in human affairs well-nigh impossible'.[74] For J. P. Stern this is the 'message Schnitzler intends to convey', namely that 'every man's soul is an enigma, to himself and to those around him' and that therefore '[n]o one can foretell how he will react to the other and to each emerging event'.[75] Austrian and German audiences watching the play in 1911 (and subsequently) will have

73 Tom Stoppard, *Leopoldstadt* (London: Faber & Faber, 2020), pp. 5, 6–7, 11–12, 26–27, 28–30, 38–39. See also Lee, *Tom Stoppard*, pp. 848–51.

74 Swales, 'Schnitzler's Tragi-comedy', p. 240.

75 J. P. Stern, 'Anyone for Tennis?', p. 29.

heard echoes of Fontane's *Effi Briest* (1895) (hence the 'Dichter'), in which Effi's father answers moral dilemmas by referring to 'ein weites Feld' and so avoids committing himself when he might otherwise feel conflicted.[76] Meanwhile the meatiness of the philosophy summed up in the phrase regurgitated by Aigner finds its counterweight in the possibility that it was a mere hotel director who first pronounced it.

Schnitzler set out, in an undated note, his response to what he considered a misunderstanding about the title: 'Das weite Land' was *not* a statement about pure chaos, in which no laws govern the action of the drama, but about the limits of possibility. He maintained: 'Das meint nicht, das als ein Gebiet absoluter Gesetzlosigkeit und Willkür aufzufassen, sondern dass die Grenzen der Möglichkeiten im allgemeinen viel weiter gesteckt sind als die Menschen im allgemeinen wissen oder als die Meisten aus Bequemlichkeit sich eingestehen'.[77] Heinrich Schnitzler had his own thoughts about the meaning of the title and duly protested over suggestions made by the BBC for its radio adaptation in 1972. The BBC's preferred title, *The Uncharted Sea*, implied 'the possibility that [the sea] can [...] be [...], mapped', by contrast to 'the original title [...] [which] suggests a vastness that can never be charted, or explored'.[78] Heinrich Schnitzler argued instead for 'The Vast Domain' or 'The Vast Land', the former having been used when the play was first published in English in 1923. Notwithstanding his opprobrium, the BBC went ahead with its initial plan and the play was broadcast as *Uncharted Sea*.

Stoppard's English title for the play removes the work even further from its perceived frame of reference and hands it over to a different, English poet. 'Undiscovered Country' is borrowed from Shakespeare's monologue for his eponymous hero in *Hamlet* beginning, 'To be, or not to be'. The 'undiscover'd country' refers to death, 'from whose bourn | No traveller returns' (*Hamlet*, III. 1. 78–80).[79] Aigner's line in the published English text thus becomes: 'Yes, [...],

76 Reinhard H. Thum, 'Symbol, Motif and Leitmotif in Fontane's Effi Briest', *The Germanic Review*, 54 (1979), 115–24 (p. 118). As well as the father's phrase, Thum identifies two themes linked to Effi which operate as repeated motifs: a swing and the need for light and air (p. 118). The two themes coincide when Effi's mother comments: 'Effi, eigentlich hättest du doch wohl Kunstreiterin werden müssen. Immer am Trapez, immer Tochter der Luft' (Theodor Fontane, *Effi Briest*, 3rd edn (Munich: Deutscher Taschenbuch Verlag, 1987), p. 8). A further intertextual reference might accordingly be found in the figure of Erna Wahl in *Das weite Land*, who, according to her mother, loves to walk a psychological tightrope and chases the thrill of high mountain climbing.

77 Arthur Schnitzler, Undated Note (CUL, A20,10).

78 Heinrich Schnitzler to Eric Glass, 7.5.1972 (Schn 21/9/68).

79 Stoppard's title is not his only reference to Shakespeare. See also 'Friends, Romans and Countrymen!' (*UC*, p. 124). A *Hamlet* allusion in Schnitzler's text ('wenn es auf Erden nach Verdienst ginge' (*DwL*, p. 250)) does not reach the published edition of *Undiscovered Country*, although Stoppard did experiment with adding 'who would "scape whipping"; etcetera?'

the soul . . . is an undiscovered country as the poet once said . . . though it could equally well have been the manager of a hotel' (*UC*, p. 112). Guy Stern has argued that the title chosen by Stoppard announces the latter's intention to 'maximize Schnitzler's game of sex, love, and death and minimize psychological explorations'.[80] Similarly, Richard Corballis sees the title choice as reflecting Stoppard's resistance to the enterprise of psychological probing: 'A vast country can be explored but an undiscovered one cannot'.[81] Corballis's assessment therefore appears to run counter to Heinrich Schnitzler's understanding of what a 'vast country' might or might not entail. J. P. Stern draws the focus back to death, interpreting the title as an indication that Stoppard understood 'that the most interesting issue is not the enigmatic unpredictability of people's souls but the profound attraction of death'.[82] Most recently, Beatrix Hesse reads the *Hamlet* reference as coinciding with Schnitzler's original comment on the soul: the quotation suggests 'a metaphorical country that has remained undiscovered because the explorers have never returned – you only find out what it is like once you get there. And this is perfectly in tune with what Schnitzler says about the human soul'.[83] Such a reading presumably relies upon a definition of 'soul' which limits it to the dead, whereas there is every reason to believe that Schnitzler's 'soul' refers to part of lived experience. In any event, sight of the drafts for Stoppard's adaptation, alongside Heinrich Schnitzler's correspondence on the topic, provides a view of the genesis of the title which undermines an interpretative regime restricted solely to Schnitzler and Stoppard; it is in this vein of exploration that this chapter proceeds.

The first feature of the drafts to note is that Stoppard used a literal translation of the play by an unknown translator before embarking on his own attempt. Stoppard cannot read German and has been transparent about his reliance on others when adapting foreign-language plays.[84] In this case, the literal translation provided as a provisional title 'The Open Country'. Heinrich Schnitzler must have caught wind of this first idea, as he was quick to voice his disapproval of a title he considered 'entirely misleading' and to stress that he would 'insist on being shown [Stoppard's] adaptation'.[85] The practice of commissioning an established playwright to adapt from a literal

when drafting (see first typed draft, *Undiscovered Country*, February 1979 (Container 32.3, p. 81); and further typed draft, n.d. (Container 32.5, p. 61)). See Shakespeare, *Hamlet*, II. 2. 524–25: 'Use every man after his desert, and who should 'scape whipping?'.

80 Guy Stern, 'From Austria to America', p. 71.

81 Richard Corballis, *Stoppard: The Mystery and the Clockwork* (Oxford: Amber Lane Press; New York: Methuen, 1984), p. 175.

82 J. P. Stern, 'Anyone for Tennis?', p. 29.

83 Hesse, 'Rediscovered Country', p. 173.

84 Guppy, 'Tom Stoppard: The Art of Theater VII', p. 189.

85 Heinrich Schnitzler to Eric Glass, 3.2.1979 (Schn 21/12/18).

translation of a foreign-language play is far from unusual in contemporary theatre productions.[86] Indeed, the BBC radio adaptation must also have been based on a literal translation, given that Ronald Adam, like Stoppard, did not speak German.[87] Often unbeknown to the audience the script performed is the result of a collaborative effort from (at least) two contributors: translator and playwright. Stoppard's method of adapting *Das weite Land* took this approach a step further: not only do his papers include a copy of *The Vast Domain*, so that we might assume he at least included the translation from 1923 in his preparatory reading, but he also enjoyed the services of a German linguist, John Harrison. Stoppard has described working with Harrison as follows:

> Together – he with the German text, I with the English – we went through the play line by line, during which process small corrections were made and large amounts of light were shed on the play I had before me. After several weeks of splitting hairs with Harrison over alternatives for innumerable words and phrases, the shadings of language began to reveal themselves. (*UC*, p. ix)

The drafts themselves reveal that Harrison's 'words and phrases' often survive Stoppard's almost relentless revisions to make it into the printed playscript. His handwriting can be identified at several stages in the process of adaptation, often accompanied by a backwards tick to represent Stoppard's approval. Harrison's, then, is a further voice audible in *Undiscovered Country*.

Pursuing further the enquiry into the genesis of the title, the literal translation and first draft provide concise material evidence of broader contributions made to the English 'version'. The literal translator, having suggested 'The Open Country' on the title page, adds, in the context of Aigner's reflections in Act 3, 'A BIG COUNTRY', with a note to compare that phrase with the title.[88] In pencilled marginalia alongside those words, and doubtless informed by Harrison's reading of the source text, Stoppard has noted 'psyche' and 'human spirit' (most likely as alternatives to 'the soul' forming the first half of the line) and 'vast'. By the time the first draft had been typed, the new provisional title, 'THE UNDISCOVERED COUNTRY', had replaced the literal translator's suggestion.[89] Stoppard's drafting practice involves sketching out the dialogue in hurried handwriting, which he then

86 See Susan Bassnett, 'Theatre and Opera', in *The Oxford Guide to Literature in English Translation*, ed. by Peter France (Oxford: Oxford University Press, 2000), pp. 96–103 (p. 100); Brodie, 'Indirect Translation', p. 340.

87 Adam, *Overture and Beginners*, p. 161.

88 Literal translation of *Das weite Land*, Act 3, p. 38 (Container 31.2).

89 First typed draft, *Undiscovered Country*, February 1979 (Container 32.3).

dictates (to his typist), filling in the stage directions as he goes.[90] This is presumably what took place between the initial consultation of the literal translation with Harrison and the production of the first typed draft. However, the typed title cannot have survived for long: Stoppard has drawn a line through the typed words and played with his own alternatives – 'The Importance of Being Erna' and 'Anyone for Tennis?' – as well as three suggested by Harrison (and in Harrison's handwriting on the page), namely 'Uncharted Areas', 'Unexplored Territory' and 'Match Point'. Finally, Stoppard has drawn a line through all the pencilled ideas and reverted, by re-printing in capital letters, to 'THE UNDISCOVERED COUNTRY'. The excision of 'The' from the typed title two drafts later differentiates it from previous texts with the same title[91] and this marks the moment the play acquired the name by which it is now known.[92]

Although 'Undiscovered Country' might well have emerged from Stoppard's penchant for recycling Shakespeare's words, the drafts show a process of collaborative experimentation and play engaged in by both the playwright and his German-language consultant as a means of reaching a solution. The Stoppard Papers also flag up the multiple voices distinguishable in the playscript, as clearly made visible in the microcosm of the sketched title. Not only can we see Harrison's direct input (in the pencilled suggestions on the draft and later in the concrete words and phrases adopted in the printed playscript), but we are also reminded of the influence of Oscar Wilde ('The Importance of Being Erna') and hear echoes of previous translators: Ronald Adam ('Uncharted Sea'); Caro and Woticky (the 'vast' annotating the literal translation); and, of course, the anonymous literal translator ('The Open Country' and 'The Big Country').

At the same time Heinrich Schnitzler's role as trustee of the estate cannot be missed, even if only through the absence of any radical alteration to the body of the text rather than through the presence of any particular trait. We might infer from what Stoppard has said of *Undiscovered Country* that he was aware of the control exercised from Vienna: although 'considerably shorter' than the source, *Undiscovered Country* was 'very faithful in most respects'; and Stoppard recognized that *Das weite Land* was 'not to be monkeyed about with'.[93] The very apparent sense of freedom he felt when later adapting *Liebelei* also hints at the corresponding constraint which had bound him before the

90 Guppy, 'Tom Stoppard: The Art of Theater VII', p. 185.

91 See, for example, Stephen McKenna, *The Undiscovered Country* (London: Hutchinson, 1932); Julian Mitchell, *The Undiscovered Country* (London: Constable, 1968).

92 Typed draft, *Undiscovered Country*, '~~April 1979~~' [*sic*] (Container 32.7).

93 Gussow, 'Stoppard's Intellectual Cartwheels', p. 133; Guppy, 'Tom Stoppard: The Art of Theater VII', p. 190.

expiry of copyright when writing in 1979.[94] However, perhaps the strongest evidence for Heinrich Schnitzler's hold on the process comes from his correspondence with Eric Glass, which includes a copy of the contract, dated 8 June 1979 but not in fact agreed until 26 July 1979.[95] That contract records the 'OWNERS' having approved the 'version' prepared by the 'ADAPTOR' as a preliminary to the assignment of any rights to produce or publish the same.[96] Returning to the title page of Stoppard's first draft for *Undiscovered Country*, and taking into consideration the ancillary evidence from Stoppard's and Heinrich Schnitzler's respective papers and published comments, it is possible to discern not one or two authors determining the text, but a whole team of diachronic and synchronic contributors.

There can be no doubt that Stoppard's attitude to *Liebelei* was quite different from his attitude to *Das weite Land*. The reasons for that change, and its manifestations in the published text, have already been set out above. What did not vary, however, was Stoppard's method of re-working the source text for English performance: the drafts for *Dalliance* disclose Stoppard tackling the job of adaptation in much the same way as he had in 1979. Although on this occasion not assisted by the linguist John Harrison, he was able to effect a similar triangulation strategy using a detailed, scholarly, literal translation by the respected dramaturg and translator Antony Vivis (including footnotes to explain linguistic, historical and cultural idiosyncrasies),[97] together with one of the existing published translations, *Playing with Love* (1914) by P. Morton Shand.[98] Vivis's translation had been especially commissioned for Stoppard at the latter's request:

> [I]f it is not too expensive for the N[ational] T[heater] it really would be awfully helpful to have a literal translation commissioned. The English version I have will provide one co-ordinate but I would feel more secure if I had the other one as well, because the former may well have taken some liberties of which I would not be aware.[99]

As with *Undiscovered Country*, close examination of the English sources alongside the drafts reveals Stoppard's adoption of whole phrases, or even

94 See *UC*, p. x; Guy Stern, 'From Austria to America', p. 181; Spencer, 'Translating Schnitzler for the stage'.

95 Eric Glass to Heinrich Schnitzler, 26.7.1979 (Schn 21/12/31/1).

96 Memorandum of Agreement between Tom Stoppard and Heinrich Schnitzler (not signed), 8.6.1979 (Schn 21/12/31/5).

97 Literal translation of *Liebelei* by Anthony Vivis (Container 79.7). As with *Undiscovered Country*, this translation was commissioned by the National Theatre for subsequent adaptation. Vivis was not credited with the literal translation in *Dalliance and Undiscovered Country* or in the National Theatre programme for *Dalliance*.

98 For more details of the translation by P. Morton Shand see Chapter 1.

99 Tom Stoppard to John Russell Brown, 5 August 1985 (Container 131.3).

longer passages of dialogue, from his collaborators. Once more the concept of a single author (already undermined by the very exercise of interlingual adaptation) is thrown into question by the obvious multiplicity of contributors to the playscript.

There are, however, slight variations in Stoppard's treatment of his two English-language source texts. Vivis's translation, for example, has hardly been annotated by Stoppard. His is a 'thick' translation, oriented towards the adapting playwright and hence full of cultural and historical explanations which might assist Stoppard better to understand Schnitzler's play.[100] For example, an asterisk after the title *Liebelei* directs the reader to an expansive translation, which ultimately provides Stoppard with his own title: '[L]iterally: "Love affair", "dalliance", "amour". Can be extended to cover the state of "Being in love with love", "Playing at love", "romance" or "philandering" rather than loving in the deep emotional sense'. In the event of any uncertainty or ambiguity, Stoppard was in direct contact with Vivis and so could have sought clarification.[101] The service provided by Vivis and his literal translation accordingly resembles the role played by John Harrison in respect of *Undiscovered Country* more closely than that played by the anonymous literal translator in the latter case. A reading of the published *Dalliance* alongside Vivis's text highlights the many occasions when Stoppard lifted straight from the literal translation: Stoppard's text is littered with lines that are exact or almost-exact replicas of the words provided by Vivis. A further significant departure from Stoppard's practice with *Undiscovered Country* was his reliance on the existing published translation for *Dalliance*. Notwithstanding the criticism which has been levelled at Shand's work, Stoppard adopted innumerable words, phrases and even whole sentences from the seventy-year-old translation of *Liebelei*.[102] The

100 See Kwame Anthony Appiah, 'Thick Translation', in *The Translation Studies Reader*, ed. by Venuti, pp. 389–401.

101 Antony Vivis to Tom Stoppard, 15.1.1986 (Container 80.2).

102 See, for example, Robert Cushman, who describes Shand's translation as 'ludicrously bad' (Robert Cushman, Review of *Dalliance, Plays International*, July 1986, p. 26); and Kevin Bartholomew and Katja Krebs, who found it 'irritating', 'absurd', 'stilted and lacking in sophistication' (Kevin Bartholomew and Katja Krebs, 'Arthur Schnitzler 1862–1931: Austrian Dramatist, Novelist and Short-Story Writer', in *Encyclopedia of Literary Translation into English*, ed. by Olive Class, 2 vols (London: FitzRoy Dearborn, 2000), II, 1241–43 (p. 1243). Heinrich Schnitzler also once 'recalled' the Shand translation as being 'horrid' (Heinrich Schnitzler to Eric Glass, 8.2.1954 (Schn 21/5/45)). One of Stoppard's reasons for relying more heavily on the existing published translation on this occasion might have been nervousness about sticking too closely to the literal translation. On 22 November 1984 John Faulkner, an Associate Producer at the National Theatre, had warned Stoppard: 'We have had one or two problems recently with literal translators who objected to what they thought were parts of their literal appearing in the final version' (John Faulkner to Tom Stoppard, 22.11.1984 (Container 131.3)).

mass of textual cross-overs between *Dalliance*, Vivis's translation and Shand's *Playing with Love* demonstrate the multi-authored nature of the playscript sent out to director and company for rehearsal.

Conceptions of Authorship in the Critical Reception

How were the two National Theatre productions received by their professional audiences? Were there differences in response between the pre- and post-copyright adaptations by Stoppard? The critical reception of *Undiscovered Country* presents the authorship of the play in relatively traditional terms, limited to only one writer, Arthur Schnitzler, assisted in his arrival on the British stage (or not, according to some reviewers) by Tom Stoppard. John Barber's review of the opening night, for example, may have included praise for a 'spring-heeled translation' by Stoppard, but it stressed that the real interest of the play lay in 'Schnitzler's clinical probing into the complexity of his people'.[103] This reviewer, at least, clearly considered it Schnitzler's play and not Stoppard's. Similarly, in Michael Billington's celebratory review (he considered it 'a theatrical feast'), the only reference made to Stoppard's part in the production was to the 'verbal felicity' of his 'version'.[104] A number of reviewers took up the 'undiscovered' element of the title to interrogate the neglect Schnitzler had previously suffered in Great Britain. The anonymous reviewer for the *Mid Sussex Times* considered it:

> astonishing that Schnitzler has over the years been so neglected here and the dust allowed to gather on his collected works. [...] why should the Austrian be almost as undiscovered as the human country that he wrote about with such understanding?[105]

Hugh Rank drew attention to the poor precursors to this production: besides Ophüls's *La Ronde*, on which Schnitzler's reputation abroad was founded, there had been only 'a lifeless BBC/TV series [...] which did not do him justice. Then a short run of Anatol at the Open Space in London'.[106] Stoppard's 'version' was largely regarded as an English vehicle for Schnitzler's talent; Schnitzler was the true author.

103 John Barber, 'Tragi-comical study of a philanderer', *Daily Telegraph*, 21 June 1979, p. 15. Reviews referred to in this section can be found in the National Theatre Archive, RNT/PR/4/1/181 (for *Undiscovered Country*) and RNT/PR/4/1/349 (for *Dalliance*).

104 Michael Billington, 'Vintage Wiener Schnitzler', *Guardian*, 21 June 1979, p. 12.

105 Anon., *Mid Sussex Times*, 24 August 1979.

106 Hugh Rank, '"My distrust in matters of love was universal. Faithfulness in lovers, to say nothing of married couples, was at best a lucky coincidence" – Schnitzler' (*Guardian*, 19 June 1979, p. 8).

Responses to Stoppard's influence, where acknowledged, were mixed. Jack Tinker commended Stoppard for his 'quick-witted and mellifluous adaptation';[107] and Peter Jenkins found that 'the wit of Tom Stoppard, who is credited with more than a translation of Arthur Schnitzler's original, is audible'.[108] By contrast, Peter Bennett was sceptical about the adaptor's voice in the final product: 'Between the sombre bits the evening flashes with brittle cynicism. My guess is that the best of it is Schnitzler's in origin, more or less faithfully rendered'.[109] Michael Walker was rankled by 'the dichotomy between what is obviously a period piece and Stoppard's contemporary dialogue';[110] whereas others clearly considered Stoppard's influence minimal, limited to 'one or two jokes that are [...] more Stoppard than Schnitzler'.[111] In an otherwise scathing review in *Plays & Players*, John Russell Taylor applauded the 'sensible English version by Tom Stoppard, who, a couple of Stoppardish one-liners notwithstanding, does not seem to obtrude himself noticeably on the text'.[112] Steve Grant, on the other hand, referred to 'Stoppard's deft though occasionally intrusive adaptation';[113] and Robert Cushman noted that the character of Hofreiter seemed to have 'absorbed something of Mr Stoppard', not least when speaking about 'all that fagging and cricket' in English public schools.[114]

Whereas some reviewers found any element of contemporaneity in the production jarring, others praised the play's capacity to speak across time and space. Kenneth Hurren, for example, wrote that 'apart from a few local references and mores, it could as easily have been set in the Home Counties'.[115] Peter Jenkins found it 'so chimes with the spirit of the times that it could have been commissioned yesterday'. In his view, '*Undiscovered Country* achieves simultaneously the status of a fin de siècle period piece and an exploration of human behaviour which is utterly modern and contemporary'.[116] Jack Tinker was overwhelmed to find 'that the dilemmas [Schnitzler] sets his characters have lost none of their potency'.[117] Finally, Billington was drawn to conclude with the pun: 'Old Wien [...] goes well in new bottles'.[118] The play was not of

107 Jack Tinker, 'Grand National', *Daily Mail*, 22 June 1979, p. 26.
108 Peter Jenkins, 'Theatre', *Spectator*, 7 July 1979, n. pag.
109 Peter Bennett, 'Upstage', *Gay News*, 12–25 July 1979, p. 34.
110 Michael Walker, 'Mesmerising Discovery', *Chelsea News* and *Chelsea Post*, 6 July 1979, n. pag.
111 Ian Stewart, *Country Life*, 19 July 1979, n. pag.
112 John Russell Taylor, *Plays & Players*, July 1979, n. pag.
113 Steve Grant, *Time Out*, 28 June 1979, n. pag.
114 Robert Cushman, 'Wenching in Old Austria', *Observer*, 24 June 1979, p. 14.
115 Kenneth Hurren, *What's On IN LONDON*, 29 June 1979.
116 Peter Jenkins, 'Theatre', *Spectator*, 7 July 1979.
117 Tinker, 'Grand National', p. 26.
118 Billington, 'Vintage Wiener Schnitzler'.

value merely for its anthropological interest; it had theatrical relevance to a modern, British audience.[119]

A general pattern materializes from the newspaper reviews summarized above, albeit a pattern with its inevitable discrepancies and anomalies: Stoppard's labour is secondary; the play's timelessness, when it works, is down to the genius of Schnitzler; only when the play feels too modern is responsibility attributed to the anachronistic dialogue imposed by Stoppard. Meaning and narrative force are perceived to be in the hands of the original author. Stoppard merely engineers the conduit – one ornamented with sparkling wordplay, perhaps, but a conduit nonetheless. Even more striking, however, is the fact that none of the reviews was concerned with Stoppard's lack of German and the gap that was left between source text and 'version'. Perhaps this is unsurprising given that the programme notes for the production say nothing about either the literal translation or John Harrison's role (an omission admittedly corrected in Stoppard's introduction to the published script). Heinrich Schnitzler, having approved the script sent to him in April 1979, attended the première and found it 'an excellent production'. Stoppard's translation had, according to Heinrich Schnitzler, 'contributed – of course – immeasurably to the impact of the play'.[120] Implicit in that praise is a similar assessment of authorship to that of the reviewers: Stoppard had *helped* to place Schnitzler on the stage at the National Theatre. In the eyes of the press and the trustee of the literary estate, the lone genius remained happily alone.

The critical response to *Dalliance* was generally more negative and more Stoppard-oriented. At worst, the play was regarded as too 'slight' or 'modest' to warrant production at the National Theatre; and thematically it was considered out of sync with the modern age, in which 'women are emancipated and no longer treated as sexual playthings'.[121] Milton Shulman was certainly of this view:

> The Viennese were disturbed by the sight of unchaperoned girls in a bachelor flat, shocked by the tolerance of Christine's father over the affair, intrigued about the ethics of duelling and unbridgeable class barriers.
>
> None of these matters interests us very much in our permissive, classless times, and what we are left with is a charming dramatic bauble floating in the shallow waters of the Danube.[122]

Similarly, Megan Theobald reflected that '[t]hough it must have been a daring exposé of *fin de siècle* morals when first produced in 1895, Dalliance

119 Michael Billington, 'A penchant for foreign affairs', *Guardian*, 23 June 1979, p. 11.

120 Heinrich Schnitzler to Eric Glass, 28.6.79 (Schn 21/12/24).

121 'Curtain Up', *Today*, 8 June 1986, p. 34; and 'DSC', *London Weekly Diary*, 15 June 1986.

122 Milton Shulman, 'That Fritz is a Cad', *London Evening Standard*, 26 May 1986, p. 30.

now seems fairly inconsequential'.[123] Perhaps David Shannon summed up the overriding sentiment most snappily in his review for *Today*: 'Times and filth-ratings change. Liebelei is unlikely to shock many people today'.[124] Nevertheless, it was not all doom and gloom. The major national newspapers tended to come out in favour of the adaptation. The reviewer for *The Sunday Telegraph* wrote:

> It is easy to see where Tom Stoppard's nimble wit has sewn sequins on to the already glittering fabric of the original. [...] this is one of the most enjoyable plays in London. One's only regret is that, at less than two hours, it does not go on longer.[125]

Elsewhere Stoppard's adaptation was called 'direct and simple' (*The Daily Mail*), as well as 'expert' (*The Daily Telegraph*), with attention drawn to 'Christine's suicidal agony [...] ironically counterpointed with the romantic flimflam being sung on the boards' (*The Daily Telegraph*), a 'fine theatrical dénouement' (*The Observer*).[126]

By contrast to the reviews for *Undiscovered Country*, Stoppard's name appears with frequency, often in the possessive sense of 'Stoppard's version', 'Stoppard's adaptation' or 'Stoppard's *Dalliance*', as well as being treated, in the review by *The Jewish Chronicle*, as in 'partnership' with Schnitzler.[127] Michael Billington, whilst accepting that the play 'work[ed] well', criticized a morally dubious 'transposition' of Act 3, which he considered 'a violation of Schnitzler's purpose'.[128] Whilst recognizing that it made 'for a short but emotionally affecting evening', he concluded that he still 'prefer[red] Schnitzler's play to Stoppard's'. J. C. Trewin, writing in the *Illustrated London News*, observed that '[i]n making a version for the National company, Tom Stoppard has not gone all the way with Schnitzler': whereas 'Schnitzler saw in *Liebelei* a remorseless tragedy of Christine's true love; in Stoppard's *Dalliance* [...] we have to be uncertain of her future'.[129] The *Sunday Express* reviewer described the play as 'Stoppard's rather flaccid version', while the author of the review in *Midweek* was even more scathing: 'I don't know whether the trendy little gags Stoppard inserts have leeched the real feeling from Schnitzler's play but there doesn't

123 Megan Theobold, 'Left high and dry', *West Herts & Watford Observer*, 6 June 1986.

124 David Shannon, 'Don't lock up your daughters', *Today*, 2 June 1986.

125 Francis King, 'Playing by the rules', *Sunday Telegraph*, 1 June 1986, p. 16.

126 Jack Tinker, 'Here's a girl to break your heart', *Daily Mail*, 28 May 1986, p. 3; John Barber, 'Stoppard worth the wait', *Daily Telegraph*, 19 May 1986, p. 13; Mary Harron, 'Vanessa's calculating Cleopatra', *Observer*, 1 June 1986, p. 21.

127 David Nathan, 'Too much dalliance for the National', *Jewish Chronicle*, 6 June 1986.

128 Michael Billington, 'Fiddling with a game of love: Michael Billington doubts the wisdom of Tom Stoppard's transposition of Schnitzler's play', *Guardian*, 29 May 1986, p. 10.

129 J. C. Trewin, 'The Tragic Dangers of Dalliance', *Illustrated London News*, July 1986.

seem to be much of it left'.[130] Writing for *The Sunday Times*, John Peters did not hold back in his criticism and landed on the same point as Billington: this was Stoppard's, not Schnitzler's, play.[131] Whereas *Undiscovered Country* had clearly been considered Schnitzler's play, with Stoppardian touches, the greater tendency seven years later was to apportion responsibility (and blame) to Stoppard.

The shift in critical perception of authorship from Schnitzler (in 1979) to Stoppard (in 1986) can be mapped in the publishing history of the adaptations. When *Undiscovered Country* was first published (on its own) in 1980 the name 'Arthur Schnitzler' appeared directly under the title at the top of the front cover. Although Stoppard's name appeared in the same size font as Schnitzler's, it was at the bottom of the cover, under the words 'In an English version by'. The image used was a photograph from the National Theatre production, showing Friedrich and Genia seated with Erna and Mrs Wahl standing behind them. By the time *Undiscovered Country* came to be re-published with *Dalliance* in 1986, Schnitzler's name was in a much smaller font and beneath Stoppard's on the front cover. The plays were now 'by' Stoppard and 'adapted from' Schnitzler. The image used, however, was a portrait of Schnitzler. The result is confusing, with Stoppard pitched as author in the printed text but Schnitzler's (to many, unidentifiable) face a counteracting indicator of paternity. Finally, both adaptations were published in 1999 as part of the collected plays of Stoppard, along with three other adaptations (already mentioned above) of plays by Nestroy, Molnár and Chekhov), under the title *Tom Stoppard: Plays 4*. No mention is made on the cover of the writers of the source texts and no image provided to redirect the reader.

It is tempting to explain the trajectory visible in these three publications, and in the critical reception of the two productions, by reference to Stoppard's growing fame and there is undoubtedly some merit in such an assessment. However, additional factors play into the presentation of authorship. Heinrich Schnitzler was able to dictate, to some degree, the terms of publishing *Undiscovered Country* in 1980, specifying in his contract with Stoppard that:

> THE PLAY shall at all times be announced as by ARTHUR SCHNITZLER in first position as sole author of the PLAY to be followed by TOM STOPPARD'S name as author of the English version thereof it being understood that one name should not appear without the other and both names except for the position thereof shall appear in the same size and with equal prominence.[132]

130 Clive Hirschorn, 'Theatre', *Sunday Express*, 1 June 86; and Anonymous, *Midweek*, 12 June 1986.

131 John Peter, 'For Disservices Rendered', *Sunday Times*, 1 June 1986, p. 49.

132 Memorandum of Agreement between Tom Stoppard and Heinrich Schnitzler (not signed), 8.6.1979 (Schn 21/12/31/5).

The National Theatre's commercial alliances and artistic mission would also have informed decisions taken about publishing scripts to coincide with the theatre productions in 1979 and 1986. The collected plays (published in 1999) stand out as having been published independently of any production; and they represent a celebration of Stoppard as writer, his own authority a sufficient balance to the commercial risks taken on by his publisher, Faber & Faber.

Text and Archive

Having assessed the establishment of Arthur Schnitzler's reputation on the stage, it is worth pausing to examine the writer's place in the archive. Schnitzler's notes, sketches and drafts for *Liebelei* are preserved in Vienna and have been incorporated into the *Historisch-kritische Ausgabe*.[133] Those for *Das weite Land* are preserved in Cambridge University Library and were examined in the preparation of a digitally presented critical edition of some of Schnitzler's works.[134] The *Historisch-kritische Ausgabe* and the work carried out by the editors of the digital edition reveal a writing practice which anticipates, to some degree, Tom Stoppard's method of writing, involving widespread alterations, excisions, substitutions and even overlaps between texts.[135] Schnitzler's manuscript drafts were either transcribed directly by the typist or dictated by him, on which occasions he often composed on the hoof.[136] One is reminded of Stoppard's freestyle composition of stage directions into the dictaphone.[137] Schnitzler often read excerpts or whole drafts to his wife Olga and trusted literary friends such as Richard Beer-Hofmann, Hugo von Hofmannsthal, Felix Salten and Gustav Schwarzkopf; and subsequent stages

133 Most of the manuscript material for *Liebelei* is held at the Österreichische Nationalbibliothek; some in the Handschriftenabteilung der Wienbibliothek im Rathaus; and a photograph of a one-page sketch at the Deutsches Literaturarchiv in Marbach (*Liebelei*, p. 6).

134 *Arthur Schnitzler digital*, https://www.arthur-schnitzler.de/edition/genetisch [accessed 29 March 2021].

135 At least three scholars have previously considered the papers for *Das weite Land*: Rudolf Denk, 'Arthur Schnitzlers *Das weite Land*. Theater und Film im Medienvergleich', in *Arthur Schnitzler und der Film*, ed. by Achim Aurnhammer, Barbara Beßlich and Rudolf Denk (Würzburg: Ergon, 2010), pp. 271–95; Rena R. Schlein, 'Das Duellmotiv in Schnitzlers Dramen "Ritterlichkeit," "Das weite Land" und "Das Wort"', *Modern Austrian Literature*, 8 (1975), 222–35; Sol Liptzin, 'The Genesis of Schnitzler's *Das weite Land*', *PMLA*, 46 (1931), 860–66.

136 Wolfgang Lukas and others, 'Editorischer Bericht', para. 3.1.2, 'Zur Praxis des Abschreibens, Diktierens, Korrigierens', in *Arthur Schnitzler digital*, https://www.schnitzler-edition.net/edb [accessed 23.6.21].

137 Guppy, 'Tom Stoppard: The Art of Theater VII', p. 185.

in the writing process were informed by the feedback he received.[138] Again, one thinks of the manifold voices contributing to Stoppard's drafts. We also know that Schnitzler (like Stoppard later) attended rehearsals for the first productions of his plays and hence was involved in making cuts at that point.[139] Finally, there is evidence that Schnitzler continued to revise even published playscripts, adopting an approach to the text which necessarily posited it as never finished and never fixed.[140] Stoppard similarly returned to the published script of *Undiscovered Country* to make substantial revisions for a proposed American teleplay.[141]

The contingent nature of the playscript as understood by Schnitzler makes it possible to read subsequent translations as continuations of the revisions initially carried out by the Austrian playwright. Following that idea to its logical conclusion, then, the drafts preserved among Stoppard's papers in the Harry Ransom Center, The University of Texas at Austin, come to represent a continuation of Schnitzler's own archive, so that it is possible to trace the development of a word or phrase from Vienna in 1908 (when first written) all the way to its rendition in English as recorded in the American archive, where contingency remains a defining feature. Stoppard's papers are a manifestation of his own philosophy that 'plays never quite get finished [...]; they get interrupted by rehearsal. The production impedes a process which then very often continues after that first performance has evolved and gone its way and finished and so on'.[142] At the micro-level, perhaps, some sort of finality is possible – 'Writing your own stuff, you know when a particular speech reaches its final form' – but for Stoppard it is a peculiarity of translation work that even the minutiae of the text are never quite finished: 'Each time you think it's pretty

138 Lukas and others, 'Editorischer Bericht', para. 3.1.3, 'Zur Praxis des Erzählens und Vorlesens', in *Arthur Schnitzler digital*, https://www.schnitzler-edition.net/edb [accessed 23.6.21]; Schnitzler, *Liebelei*, pp. 1–3.

139 For examples of Schnitzler's attendance at rehearsals for *Das weite Land*, see *Tagebuch*, 15.9.1911; 16.9.1911; 18.9.1911; 27.9.1911; 29.9.1911; and 30.9.1911. For references to cuts see *Tagebuch*, 8.6.1911; 2.9.1911; 21.9.1911; and 12.10.1911.

140 See Annja Neumann, 'Entstehungsgeschichte von "Zum großen Wurstel"', in Arthur Schnitzler, *Marionetten*, ed. by Annja Neumann and others, in *Arthur Schnitzler digital*, https://www.schnitzler-edition.net/entstehungsgeschichtetext/10118 [accessed 23.6.21]. This refers to the numerous cuts and manuscript alterations made by Schnitzler in his personal copy of the published text of *Marionetten* during rehearsals at the Deutsches Volkstheater in 1912 and directs the user to digital images of the copy at D^{1H}. Concerning Schnitzler's re-working of *Liebelei* for film, see also Schnitzler, *Liebelei*, pp. 1117–52.

141 *Undiscovered Country*, 'play for television', draft script, February 1983 (Container 33.3); *Undiscovered Country* (Faber & Faber, 1980), book cover and printed pages, with holograph revisions, n.d. (Containers 33.6 and 33.7).

142 Stoppard, 'The Event and the Text', p. 201.

good. Then reading it a fortnight later, you think how ludicrous – and do the whole thing again.'[143] By demonstrating the quasi-kinship between Schnitzler and Stoppard in their approaches to playwriting and in their appreciation of the unfinished nature of the text, and by drawing together the threads which connect initial drafts in Vienna to extended revisions in Austin, this chapter claims a place for Schnitzler in the ever-evolving text as iterated in Stoppard's archived papers.

One line from early in *Undiscovered Country* proves an illuminating example of the aforementioned textual evolution through Stoppard's apparently never-ending capacity to revise. It arises from a metaphor in *Das weite Land* with which Mrs Wahl comments on her daughter's tendency to psychological analysis:

> Wissen Sie, Frau Genia, wie mein seliger Mann solche Bemerkungen von Erna zu nennen pflegte? Ihre Produktionen auf dem psychologischen Seil. (*DwL*, p. 221)

Metaphors have acquired a reputation (not without some justification) for being difficult to translate, often leading translators to be tempted by 'the powerful gravitational pull of source-language patterns that may give rise to an unwillingness to seek out functional equivalents in the target language.'[144] In this case, the anonymous literal translator provided the following:

> late used to call
> Do you know, Mrs Hofreiter, what my ~~dear~~ husband ~~calls~~ remarks
> pirouette
> like those by Erna? Her performances on the psychological tightrope.[145]

The underlining and grey text represent pencil additions and substitutions (and, indeed, a correction – from 'dear' to 'late') made in Stoppard's hand but most probably informed by Harrison's reading of the source text. By the time the first draft came to be typed up, further thought had apparently been given to the line, only to be reworked once more in pencil:

> Do you know, Mrs Hofreiter, what my late
> say about of hers? –

143 From an interview with Nicholas Shakespeare, 'A New Wineskin from Old Vienna: Reworking Other People's Plays Makes a Welcome Change for Tom Stoppard', *The Times*, 17 May 1986, p. 18.

144 Mark Shuttleworth, *Studying Scientific Metaphor in Translation* (New York & London: Routledge, 2017), p. 5; for a detailed theoretical discussion of metaphors in translation see pp. 47–62.

145 *Undiscovered Country* [*Open Country*], photocopy typescript with holograph revisions, 23.2.1979 (Container 32.1, Act 1, p. 6).

husband used to ~~call~~ those remarks ~~by Erna?~~
there goes Erna, treading the
~~– her~~ psychological tightrope ~~act~~.[146]

Once again, further revision is represented in the typed second draft, when Erna is described as: 'clodhopping along … in her lead boots'.[147] In the prompt script yet more revision is marked (by an unknown hand) on the otherwise typed page:

> my dear Genia,
> Do you know, ~~Mrs. Hofreiter~~, what my late
> husband used to say about those remarks?
> pirouetting
> – there goes Erna, ~~clodhopping~~ along the psychological tightrope.[148]

The published text, which might usually be seen to conclude matters, matches the revised prompt script and 'records' the performance as:

> Do you know, my dear Genia, what my late husband used to say about those remarks? – there goes Erna, pirouetting along the psychological tightrope.[149]

Given that the text is usually sent for publication several weeks before performance, approximately when rehearsals begin, this coincidence between prompt script and published script suggests the revisions noted above were made relatively early in the rehearsal period. However, there was to be more. When later re-working the text from its published version (i.e., post-1980) for the American teleplay, Stoppard changed the line to: 'there goes Erna, tripping along on the psychological high wire'.[150] The alterations made in the margins of the published text were then typed up and re-worked yet again in pencil in a document dated February 1983:

> […] ~~there goes Erna, tripping along on the psychological high wire.~~
> There's our Erna, going out on her psychological limb.[151]

146 First typed draft, *Undiscovered Country*, February 1979 (Container 32.3, p. 7).
147 *Undiscovered Country*, typed draft, n.d. (Container 32.5, p. 6).
148 Prompt "Bible" Script, *Undiscovered Country*, National Theatre Archive, RNT/SM/1/152, p. 6.
149 Stoppard, *Undiscovered Country* (1980), p. 15. For Stoppard's description of the published playscript as a 'record of what was performed' see *UC*, p. x.
150 *Undiscovered Country* (1980), book cover and printed pages with holograph revisions, n.d. (Container 33.6, p. 15).
151 *Undiscovered Country*, 'play for television', draft script, February 1983 (Container 33.3, 'Part One', p. 5).

The most striking changes Stoppard makes are to the style of Erna's movement. Whereas the source line merely refers to 'Produktionen', without any reference to motion, Stoppard cannot resist letting Erna 'pirouette', 'tread', 'clodhop' and 'trip' along the psychological tightrope, before she eventually goes 'out on her psychological limb'. The last of these suggests Erna is on her own, and therefore possibly vulnerable, in her socially anomalous psychologizing, whereas the earlier iterations present Erna's analysis first as artistry ('performances', 'her psychological tightrope act') and then amateurish psychobabble ('clodhopping' in 'lead boots'). Form and, in particular, any resulting humour seemingly take priority for Stoppard over the potential shifts in substance produced by these alterations. Nevertheless, and whether intended or otherwise, each of Stoppard's textual tweaks unavoidably alters Erna's character. She is, in Stoppard's different drafts, at once intellectually elegant, conversationally blunt and socially reckless.

Each of the revisions set out above represents a further echo of a line whose earlier manifestations are to be found in the drafts for *Das weite Land*. These innumerable additions, substitutions and excisions provide a compelling illustration of the teleology of the modern writer, who no longer imagines 'the text existing in its fullest form in the past, in pre-linguistic shape' but instead posits 'the ideal text [...] as existing just out of grasp'.[152] Stoppard's pencil never truly settles. His back-to-front ticks (applied to his own revisions as well as to those by Harrison) might signal a temporary conclusion, one that will suffice for the immediate purpose of performance or even publication, but even that is not truly final. Hans Walter Gabler makes a similar point in respect of Joyce's *Ulysses*, focusing on the later stages of production and dissemination:

> The process by which *Ulysses* grew at the same time as it became subtly but persistently deformed in transmission [...] helps us to understand that the literary text itself never wholly achieves a definitive state. Neither do scholarly and critical procedures of editing in their turn bring forth definitive texts, but at the most approximations to the best possible text.[153]

Unlike more Romantic ideas of the lone genius rushing out words onto a page as the moment of inspiration hits him or her, these drafts provide evidence of Stoppard (and others) thrashing out and playing with different ideas in what

152 Hannah Sullivan, *The Work of Revision* (Cambridge, MA and London: Harvard University Press, 2013), p. 3.

153 Hans Walter Gabler, 'Note on the Second Impression', in James Joyce, *Ulysses: A Critical and Synoptic Edition*, ed. by Hans Walter Gabler, Wolfhard Steppe and Claus Melchior (New York: Garland, 1986), pp. vii–ix (p. vii).

Hannah Sullivan has called the 'fervent commitment to continued process rather than completed product'.[154] The roots of that 'continued process' can be traced back to Schnitzler's own papers.

Humour as a Marker of Textual Evolution

One of the most prominent alterations which the texts experience in Stoppard's hands is the accentuation of, and addition to, the existing humour. The text evolves, as a result of Stoppard's relentless creative labour, into sharper, wittier repartee, affecting some characters more than others. Traces of the thinking behind that evolution are scattered throughout the archived drafts. In the opening moments of *Dalliance*, for example, Theo comments on Fritz's frantic opening of letters. In the source text Schnitzler's Theo says:

> Na, na! . . . Du erschrickst ja förmlich. (*Liebelei*, p. 926)

Shand translated this as:

> Come, come . . . you are in a regular fright. (*PwL*, p. 10)

Vivis's literal translation provided:

> Well, well! You're really alarmed.[155]

In or around February 1986 Stoppard worked on a typed draft (Container 3.8) which had been produced from corrections made to an earlier typed draft (Container 3.9, January 1986). At this stage, the line in question was presented as:

> I say, you are in a state.

In pencil, Stoppard has drawn a line through that typed text and experimented, by hand, with the following:

> [~~postal~~
> ~~post-~~] ~~post haste~~
>
> steady on? ~~Post-haste, less speed. Post chase – post facts~~
> oh never mind –
>
> Expecting a letter? ~~Post-haste~~. This is the post-coital state
> one hears so
> much about.
>
> ~~You seem to be in a state of post~~

154 Sullivan, *The Work of Revision*, p. 2.
155 Literal translation of *Liebelei* by Anthony Vivis (Container 79.7, p. 1).

The sketching continues on the verso of the previous page, where Stoppard has written in pencil:

> Expecting a letter? –
>
> I say, you are in a state – ~~it~~ is it
> the same with
> all your
> correspondents

The alterations do not end there. In the prompt script there is evidence of amendments having been made during rehearsal:

> FRITZ Well . . . why don't you take your coat off?
> AH – THE POST.
> FRITZ sees that the post has arrived. He approaches the desk nervously, puts the gun in a drawer in the desk. He seizes the letters and goes through them rapidly.
> IT
> THEODORE ~~Love letter?~~ I say, you are in a state. Is ~~this~~ the post-coital one hears so much about?
> SERVANT GOOD NIGHT SIR
> ~~FRITZ: Nothing.~~
> THEODORE LOVE LETTERS?
> Whatever FRITZ might have been expecting is not there. He is relieved. He starts to open letters.
> FRITZ NOTHING.
> THEODORE I always say one should never put it in writing.
> FRITZ Nothing. One from Lensky . . . and my father . . ..[156]

The text in grey, together with the lines struck through, has been executed in either pencil or pen – it is difficult to say which, as the National Theatre Archive holds only a black and white photocopy. The handwriting is not Stoppard's. These markings on the page, therefore, very probably represent the influence of yet more agents in the writing process. Stoppard, like Heinrich Schnitzler and Arthur Schnitzler before him, was only too aware that the script delivered for rehearsal was only the starting point in determining what would be performed on any given night.

Further changes are evident in the published text made available to the reading public:

> Love letters? I say, you are in a state. Is this the post-coital one hears so much about? (*Dall.*, p. 6).

156 Prompt "Bible" Script, *Dalliance*, National Theatre Archive, RNT/SM/1/265.

The draft scripts bear witness to the production of playful puns for which Stoppard is famous, what J. P. Stern refers to as his 'immensely verbal imagination'.[157] The pun does not come to Stoppard instantly, in a flash of inspiration. Instead, he can be seen here to be labouring over the word 'post' and its potential ambiguities and multiple extensions. Evidently Stoppard needs to see his wit worked out on the page rather than, or perhaps as well as, hearing it in his own mind. The archive thus reveals the mechanics of transforming a text from German-language published drama to English-language rehearsal script and beyond.

The seeds of Stoppard's joke are scarcely present in Schnitzler's words. The only humour legible is Theo's amusement (or perhaps bemusement) at Fritz's apparent panic. Nevertheless, Stoppard does not pluck his pun from thin air. The material for it is there in Schnitzler's dialogue and has to be interpreted and re-created by other writers, namely Vivis and Shand, before Stoppard can impose his own narrative, and his own playful attitude, onto Theo's line. By doing so, Stoppard alters Theo's character. He gives him a wit and capacity to pull language around that is far sharper, faster and perhaps more contemporary than in the source text. This loan of Stoppard's own comic brilliance to others' creations can have incongruous consequences, rendering otherwise apparently dim-witted characters anomalously funny and thereby diluting the particular features of individual figures.[158] To a large degree in *Dalliance*, however, Stoppard limits the additional humour to Theo, who in Schnitzler's hands is already the dry observer of Fritz's romantic relations. The jokes introduced into the text serve only to add force to a pre-existing feature of Theo's character and of course provide additional entertainment for the audience.[159]

Stoppard's comic augmentation is sometimes achieved at Theo's expense. In Act 1 Theo shows off that he knows (or at least thinks he knows) who Christine's father is:

> THEODOR: Nicht wahr, der Vater von der Christin', das ist so ein kleiner Herr mit kurzem grauen Haar –

157 J. P. Stern, 'Anyone for Tennis', p. 27.

158 See Schippers, 'Stoppard's Nestroy, Schnitzler's Stoppard', pp. 262–63. Stoppard has said about his plays, more generally, that he 'rel[ies] quite a lot on the actors differentiating between the characters because characters with a capital "K" isn't something that interests [him] very much. Quite a lot of [his, i.e., Stoppard's] lines could be given to different people in the play without anything odd' (Nancy Shields Hardin, 'An Interview with Tom Stoppard', *Contemporary Literature*, 22 (1981), 153–66 (p. 158)).

159 For a striking contrast, see David Harrower's *Sweet Nothings*, in which a far less attractive aspect of Theo's character, his misogyny, is accentuated (David Harrower, *Sweet Nothings* (London: Faber & Faber, 2010)).

> MIZI: [. . .] Nein, er hat ja lange Haar'.
> FRITZ: Woher kennst du ihn denn?
> THEODOR: Neulich war ich mit dem Lensky in der Josefstadt und da hab' ich mir die Leut' mit den Baßgeigen angeschaut.
> MIZI: Er spielt ja nicht Baßgeigen, Violin' spielt er.
> THEODOR: Ach so, ich hab' gemeint, er spielt Baßgeige. *Zu Mizi, die lacht* Das ist ja nicht komisch; das kann ich ja nicht wissen, du Kind.

Vivis provided Stoppard with the following translation of the last line:

> Oh, I see, I thought he played the double-bass. (*to MIZI, who laughs*) It's nothing to laugh at, how could I possibly know, you child.[160]

Mizi mocks Theo's misplaced confidence and the resulting mistaken identity may raise a smile in the audience. Arguably the main purpose of this exchange, however, lies in illustrating the nature of the relationship between Mizi and Theo: Mizi does not fawn at Theo's feet but teases him as one might an equal.

Stoppard brought out additional humour in the dialogue by rendering more easily imaginable the physical comedy inherent in the underlying idea that Theo confused violin and double-bass. From the second typed draft it is possible to see how Stoppard has first altered Vivis's words, cutting out 'I see' and 'you child' and tightening up the remaining syntax, in order to turn them into phrases which more easily roll off the tongue.[161] He then re-works the typed line in pencil, experimenting with a joke about a stoop before settling on the words that would survive in the printed script:

> Well,
> ~~Hence the stoop~~. I said he was small
> (Oh, I thought he played the double-bass.)
> ~~(MIZI laughs) There's no need to laugh, I can't know everything.~~

Thus, in *Dalliance* the whole exchange has become:

> THEODORE: Christine's father – little man with long, grey hair?
> MIZI: No, he's got short hair.
> FRITZ: How would you know him?
> THEODORE: I was watching the show at the Josefstadt with Lensky the other day and I had a good look at the chap playing the double-bass –
> MIZI: It's not a double-bass, it's a violin.
> THEODORE: Well, I said he was small. (*Dall.*, p. 10)

160 Literal translation of *Liebelei* by Anthony Vivis (Container 79.7, p. 10).
161 Container 3.8, p. 11.

A pattern emerges from these traces of Stoppard's drafting practice. He begins by modifying the literal translation into something still quite close to his English sources (i.e., including existing translations like Shand's), in effect producing approximately one line for every line in the German text. He then experiments and plays with the new, adapted and typed text, creating new puns, supplementing the existing humour, but also making (at times quite extreme) cuts. He revises and cuts his own words as well as those adopted from the sources. Whole (Stoppardian) puns can disappear by the time the text comes to be published in book form. In *Undiscovered Country*, for example, Stoppard toyed with introducing a play on death in an exchange between Genia and Mauer about the latter's plan to take Friedrich mountain-climbing:

> GENIA: Zu Dolomitentouren– ? . . . Was sagt er denn dazu . . .?
> MAUER: Er scheint nicht gänzlich abgeneigt. (*DwL*, p. 224)

The literal translator rendered Mauer's response as: 'He doesn't seem to be absolutely against it'.[162] In pencil Stoppard has written over the typed text: 'exactly seem to be exactly against it dead against'. The idea is developed further, so that it is typed up as:

> ~~seem to be~~
> ~~He doesn't give the impression of being~~
> ~~absolutely~~ He's not exactly dead against it.
> ~~dead set against~~ it.[163]

The pencil revisions (shown in grey above and the struck-through lines) demonstrate yet further re-thinking on Stoppard's part. For the prompt script (p. 11) and the published version, however, the reference to death was dropped altogether, along with the rest of the two-line exchange between Genia and Mauer (*UC*, p. 65).

Infinite Extensions

The drafts show not only the gradual re-working of humour across the dialogue, but also shifts in character and mood as the text is transformed into its various English embodiments. Christine's eventual metamorphosis into something akin to a modern-day heroine has been commented on above. The drafts show that the alternative ending, which injects Christine with new attitude, did not appear until quite late in the writing process. In the initial

162 Container 32.1, Act 1, p. 13.
163 First typed draft, *Undiscovered Country*, February 1979 (Container 32.3, p. 15).

drafts (from January to March 1986) Stoppard kept the ending as conceived by Schnitzler: Christine rushes from the stage, leaving her father '[s]obbing loudly [as] he sinks to the floor'.[164] The first signs of revision appear in Stoppard's rehearsal copy, in typescript: 'What? That I loved him? You bastard, Theo. You fat, ugly, ignorant, lecherous, selfish, dirty-minded little help yourself groper, your breath stank of stale women when you kissed me, I was nearly sick'.[165] The rehearsal copy contains extensive re-drafting, in manuscript, on the versos of the final pages. Stoppard was apparently unsure of how the play should finish. He tried out 'charlatan' six times within a few sides of paper (subsequently settling for 'shit-bucket'), along with 'wheezing', 'sweaty', 'self-satisfied', 'pig', 'your breath stank of stale sluts' and 'you're all uniform', as well as multiple other alternatives. In the prompt script Christine's final outburst changes again:

> You fat, ugly, ignorant, lecherous, dirty-fingered
> how could you know
> God's gift to the female race,^ your breath stank of
> stale women when you kissed me, I was nearly sick! (*Dall.*, p. 71)

Not only do these archived papers demonstrate the means by which Stoppard arrives at his 'baroque linguistic precision', but they also chart the extended development of sometimes significant changes to the source material.[166] Examination of the genesis of *Dalliance* reveals that Stoppard's decision (if indeed it was his) to alter Christine's destiny at the close of the play was only made towards the very end of the process of re-writing Schnitzler's *Liebelei*.

This chapter accordingly reinforces the argument of such scholars as Munday, Cordingley and Montini that we should include within the research landscape not only published play texts but also the correspondence, drafts and revisions, prompt scripts and reviews for translated texts. Such a comprehensive analysis of textual production challenges those more traditional models for translation that limit their remit to '(final text) A' into '(final text) B'; it also undermines conceptions of authorship restricted to individual voices of authority. The material book, the archived draft and the live performance each represent a single instantiation of textual meaning, but also a palimpsest, haunted by both past and future iterations. Each posits, as theatre translator David Johnston has said, 'an infinity of possible extensions, of possible completions'.[167] Individual agents may control the text, and therewith its meaning, from one moment to the next, but that

164 Container 3.8, p. 97.
165 Container 79.10, p. 71.
166 Demastes, *The Cambridge Introduction to Tom Stoppard*, p. 3.
167 David Johnston, 'Historical Theatre: The Task of the Translator', *Trans*, 13 (2009), 57–70 (p. 66).

control is not final and accordingly it cannot be authoritative. By observing the shifts from one adaptation to the next over a period of seven years, it has been possible to identify factors informing the process, production and reception of Schnitzler's plays translated for Britain. Copyright has emerged as a clear and decisive factor in determining whether and how plays are translated. The next chapter shows what happens when copyright in *Reigen* drops away, leaving translators, playwrights and directors to treat Schnitzler's plays with abandon.

CHAPTER 4

Reigen: Contagion and Identity

In 2009 there were no fewer than four plays produced in London that claimed to be adaptations of Schnitzler's *Reigen*. One of these was set in post-apartheid South Africa; two incorporated stretches of modern dance and tango; and yet another cast all the characters (originally five male and five female) as men. *Reigen* occupies an extreme position when it comes to generating new interpretations. It seems endlessly open to adaptation, feeding an insatiable hunger among theatre-makers to make it their own. The attraction of the play today can in part be explained by the absence of authorial control or copyright protection and the consequent freedom for re-writers to do with it as they please. A further important contributing factor to the play's appeal to modern playwrights and directors is undoubtedly its scandalous history and the decades-long ban on its performance (details of which are set out below): its reputation as an obscene, indecent play continues to function as a draw to theatre-makers, producers (for whom it reduces commercial risk) and audiences alike. A third source of the play's allure is its innovative form (ten duologues linked as a daisy chain), so that very 'loose' adaptations take that from it if nothing else. Finally, a possible explanation for its capacity to generate hundreds of different interpretations is its treatment of identity as fluid and changeable. In this respect, it might productively be read from a queer perspective, anticipating contemporary discourses that challenge traditional ideas of sexuality and gender.

The openness which *Reigen* presents to translators and interpreters across the anglophone world is a reflection of the themes portrayed in the play itself: in *Reigen* Schnitzler exposes the porous nature of boundaries, both physical and social, between individuals, as well as the vulnerability of the self in a state of 'Kernlosigkeit'. Through the commonality of sexual desire and the diseases which can spread through sexual intercourse, Schnitzler confronts his audiences with the many ways in which we are not unique, authentic or original; at the same time, he illustrates how personal borders can be permeated and identities altered, as well as exploring the consequences of the self as unfixed and 'impressionistic'.

Such an analysis of Schnitzler's famous play is not entirely new. Work done by scholars such as Laura Otis and Marie Kolkenbrock highlights the many points at which Schnitzler's medical understanding of contagious disease informs his literary writing, recognizing it also in the context of a broader tendency for modernism to engage with contemporary bacteriology.[1] Similarly, Hunter G. Hannum has read *Reigen* as addressing Modernist concerns with continuity through time and the role of forgetting and remembering in establishing a coherent identity, anticipating the significant work of Konstanze Fliedl in her monograph *Arthur Schnitzler: Poetik der Erinnerung*.[2] This chapter applies those medically and philosophically inflected readings of Schnitzler to British translations of *Reigen*, not only to explain the appeal of that play to its interpreters but also as a lens through which the translations and adaptations might themselves be read. After setting out the historical and theoretical context for such a reading of *Reigen*, this chapter focuses on three contemporary British adaptations of the play to illustrate the way in which today's playwrights take up the core idea of permeable identity in their re-interpretations.

Power is far less easy to discern when tracking the production and dissemination of translations from the last twenty years. The archive cannot help in such a context and so the research and analysis possible for earlier periods cannot be repeated here. Instead, this chapter investigates what happens in the absence of authorial (or quasi-authorial) power on the expiry of copyright. This is not to deny that power is still exercised, institutionally and individually, over the text – theatres, directors, translators and actors will still have influenced what is ultimately performed on the stage – but the decisions informing what an audience sees must remain, for now, largely inaccessible to the academic researcher. This chapter therefore explores what happens when one particular agent (whether author or legatee) is removed from the negotiating process. As part of that investigation this chapter considers, more specifically, how power is revealed in the relationships between characters and how, in the case of *Reigen* adaptations, it can be inverted, or even queered.[3]

1 See Marie Kolkenbrock, 'Gothic Infections: Arthur Schnitzler and the Haunted Culture of Modernism', *Modern Language Review*, 113 (2018), 147–67, esp. pp. 151–52. See also Laura Otis, 'The Language of Infection: Disease and Identity in Schnitzler's "Reigen"', *The Germanic Review*, 70 (1995), 65–75; Laura Otis, *Membranes: Metaphors of Invasion in Nineteenth-Century Literature, Science, and Politics* (Baltimore, MD: Johns Hopkins Press, 1999).

2 Hunter G. Hannum, '"Killing Time": Aspects of Schnitzler's "Reigen"', *Germanic Review*, 37 (1962), 190–207; Konstanze Fliedl, *Arthur Schnitzler: Poetik der Erinnerung* (Vienna: Böhlau, 1997).

3 As indicated above, 'queer' is used with reference to queer theory so that the verb can include the act of 'mak[ing] (more) relevant, accessible or susceptible to audiences or perspectives representing diverse sexual and gender identities' ('queer, *v.2* [entry 4]', in *Oxford English Dictionary*, https://www.oed.com/ [accessed 26 July 2021]).

The Play and its Historical Context

Even as *Reigen* was being written, in the winter of 1896 to 1897, Schnitzler was concerned it was a work that could be neither published nor performed in the contemporary German-speaking world.[4] The play comprises ten scenes, in all but one of which a man and a woman are shown in the build-up to, and the come-down from, sexual intercourse. The coital act itself is represented in the text by a line of dashes. A daisy chain is effected by one of each pair appearing in the subsequent scene with a new partner. Thus the *Soldat* (Franz) from the first scene, in which he appears alongside the *Dirne* (Leocadia), returns in the second scene with the *Stubenmädchen* (Marie), who in turn appears in the third scene with the *Junger Herr* (Alfred). The chain of sexual encounters continues with the *Junge Frau* (Emma), her husband, the *Gatte* (Karl), the *Süßes Mädel*, the *Dichter* (Robert), the *Schauspielerin* and the *Graf* until the play comes full circle with a post-coital meditation between the *Graf* and the *Dirne* of the opening scene (there are no charged dashes in this final scene).[5]

Wittily revealed via this unusual episodic structure are the shared rituals of seduction and the common patterns of post-coital awkwardness and regret found at all levels of society. Thus each encounter begins with a sense of excitement and anticipation, but (generally) ends with disappointment, self-disgust or indifference. Schnitzler's script recognizes and applies the subtle nuances of address and gesture that belie words and actions otherwise deployed: it contrasts 'the naked truth with the rhetorical veils thrown over it'.[6] Hence, for example, the *Junge Frau* declares her wish to leave almost as soon as she has arrived at her rendezvous with the *Junger Herr*, but she has had the foresight to bring her button-hook with her in order to re-fasten her shoes after an anticipated undressing (*Reigen*, p. 966).[7] Similarly, the *Stubenmädchen* feigns innocence before the flirtatious *Junger Herr*, but preens herself in front of a mirror before taking him a glass of water (*Reigen*, p. 946). Inconsistent claims made by characters about their desires, their expectations,

4 *Briefe* I, 314–15, 26.2.1897; *Briefe* I, 309–11, 7.1.1897.

5 The original, generic character names are retained (rather than translated) to avoid the risk of reducing and/or adding to the range of cultural meanings encapsulated in the German. '*Süßes Mädel*', most obviously, has unavoidably lost its cultural specificity even in such close translations as 'The Sweet Girl' (Arthur Schnitzler, *Merry-Go-Round*, trans. by Frank and Jacqueline Marcus) and 'Sweet Maid' (Arthur Schnitzler, *Round Dance and Other Plays*, trans. by. J. M. Q. Davies (Oxford: Oxford University Press, 2004)). The first names, given here in parentheses, emerge from the dialogue during the course of the play.

6 Fliedl, 'Love's Labour's Lost', pp. 68–69.

7 Page references for *Reigen* are from *Reigen*, ed. by Marina Rauchenbacher and Konstanze Fliedl, in *Werke in historisch-kritischen Ausgaben*, ed. by Konstanze Fliedl, 12 vols (Berlin and Boston, MA: de Gruyter, 2011–), XII (2019).

their previous experiences and, most obviously, their subscription to social norms highlight the game-like nature of the encounters and the underlying hypocrisies of a society outwardly determined to maintain strict boundaries between social groups. Each spends at least some, if not all, of their time on stage playing a role, lending a metatheatrical veneer to the entire cycle.

Much has been written about the shift between formal and informal modes of address (i.e., 'Sie' and 'Du') as markers of the differing levels of emotional intimacy and their sometimes inverse relationship to the levels of physical intimacy on display.[8] A similar strategy is legible in the contrasting anonymity and select scattering of names, formal and informal, throughout the scenes.[9] The *Soldat* refuses to give his name to the *Dirne* and so maintains the upper hand even at the end of their encounter; the *Dirne* perseveres with her attempt at intimacy by volunteering her own name, only for it (and therewith her claim to selfhood) to be ridiculed and implicitly denied (*Reigen*, p. 936). In his haste to seduce her the *Soldat* then stumbles over the name of the *Stubenmädchen*: 'Wie heißen S'? Kathi? [...] Ich weiß, ich weiß schon . . . Marie' (*Reigen*, p. 937). The *Stubenmädchen* meanwhile flits between the semi-formal 'Herr Franz' and 'Franz' in her post-coital confusion. The *Dichter* cannot decide whether he wishes to be recognized as the famous 'Biebitz' or known for himself, as 'Robert', in his affair with the *Süßes Mädel*, but he is subsequently subjected to unwanted diminutive name-calling by the *Schauspielerin* ('Grille', 'Frosch' and 'Kind') as part of her reversal of the more conventionally understood power dynamic between man and woman. The varying acts of name-giving and name-hiding function as an index of register and emotional intimacy while at the same time establishing power relations between players.[10] Most importantly from the perspective of this study, however, they act as counterweights to the tendency to read the play as inhabited by stereotypes: the characters are not nameless caricatures but individuals with their own concrete, identifiable places in the world.[11]

8 See, for example, Janz and Laermann, *Arthur Schnitzler*, p. 73; Otis, *Membranes*, pp. 137–38.

9 See Iris Denneler, *Von Namen und Dingen. Erkundungen zur Rolle des Ich in der Literatur am Beispiel von Ingeborg Bachmann, Peter Bichsel, Max Frisch, Gottfried Keller, Heinrich von Kleist, Arthur Schnitzler, Frank Wedekind, Vladimir Nabokov und W.G. Sebald* (Würzburg: Königshausen & Neumann, 2001), pp. 99–111.

10 Denneler, *Von Namen und Dingen*, pp. 101–02; Janz and Laermann, *Arthur Schnitzler*, pp. 65–67.

11 Cf. Yates, *Schnitzler, Hofmannsthal, and the Austrian Theatre*, pp. 135–36. Ilsa Barea identifies in *Anatol* an oxymoronic tension arguably echoed in *Reigen*: Max and Anatol are 'individuals and types at the same time'. See 'Viennese Mirage', *The Times Literary Supplement*, 15 June 1951, p. 365. For a contrasting view, i.e., of the names as stereotypes, see Denneler, *Von Namen und Dingen*, p. 101.

Schnitzler's play can, of course, be read as including a commentary on the universal 'discourse of love' and the nature of sexual desire, but he does not achieve this at the expense of his figures' humanity. A tension undoubtedly obtains, therefore, in the text between the particular and the universal, the individual and the communal. It is a tension that has informed critical and scholarly responses since first publication and has, unsurprisingly, led to polarized views on those very issues of specificity and universality. The play has, for example, often been compared with the medieval *Totentanz*, by virtue of, among other things, its circular form and what some have interpreted as a repeated concern with death. In a letter to Eric Glass on the failings of a translation of the play by Charles Dyer, Heinrich Schnitzler cited with approval the epithet supposedly given to the play by his father's contemporary, Felix Salten, namely a 'deathdance of love'.[12] Heinrich Schnitzler noted that the English translation in question therefore failed to capture the bitterness implicit in the descriptor. Richard Alewyn has likewise drawn comparisons between Schnitzler's *Reigen* and the *Totentanz*, focusing on the representative sameness of the characters, which he considers to be like figures in a puppet theatre, pulled by unseen strings and so rendered nameless 'types' in a dance of death.[13]

Rolf-Peter Janz denies the validity of such an analogy, pointing to the theological and historical distance between the medieval trope and Schnitzler's play, as well as the substantive differences in their treatment of death: the brief references to death at the beginning and end of Schnitzler's cycle (in the mouths of the *Soldat*, the *Dirne* and the *Graf*) point to the theme of transience, a central theme of the Impressionists, rather than a consciousness of human mortality specifically.[14] Similarly, Konstanze Fliedl has questioned the helpfulness of the analogy, which centres attention on Eros and Thanatos as the great levellers and ignores the social and gender-specific asymmetries in the text: it is the men who benefit from the patriarchal morality, with its permissive attitude to male philandering, whereas the women of the play generally have to take on

12 Heinrich Schnitzler to Eric Glass, 19.9.1979 (Schn 21/12/37). The memory of the epithet appears to have been false. Felix Salten's review of the published play does not include any reference to a 'deathdance of love' (Felix Salten, 'Arthur Schnitzler und sein "Reigen"', *Die Zeit* (Vienna), 7 November 1903, pp. 1–2). Heinrich Schnitzler might instead have been thinking of later reviews, such as that by Carl Müller-Rastatt, 'Totentanz. Zur Uraufführung von Schnitzlers Reigen in den Hamburger Kammerspielen', *Hamburger Correspondent*, 8 January 1921; or of the chapter '"Reigen" und Danse Macabre' in Theodor Reik's study, *Arthur Schnitzler als Psycholog* (Minden: Bruns, 1913), pp. 67–84.

13 Cf. Richard Alewyn, *Probleme und Gestalten* (Frankfurt a. M.: Insel, 1974), pp. 302–03.

14 Janz and Laermann, *Arthur Schnitzler*, pp. 56–57.

the far greater risks associated with their liaisons;[15] and the couplings are by no means socially random – unlike the men, the women liaise only with their social equals or those above them in the hierarchy, never below.

Both Fliedl and Yates see in *Reigen* an essentially chronotopically rooted drama, from which abstraction into generalization risks destroying the very essence of the enterprise.[16] Fliedl is particularly critical of the 'moralising interpretation of *Reigen*' that manifests itself in translators' concentration on the 'universally human' content of the play at the cost of its locally oriented form:

> If our sole concern is with the 'anthropological constants' in Schnitzler's cycle, the depiction of crude instinctual behavior that has not been culturally moulded, [then] cultural differences between the languages of the original and of the translation are of no importance. Schnitzler is then regarded as a critic of all-too-human weaknesses and a defender of eternally human values.[17]

It is by reason of its necessarily local flavour that, for Fliedl at least, *Reigen* eludes easy translation.[18]

If anything, these conflicting assessments of *Reigen* demonstrate that it is neither one thing nor the other, neither straightforwardly a comedy of its time and place nor an allegorical drama addressing the animal lusts driving us all. Günther Rühle rationalizes the tendency for polarized interpretations thus:

> Zu Schnitzlers 'Reigen' muß man sich seine Nähe oder seine Entfernung selbst bestimmen, und je nach der Distanz wird sich die Erscheinung des Stücks verändern. Je größer sie wird, desto stärker drängt der Ewigkeitszug sich im Arrangement hervor: das Sinnbild von der immerwährenden Wanderschaft auf der Suche nach Glück wie

15 Fliedl, *Arthur Schnitzler*, p. 87. Whilst the unmarried women in the play are undoubtedly vulnerable to pregnancy and disgrace, and the *Junge Frau* to the unwanted collapse of her marriage (with probable financial consequences), the men do not always avoid serious risk: the *Junger Herr*, if challenged by the *Ehegatte*, faces the prospect of death by duel.

16 Yates asserts that the 'special flavour of Reigen [...] derives from the fact that [...] it is firmly rooted in Viennese reality' (Yates, *Theatre in Vienna*, p. 135).

17 Fliedl, 'Love's Labour's Lost', p. 63. See also Hilde Spiel, for whom *Reigen* is a mirror of 'das Gewebe sozialer Beziehungen in jenem todgeweihten Alt-Österreich' (Hilde Spiel, 'Die geselligen Eigenbrötler', in *Wien. Spektrum einer Stadt*, ed. by Hilde Spiel (Munich: Biederstein, 1971), pp. 110–23 (p. 117)). Spiel's interpretation of the play sees it as rooted in *fin-de-siècle* Vienna; thus even the recognized 'Vermischung und Nivellierung der Typen' are located 'im damaligen Wien'.

18 Fliedl asserts that 'the profundity [of a work like *Reigen*] is situated in its untranslatable surface' (Fliedl, 'Love's Labour's Lost', p. 64).

> das Schreckbild von der Mechanik im beseelten Körper. Und je näher man bleibt, desto mehr tut sich auf von der Fülle der Beobachtungen, Entdeckungen, Beschreibungen und Erkenntnisse über menschliche Typologie und Individualität, über das Verhalten der Personen, die Formen ihres Lebens und ihre sozialen Prägungen.[19]

Those who see in *Reigen* keen observations of the local, contemporaneous society in which Schnitzler wrote more often than not view those observations (and subtle criticisms) as representing the play's essence, thereby setting up any translation for failure. However, such failure is not inevitable. Rühle concludes his thoughts on the subject with the following, probably inadvertent, encouragement for the prospective translator:

> Der 'Reigen' ist aber kein Stück aus einer vergangenen, abgelebten Welt, sosehr soziales Gefüge, Habitus und Interieur, Sprache und Ambiente die Welt von 1900 auch festhalten. Die Modernität des 'Reigen' besteht in der Aufdeckung der Ängste und Widersprüche, der Transzendenzlosigkeit der Personen, der Berührungszwänge, der Flucht in den Sexus, ohne daß in deren Darstellung die Personalität dieser Menschen verletzt wird.[20]

According to Rühle, Schnitzler's great achievement in *Reigen* is in showing us our common fears and contradictions, in essence our common humanity, while not allowing our individuality to disappear. We shall return to these entangled concepts of specificity and universality, and their origins in Schnitzler's medical work, in due course.

Schnitzler was advised by his Berlin-based publisher Samuel Fischer not to publish the play in Germany, where it was certain to attract the unwanted attention of the authorities.[21] Instead Fischer suggested Schnitzler print it privately in Vienna, where a more liberal attitude to the literary treatment of sex would likely allow a limited publication. This advice was taken and in early 1900 *Reigen* appeared in a privately printed edition of two hundred copies, available to Schnitzler's (male) friends only.[22] Schnitzler provided a foreword to the printed play, asking the recipients to view it as a gift from the author and, implicitly, not to distribute it further. Notwithstanding the very un-public nature of that print, the play was reviewed and, indeed, praised

19 Günther Rühle, 'Der ewige Reigen', in Arthur Schnitzler, *Reigen / Liebelei* (Frankfurt a. M.: Fischer, 1996), pp. 7–21 (pp. 18–19).

20 Rühle, 'Der ewige Reigen', p. 21.

21 Fischer, rather than Schnitzler, would have faced any legal penalties by virtue of his position as publisher of the offending material (Schneider, *Die Rezeption von Arthur Schnitzlers Reigen*, p. 10).

22 Schneider, *Die Rezeption von Arthur Schnitzlers Reigen*, p. 37.

by some in the press.[23] It was perhaps unsurprising, then, that Schnitzler was eventually persuaded to publish the play more widely with the Wiener Verlag in 1903: 'Die Szenen fanden viel Beifall, meine Bedenken wurden allmählich beschwichtigt'.[24] Within the first eight months 14,000 copies had been sold. The play was the talk of the town; everyone wanted to read the drama 'das [...] Illusionen zerstört und den Zauber unserer glücklichsten Stunden entlarvt'.[25] However, in March 1904 the Berlin Prosecuting Attorney's Office ordered its confiscation throughout the Wilhelmine Empire; and in September of the same year two book dealers were charged by the Leipzig Criminal Court with having sold copies of the prohibited *Reigen*.[26] Thus began a period of interrupted public readings and performances, pre-emptive bans and an increasing and understandable reluctance on Schnitzler's part to allow further productions to be mounted.[27]

Eventually, after the conclusion of the First World War and the fall of both the German and the Austrian Empires, Schnitzler felt more confident that the play could be staged. According to a decision passed by the provisional National Assembly of the new Austrian Republic on 30 October 1918, censorship was to end, having been deemed contrary to the basic rights of the citizen.[28] Although a decision by the Constitutional Court in December 1919 clarified that the new dispensation applied only to the press, in practice the advisory committee responsible for theatre censorship adopted a relatively liberal stance in the exercise of its powers.[29] A similar relaxation of censorship was announced by Germany's post-war interim government and confirmed in the Weimar Constitution, although the controversial *Lex Heinze* regulating obscene works (Article 184a of the National Code of Criminal Law) remained

23 See, for example, Berlin theatre critic Alfred Kerr's review in the *Neue deutsche Rundschau*, November 1900, an excerpt of which is re-printed in Thomas Koebner, *Arthur Schnitzler: Reigen: Erläuterungen und Dokumente* (Stuttgart: Reclam, 2012), p. 11. Generally, Schnitzler was disappointed by the lack of interest shown by the press, even after the play's wider publication by the Wiener Verlag (*Tagebuch*, 27.7.1903).

24 See *Briefe* ii, 223–28, 30.12.1920, for Schnitzler's own recollections of the scandal around *Reigen* and his reasons for deciding to publish in 1903. Fischer, acting on the advice of his lawyer, refused once again to publish, notwithstanding the success of the private distribution (Schneider, *Die Rezeption von Arthur Schnitzlers Reigen*, p. 39).

25 Salten, 'Arthur Schnitzler und sein "Reigen"', p. 1.

26 Otto P. Schinnerer, 'The History of Schnitzler's *Reigen*', *PMLA*, 46 (1931), 839–59 (p. 844).

27 For an example of the problems faced by those aspiring to produce *Reigen*, see Hermann Bahr's thwarted attempt at a public reading of the play in November 1903, as documented in Hermann Bahr and Arthur Schnitzler, *Briefwechsel, Aufzeichnungen, Dokumente 1891–1931*, ed. by Kurt Ifkovits and Martin Anton Müller (Göttingen: Wallstein, 2018), pp. 267–78.

28 Johannes Schober, 'Zensur. Eine aktuelle Betrachtung', *Neue Freie Presse*, 4 April 1926, pp. 10–11.

29 Yates, *Theatre in Vienna*, pp. 46–47.

enforceable.[30] Two productions of *Reigen* were subsequently put on, one in Berlin at the Kleines Schauspielhaus in December 1920 and the other in Vienna at the Kammerspiele of the Deutsches Volkstheater in February 1921, both with Arthur Schnitzler's authorization and co-operation and the later production with his involvement in rehearsals.[31]

The Berlin production was the subject of criminal proceedings and led to an infamous six-day trial in November 1921, at which the anti-Semitic motivation of those driving and giving evidence for the prosecution quickly became apparent. The directors and actors of the Kleines Schauspielhaus were eventually acquitted.[32] In the meantime, however, the Viennese production was attacked in the local press in a similarly anti-Semitic vein. Encouraged by those printed assaults, a small group of young men stormed the theatre on 7 February 1922, during the penultimate scene, with the intention of interrupting the performance; on 13 February hundreds gathered outside the theatre to protest and had to be dispersed by the police; finally matters reached crisis point on 16 February, when around six hundred people rushed into a sold-out performance and caused utter chaos:

> The mob entered, swinging canes. From the boxes they hurled paper balls soaked in tar and eggshells filled with tar, and even seats, into the auditorium and onto the stage. A panic ensued with scenes that can hardly be described. Men trying to defend their escorts were clubbed. Ladies were slapped in the face and insulted. The stagehands hurried to the hydrants and turned the hose on the invaders. Soon the stage and the dressing rooms were flooded. The theatre looked as if it had been wrecked.[33]

30 See Kara L. Ritzheimer, *'Trash', Censorship and National Identity in Early Twentieth-Century Germany* (Cambridge: Cambridge University Press, 2016), pp. 1, 54–55 and 193.

31 Schneider, *Die Rezeption von Arthur Schnitzlers Reigen*, pp. 116–17. Arthur Schnitzler was involved in the preparation of the Berlin production as well. Two of the directors of the Kleines Schauspielhaus, Maximilian Sladek and Hubert Reusch, travelled to Vienna before rehearsals to discuss the play with Schnitzler. This led to forty-one alterations being made to the text in order to prevent it from causing offence. One of these included the *Junge Frau* in the fourth scene asking the *Junger Herr* to pass her her shoes, instead of her stockings (Schinnerer, 'The History of Schnitzler's *Reigen*', p. 847).

32 For documents from and an analysis of the trial see *Schnitzlers 'Reigen'. Zehn Dialoge und ihre Skandalgeschichte*, ed. by Pfoser, Pfoser-Schewig and Renner. For an analysis of the trial which highlights the problematic nature of the defence witnesses' interpretation of the play, see Ludwig Marcuse, *Obscene: The History of an Indignation*, trans. by Karen Gershon (London: Macgibbon & Kee, 1965), pp. 167–214 (orig.: *Obszön: Geschichte einer Entrüstung* (Munich: List, 1962)). See also Fliedl, 'Love's Labour's Lost', for an evaluation of the effect of this problematic interpretation on subsequent anglophone translations.

33 Schinnerer summarizes the report from the *Neues Wiener Journal*, 17 February 1921 (Schinnerer, 'The History of Schnitzler's *Reigen*', p. 852). An account is also given by Schnitzler in *Tagebuch*, 16.2.1921.

Further performances were, unsurprisingly, prohibited by the police on the grounds of maintaining public order. Although the prohibition was lifted within twelve months (on an application by the theatre) and performances recommenced on 7 March 1922, the revival was short-lived. Schnitzler withdrew permission for the production and the performance on 30 June 1922 was the last in Vienna for almost sixty years.[34]

Pfoser explains Schnitzler's decision by reference to the shadow of anti-Semitism that now lingered around all his work and the author's wish to avoid giving the anti-democratic powers a cheap scandal to fuel their cause.[35] Heinrich Schnitzler, who had been with his father at the performance in Vienna in 1921,[36] upheld the ban for the entirety of his half-century in control of the estate, notwithstanding the fact that the said 'ban' had never been put in writing by the author.[37] Heinrich Schnitzler's own justification for continuing the prohibition was, he claimed, his respect for his father.[38] He explained the latter's stance in correspondence with Eric Glass: 'My father realized that any stage production of this particular work will be liable to be misunderstood and that there undoubtedly exists a staging problem, namely in relation to the famous "dashes", which cannot be solved satisfactorily'.[39]

34 For a summary and analysis of the events leading up to, coinciding with and following the Berlin and Vienna productions, including key aspects of political and press activity in both Germany and Austria, see Theodore Ziolkowski, *Scandal on Stage: European Theater as Moral Trial* (Cambridge: Cambridge University Press, 2009), pp. 85–99.

35 Alfred Pfoser, 'Wer hat Angst vor Arthur Schnitzler? Der Wiener *Reigen*-Skandal 1921 – ein unerledigtes Drama', *Die Presse. Literaricum* (2/3 May 1981), p. v.

36 *Tagebuch*, 16.2.1921.

37 Heinrich Schnitzler to Eric Glass, 17.10.1953 (Schn 21/5/34).

38 Heinrich Schnitzler to Eric Glass, 13.4.1976 (Schn 21/11/81). Also, see Heinrich Schnitzler to Eric Glass, 4.9.1954 (Schn 21/5/65), in which Heinrich Schnitzler expresses his need to protect his father's memory 'against complete identification with REIGEN'. He admits that he was particularly sensitive where *Reigen* was concerned because of the history of misunderstandings and misrepresentations of the play (Heinrich Schnitzler to Eric Glass, 17.10.1953 (Schn 21/5/34)).

39 Heinrich Schnitzler to Eric Glass, 20.5.1951 (Schn 21/5/1). The withholding of permission was only effective in those parts of the world where Heinrich Schnitzler held enforceable copyright. In France and America, therefore, *Reigen* and translations of the same could be performed without Heinrich Schnitzler's consent. (America was not a signatory to the Berne Convention; and Arthur Schnitzler's rights in respect of France had, anomalously, been given to his French translator Suzanne Clauser under the terms of his will (Zieger, *Arthur Schnitzler et la France*, pp. 75–76). The author's son also gave permission for private readings, radio productions and eventually film adaptations even where copyright was effective, on the basis that the 'dashes' need not cause difficulties in these media. The constraint exercised by Heinrich Schnitzler is apparent in his refusal of permission even to high-profile applicants. In January 1964 Kenneth Tynan (newly appointed Literary Manager to the National Theatre), Harold Pinter and Ronald Duncan expressed an interest in adapting *Reigen* (presumably for the National Theatre) but were refused (Heinrich Schnitzler to Eric Glass, 18.1.1964

The result of the ban from 1922 until 1982, when copyright expired in the UK and parts of the German-speaking world, was that the play's reputation as provocative, scandalous, obscene and daring survived and retained its novelty for far longer than it might otherwise have done, thereby contributing to a growing sense of excitement around the year that the play could finally be produced on stage.

Reigen in Britain

Reigen did not pass the years to 1982 without any presence in the UK. There was at least one private reading in 1924, presumably using the American translation, *Hands Around*, by F. L. Glaser and L. D. Edwards.[40] A further English-language translation, *Couples*, was made (with Schnitzler's knowledge) in 1927 by an American publisher in Paris, Edward W. Titus, with Lily Wolfe, and might well have made its way onto the British market. More significantly in terms of reach, Max Ophüls's film adaptation *La Ronde* made a huge splash globally in 1950. As the *Observer*'s film critic Philip French put it in 1982, the film starred 'five of Europe's most desirable women making love with five of France's most engaging actors, under the amused gaze of a sixth man, the Austrian master of ceremonies, Anton Walbrook'.[41] Walbrook's narration opened and closed the film and acted as a bridge between scenes; a carousel operated by Walbrook (ostensibly as fairground worker) provided a central visual trope. The film's significance within British cinema and its popularity among British audiences are evident in the fact that the British Film Academy awarded it the prize for 'Best Film of the Year' in 1952. Indeed, such was its impact on the anglophone

(Schn 21/7/81); Heinrich Schnitzler to Eric Glass, 9.2.1964 (Schn 21/7/84); and Heinrich Schnitzler to Eric Glass, 16.11.1964 (Schn 21/7/101)). See also Heinrich Schnitzler to Eric Glass, 16.11.1964 (Schn 21/7/101); and Eric Glass to Heinrich Schnitzler, 30.3.1976 (Schn 21/11/78).

40 Anne Chisholm, *Frances Partridge: The Biography* (London: Weidenfeld & Nicholson, 2009), p. 88. *Hands Around* was the only English translation Arthur Schnitzler could have seen. His approval of the same is recorded in his diary: 'Las den englischen Reigen zu Ende. Ein wirklich amüsantes Buch, mit mancherlei Köstlichkeiten – und es könnte doch besser sein;– an manchen Stellen ins höhere und weitere gehen' (*Tagebuch*, 2.11.1920). (According to a diary entry on that day, Schnitzler started reading the translation on 25 October 1920, referring to it as the 'Amerik. Subscr.-Ausgabe'.) The English text could not have been performed publicly, regardless of Schnitzler's prohibition, by virtue of the Lord Chamberlain's powers (see Introduction). For an assessment of Schnitzler's very brief comment on the English translation *Hands Around*, see Fliedl, 'Love's Labour's Lost', p. 64.

41 Philip French, 'Returning to Eboli: Philip French on a film by Francesco Rosl and the revival of Ophuls's [*sic*] "La Ronde"', *Observer*, 2 May 1982, p. 32.

world that the film's title quickly became (and continues to be) the most widely recognized name for *Reigen* in English.[42]

Finally, a British translation written by Frank and Jacqueline Marcus and approved by Heinrich Schnitzler was published in 1953 as *Merry-Go-Round* and broadcast on BBC radio's Third Programme in 1964.[43] The Audience Research Report for the production reflects once more the significance of Ophüls's film for the global reception of Schnitzler's play and its translations:

> Although the opportunity of hearing Merry Go Round (the play on which the film La Ronde was based) was widely welcomed, this version was often felt to lack the wit and effervescence of the film. [...] – in the words of a Local Government Officer, for instance: 'This piece surely depends for its effect on its novelty and the fact that it is perhaps naughty. Take away its novelty, as nearly everyone has seen La Ronde and in 1964, nothing is naughty'.[44]

Notwithstanding the judgment of this rather grumpy-sounding Local Government Officer, there was sufficient excitement surrounding the expiry of copyright at midnight on 31 December 1981 to propel three major theatres to produce English-language translations in 1982 and the BBC to adapt the play for television broadcast in the same year.[45]

The Royal Exchange in Manchester was the first to raise the curtain on a British stage performance, doing so the minute copyright expired (i.e., it was a midnight show on 31 December 1981). *Round Dance* was translated by Charles Osborne, produced by Caspar Wrede and 'moved the action to Britain during the past 40 years' so that it shifted 'from London in the

42 The name association was a constant source of consternation for Heinrich Schnitzler, who grew increasingly irate with publishers and promoters determined to link new English translations of the play with the film by adopting the same, French, title. See, for example, letters from Heinrich Schnitzler to Eric Glass, 5.1.1953 (Schn 21/5/12); 3.1.1963 (Schn 21/7/44); 2.5.1963 (Schn 21/7/54); and 2.12.1964 (Schn 21/7/104).

43 Heinrich Schnitzler refers to the Marcus translation of *Reigen* as being 'excellent', a 'fine achievement' and of 'high quality' (Heinrich Schnitzler to Frank Marcus, 11.6.1951 (Schn 34/18/2)).

44 Audience Research Report for 'Merry Go Round' ('Adapted and produced by Martin Esslin'), 22.5.1964 (BBC Written Archives Centre, R9/6, Merry Go Round, 25/05/64, TP). According to Heinrich Schnitzler's correspondence with Glass, Esslin was a friend of the trustee's and the two spoke in person about the *Reigen* radio adaptation during a visit by Heinrich Schnitzler to London in 1963 (Heinrich Schnitzler to Eric Glass, 2.5.1963 (Schn 21/7/54); 6.10.1970 (Schn 21/8/73)).

45 Bryan Appleyard summed up the excitement in the title to his long article in the *Times*: 'The race to stage a liberated *La Ronde*' (*The Times*, 7 September 1981, p. 11). The flipside of that race was that the play was 'forced to carry more expectations than it can decently bear' (Patrick Ensor, 'La Ronde', *Guardian*, 3 April 1982, p. 10).

Forties to [...] Liverpool in the Seventies, thence to London in the Eighties'.[46] This approach to modernization and translocation was criticized by the reviewers: it had the effect of 'homogenising the characters' so that they 'all appear of roughly the same social rank and even age'[47] and it betrayed a lack of trust on the part of the director that audiences could understand Vienna at the turn of the century.[48] The Royal Shakespeare Theatre's production of a translation by John Barton and Sue Davies (*La Ronde*, directed by Barton) was accordingly deemed superior merely by virtue of the fact that it left the play in its original time and place.[49] Nevertheless, the conclusion among reviewers of the RSC's attempt was that it proved *Reigen* had nothing more to say to modern audiences. It was considered 'dated' and whereas it might have been 'emotion-provoking' when written, it was 'fairly tame now'.[50]

The third, chronologically, of the three British theatre productions in 1982 was a translation by Mike Alfreds (another *La Ronde*), which opened at the Crucible Theatre in Sheffield on 16 February.[51] By contrast to the earlier two productions, Alfreds cast only one male and one female actor to play all the applicable roles. As a result, costume changes had to be slick, the two actors highly versatile and the staging straightforward. From the critics' perspective, this was the most successful of the three theatre productions. The 'quick [costume] changes' accompanied by Ilona Sekacs's music, described as 'the musical equivalent of rancid fruit', gave 'an extra dimension to the play's obsession with costume and how to get out of it'.[52] The production was hailed as having made the play 'many more of the things that were previously claimed for [it]': 'witty and insightful, sensual and tinged with sadness'.[53] This last of the three productions in 1982, by removing the play from a chronotopically fixed set, most successfully bridged the passage of time and space, i.e., it allowed Schnitzler's play to speak to modern audiences in Britain. By providing new emphases to the play (highlighting the gendered performativity of social roles, for example, as well as the relationship between clothing, class and the 'inaccessibility' of skin) and avoiding excessively laboured

46 Victoria Radin, 'Nudge-nudge, wink-wink', *Observer*, 10 January 1982, p. 27.

47 Radin, 'Nudge-nudge, wink-wink'.

48 Hugh Rank, 'Der *Reigen* begann sich zu drehen', *Wiener Zeitung*, 28 January 1982.

49 The production opened at the Aldwych Theatre in London on 11 January 1982.

50 'Pit', 'La Ronde', *Variety*, 27 January 1982, p. 90. Schneider summarizes the position more generally (Schneider, *Die Rezeption von Arthur Schnitzlers Reigen*, p. 304).

51 The production subsequently moved to the Drill Hall, London, on 31 March 1982.

52 Michael Coveney, 'La Ronde', *Financial Times*, 5 April 1982, p. 17, as recorded in *London Theatre Record*, 10 vols (London: Herbert, 1981–90), II (1982), 154.

53 Suzie Mackenzie, *Time Out*, as recorded in *London Theatre Record*, II, 154.

attempts at specificity, Alfreds rendered the work relevant and engaging to English-language audiences more than eighty years after its inception.[54]

The BBC's television adaptation of *Reigen*, directed by Kenneth Ives, was (like the earlier radio adaptation) based on Jacqueline and Frank Marcus's translation and was broadcast as 'The Play of the Month' on 19 April 1982. Period costumes and set design were used; it was, according to one reviewer, 'naughty – but [...] in the best possible taste' (most likely a reference to comedian Kenny Everett's regular television sketch as 'Cupid Stunt', an American B-film actress whose catchphrase this was).[55] Nancy Banks-Smith, reviewing the adaptation for the *Guardian*, wrote: 'It could hardly have been done more beautifully – delicious, disinfected by fun, and cutting away at every copulation to the curves of an art nouveau window'.[56] One is left with the impression that the BBC restricted the dark and contagious elements of the play to the spoken text and kept the *mise-en-scène* clean, light and unthreatening. That has not been the case with subsequent translations of *Reigen*. After the initial flurry of relatively careful and closely translated English-language productions in 1982, re-writers and directors have become increasingly bold in the apparent distance they are willing to put between Schnitzler's text and their own adaptations. David Hare's *The Blue Room* is surely the most significant of these, not least because of the strong evidence suggesting Hare's is now the 'source text' to which many playwrights turn when making their own English versions of *Reigen*.[57] It has also been translated into German, which gives an indication of the degree to which Hare made Schnitzler's play his own.[58]

Subtitled as 'freely adapted from Arthur Schnitzler's *La Ronde*', *The Blue Room* was directed by Sam Mendes for the Donmar Warehouse and, famously, starred Nicole Kidman opposite Iain Glen, with each playing five of the ten roles. The production opened on 10 September 1998 and was set 'in one of the great cities of the world, in the present day'. The characters are listed in the published script by generic labels ('The Girl', 'The Cab Driver', 'The Au Pair', 'The Student', 'The Married Woman', 'The Politician', 'The Model', 'The

54 From author's correspondence with Pam Ferris, 11.3.2019 (with permission).

55 James Murray, 'So naughty – but it's in the best possible taste', *Daily Express*, 19 April 1982, p. 19.

56 Nancy Banks-Smith, 'Vienna's bitter-sweet taste', *Guardian*, 20 April 1982, p. 9.

57 Examples of this evidence are given below, in discussion of more recent adaptations.

58 David Hare, *The Blue Room*, trans. by Michael Walter, published online by Deutscher Theaterverlag as a manuscript for performance: https://www.dtver.de/downloads/leseprobe/f---1123.pdf [accessed 1 August 2018]. Hare, like Stoppard, cannot have had sufficient German to translate the play for himself, but instead relied on a literal translation by Julian Hammond, as credited in the (unpaginated) opening pages of the published script (David Hare, *The Blue Room* (London: Faber and Faber, 1998)).

Playwright', 'The Actress' and 'The Aristocrat'), but also, in brackets, by first names: Irene, Fred, Marie, Anton, Emma, Charles, Kelly, Robert and Malcolm. Many of these echo or mimic wholly the names of Schnitzler's characters (thereby extending the parody of *Madame Bovary* through the names of the *Junge Frau* and the *Gatte*).[59] As with the *Schauspielerin*, the Actress is not allocated a first name. The dialogue is undoubtedly modernized and, at times, Hare seems to write without reference to the source at all.[60] Nevertheless, more often than not it is possible to trace a direct relationship between the source material and Hare's adaptation. A brief comparison with another play produced in 1998 and also based on *Reigen* highlights the relative closeness of Hare's work to that of Schnitzler.

Sleeping Around was written collaboratively by Hilary Fannin, Stephen Greenhorn, Abi Morgan and Mark Ravenhill for Paines Plough, a touring theatre company known for commissioning and producing new plays. It was first performed at the Salisbury Playhouse in early March 1998 and continued its nationwide tour with a weeklong run at the Donmar Warehouse at the end of the month. Like *The Blue Room*, the play was set 'in a city and the time is present day';[61] and its cast comprised only one female and one male actor, each playing half the roles. Unlike *The Blue Room*, however, there were twelve scenes and hence twelve different characters; the cast list provides first names and, as additional information, ages and occupations for the characters; and the couples engage in sexual intercourse of one kind or another in some but not all of the scenes. Whilst echoing some of the themes explored in *Reigen*, such as desire and fidelity, the play makes more of the commodification of sex and the loneliness which often accompany modern city life. A woman longs to sleep with her dying, HIV-positive partner to demonstrate her commitment to him; a bulimic student subjects herself to brutal sexual intercourse with her lecturer; and a marketing manager fails to make contact with the night-shift garage cashier, who is protected by a Perspex security screen. The view is altogether less funny and more depressing than Schnitzler's light-hearted and witty meditation. Although the daisy-chain structure leaves no shadow of a doubt that *Reigen* was at least a major, if not the main, source of inspiration for *Sleeping Around*, the dialogue cannot be traced back to *Reigen* in any way

59 See Denneler for a reading of the Flaubert imitation in *Reigen* (Denneler, *Von Namen und Dingen*, p. 101).

60 See, for example, the conclusion to the scene between the Au Pair and the Cab Driver, in which instead of abandoning his latest conquest in search of the next, the Cab Driver offers the Au Pair a lift home and seems keen to maintain a connection with her (Hare, *The Blue Room*, pp. 11–12).

61 Hilary Fannin, Stephen Greenhorn, Abi Morgan and Mark Ravenhill, *Sleeping Around* (London: Methuen, 1998), n. pag.

and leaves the distinct impression that Schnitzler's play (or a translation of it) can only have played a fleeting role at the beginning of the writers' creative process.[62]

Both *The Blue Room* and *Sleeping Around* were written at a time when copyright in *Reigen*, as in Schnitzler's other works, had been revived by virtue of the Duration of Copyright and Rights in Performance Regulations 1995, which implemented the European Union-wide harmonization of copyright protection and came into effect on 1 January 1996. It is, therefore, unsurprising to see no reference to *Reigen* as a source in the published script for *Sleeping Around*. It seems quite possible that permission was not sought or granted for a new translation; and the writers of *Sleeping Around* would have had grounds for arguing that their play did not fall into the restricted definition of adaptation prescribed by the 1988 Act. The 'revived' copyright protection finally expired on 31 December 2001; this chapter now focuses on the translations and adaptations made after that date. In these newer interpretations the medically inflected tropes of contagion and fluidity in identity pick up fresh momentum.

Medical and Philosophical Readings of *Reigen*: Contagion and the Self

Marie Kolkenbrock and Laura Otis illuminate, through their respective studies of Schnitzler's prose and dramatic works, the intersection between the bacteriological discourse of the period, contemporary experimentation with hypnosis and Schnitzler's literary output. Whereas Schnitzler's interest in hypnosis is well documented, his attention to developments in somatic medicine had previously been somewhat neglected. By looking at Schnitzler's *Medizinische Schriften*, which include a number of reviews of published research concerned with syphilis, Kolkenbrock and Otis persuasively demonstrate the writer's interest in, and familiarity with, nineteenth-century thought in the field of bacteriology.[63] This in turn invites an interpretation of the literary corpus as a response to public perceptions of the germ as, among

62 Something of that process is recorded in the (unpaginated) Introduction to the published script: 'The kernel [...] came from an idea by Mark Ravenhill [...]. The four writers then began working together during August 1997, when they took part in the first of a series of developmental workshops at the Royal National Theatre Studio. Much research and debate later, *Sleeping Around* draft one emerged. Only one line from that original draft is present in this play'.

63 Arthur Schnitzler, *Medizinische Schriften*, ed. by Horst Thomé (Vienna: Zsolnay, 1988). Schnitzler also had personal experience of the impact syphilis could have: his friend Richard Tausenau contracted the illness; and his own father, on discovering his son's diaries, presented him with medical volumes on syphilis by way of a prophylactic (Schnitzler, *Jugend in Wien*, pp. 86 and 176).

other things, 'evil, menacing, [and] invading'.[64] The discovery that invisible microbes could move from one person to another without explanation, that these microbes could infect populations on a large scale and that they were, essentially, uncontrollable, fed into existing discourses around identity. Out of the 'golden age of bacteriology'[65] emerged a sense of 'the terrible sameness of all people, defeating any illusion about personal uniqueness'.[66] Class boundaries threatened to become blurred and meaningless; and social differences suddenly seemed arbitrary, no longer self-evident, their culturally constructed quality dangerously exposed.[67]

The discovery of microbes also brought to light the permeability of personal and social borders and the body's vulnerability to infection from any source. These consequences flow similarly from the clinical work that was being done with hypnosis during the same period: if the mind was susceptible to external suggestion, where were the fixed edges of identity?[68] Whereas some critics saw in the medical use of hypnosis 'subversive invasions of the psyche',[69] Schnitzler argued that suggestibility was, in fact, an everyday occurrence in the mind's encounter with the world:

> Die Pädagogik ist Suggestion, die großen Männer waren eigentlich Suggerenten. Die Religionsstifter haben suggeriert, und ganze Völker waren ihre Medien. Die unwillkürliche Tyrannei, die der bedeutende Geist über den kleineren ausübt, ist Suggestion, und wenn wir uns vornehmen, um fünf Uhr früh aufzustehen und uns tatsächlich nicht verschlafen, so haben wir eine Autosuggestion ausgeführt.[70]

Unsurprisingly, given his professional interest in both bacteriology and hypnosis, the problems of selfhood and free will, and the problem of 'where one individual ends and the next one begins', can be seen as central to Schnitzler's medical and literary writings.[71]

Like many of his peers in Vienna, Schnitzler was intrigued by the discontinuities of the self and what Robertson refers to as the 'disintegrative

64 Martina King, 'Anarchist and Aphrodite: On the Literary History of Germs', in *Contagionism and Contagious Diseases: Medicine and Literature 1880–1933*, ed. by Martina King and Thomas Rütten (Berlin: de Gruyter, 2013), pp. 101–29 (p. 103). King demonstrates the surprising breadth of cultural meanings attributed to bacteria, far from all of them negative.

65 King, 'Anarchist and Aphrodite', p. 102.

66 Otis, 'The Language of Infection', p. 65.

67 Kolkenbrock relates the cultural response to this scientific discourse to the Romantic *Grauen*, which 'occurs when a subject is confronted with a fading of differences which had been taken as given' (Kolkenbrock, 'Gothic Infections', p. 150).

68 Cf. Otis, *Membranes*, pp. 25–26; Kolkenbrock, 'Gothic Infections', p. 152.

69 Otis, 'The Language of Infection', p. 66.

70 Schnitzler, *Medizinische Schriften*, p. 179.

71 Otis, 'The Language of Infection', p. 73.

implications of impressionist psychology'.[72] The 1890s witnessed a number of writers (in literature and cultural journalism) engaging with and challenging Kantian notions of stable selfhood. At the critical vanguard Hermann Bahr published his essay 'Die Moderne' (1890), in which he advanced a subjective, rather than objective, measure of truth and, correspondingly, recognized a sensitivity to experience as the proper measure of the artist.[73] When Bahr discovered and promoted the work of physicist and psychologist Ernst Mach at the beginning of the twentieth century, the latter gave scientific, systematic credence to a world view already well established among the literati of Vienna.[74]

Schnitzler's ideas of the self differ from those of Mach and Bahr in a number of significant respects. Machian phenomenology presents a universally unsalvageable self: of primary importance are the elements, i.e., sensory experiences, which in turn form the notion of the 'Ich', so that the 'Ich' changes with every new experience. Thus the 'Ich', according to Mach, 'ist keine unveränderliche, bestimmte, scharf begrenzte Einheit'.[75] For Bahr, also, the common conceit of a fixed, concrete 'Ich' serves only for us to orient ourselves; in reality 'alles ist nur eine ewige Flut'.[76] Although Schnitzler's works clearly concern themselves with the impressionistic self in general terms, there are two respects in which he departs from Mach and Bahr (albeit unwittingly – Schnitzler did not read Mach's work until 1904 (*Tagebuch*, 28 and 29.9.1904)).

First, in Schnitzler's view 'Kernlosigkeit', which Mach regards as afflicting all selves, was a condition experienced by some, possibly even the majority of, individuals, but not all:

> Die Seele mancher Menschen scheint aus einzelnen gewissermaßen flottierenden Elementen zu bestehen, die sich niemals um ein Zentrum zu gruppieren, also auch keine Einheit zu bilden imstande sind. So lebt der kernlose Mensch in einer ungeheuren und ihm doch niemals völlig zu Bewußtsein kommenden Einsamkeit dahin. Die große Mehrzahl

72 Robertson, 'Modernism and the Self', p. 166.

73 Hermann Bahr, 'Die Moderne', *Moderne Dichtung*, 1 (1890), 13–15. See Andrew W. Barker, '"Der Grosse Überwinder": Hermann Bahr and the Rejection of Naturalism', *Modern Language Review*, 78 (1983), 617–30 (pp. 626–28).

74 Ernst Mach, *Die Analyse der Empfindungen und das Verhältnis des Physischen zum Psychischen* (Jena: Fischer, 1886). Although first published in 1886, Mach's work initially made little impact. Bahr's essay 'Das unrettbare ich' was first published in the *Neues Wiener Tagblatt*, 10 April 1903, pp. 1–4, then as part of his collection *Dialog vom Tragischen* (Berlin: Fischer, 1904), pp. 79–101. It followed reprints of Mach's work in 1901 and a further impression in 1902 (Barker, '"Der Grosse Überwinder"', p. 629 n. 39).

75 Ernst Mach, *Die Analyse der Empfindungen und das Verhältnis des Physischen zum Psychischen*, 9th edn (Jena: Fischer, 1922 [1886]), p. 19. See also p. 10.

76 Hermann Bahr, 'Philosophie des Impressionismus', in Hermann Bahr, *Dialog vom Tragischen* (Berlin: Fischer, 1904), pp. 102–14 (p. 113); Bahr, 'Das unrettbare Ich', p. 98.

> der Menschen ist in diesem Sinne kernlos, doch erst an merkwürdigen und bedeutenden Menschen fällt uns eine solche Kernlosigkeit auf, die übrigens vorzugsweise bei reproduzierenden Talenten, vor allem bei genialen Schauspielern, insbesondere Schauspielerinnen, zu beobachten ist.[77]

By extension, 'Kernlosigkeit' could be diagnosed as a medical symptom rather than as an ontological state, thereby diminishing its meaning and effect.[78] Nevertheless, both condition and resulting solitude were widespread: Schnitzler notably uses the plural 'Einsamkeiten' in the title for the section in which the above-quoted aphorism was first published, as if struck by the sheer mass of 'lonelinesses' around him. The visibility of centrelessness in actors (or more particularly, actresses) is rendered dramatically by the *Schauspielerin* in *Reigen*. As Hannum observes, in her scene with the *Dichter* the *Schauspielerin* 'voices changing opinions in virtually every speech'.[79] The significance of role-play to Schnitzler's Impressionism will be examined further in the close readings below. The gendered specificity of Schnitzler's observation above can perhaps be best understood when considered in its historical context, most notably in light of the cultural overlap with Otto Weininger's *Geschlecht und Charakter* (1903), in which Weininger argues that Mach's 'Zeichnung des Ich' describes perfectly the female ego.[80]

The second respect in which Schnitzler diverges from Mach and Bahr is in his resistance to the ethical consequences of an entirely centreless self. A similar resistance can be read in his rejection of the Freudian self – Schnitzler insists on attributing moral responsibility to individuals.[81] In respect of 'Kernlosigkeit', Schnitzler stresses the role of memory and therewith responsibility.[82] Whereas for Mach memory serves only to provide a semblance of constancy,[83] so that our sense of slow change and fixed identity is mere illusion, Schnitzler reads the role of memory more substantively. Memory compels us to accept

77 Schnitzler, *Aphorismen und Betrachtungen*, pp. 53–54. This aphorism was first published in Arthur Schnitzler, *Buch der Sprüche und Bedenken. Aphorismen und Fragmente* (Vienna: Phaidon, 1927), pp. 95–96. However, it may have been written years or decades earlier.

78 Horst Thomé, 'Kernlosigkeit und Pose. Zur Rekonstruktion von Schnitzlers Psychologie', in *Fin de Siécle. Zu Naturwissenschaft und Literatur der Jahrhundertwende im deutsch-skandinavischen Kontext / Vorträge des Kolloquiums am 3. und 4. Mai 1984*, ed. by Klaus Bohnen, Uffe Hansen and Friedrich Schmöe, *Text & Kontext*, Sonderreihe, 20 (Copenhagen and Munich: Fink, 1984), pp. 62–87 (p. 64).

79 Hannum, '"Killing Time"', p. 203.

80 Otto Weininger, *Geschlecht und Charakter* (Vienna and Leipzig: Braumüller, 1903), p. 259.

81 Thomé, 'Kernlosigkeit und Pose', pp. 78–80.

82 Robertson, 'Modernism and the Self', p. 166.

83 Mach, *Die Analyse der Empfindungen*, pp. 2–3.

our nature as ethical beings. Schnitzler arguably rescues 'das unrettbare Ich' from the moral abyss and simultaneously provides a balm for the existential panic spreading among the educated public at the beginning of the twentieth century.[84]

It is in his literary works that Schnitzler explores the implications of the self as physically and psychologically permeable and of many individuals as being 'kernlos'. Thomé has shown, for example, how many of his characters, while enjoying a level of stability through the socially normalized roles they occupy, are disrupted by a single shocking event which, in its nonconformity with the adopted role, provokes a dissociation of the parts of the self.[85] In her study of the Gothic in Schnitzler's works, Kolkenbrock highlights the way in which biological sameness interrupts (through an infection of sorts) 'the culturally constructed quality of social boundaries' normally experienced by the protagonist in 'Andreas Thameyers letzter Brief'.[86] Similarly, an 'infection anxiety' in *Traumnovelle* is linked to the doctor Fridolin's 'emerging identity crisis', which is made manifest in his feeling that 'the protective boundaries around his sense of self have become permeable'.[87] Fridolin is exposed, through his house-visits and street-wanderings, to various situations in which he either faces or recalls threats to his physical integrity; these threats appear in the infectious patients he treats, a group of fraternity students he encounters, a prostitute to whom he is attracted and even the air of the city around him. *Reigen* provides a ten-fold portrait of this crisis of the 'minimal self'.[88] Indeed, the very structure of the play presents in its form, in its episodic and connected framing, what gradually materializes from the content. There is no real centre to the play (although the deceit-filled marriage in the fifth scene admittedly provides a thematic focus) and no central character or characters. Seen on their own, each part seems disconnected from any other; yet they are, of course, linked through the characters' engagement in sexual intercourse.

The ten characters of *Reigen* are, through their actions and their words, exposed as vessels of sameness, spouting variations on repeated themes or

84 Judith Ryan, *The Vanishing Subject: Early Psychology and Literary Modernism* (Chicago, IL and London: University of Chicago Press, 1991), p. 21. See also Fliedl on Schnitzler's concern, from 1900 onwards, with the role art could play in rescuing memory (Fliedl, *Poetik der Erinnerung*, p. 25).

85 Horst Thomé, 'Vorwort. Arthur Schnitzlers Anfänge und die Grundlagenkrise der Medizin. Walter Müller-Seidel zum siebzigsten Geburtstag', in Schnitzler, *Medizinische Schriften*, pp. 11–59 (pp. 52–53).

86 Kolkenbrock, 'Gothic Infections', p. 157.

87 Kolkenbrock, 'Gothic Infections', p. 160.

88 Ritchie Robertson's term is especially useful if extended to include concepts of the self informed by the bacteriology, hypnosis and Impressionist philosophy current at the end of the nineteenth century (Robertson, 'Modernism and the Self', p. 162).

even, on occasion, exact replications.[89] 'Engel', for example, appears in the first line spoken in the play, that uttered by the *Dirne* as she calls to the *Soldat*, and is subsequently deployed as part of the pre- and post-coital rituals by the *Junger Herr* in respect of the *Junge Frau*, the *Dichter* in respect of the *Süßes Mädel* and the *Graf* in respect of the *Schauspielerin*. Nevertheless, the characters long to be regarded as different and unique; and in each sexual encounter they seek an irreplaceable experience.[90] This gives rise to the oft-repeated enquiries into former lovers and the desperate pleas for post-coital confirmation of genuine affection. They want to be known by their names and as themselves, but names, like bodies, are exchangeable and recyclable. Even the *Gatte* must face the fact that his own name, 'Karl', as well as referring intertextually to his forebear in Flaubert's *Madame Bovary* (1856), is a repetition in the catalogue of sexual encounters already collected by the *Süßes Mädel* (*Reigen*, p. 990). *Reigen* exposes the uncontrollable drives that lead one person to make a connection with another, even when those very connections threaten the individual's identity (through the risk of infection) and undermine the stability of established social structures.

Although only indirectly referred to in the play, venereal disease, and syphilis in particular, were a stark reality in Europe at the end of the nineteenth century, with one estimate putting the number of syphilitic adult men in Paris in 1899 at seventeen per cent.[91] Although Schnitzler alludes to sexually transmitted diseases only indirectly in *Reigen* (perhaps as a form of self-censorship),[92] the prevalence of the disease at the turn of the century has undoubtedly informed subsequent interpretations of the play. Intensive research into and media coverage of AIDS in the 1980s provided the background for a succession of productions which made a feature of the haptic aspect of contamination. Florence Hetzel's survey of the reception of

89 See Erna Neuse, for whom the repeated idioms emphasize acoustically the various partners' 'Gleichheit' (Erna Neuse, 'Die Funktion von Motiven und stereotypen Wendungen in Schntizlers *Reigen*', *Monatshefte*, 64 (1972), 359–70). Such 'Gleichheit' is, however, far from a political, liberal ideal. As Janz stresses, neither the *Junge Frau* nor the *Schauspielerin* looks below her social standing for her lovers (Rolf-Peter Janz, 'Reigen', in Janz and Laermann, *Arthur Schnitzler*, pp. 55–75 (pp. 57–58)). (In fact, no woman does in *Reigen*.) The *Soldat* sleeps with a prostitute and a chambermaid – nobody else.

90 Cf. Helga Schiffer, who argues that the characters' desire for individuality is the very thing that makes them human (Helga Schiffer, 'Arthur Schnitzlers *Reigen*', *Text & Kontext*, 11 (1983), 7–34 (p. 12)). See also Richard Alewyn, for whom the endless enquiries about former partners and angst about future partners are explained by 'das Zittern um die Illusion der Einmaligkeit und Ewigkeit' (Alewyn, *Probleme und Gestalten*, p. 303).

91 Peter Baldwin, *Contagion and the State in Europe 1830–1930* (Cambridge: Cambridge University Press, 1999), pp. 424–25.

92 Anja Schonlau, *Syphilis in der Literatur. Über Ästhetik, Moral, Genie und Medizin* (Würzburg: Königshausen & Neumann, 2005), p. 101.

Reigen in France includes two historicist stagings, in 1988 and 1993, which both 'introduced a symbolic object that passed from hand to hand in each scene, alluding to the transmission of contagion – [...] most obviously syphilis – from person to person'.[93] In 1993 an adaptation for opera (with a libretto originally written in German by Luc Bondy and produced in Brussels) incorporated a handkerchief passed from hand to hand to represent the transmission of disease.[94] A more recent production in Vienna at the Burgtheater (1999/2000) similarly incorporated props, this time linked to individual characters, to symbolize contagion.[95] As will be shown below, a contemporary English-language adaptation, *Fucking Men*, explicitly enlists AIDS as the successor to syphilis.

However, contagion is not only physical. Schnitzler's figures are infected by memories of the past and thoughts of the future. Contrary to the Machian self, which can live only in the moment and is therefore incapable of fidelity, Schnitzler's characters are plagued by the recognition of their own continuity. Max captures the undesirability of such continuity (from his perspective) in the following passage from *Anatol*:

> Deine Gegenwart schleppt immer eine ganze schwere Last von unverarbeiteter Vergangenheit mit sich . . . Und nun fangen die ersten Jahre Deiner Liebe wieder einmal zu vermodern an, ohne daß Deine Seele die wunderbare Kraft hätte, sie völlig auszustoßen – Was ist nun die natürliche Folge–? – Daß auch um die gesundesten und blühendsten Stunden Deines Jetzt ein Duft dieses Moders fließt – und die Atmosphäre Deiner Gegenwart unrettbar vergiftet ist. [...] Und darum ist ja ewig dieser Wirrwarr von Einst und Jetzt und Später in Dir.[96]

For Max, a past which has not been processed and properly concluded becomes a burden. If not fully left behind, decaying elements of that past can infect, even poison, the otherwise healthy present. To live without a sense of the temporally extended self, however, is to lose a sense of one's own centre, to become 'minimal'. According to Hannum, this is precisely what the characters in *Reigen* seem to desire, namely to lose themselves in the 'poetic infinitude' of the erotic moment.[97]

93 Hetzel, 'The Reception of Arthur Schnitzler on the French Stage', p. 196.

94 Hetzel, 'The Reception of Arthur Schnitzler on the French Stage', p. 208.

95 Hetzel, 'The Reception of Arthur Schnitzler on the French Stage', p. 197.

96 Schnitzler, *Anatol*, pp. 974–75.

97 Hannum, '"Killing Time"', p. 200, citing Søren Kierkegaard, 'Either/Or: A Fragment of Life' (1843), in *A Kierkegaard Anthology*, ed. by Robert Bretall (Princeton, NJ: Princeton University Press, 1946), pp. 19–108 (p. 30).

In the *Graf* we find the avatar of that philosophy and discover that 'losing oneself' is precisely the consequence. Having determined that happiness is impossible, the *Graf* pursues only isolated, fleeting pleasures (*Reigen*, p. 1031). Nonetheless, without memory, Hannum suggests, characters cannot be certain of their own existence. In the last scene the *Graf* cannot remember the presumed instant of gratification with the *Dirne*; '[t]he motif of forgetfulness takes on nihilistic proportions' as the *Graf* 'fight[s] for his existence and meet[s] only blank nothingness'.[98] Notwithstanding the drive towards the supposedly ideal, unique moment between two individuals, therefore, *Reigen* is littered with references to before and after, to forgetting and remembering. Once more, theme is reflected in form: the scenes in *Reigen* are, as Hannum puts it, Janus-faced, 'point[ing] to both past and future'.[99] It is only by understanding the self as continuing through time that identity is possible.

With *Reigen* Schnitzler brings together contemporary discourses of bacteriology, psychology and philosophy in his exploration of ten individuals and their unavoidable connectedness, to each other and to their own pasts and futures. The preceding section shows how those discourses overlap in the play through reference to contagion, permeable identities, role-play and loneliness. The reading below of three recent English translations examines the degree to which those themes are picked up in modern interpretations and even motivate the continuing interest in *Reigen* more than a hundred years after its first publication.

Post-2002 Adaptations

On 1 January 2002 the revived, extended copyright in Schnitzler's works expired, leaving those wishing to experiment with any element of Schnitzler's corpus free to do so. The previous decade had witnessed the boom years of what came to be known as 'in-yer-face' theatre, paving the way for a new, anything-goes approach to theatre-making.[100] London audiences have since seen a huge range of new interpretations of *Reigen*, predominantly in off-West End or fringe theatres. The following summary gives a flavour of that breadth.

In 2002 itself Carlo Gebler's *Ten Rounds* premièred at the Tricycle Theatre, transposing the action to Northern Ireland and the focus of

98 Hannum, '"Killing Time"', p. 204.

99 Hannum, '"Killing Time"', p. 198.

100 See Aleks Sierz, *In-Yer-Face Theatre: British Drama Today* (London: Faber & Faber, 2001).

attention to contemporary politics.[101] In the same week Sarah Phelps's adaptation, *Modern Dance for Beginners*, played at the Soho Theatre, reducing the number of actors to two and the scenes to six. In 2009 *Foreplay*, a re-location of the play to post-apartheid South Africa, was written and directed by Mpumelelo Paul Grootboom and performed by the South African State Theatre at the Theatre Royal Stratford East; in the same year a part-dance, part-drama production at the Gate Theatre, *Unbroken*, was adapted by Alexandra Wood and directed by Natalie Abrahami. Once again in 2009, Neil Sheppeck produced *La Ronde* at Riverside Studios, employing tango as a means to navigate the dashes and playing with gender: two of the normally female roles were played by men, so that the prostitute became a rent boy and the sweet young thing a male 'youth', while the soldier was played by a woman.[102] *Fucking Men*, by American playwright Joe DiPietro, was the fourth adaptation to be produced in 2009 (after an initial run at the Finborough Theatre in 2008) and is one of the three plays examined in more detail below.

The year 2011 saw a musical version of *Reigen*, set in a gay bar, at the Rose Branch Theatre (another *La Ronde*), written by Peter Scott-Presland and David Harrod. Lukas Raphael's 'new translation' for the Harbinger Company set the play in the 1950s and was produced at the White Bear Theatre, also in 2011. It apparently fused 'theatre, live music and dance'.[103] Richard Listor wrote and directed *Swings and Roundabouts* at the White Bear Theatre in 2014, updating the maid to an intern and the count to a movie producer. *Love to Love to Love You*, by Florence Keith-Roach, was shown at a private club, The Library in St Martin's Lane, in 2014 and was billed as being produced 'In Response to Arthur Schnitzler's "Der Reigen"'; it was summarized on the writer's website as '[a] comedy about sex, disco and loneliness'.[104] Finally, in 2017 London once again witnessed four different productions of *Reigen* in translation. One of these was a revived *Fucking Men*, staged at The Vaults (a fringe theatre near Waterloo) and with a

101 Few of these adaptations have been considered within Schnitzler- or translation-oriented scholarship. *Ten Rounds* is a rare exception, having been analysed in detail in Zojer, 'Vienna-London-Belfast'.

102 John Thaxter, 'La Ronde', *British Theatre Guide*, https://www.britishtheatreguide.info/reviews/laronde-rev [accessed 6 March 2019].

103 'La Ronde by Harbinger Company at White Bear Theatre', *London Theatre*, 3 August 2011, https://www.londontheatre.co.uk/theatre-news/news/la-ronde-by-harbinger-company-at-white-bear-theatre [accessed 6 March 2019].

104 'Love to Love to Love You', *Florence Keith-Roach*, http://web.florencekeithroach.co.uk/love-to-love-to-love-you [accessed 6 March 2019]. The title echoes and extends Donna Summer's 1975 disco hit 'Love To Love You, Baby'.

reduced cast of three. In addition, newcomer Max Gill wrote and directed *La Ronde* for The Bunker (London Bridge); the Acting Gymnasium performed an adaptation by Gavin McAlinden at the Theatro Technis (Camden); and *Roundelay* by Sonja Linden broke the final taboo – 'sex between those whose bodies are no longer young' – in a production by the Visible Theatre Ensemble at Southwark Playhouse.[105] The second of these four, *La Ronde*, is also considered more closely below. Evident even from this very brief survey is the readiness with which recent directors and writers have used *Reigen* to address twenty-first-century concerns such as ageing, homosexuality, loneliness, gender performativity and geopolitical apartheid (whether in South Africa or Northern Ireland).

This chapter will now concentrate on two of these recently staged productions and *Cashcows*, a radio adaptation broadcast in 2005. Consideration of the published texts (in the cases of Joe DiPietro's *Fucking Men* and *La Ronde* by Max Gill) and the archived script (in the case of *Cashcows* by April de Angelis) draws out some of the common features of the post-Millennium approach to adapting *Reigen*. More specifically, these three adaptations invite comparison by virtue of their shared attention to gender and sexuality, a focus which becomes apparent as soon as the casting is considered: *Fucking Men* is an all-male play; *Cashcows* all-female; and *La Ronde* casts gender (and hence also sexuality) differently with each performance. The binary arrangement of the original daisy chain is duly queered and Schnitzler's historically-rooted approach to gender modified.[106] All three plays explore questions of identity, connectedness and contagion, themes already shown to be prevalent in Schnitzler's writing more generally and especially in *Reigen*. The last of these themes emerges most clearly in *Fucking Men*, in which AIDS replaces earlier established venereal diseases as the condition through which individuals' physical porosity and vulnerability are exposed. As in the source text, the desire for contact with others, whether sexual or not, overwhelms any prior sense of self-preservation.

All three adaptations depart significantly from *Reigen* in terms of time, place and culture, transposing the play into the twenty-first century with the result that all 'bring [...] the text closer to the audience's personal frame of reference'.[107] In *Cashcows* the physical locations referred to include London NW4, Primrose Hill and Harringay; cultural references made are to Norah Jones, New Labour and

105 'Roundelay by Sonja Linden: Note from the author', *Visible Theatre Ensemble*, http://www.visible.org.uk/2017/05/22/roundelay-by-sonja-linden/ [accessed 30 July 2018].

106 Schnitzler's approach to gender is best understood in its historical context, most notably in light of the cultural overlap with Otto Weininger's *Geschlecht und Charakter* (1903).

107 Julie Sanders, *Adaptation and Appropriation* (London & New York: Routledge, 2006), p. 26.

Victoria Beckham;[108] and one scene takes place entirely via email. Through these allusions it is quickly possible to locate *Cashcows* in mid-2000s London. Gill's *La Ronde* is similarly rooted, geographically and temporally, in the post-Millennium capital city: characters talk about Tottenham, Southwark, London Bridge, Piccadilly Circus, the British Library and Bart's Hospital; the national shop chains Poundland, DFS, Cath Kidston and Waitrose enter the dialogue; two characters meet via a dating app; another couple's liaison takes place in a Premier Inn hotel room in Hillingdon; and a terminally ill patient is advised by the doctor not to 'look online' for information.

Fucking Men prescribes 'Place & Time' as 'Here & Now'.[109] Although played as if in London for the production at The Vaults (with a variety of British accents and local allusions), the published script makes reference only to contemporary American culture.[110] American brands such as Bengay pain relief and Starbucks, and locations which included 'Philly', Hollywood, Broadway and 'downtown', led reviewers of the King's Head production to conclude that this was a play specifically about the modern New York gay scene.[111] The men used mobile phones on stage to take photographs, check their calendars and send text messages; and, as in Gill's *La Ronde*, two characters had met through a dating app. Whether set in New York or London, then, there can be no doubt about the era with which DiPietro's play is concerned. In each case, the translocation of the action to modern-day metropolises enables the adapter to use his or her adaptation as a commentary on the politics and culture of the new *mise-en-scène*.[112] Furthermore, for those members of the audience for whom the relationship with Schnitzler's text was apparent, the updating of the play draws attention to the continuities between the two turn-of-the-century contexts.[113]

108 Norah Jones, a jazz singer and daughter of Ravi Shankar, the sitar-player who influenced the Beatles, launched her solo career in 2002; 'New Labour' refers to the more centrist brand of Labour party politics promoted by and associated with Tony Blair and Gordon Brown between 1995 and 2010; Victoria Beckham was, in 2005 (when *Cashcows* was broadcast), perhaps best known for her membership of the (by then disbanded) pop group The Spice Girls as well as her marriage to the international footballer and fashion icon David Beckham.

109 Joe DiPietro, *Fucking Men* (New York: Dramatists Play Service, 2014), p. 4. Hereinafter references will be included in the text as *FM* followed by the page number.

110 Textual alterations to re-localize the play were made with DiPietro's agreement (author's correspondence with Richard De Lisle, one of the three actors in the Vaults production, 11.7.2018, with permission).

111 See, for example, Lyn Gardner, 'Fucking Men', *Guardian*, 10 January 2009, https://www.theguardian.com/stage/2009/jan/10/review-fucking-men [accessed 27 October 2018]. This conclusion is supported by the synopsis on the back cover of the published script, which locates the play in 'the gay subculture in contemporary Manhattan'.

112 Sanders, *Adaptation and Appropriation*, p. 27.

113 The importance of audience familiarity with the source, or adapted, text has been discussed by various theorists within Adaptation Studies. See, for example, Hutcheon and O'Flynn, *A*

Structurally, all three adaptations maintain the ten encounters between ten pairs that are so strongly associated with *Reigen*. Although in *Cashcows* none of the couples has sexual intercourse, in both Gill's *La Ronde* and in *Fucking Men* sex remains a crucial part of every scene. As in the source text, the published adaptations do not spell out explicitly what might or might not take place on stage. DiPietro's directions provide a blackout, during which one of the other men appears briefly and delivers an excerpt from his earlier or later scene; and Gill similarly directed that the lights go 'down' and then 'up', substituting a row of asterisks in the text for Schnitzler's dashes. As well as this structural mirroring, there are clear relationships between the characters in Schnitzler's play and those in the adaptations; and, similarly, themes dominant in the source text are retained, developed or updated in the adaptations. Thus, although these modern interpretations cannot be mapped onto the source text line for line, the combination of the formal replication with significant character overlaps and thematic echoes supports a claim for each of the later works being a rewriting of the earlier Schnitzler text. The following analysis of the three plays illustrates some of the common threads connecting the English texts with *Reigen*, while also drawing out significant points at which the adaptations depart from the source.

Fucking Men

Before diving into the adaptive text, it is worth briefly assessing the paratexts accompanying performance. First and foremost, the title, which refers enigmatically to the homosexual content of the play ('Fucking' could here be an expression of disgust), omits to bring to light the relationship with *Reigen*. The role of Schnitzler's play as its source is, however, spelt out on the front and back covers of the published script, where it states, 'Adapted from *La Ronde* by Arthur Schnitzler' and 'a free-wheeling adaptation of the 19th century play'; and in the double-page, centrally-located 'Timeline' in the 2017 programme. The subheading to the timeline informs the audience that the chronology moves 'From *La Ronde* to *Fucking Men*', to which the explanation is added: 'Joe DiPietro based the structure of this play on the Arthur Schnitzler classic *La Ronde*'. Among the pertinent dates subsequently included are those for the 'first gay version of the play' (*Round 2* by Eric Bentley, 1992), the 'first version to mix straight, gay and bisexual characters in its take on Schnitzler's

Theory of Adaptation, p. 116; Sanders, *Adaptation and Appropriation*, pp. 10, 28–29 and 34; Margherita Laera, 'Introduction', in *Theatre and Adaptation: Return, Rewrite, Repeat*, ed. by Margherita Laera (London and New York: Bloomsbury, 2014), pp. 1–18 (pp. 3–4).

tale' (*Circle*, 2002) and 'a gay version advocating safe sex' (*Complications* by Michael Kearns, 2004). DiPietro's adaptation is unambiguously presented as continuing an extant tradition of undoing the heteronormative binaries of *Reigen*.

In the opening scene the parallels between Schnitzler's and DiPietro's worlds are already easily drawn: Schnitzler's *Dirne* becomes John, 'the escort', who picks up Steve, 'the soldier', while hanging around on a park bench at night. Somewhat less clear cut, the *Stubenmädchen* becomes Marco, 'the graduate student', who after an encounter with Steve in a sauna is hired by the parents of Kyle, 'the college kid', to tutor their son. Although Marco is not an obvious modern version of a chambermaid, the triangular arrangement of power between parents, servant and son is preserved. The scene between tutor and college student echoes that between the *Stubenmädchen* and the *Junger Herr*: as in the source text, physical heat is relevant – Marco is sweaty on arrival and has to change into a clean shirt (*FM*, p. 12), while in Schnitzler's play the *Stubenmädchen* is initially summoned to lower the blinds in order to cool the room (*Reigen*, p. 944). The Doktor Schüller expected by the *Junger Herr* is made partially manifest in Marco as tutor (i.e., Marco embodies elements of both the *Stubenmädchen* and the awaited visitor); and the doorbell interruption (possibly the anticipated Doktor Schüller) (*Reigen*, p. 949) is transposed into the sound of a door shutting (signalling the arrival of Kyle's parents) at the end of the scene (*FM*, p. 16). The couple are susceptible to the influence of the outside world, whether in the form of other people bursting in, or merely the sun's heat affecting their own body temperature.

The relationship between source and adaptation continues to be established in the next scene when Kyle has a speedy fling with Leo, 'the married guy', the two having found each other through a dating app. This is followed by the marital bedroom scene between Leo and Jack, his husband. Jack then sleeps with Ryan, 'the porn star', who subsequently invites Sammy, 'the playwright', to come home with him. Sammy tells Ryan repeatedly that he is an 'angel' (*FM*, pp. 33–34), a direct translation of the 'Engel' used by the *Dichter* to seduce the *Süßes Mädel* (*Reigen*, pp. 1002, 1005, 1009). Sammy's secret liaison with Oscar-winning actor Brandon in a backstage store cupboard results in an exposé that threatens to ruin the latter's marriage and career. In the penultimate scene, television journalist Donald advises Brandon to forget any plans to reveal his sexual orientation and instead to deny everything asserted by Sammy. Just as in the final scene of *Reigen*, where the sexual encounter between the *Graf* and the *Dirne* has already taken place when the action begins, in *Fucking Men* we see Donald working at his desk after a night spent with John. The scene ends with Donald's gift to John of money to start renting a flat, thereby enabling him to settle down with the soldier, Steve. John's dream of domestic stability seems set for realization but is undermined by the audience's memory of the fragile fidelity displayed by the married couple at the centre of the play. Although much of the dramatic development occurs in the final three scenes of DiPietro's adaptation, it is in the central three scenes involving Leo and Jack that the key concerns of the play are focused.

Leo, like the *Junge Frau*, is outwardly uneasy about his rendezvous with Kyle. At one point he seems on the verge of leaving and at the end of the scene he announces his intention not to see Kyle again (*FM*, pp. 17 and 20). However, whereas the understandable caution shown by the *Junge Frau* also transpires to be part of her flirtation with the *Junger Herr*, Leo is genuinely disconcerted by his own infidelity; his selfhood is clearly shaken by his actions. Contrary to his own principles, Leo has embarked upon the extra-marital dalliance with the encouragement of his husband, Jack, whom we later hear advocating promiscuity as a cure for the monotony of marriage. This is just one of several ways in which DiPietro re-orients Schnitzler's central scene between the married couple.

It is Leo, not Jack, who suggests they have sex and Jack who claims to be too tired. Unlike the *Gatte*, whose ignorance of his wife's worldliness and romantic adventures increases the comedic irony at the centre of *Reigen*, Jack knows about Leo's fling with Kyle and tells him as much (he has seen explicit photographs sent by Kyle in an email). Moreover, rather than berate Leo, Jack assures him 'it's fine'. By contrast to the sermon delivered by the *Gatte* to his wife in *Reigen*, Jack argues in favour of adultery: 'Look, do you honestly think we're made to have sex with the same person over and over again for the rest of our lives' (*FM*, p. 23). Continuity through time is, accordingly, a misconceived fantasy. In this respect, Jack and the *Gatte* are aligned, with Jack's series of extra-marital affairs echoing the intra-marital affairs (separated by 'Freundschaftsperioden') promoted by the *Gatte* (*Reigen*, p. 971). When Leo suggests they could 'try other things', Jack's answer purports to solve a paradox at the heart of the play:

> JACK: That's what straight people do. The wife wears Saran Wrap and surprises the husband. But that's one of the great things about being gay.
> LEO: What?
> JACK: We don't have to be trapped by monogamy.[114]

Jack's argument is that he and Leo can have their cake and eat it. They can enjoy the benefits of both marriage and sexual liberty. As the scenes play out,

114 DiPietro, *FM*, p. 23. 'Saran Wrap' is the American name for cling-film. When the play was performed at the Vaults, overtly American cultural references were swapped for either generic terms or alternative British brands.

however, the incompatibility of the ten men's sometimes simultaneous desires for domestic stability and erotic adventure is exposed.

According to Monica B. Pearl's account of AIDS in American literature, marriage represented the antidote to the AIDS epidemic, especially in post-2000 narratives.[115] In turn, gay marriage opened up gay literature to one of the otherwise absent Grand Narratives of that genre, namely adultery: '[W]ithout the story of marriage, there [had been] no possibility of the story of adultery'.[116] Both these developments feature in the central relationship between Jack and Leo, although marriage has not kept AIDS at bay. Jack, we discover, is HIV-positive. His contagious condition inevitably has a bearing on his extra-marital activities. Jack has promised Leo that he will always disclose his status before putting a new lover at risk. The married couple have also agreed that each sexual encounter with another man should be a one-off fling. By avoiding return visits to particular lovers, Leo and Jack aim to protect the emotional core of their marriage. Although the norms surrounding sexual behaviour might have changed when compared with those portrayed in *Reigen*, the men in DiPietro's play still struggle to live happily with or observe the new rules. Whereas Leo only wants to have sex with Jack and sleeps with Kyle by way of perfunctory compliance with this new system of fidelity, he is ultimately betrayed when Jack allows his one evening with Ryan 'the porn star' (occupying the same position as the *Süßes Mädel*) to turn into something longer-term and potentially more meaningful.[117] The deceit is doubled when Jack denies his infected status to Ryan.

Promiscuity and monogamy thus provide two of the key topics for the couples in DiPietro's adaptation. Whereas Schnitzler's lovers are uneasy at the idea of the current partner having previous, or indeed future, sexual partners, promiscuity is the accepted starting point for most of DiPietro's characters. Indeed, the illusion of monogamy at times falls away entirely. Nevertheless, in DiPietro's imagined world the fantasy for several characters remains complete fidelity and they feel trapped in a culture of constant change and exchange. Thus, the lie is given to the common fiction (in the play, at least) that promiscuity frees the modern gay man. Instead, it leaves him lonely and often alone, a victim of the 'Einsamkeit' identified by Schnitzler as an otherwise unappreciated consequence of 'Kernlosigkeit'.

115 Monica B. Pearl, *AIDS Literature and Gay Identity: The Literature of Loss* (New York & London: Routledge, 2012), p. 127.

116 Pearl, *AIDS Literature*, p. 127.

117 Just as in *Reigen* the *Gatte* suggests arranging a flat for the *Süßes Mädel* on the understanding that he will thereby obtain exclusive access to her (*Reigen*, p. 999), Jack offers to set up Ryan in his 'own place' (DiPietro, *FM*, p. 27) and the relationship has become 'serious' by the time Ryan and Sammy meet (*FM*, p. 31).

The men in DiPietro's adaptation seek in their encounters with each other a meaningful human connection, but they are unsure of how it should be achieved. During the blackout in Jack and Ryan's scene, Sammy 'the playwright' delivers an anticipatory excerpt from his subsequent dialogue with Ryan:

> I'm just saying that sex – well, it's just about connecting, isn't it? 'Only connect!' That's not me, E. M. Forster wrote that. I hate that – two words and he sums up the entire human condition! But that's [what] we're doing here tonight – only connect. When people tell me they're monogamous, I always feel bad for them. I always think – My god, how much you're missing. Just think, if I was monogamous now – I would've missed you. (*FM*, p. 27)

The intertextual reference is intriguing: the two words provide the epigraph for *Howard's End* (1910) and are repeated in the body of the novel (written by E. M. Forster, himself a closet homosexual) as part of a 'sermon' by Margaret Schlegel which ends on the instruction to '[l]ive in fragments no longer'.[118] For Sammy the possibilities for connection are severely limited by monogamy. An episodic, disrupted approach to relationships, he seems to argue somewhat perversely, merely multiplies the opportunities to avoid loneliness. For others in the play, though, the promised land is the connectedness only available in a stable and constant relationship.

Ryan daydreams about the possibility that he might one day find himself with such a settled arrangement, referring to himself in the third person: '[S]omeday I bet he's going to move on and find someone and fall in love. And it's just gonna be the two of them. And they're never gonna fuck around with anyone else. And they're gonna be happy' (*FM*, p. 34). Models of more traditional committed relationships are visible in Donald's long partnership with Phillip (*FM*, p. 43) and in the burgeoning domestic relationship between John and Steve (*FM*, pp. 46–47). However, the only married couple represented fully in the play reveal the tough realities of that fantasy: domestic bliss can become just domestic. Leo worries: 'I just don't want our life together to be nothing but, you know, who does the laundry and who's cooking dinner' (*FM*, p. 24). The die has already been cast. The scene ends, after marital sex, with Jack asking Leo if he is 'doing a wash tomorrow' and telling him 'I got whites' (*FM*, p. 24). The mystery of (sustained) meaningful human connection remains unsolved.[119] DiPietro, like Schnitzler,

118 E. M. Forster, *Howard's End* (London: Penguin, 2000), p. 188.

119 This is not the only play in which DiPietro has engaged with the subject of troubled relationships. See, for example, the musicals *I Love You, You're Perfect, Now Change* (1996) and *Memphis* (2002). DiPietro has said in interview: '[W]hat writing has taught me is that we're all the same inside. We all want to have a purpose in life, we want to love someone,

denies his audience easy answers to perennial questions about how we should live in relationship with others. His explicit employment of AIDS as a threat overshadowing each homosexual encounter exposes Forster's 'Only connect!' as ethically more ambiguous than it first appears.

Jack's initial denial of his positive HIV status to Ryan is accompanied by the suggestion that they 'use a rubber anyway' (*FM*, p. 27). DiPietro alters the power dynamic at play in the source scene from *Reigen*, reversing the lack of caution exercised by the *Gatte* with the *Süßes Mädel*. In one of the rare instances of Schnitzler making reference to venereal disease (albeit only implicitly), the *Gatte* comments to himself, post-coitally: 'Wer weiß, was das eigentlich für eine Person ist – Donnerwetter . . . So schnell. . . . War nicht sehr vorsichtig von mir . . . ' (*Reigen*, p. 993). He is aware that his young lover might be syphilitic or otherwise infectious. By sleeping with her, therefore, he has exposed himself (and therefore also his wife) to possible disease. Although socially and economically the *Gatte* is the more powerful one in the couple, in this instance of physical vulnerability he becomes the weaker partner. In *Fucking Men* it is Jack who knows that he is already infected and Jack who must therefore decide how to employ that knowledge. By disclosing his status as HIV-positive he risks scaring Ryan away; but by denying it he risks infecting his new, innocent lover (as well as breaking the promise of transparency he made to Leo). Jack's solution (deceiving Ryan but also insisting that they use protection) provides, at least momentarily, an interruption in the transmission. By contrast, Sammy declares his contagious status to Ryan before their first kiss (*FM*, p. 32), only to be told by Ryan that it is '[n]o problem'. When Sammy suggests that Ryan must be 'very open-minded', the latter replies simply: 'I don't want you to leave' (*FM*, p. 33). Ryan is lonely and will expose himself to possible infection, whether through Jack or Sammy, to alleviate that pain. The very real and serious threat which AIDS posed to gay men in the 1980s and 1990s accentuates, through Ryan's refusal to pay heed to it, the pressing need to escape loneliness by connecting to others.

AIDS proves itself in many ways the cultural heir to syphilis in the adaptation, a model of succession recognized in some of the scholarship on AIDS in literature. Pietzrak-Franger has observed, for example, how 'syphilis has bequeathed its phantasmic significance to AIDS, which is not only characterized in terms earlier reserved for syphilis, but which also partakes of

---

and we want to be loved. Everything from gender to sexuality to nationality is just the exterior' (Ryan Leeds, 'Clever and Eclectic: An Interview with Playwright Joe DiPietro', *Manhatten Digest*, 16 January 2016, https://www.manhattandigest.com/2016/01/16/clever-and-eclectic-an-interview-with-playwright-joe-dipietro/ [accessed 14 July 2018]).

its iconographic heritage'.[120] Susan Sontag has also examined the medical and metaphorical overlaps between syphilis and AIDS.[121] It is perhaps unsurprising, then, that Sontag's assessment of how AIDS alters our awareness of time feels as though it could have been written with *Reigen* in mind:

> The fear of AIDS imposes on an act whose ideal is an experience of pure presentness (and a creation of the future) a relation to the past to be ignored at one's peril. Sex no longer withdraws its partners, if only for a moment, from the social. It cannot be considered just a coupling; it is a chain, a chain of transmission, from the past.[122]

DiPietro undoubtedly deals with AIDS in more explicit terms than Schnitzler with venereal disease: not only is the condition referred to and named in a number of scenes, but two of the characters are HIV-positive. Whereas Jack's condition is only alluded to ('[D]o you tell them you're positive?' (*FM*, p. 22)), Sammy declares himself, almost playfully, as 'HIV-enhanced. HIV-gifted. Poz. Positive-o' (*FM*, p. 32).[123] By focusing on a condition with at least some of the cultural significance previously attached to syphilis, DiPietro renders the anxieties around contagion and identity experienced at the turn of the last century more accessible to twenty-first-century audiences.

Death as a result of AIDS articulates the threat even more clearly (just as death features subtly in the opening and closing scenes of *Reigen*). In the penultimate scene we learn that Donald's long-term partner Philip died a few years earlier from AIDS (*FM*, p. 43); and in the last scene of the play, in ignorance of the death but aware of Philip's significance to Donald, John the escort offers to sleep with Philip 'without a rubber, yeah, even if he's got AIDS' (*FM*, p. 46). Notwithstanding a communal awareness of the prevalence of the (still potentially fatal) condition, the characters in *Fucking Men* repeatedly expose their bodies to the risk of infection. As in *Reigen*, the vulnerability of the body competes with the desire (or need) for physical and emotional contact. To a lesser degree the dangers of exposure could also be said to compete with

120 Monika Pietrzak-Franger, *Syphilis in Victorian Literature and Culture: Medicine, Knowledge and the Spectacle of Victorian Invisibility* (Basingstoke and New York: Palgrave Macmillan, 2017), p. 4.

121 Susan Sontag, 'AIDS and its Metaphors', in *Illness as Metaphor and AIDS and its Metaphors* (London: Penguin Classics, 2002 [1979/1989]), pp. 89–180. Sontag suggests that AIDS is, like syphilis, a disease or condition 'to which sexual fault is attached' and it therefore 'always inspire[s] fears of easy contagion and bizarre fantasies of transmission by nonvenereal means in public places' (Sontag, 'AIDS and its Metaphors', pp. 112–13; see also pp. 102, 107, 131–32 and 151). See also Schonlau, *Syphilis in der Literatur*, p. 492.

122 Sontag, 'AIDS and its Metaphors', p. 158.

123 Cf. Sontag, who catalogues cultural representations linking tuberculosis with heightened levels of creativity and a bohemian life ('AIDS and its Metaphors', pp. 32–37).

the economic gains to be made. Most notably, John's offer to sleep with Philip without protection is made with dollar signs in his eyes: the risk has a concrete financial value of 'a thousand' (*FM*, p. 46). However, John's need for cash is itself related directly to his desire for connection with Steve. He is 'saving up' to 'get a place for ourselves. Someplace decent, with like a kitchen' (*FM*, p. 47).[124] Once again, the potential dangers of contagion are deemed insignificant when compared to the value of human contact. In the effort to create a stable and meaningful relationship with Steve, John will open himself up to the risks of illness.

Finally, *Fucking Men* echoes its source in *Reigen* by exposing the social hypocrisies underlying the continuedly closeted nature of homosexuality in Western society. What is perhaps only hinted at in Kyle's claim to bi-sexuality – he has a girlfriend who does not know that he sleeps with men (*FM*, pp. 13 and 17) – is violently displayed when Steve attacks John for suggesting that he enjoyed the service he has paid for (*FM*, pp. 7–8). No less poignant a form of self-denial is legible in Brandon's marriage to Julie and Donald's twenty-eight-year marriage to Francis (*FM*, pp. 39–40). The metaphor of the closet is made literal when Sammy has sex with Brandon in a 'broom closet' backstage 'at a dingy theatre' (*FM*, p. 34), recalling some of the clandestine arrangements in *Reigen* (the *Dirne* and the *Soldat*; the *Junge Frau* and the *Junger Herr*; and the *Gatte* and the *Süßes Mädel*). When Sammy then publishes the story he forces Brandon either to deny his hitherto hidden sexuality and continue that part of his life in secrecy (as Donald has done) or to risk personal and professional disruption by confirming the fling with Sammy. Brandon informs Donald of his intention to come out on Donald's current-affairs show, in response to which Donald warns the actor:

> I know I sound like a dinosaur to you but there are benefits – undeniable benefits – to being closeted. The times have changed, yes, you're right. But you don't realize – they haven't changed enough. They still hate us out there. Not all. But most – most do. (*FM*, p. 43).

The TV producer is proved right when Brandon's voluntary confirmation of Sammy's exposé is greeted by his studio swiftly dropping the film he was scheduled to make. We are left to conclude that he has become, as Donald anticipated, 'a joke, a box-office disaster, a man defined by what he does in the bedroom' (*FM*, p. 43).

124 John's keenness to explain his aspirations to Donald are reminiscent of the *Dirne* responding to the *Graf* as he looks around her room: 'Im nächsten Monat ziehn wir in die Stadt, in die Spiegelgasse' (*Reigen*, p. 1044). Both characters, at the bottom of the socio-economic ladder, dream of the material comforts apparently available on the next rung up.

The hypocrisies surrounding sexual behaviour evident in Schnitzler's work are given fresh resonance in this modern adaptation. Whereas the double standards of contemporary Viennese society are best encapsulated in *Reigen* by the figure of the *Gatte*, with his spousal lecture on the evils of extra-marital sex contrasted to his infidelity (theatrical) moments later, DiPietro deploys Brandon to highlight the duplicity behind the public view (that homosexuality is now accepted and acceptable), a duplicity revealed in the harsh reality that an openly gay actor cannot enjoy the same success as his straight colleagues. The protection offered by life in the closet remains necessary for many, even in the apparently liberal West, and the possibilities of living a connected life accordingly remain restricted for twenty-first-century gay men. Deception and desire are accompanied, as in *Reigen*, by fluctuating power dynamics, most visible in the figure of Sammy and his blackmailing activities. *Fucking Men* brings this feature of Schnitzler's play to the fore, laying bare for today's audiences the irresolvable and uncomfortable entanglements created by the human need for connection against a background of unstable and porous selfhood.

Cashcows

April de Angelis's very different re-working of *Reigen* in her radio adaptation *Cashcows* benefits from consideration alongside, first, the themes treated in her larger corpus and, second, the programming of the drama in BBC Radio 4's broadcast schedule. Whereas DiPietro has built up a reputation for writing comedic musicals and light entertainment (but has clearly brought in his own open homosexuality to his adaptation of *Reigen*),[125] De Angelis is known for her 'lifelong concerns with feminism, history and community' and her plays are overtly political in nature.[126] Indeed, *Cashcows* was not the first all-female play De Angelis had written.[127] *Playhouse Creatures* was originally written for

125 DiPietro has acknowledged autobiographical elements to *Fucking Men*, stating that some of the dialogue about infidelity was 'typing, not writing' (Robert Hofler, 'The L.A. side of DiPietro', https://variety.com/2009/legit/news/the-l-a-side-of-dipietro-1118010074/ [accessed 17 July 2018]).

126 Rebecca D'Monté, 'April de Angelis', in *Methuen Drama Guide to Contemporary British Playwrights*, ed. by Martin Middeke, Peter Paul Schnierer and Aleks Sierz (London: Methuen Drama, 2011), pp. 123–43 (p. 123).

127 Neither was *Cashcows* the first all-female adaptation of *Reigen*. As early as 1904 a 'Wienerin' (otherwise anonymous) published her parody *Duo-Szenen im Dampfbad. Ringel-Reigen-Rosenkranz nach berühmtem Muster* with the Magazin-Verlag Jacques Hegner. It comprises ten scenes between ten different pairs of women (Schneider, *Die Rezeption von Arthur Schnitzlers Reigen*, p. 72; Gerd K. Schneider, 'Zur künstlerischen Umsetzung von

an all-female cast (Haymarket Theatre, 1993)[128] and was concerned with the first appearance of actresses on the English Stage; and *Ironmistress* (1989) was a female two-hander exploring a mother-daughter relationship in industrial Victorian Britain. *Cashcows* was broadcast in September 2005 as Radio 4's 'Woman's Hour Drama'. As such, the play was divided into five fifteen-minute episodes and broadcast over five consecutive weekdays at the end of *Woman's Hour*. The editorial agenda for *Woman's Hour* has been summarized as 'covering women's issues; addressing general issues from a female perspective; and choosing to interview predominantly women on the widest range of topics'.[129] The listeners would accordingly have had certain expectations prior to listening to *Cashcows*, especially if already familiar with De Angelis's work.

The play's relationship with *Reigen* was established in advance of the broadcast by the BBC's 'official organ' or programme of radio and television listings:[130] the brief synopsis of the play in the *Radio Times* explained that it was 'about a circle of women who are bound together by guilt – and cash' and that it was '[b]uilt on the same model as Schnitzler's La Ronde, each episode contain[ing] two two-handed comedies, until the last character meets the first'. The connection between the radio play and *Reigen* was also made retrospectively in a review in *The Stage* by Moira Petty, published on 22 September 2005:

> The vital role of money in women's lives was also the theme of a clever Woman's Hour Drama, Cash Cows. Author April de Angelis based it on Schnitzler's La Ronde, in which a series of sexual encounters come full circle. Here, it is a £20 note and the lives of women on various rungs of the financial ladder, which rotate through five scenes.[131]

Notwithstanding these paratextual hints, one might think on first listening (or reading) that the only connection between *Cashcows* and *Reigen* was the structure of ten characters meeting in a daisy chain of scenes. There is otherwise very little obvious resemblance between the Austrian play and this English radio drama. However, closer inspection reveals that the two works share far more than mere form. As in *Fucking Men*, numerous features and

---

Arthur Schnitzlers REIGEN in Europa und den Vereinigten Staaten', *Internet-Zeitschrift für Kulturwissenschaften*, 3 (March 1998), http://www.inst.at/trans/3Nr/schneider.htm [accessed 14 November 2018]).

128 Two male parts were subsequently added for a revival at the Young Vic in 1997.

129 Danica Minic, 'What Makes an Issue a Woman's Hour Issue? The Politics of Recognition and Media Coverage of Women's Issues and Perspectives', *Feminist Media Studies*, 8 (2008), 301–15 (p. 302).

130 'History of the BBC: The Radio Times', https://www.bbc.com/historyofthebbc/research/radio-times [accessed 12 June 2021].

131 Moira Petty, 'Fine start to lifting curse of Austen's Abbey', *Stage*, 22 September 2005, p. 15.

themes from Schnitzler's play are repeated, extended and challenged in De Angelis's work.

Cashcows opens in its first episode with a cleaner, Marta, explaining to her boss Shirley why she used a Brillo pad on a client's Aga.[132] Marta has to pay Shirley a £20 fine because of the 'verifiable complaint' (Ep. 1, p. 4), which banknote is passed on, in the following scene, to Shirley's mother-in-law Barbara on an outing from Barbara's old people's home. The two women clearly do not get on and an off-stage scuffle as Shirley tries to dress Barbara for the rain results in Barbara's waterproof jacket being ripped. The £20 is offered both to replace the jacket and as a bribe, as Shirley asks Barbara not to tell her husband (Barbara's son) what had happened. The second episode introduces the listener to Kerry, a carer at Barbara's home, who is given £20 by Barbara for a textbook for her Humanities course at college. Kerry, we discover, is pregnant and in the following scene she is assisted in her childbirth by midwife, Adjoa.[133] A bet on the probably positive outcome of labour moves the £20 on to the midwife, who uses it in the third instalment to pay Helen, a jobbing actress, for attendance at a drama course Helen organizes. The same £20 is then left by Helen to pay for her half of an abandoned restaurant meal with her sister, Jules, who had arranged the lunch to discuss their inheritance from a great aunt. In the fourth instalment, a scene between Jules and her friend Jo (a frustrated poet), is played out in an exchange of emails. After agreeing to look after Jules's two children for her, Jo has apparently been remunerated with the £20 note, to which she responds: 'Haven't women been doing unpaid childcare for each other from time immemorial?' (Ep. 4, p. 5). When Jo then leaves a massage session with Sky early, unable to cope with the emotions released by the experience, she pays £20 for Sky's time. In the fifth and final instalment Sky is joined by Geri, her adult daughter, while gardening and lends her cash for petrol; finally, Geri pays Marta for cleaning her home and so the £20 note comes full circle.

The sexual intercourse which is repeated on stage in all but one of Schnitzler's scenes is very obviously missing from the radio play. As the reviewer for *The Stage* points out, the (ostensible) link between the women is instead the £20 note. Beneath the surface exchanges of cash, however, De Angelis reveals a stubborn, sometimes forced, social interdependence, which

132 The only publicly available copy of this script is a microfiche (BBC Written Archives Centre, *Cashcows*, tx 19/09/05, Woman's Hour, R4). References in the body of the text are to Episodes (five in total) and page numbers (starting from 1 at the beginning of each Episode).

133 The aural similarity of the name 'Kerry' to 'Kelly' ('the Model' in *The Blue Room*), together with both Shelley's absent husband Tom and her mother-in-law Barbara being Members of Parliament (active and retired, respectively), strongly suggests that De Angelis's source was David Hare's adaptation of *Reigen* rather than Schnitzler's text itself.

is made manifest in a number of scenes in the form of physical contact; the sexual connections of *Reigen* are replaced by some of the other physically intimate encounters which can take place between two women. In the second scene, for example, Shirley pushes Barbara around in a wheelchair; tussles with her 'off-stage' while forcing a 'pac a mac' on her to protect her from the driving rain; offers to cut up her food; gives her a tissue when she starts crying; and then picks up her dropped fork and wipes it clean for her. Together these perhaps individually unremarkable acts hint at an unwanted physical dependency by the older woman on her daughter-in-law. Indeed, for all her complaints it seems Barbara most wants to live with Shirley and her husband, i.e., to become more, not less, dependent and so to minimize the loneliness that so often accompanies old age (Ep. 1, p. 15). In the subsequent duo scene between Barbara and the care worker Kerry this dependent element in female intimacy is taken a stage further. Kerry wipes Barbara's face, brushes her hair, offers to wipe her bottom after a visit to the toilet and helps her to pull up her underwear. There is a sort of reciprocation: when Kerry is confident that Barbara has fallen asleep, she reveals that she has missed two menstrual periods, i.e., that she is pregnant. Kerry needs to share this very private and physically intimate news with someone, but can only muster the courage to disclose it to a sleeping Barbara.

Again, the kernel of intimacy suggested in the earlier scene is pursued and enlarged upon in the follow-up. When Kerry next appears, she is in labour, being looked after by Ghanaian midwife Adjoa. During the course of the scene Adjoa carries out an examination of Kerry's cervix, commenting at the end that she is 'fully dilated' (Ep. 2, p. 13). The dialogue includes references to pushing, pain, epidurals and caesarean sections; and Kerry, in the throes of delivering the baby, gasps, screams and expresses a need to urinate. Here De Angelis shows us the consequences of the sexual intercourse repeated time and again in Schnitzler's play, using it as a vehicle for exploring another sort of intimate act, that of delivering a baby. The scene is far from sentimental, however. De Angelis's work can, like Schnitzler's, easily be categorized as comedy and this scene is particularly funny.[134] The radio script invites us to visualize the ironic juxtaposition of Adjoa's examination of Kerry with her legs akimbo and Kerry calmly reading about celebrity birth stories in a gossip magazine.[135]

Two other scenes in De Angelis's play, both involving the character called Sky, show acts of physical intimacy between women. In the first, Sky massages her

134 See Ian F. Roe, 'The Comedy of Schnitzler's "Reigen"', *Modern Language Review*, 89 (1994), 674–88.

135 Tim Crook persuasively refutes the myth that radio is a 'blind' medium (Tim Crook, *Radio Drama: Theory and Practice* (London & New York: Routledge, 1999)).

new client, Jo. In an echo of the earlier scenes showing Barbara as a vulnerable older woman, Jo's body is laid bare for Sky to manipulate at her will. Sky massages Jo's shoulders and stomach, warning her client that her emotions might thereby 'come to the surface' and advising that she '[j]ust go with the hysteria' (Ep. 4, pp. 16 and 15). The contact ultimately provokes a physical eruption from Jo (she punches a folded-up towel then uses it to muffle her own scream). As in the earlier scene between Shirley and Barbara, Jo cries and is offered a tissue by Sky. In the next scene Sky is visited by her daughter Geri. While trying to leave her mother's garden in a rage, Geri hurts herself and has to be tended to by her mother, her ankle wrapped up in a sock bandage. Finally, in both scenes Sky encourages the other women to 'breathe' – Jo 'through [her] hands' (Ep. 4, p. 9) and Geri 'through the top of [her] head' (Ep. 5, p. 4).

The physical acts that are shown in the play portray women not only as comforters and carers but also as provocateurs and pugilists, ready to use their bodies to express their anger and frustration, to defend themselves and to take whatever control is within their reach. De Angelis thereby extends Schnitzler's *Reigen* model to consider those acts of physical intimacy which occur beyond desire and between women, at what Eve Kosofsky Sedgwick calls the 'homosocial' end of the continuum of women's relationships.[136] The scenes of corporeal contact also show explicitly what is only implicit in some of the other scenes, namely the unavoidable relatedness of the characters. The women affect one another. From one link in the chain to the next, cause and effect are legible in their thoughts and actions.

Sex is not needed as the instigator of connection (contrary to Sammy's philosophy in *Fucking Men*); indeed, it is almost wholly absent as a concern for De Angelis's characters. Rather, their interrelatedness and interdependence appear to emerge at times *in spite of* their desires. Although most readily perceivable in the intimate exchanges catalogued above, this connectedness is also a feature of the one scene in *Cashcows* in which the characters do not occupy the same physical space. The dialogue between Jules and Jo is performed in a relay of emails, which medium is employed by the women not only for the practical purposes of arranging childcare but also as a channel for confession. Jules admits that she no longer has the energy required to sleep with her husband Zeb; and Jo worries about the psychological consequences of her daughter being an only child. The aurally projected image of the two women, sitting alone at different times at their different computers, brings into sharp focus the loneliness underlining each character's grasp at connection and intimacy.

136 Eve Kosofsky Sedgwick, *Between Men: English Literature and Male Homosocial Desire* (New York: Columbia University Press, 1992), p. 23.

The tentacles of connectedness in the play extend across geographical and socio-economic borders. Both Marta (Polish) and Adjoa (Ghanaian), for example, are economic migrants in low-paid jobs, regularly sending money back to family at home. They represent the 'new forms of entanglement' which are, according to Wolfgang Welsch, 'a consequence of migratory processes, as well as of worldwide material and immaterial communications systems and economic interdependencies and dependencies'.[137] Many of De Angelis's duologues illustrate to a greater or lesser degree the realities of that entanglement. *Cashcows* also shows how the boundaries between the socially powerful and those in apparently weaker positions are undone by the sometimes uncomfortable need for connection. That need has already been demonstrated by Barbara's dependence on Kerry. A slightly different role reversal is visible in the failed confrontation between Geri and Marta (Geri's cleaner) about Marta's unauthorized use of the telephone to call relatives in Poland. During the confrontation Geri's authority is totally undermined by her own nervous verbosity, which contrasts with Marta's unembarrassed straight-talking. Instead of sacking Marta, or insisting that she pay for the calls made, Geri ends up giving money to her (the final handover of £20) and gratefully accepting Marta's offer of a cup of tea.

The play ends with Geri's whimpering request to Marta: 'Tell me you don't hate me' (Ep. 5, p. 22). De Angelis's adaptation problematizes and upsets the 'normal' social order by revealing how the carers in the play – Marta, Kerry, Adjoa and Sky – who occupy low-ranking positions (cleaner, auxiliary nurse, midwife and masseuse) are the main enablers of meaningful social connection. To be alone is scarcely an option for De Angelis's women; and to die on one's own, as Helen's and Jules's great aunt has died, would be 'awful' (Ep. 3, p. 15). De Angelis's treatment of her characters' relatedness (and need for relatedness) provides dramatic form to what Welsch calls the 'extremely interconnected and entangled' nature of cultures and individuals today.[138] *Cashcows* shows how such shifts in the way people and money move around the world play out in individual lives, employing a crude representation of exchange, namely the £20 note, as an unambiguous illustration of the chain of relations. As the world becomes smaller through globalizing technological advances and free market practices, our opportunities for connection increase; and, far from intensifying the control exercisable over the spread of ideas, people and disease, modern technology in particular has lent itself to an increased potential for physical and social contagion.

137 Wolfgang Welsch, 'Transculturality – the Puzzling Form of Cultures Today', in *Spaces of Culture: City, Nation World*, ed. by Mike Featherstone and Scott Lash (London: Sage, 1999), pp. 194–213 (p. 198).

138 Welsch, 'Transculturality', p. 197.

Radio presents itself as a medium especially well-suited to both *Reigen* and *Cashcows*. The awkward, shocking nature of showing a live theatre audience a woman being subjected to an internal examination and then reaching the final stages of labour would arguably distract the viewer from the funnier (and in places more tragic) elements of De Angelis's dialogue. Just as in *Reigen*, the physically intimate act is important in *Cashcows*, but not to the exclusion of the spoken dialogue. Richard J. Hand points out the fruitful paradox of radio creating a greater sense of intimacy between writer/producer and listener whilst also allowing more explicit material to be presented without the need for an evening "watershed".[139] It is precisely this capacity in radio drama, in which the microphone is treated as 'the ear of the listener' and actors and action enter the 'domestic space of the listener', that renders it an ideal medium for Schnitzler's plays and in particular *Reigen*. Indeed, it is notable that it was on BBC Radio's Third Programme that an English translation of *Reigen* was first performed for a British audience almost twenty years before the end of copyright gave free rein for theatre performances.

The Audience Research Report for the 1964 production of *Merry-Go-Round* disclosed that a number of those members of the public surveyed thought it 'ideally suited to radio' and one commented:

> If ever a play called for performance on the Third, Reigen is surely that play. It is quite unsuitable for public performance, as one can never be sure where unfortunate giggling might occur, but for enjoyment in the privacy of one's home it is a delightful, enlightening and altogether <u>respectable</u> piece.[140]

Private listening was clearly deemed a more suitable means of witnessing the perceived 'private' nature of the encounters portrayed in the play. The praise was not unanimous. Some members of the surveyed audience found the play boring and 'too long for its material', while others commented that the original shock value was lost on a more permissive public already familiar with Ophüls's film.

De Angelis's adaptation counters both these criticisms. The division into five episodes imposed by the format of the Woman's Hour Drama works to the play's advantage by giving the audience time to reflect and, to some degree, forget between pairings, so that the chain of encounters does not become tedious or feel unduly repetitive. The new rewriting of Schnitzler's play also

139 Richard J. Hand, 'Radio Adaptation', in *The Oxford Handbook of Adaptation Studies*, ed. by Thomas Leitch (Oxford: Oxford University Press, 2017), pp. 340–55 (p. 347).

140 Audience Research Report for 'Merry Go Round', 22.5.1964 (BBC Written Archives Centre, R9/6, Merry Go Round, 22/05/64, TP). Emphasis in original.

recognizes that the shocking element in the original was not just the sexual act itself but also the nature of the social relations in the midst of which it took place: Schnitzler held up an unflattering mirror in which Viennese society could contemplate its faults. The *imagined* acts in *Cashcows* – the bottom-wiping, the cervix-measuring – are far more graphic, and therefore shocking, than anything we might *see* on a television screen.[141] Similarly, the accompanying critique of contemporary society might well have disturbed the listening audience in 2005: according to De Angelis's portrait, we can be physically and emotionally remote from each other but nevertheless always connected by cash; capitalist self-interest trumps meaningful relationships. As Frances Gay and Janet Bray put it, 'radio's intimacy also means it is uniquely qualified to show the point at which the personal becomes political'.[142] *Cashcows* reveals how the problems encountered by women in their day-to-day lives are as much a reflection of public structures of power as anything else.[143]

La Ronde

The coincidence of personal and political comes to the fore in Max Gill's *La Ronde*, an adaptation more obviously concerned with identity politics than *Cashcows* or *Fucking Men*, but also more explicitly derived from Schnitzler's play through its (admittedly French) title.[144] Gill was, in 2017, a relatively young playwright whose production of *La Ronde* that year was his first foray onto the London stage as writer and director. Like DiPietro and De Angelis before him, Gill re-locates and modernizes the play, as well as altering the gender arrangement of the cast.[145] In respect of the latter his approach was the most radical: Gill's company of two male and two female actors spun a wheel

141 Crook describes the imagination of the listener as 'the fifth dimension' (coming after the 'fourth dimension' of the 'previously recorded archive'), with the 'power to recreate a full sensory spectrum of experience' (Crook, *Radio Drama*, p. 62). See also Martin Shingler and Cindy Wieringa, *On Air: Methods and Meanings of Radio* (London: Arnold, 1998), pp. 73–93.

142 Frances Gay and Janet Bray, 'The Mind as a Theatre: Radio Drama since 1971', *New Theatre Quarterly*, 1 (1985), 292–300 (p. 296).

143 For further examples of the personal as political in De Angelis's works, see *Ironmistress* (1989) and *The Positive Hour* (1997).

144 Max Gill, *La Ronde* (London: Oberon, 2017). Hereinafter references are included in the body of the text as *LR* followed by the page number.

145 Also, as for De Angelis, it seems quite possible that Hare's *The Blue Room* was at least one of Gill's sources. See, for example, the character of the 'Bus Driver' (reminiscent of 'the Cab Driver') and the characterization of the 'Cleaner' as a speaker of English as a foreign language (reminiscent of 'the Au Pair') who speaks 'with a foreign accent' (Hare, *The Blue Room*, p. 6).

of fortune at the beginning of each scene to determine which of them would play each part.[146] According to the published script, '[o]ver three thousand different realisations of the play were possible' (*LR*, p. 6). The results might therefore include two women playing any given scene, or two men. In fact, the stage directions suggest that the whole play could be performed by a company of only men, or only women: '*All characters can be played by either gender and pronouns in stage directions reflect this*' (*LR*, p. 6). Fate determines on each spin of the wheel the gender and sexual orientation of the players.[147]

Gill's conceptualization of *Reigen* thereby challenges our continuing idealization of fixed gender identities and, more broadly, invites consideration of identity as performative. The categories of 'male' and 'female' are released from their biologically restricted parameters and gender is portrayed as socially constructed. Because any of the cast can find themselves playing any of the characters, we have to conclude that neither 'male' nor 'female' can determine who they (or we) are. The words will be spoken, the character played, regardless of whether by a male or female cast member. Gill has made the point in interview that:

> Whilst this in theory means the script is non-gender specific, it means that in performance an audience's reaction to it is likely to be highly gendered. How do we digest a woman as opposed to a man visiting a female prostitute? And how might we react differently to a male stay-at-home parent philandering than to a female? How then might our appreciation of this relationship transform if both the parents are

146 An analogous method was employed by Robert Icke in his adaptation of Schiller's *Maria Stuart*, produced at the Almeida Theatre, London, in December 2016. At the opening of each performance the two lead actresses, Lia Williams and Juliet Stevenson, tossed a coin to decide who would play Elizabeth I and who Mary Stuart. See also Maria Aberg's production of Marlowe's *Doctor Faustus* for the Royal Shakespeare Theatre Company in 2016, in which the two actors playing Doctor Faustus and Mephistopheles each lit a match: the actor whose match went out first 'lost' and played Faustus. Arguably Danny Boyle's production of *Frankenstein* for the National Theatre in 2011 applied a similar technique, casting Benedict Cumberbatch and Jonny Lee Miller in the roles of Frankenstein and the Creature on alternating nights. This increasingly popular theatrical trick injects productions with unpredictability and provides audiences with the impression of having seen something unique and improvised; paradoxically such practices require more, rather than less, preparation and rehearsal. The use of only two men and two women to play all the roles in *Reigen* had been proposed to, and rejected by, Heinrich Schnitzler more than forty years earlier. Schnitzler asked Glass to refuse permission to the Artistic Director of the Stratford Shakespeare Festival in Canada, Robin Phillips, to adapt *Reigen* (Heinrich Schnitzler to Eric Glass, 8.1.1975 (Schn 21/11/2)).

147 Although not referred to in the published text, the casting of the production in 2017 (directed by Max Gill) included two non-White actors. Race-related power structures were thereby similarly rendered subject to the spinning wheel.

> men? What inadvertent expectations or prejudices does this throw up for you?[148]

In challenging our preconceptions about gender, *La Ronde* also tests our ideas about infection, in particular in a post-AIDS age when responsibility is so often attributed, and therefore stigma attached, to gay men and sex workers.

Questions surrounding identity are raised in the translated text itself, as well as at the moment of assigning roles. Just as in *Reigen*, the importance of names, for example, and the possibility of illusion, disguise and role-play are explored. In the fourth scene, between the Student and the Spouse, the opening exchange is based almost exclusively on first names and repetition (*LR*, p. 38):

> STUDENT: Jerry.
> SPOUSE: Oh George.
> STUDENT: Jerry.
> SPOUSE: Yes, George.
> STUDENT: This is heaven.
> SPOUSE: George.
> STUDENT: Oh Jerry.
> SPOUSE: George.
> STUDENT: Yes, Jerry.
> SPOUSE: This is heaven.

The mantra is repeated after the first of three lines of asterisks in the text, each of which indicates sexual intercourse (*LR*, p. 39):[149]

> SPOUSE: George.
> STUDENT: Oh Jerry.
> SPOUSE: George.
> STUDENT: Yes, Jerry.
> SPOUSE: Imagine if I got caught. What are we doing.

148 'Interview: Max Gill, La Ronde', in *Theatre Things*, 14.1.2017, https://theblogoftheatrethings.com/2017/01/14/interview-max-gill-la-ronde/ [accessed 15 November 2018].

149 According to the preliminary stage directions, '*Sections marked with *** are filled with verbatim accounts*'. Gill has explained: 'Integral to the play are verbatim testimonies from real life prostitutes, lovers, fetishists, people who have committed incest and so on, that we have collected over many months in London. […] They are a curation of sexual appetites today and I hope their voices give the play a vibrant relevance' ('Interview: Max Gill, La Ronde', in *Theatre Things*, 14.1.2017). These aspirations to a documentary interpretation arguably found satisfaction in the Radio 4 broadcast of *Full Circle* in January 2019, a five-part 'modern day retelling' of *Reigen* using the stories and voices of real people: https://www.bbc.co.uk/programmes/m00028c3 [accessed 11 June 2019].

Finally, the last words before the third line of asterisks picks up the motif once more with the Spouse's command: 'Say my name' (*LR*, p. 40). Naming and desire are bound together, as if the two identities need to be fixed before the contact can begin. The concrete names are momentarily dropped later in the scene, however, when the two characters riff on the film *The Graduate* (1967). The Spouse refers to the Student as a 'poor little student' and is corrected with 'Graduate', to which the response comes: 'You must be so tired from all that reading. Have a little snooze. Mummy will be right here when you wake up' (*LR*, p. 41).[150] The line between authentic self and role-play becomes blurred and the identities fixed by repeated first names falter. Finally, the Spouse asks the Student to '[h]urt me. [....] And pretend to be Charlie' (*LR*, p. 47). The Student refuses to adopt the character of the Spouse's husband/wife as requested, '[b]ecause I'd be doing it out of love' (*LR*, p. 48). By introducing genuinely felt emotion into their play-acting, the Student recalls the fragility of the façade. The couple have reached the limits of feasible pretence and the Student leaves.

By contrast to the scene between the Student and the Spouse, which is verbose and full of lust, language and naming, the scene following immediately afterwards, that between the Spouse and the Doctor ('Charlie'), is completely lacking in any verbal or even physical contact. Gill paints a particularly pessimistic picture of married life. There is no spoken text and no sign of affection; from the stage directions it is possible the characters do not even make eye contact. On the contrary, when the Spouse wakes and turns on a bedside lamp, the Doctor covers his/her head and masturbates. After the Doctor climaxes, the Spouse pulls the cover from the Doctor's head, but the Doctor immediately rolls over and the Spouse switches the light off once more. Even these few gestures, however, can be seen as iterations of patterns of pretence and self-denial articulated verbally elsewhere in the play.

The duologue between the Screenwriter ('Toni') and the Actor ('Alex Gold') presents numerous further examples. With the words 'the people you pretend to be' (*LR*, p. 69), Toni accuses the Actor of having multiple personalities while assuming that there must be an authentic core distinct from the named figure: '*you*, not Alex Gold, *you*' (*LR*, p. 69). The Actor likewise remarks upon Toni's capacity to occupy different roles: 'I have equipped myself to see you as the person you are. An aggressor, [...]. And a baby. And a people pleaser. And a passive aggressor. And a negator. And an enabler' (*LR*, p. 66). Alex's surname suggests the possibility of a verifiable, solid identity, but he/she is a professional

150 There then follows what could be a nod to the *Süßes Mädel/Gatte* scene when the Student asks whether they can have dessert and the Spouse suggests, 'We'll get you an ice-cream', before ordering a 'large mint choc chip sundae' (*LR*, p. 41).

alchemist who claims: 'I turned lead into gold in that movie' (*LR*, p. 67). Hence everything is changeable and nothing stable. Alex has to resort to recreational drugs in order to cope with the confusion between authentic and fake: 'Because how the fuck else am I supposed to know who or what is *real* otherwise?' (*LR*, p. 69). Alex's own psyche has been 'tor[n] up' by Toni, whom Alex accuses of having 'pulled down your pants and shitted on my shattered selfdom' (*LR*, p. 65). Alex is now 'merely a vessel for other people's minds' and 'bodily fluids' (*LR*, p. 67), the most suggestible of subjects and so vulnerable to infection. An empty vessel, of course, has nothing tangible at its centre: it is in many ways a perfect representation of the 'kernloser Mensch', including the orifice(s) through which inner content is poured out and the external world allowed to seep in. Through Alex, among others, the Schnitzlerian notion of selfhood retains a marked presence in Gill's text. Alex is the model 'Schauspieler' (or 'Schauspielerin') referred to in Schnitzler's aphorism, readily displaying all the skills of the 'reproduzierenden Talenten' and all the symptoms of loneliness which accompany that role-playing life.

Acting is not the exclusive territory of Alex in the play, as has already been seen in the allusive exchange between the Student and the Spouse. In addition, Gill's Bus Driver claims to be a surgeon when on a date with the Cleaner (*LR*, p. 21); and the Royal tells the Prostitute that he/she 'drive[s] a bus' for a living (*LR*, p. 74). There are also more transparent (i.e., less deceptive) acts of pretence. In the opening scene the Prostitute offers to 'be whoever you want' (*LR*, p. 11), a willingness already proved by his/her performance of the Bus Driver's sexual fantasy (*LR*, pp. 7–9). The Royal is likewise prepared to adopt a more substantial alternative role: the entirety of the pre-coital dialogue between the Royal and the Actor in the latter's dressing room is lifted from Act 4, Scene 15 of Shakespeare's *Antony and Cleopatra*; and even the post-coital exchange is styled as if a theatrical performance. These metatheatrical moments and intertexts function as reminders of the smudged boundary between authentic and fictitious self, the latter imposing a temporary veneer of order and coherence onto an otherwise chaotic world.[151]

The delineation between authentic and fictitious, already rendered fragile through frequent acts of pretence, becomes all the more difficult to maintain in the face of sameness and repetition. Dialogue, noises, calendar dates and props are reiterated or reappear throughout the play, creating an uncanny sense of *déjà vu*. Both the Prostitute and the Spouse *miaow*

151 Cf. Arthur Schnitzler, who wrote: '[W]ir [sind] stets auf der Flucht aus der chaotischen Wahrheit, die wir weder zu fassen noch zu ertragen imstande gewesen wären, in den trügerischen Trost einer willkürlich geordneten Welt' (Schnitzler, *Aphorismen und Betrachtungen*, p. 26).

as part of their foreplay (*LR*, pp. 10 and 43); the Cleaner drinks Bollinger with the Bus Driver (*LR*, p. 19), anticipating the Spouse ordering 'Bolli' to drink with the Student (*LR*, p. 41); the 'goulash' used (as simile) by the Bus Driver to recall the face of a run-over pedestrian (*LR*, p. 15) reappears as post-date fodder in the Cleaner's flat (*LR*, pp. 18–19) and as a suggestion for a dinner-party dish from the Doctor (*LR*, p. 50).[152] Even birthdays are shared: the Doctor tells the Professor he/she has the same birthday as the Doctor's mother (*LR*, p. 55).

The more extended textual repetitions operate to similar effect. An exchange about a gold necklace ('can't have come cheap. | Nothing does') appears in the first and last scenes, initially between the Prostitute and the Bus Driver and then between the Royal and the Prostitute (*LR*, pp. 14 and 74). The Doctor answers the Professor's enquiry as to the timeline to death in words which anticipate the following scene: 'Every patient is different. It is difficult to say' (*LR*, p. 53). In the next scene the Professor asks the Screenwriter how long their father has before his illness 'get[s] really bad' and is told: 'Difficult to say. Doctor says every patient's different' (*LR*, p. 58). The repeated themes, phrases and props recall the reiterations of motifs throughout *Reigen*.[153] Nonetheless, the result is altogether eerier. Whereas in Schnitzler's cycle certain themes come up with such frequency that they acquire comic dimensions, in Gill's adaptation the repetitions are mostly limited to pairs, i.e., one-off iterations, generating a brief sense of haunting before the scene moves on. The effect is amplified by chronological disruption: although an underlying plot connects the characters in a complex network far beyond the chain legible on the surface, temporal order has been abandoned, leaving the audience struggling to join the dots. While Schnitzler's play reveals its author as social critic, Gill emerges from *La Ronde* as social enquirer, at this stage prepared only to raise questions around identity as they arise from his survey of twenty-first-century Londoners, but not yet to draw conclusions.

The Professor is the character most obviously concerned with the repeated nature of his/her experiences and, in particular, the sameness of relationships with other people:

> Whoever I'm with always ends up being the worst person I could possibly ever have chosen. Eventually. Which only makes it worse that it takes me so long to realize. Every time. Fascist or socialist, all our friends without exception are ghastly, self-seeking, almond-croissant-guzzling, Cath Kidston cunts. (*LR*, p. 59)

152 The Cleaner describes the homemade goulash as 'Just beans' (*LR*, p. 20), recalling the baked beans poured over the Bus Driver in Scene 1 in the enactment of a sexual fantasy.

153 Cf. Neuse, 'Die Funktion von Motiven'.

As with Charles Marowitz's reading of *Anatol*, the Professor's comments on the sameness of his/her partners suggest a dissatisfaction with him/herself more than with others – the Professor cannot change or be different and so cannot help but find the same features in each partner. Notwithstanding this recognition, the Professor longs for difference. Like many of Schnitzler's lovers in *Reigen*, the Professor hopes that *this* relationship, as experienced in the present, is meaningful, as if the past and future could somehow be forgotten. As the Professor and Screenwriter kiss, they recall a previous moment together on holiday in Spain. The Professor adds, 'But this is different' (*LR*, p. 61). Then the lights go down and the asterisks appear in the text. When the lights go up, however, the Screenwriter asks: 'That was the right decision, wasn't it? Not to' (*LR*, p. 61). The dream of difference has come to nothing. The illusion of uniqueness is finally laid bare for the audience when the Professor tells the Screenwriter that he/she is the only person who knows how ill the Professor is: '[Y]ou're the only person who knows' (*LR*, p. 63). The Screenwriter repeats, as if it were a mantra, 'I'm the only person' (*LR*, p. 63). The audience, however, remembers the truth: the Doctor in the previous scene was, of course, the original informant and so shares the same knowledge.

Whereas faces might normally be relied upon to indicate individuality and difference, the faces in Gill's adaptation are as often sources of confusion and haunting as they are transparent markers of the self. The final scene of the play opens with the Royal and the Prostitute in bed together, as the Royal '*withdraws and dresses*' (*LR*, p. 74). Presumably for the first time, the Prostitute sees the Royal's face and is confident he/she recognizes it, explaining in response to the Royal's scepticism: 'I swear I don't forget a face' (*LR*, p. 74). The exchange is reminiscent of the moment in *Reigen* when the *Graf* recognizes in the face of the *Dirne* a previous acquaintance: 'Ganz dasselbe G'sicht, ganz dasselbe G'sicht' (*Reigen*, p. 1046). It is, of course, not the same face, just as it is not the same woman. The *Dirne*, who has been asked by the *Graf* not to speak while he carries out his review, is thereby reduced to that part of her body. By contrast, in *La Ronde* it is the Royal who squirms under the interrogative gaze of the Prostitute and has to deny being 'famous' (*LR*, p. 74).

When the Doctor covers his/her face and head while masturbating, the Spouse uncovers it. In this case, revealing the face provides the Spouse with a means of shaming the Doctor. Faces can show self-knowledge, even if involuntarily. The Bus Driver is unable to forget the face of an accident victim (*LR*, p. 15) who we later discover to have been the Professor (*LR*, p. 46). Given that the face haunting the Bus Driver looked '[l]ike goulash' (*LR*, p. 15), it is most probably featureless and hence impossible to identify. The shock of the accident had been enough to set the Bus Driver's '[h]ead spinning like a fucking carousel' and sent him/her in search of contact: 'I wanted to touch someone. To feel skin. To feel red inside'

(LR, p. 14). The desire, even need, for physical contact has led the Bus Driver to the Prostitute. As discussed above, however, that contact is with someone who is always ready to play a part and whose 'real' self might never be touched.[154] A victory appears to have been won for transparency when the Cleaner notes that the Bus Driver is the 'first person I meet who actually looks like photo' (on a dating app) (*LR*, p. 22). When they take their tops off, however, to reveal a scar and tattoo respectively, neither will divulge what the marks signify and so their bodies remain illegible (*LR*, p. 25). Ultimately, although the Bus Driver has been honest in using a representative photograph of his/her face, the disclosure of his/her duplicity regarding his/her occupation effectively ends the date and therewith the connection (*LR*, p. 27). As in *Reigen*, the characters in Gill's *La Ronde* struggle to form lasting relationships in circumstances in which their own selfhood is experienced only precariously.

Coda: Bursting through the Membrane

Two images used in the adaptations warrant isolated attention. Although the images do not appear in the source text, they each appear in more than one adaptation and they speak to the themes of identity and contagion considered above. The first, clingfilm, has already been mentioned in the context of Jack explaining to Leo (in *Fucking Men*) the benefits of a promiscuous gay marriage by comparison with heterosexual fidelity: Jack feels no need for them to spice up their love lives by wrapping themselves in clingfilm (*FM*, p. 23). The transparent, paper-thin plastic sheeting acts as a second skin in this imagined erotic act, both showing and withholding the desired object, the wife. It gives the impression of being impregnable but would, of course, only be effective if in fact breaches could be forced and intercourse enabled. It is, to return to Otis's analysis, an illusory, permeable membrane.[155] Gill employs the same image in his dialogue between the Professor and the Screenwriter. Boredom, the result of the sameness of relationships, drives the Professor to want to '[s]mash through that sweaty clingfilm boundary that tells us what we should and shouldn't do' (*LR*, p. 60). In this instance, the plastic sheeting, which sweats like human skin, enforces social norms whilst also, in its transparency, revealing its own fragility. It can be 'smash[ed]' through; its integrity is illusory.

The second image to be found repeated in two of the adaptations is that of a cyst, or boil ready to burst. When Jo (in *Cashcows*) starts sobbing while being

154 See also the Actor's reference to him/herself as '[t]he pock-marked and grease-painted whore' (*LR*, p. 72).

155 Otis, *Membranes*, p. 5.

massaged, she stutters by way of explanation that it 'just sort of burst out . . . of me . . . [...] like a huge . . . I don't know . . . thing bursting out of me ...' (Ep. 4, p. 12). In *La Ronde* the Bus Driver feels 'like a fucking cyst. Whatever's inside it's gotta come out' (*LR*, p. 10). The final echo is heard when the Screenwriter cites an article by the Actor: 'It feels like I'm a cyst ready to burst' (*LR*, p. 68). Once more, Schnitzler's twenty-first-century adaptors highlight the instability of the self and the frail nature of the walls containing that self. The boil/cyst image resonates particularly strongly in these post-AIDS works as both a symptom of infection and as a source of further potential contagion; the individual character is both a victim and an agent of disease.

Even when *Reigen* is adapted loosely, when a line-for-line analysis is impossible and when source characters merge, disappear or mutate, it remains possible to read *across* contemporary interpretations and pinpoint common approaches to questions of identity, desire and contact. Recognizable within the three adaptations analysed above are writers grappling with the same conundrums tackled by Schnitzler over a hundred years earlier: how do we connect with others without jeopardizing our physical or psychological integrity? Are authenticity and uniqueness necessarily illusory? Can power be shared equally where desire is at large? The appeal of *Reigen* to contemporary adaptors is that it provides an ideal format for tackling those issues, whilst demonstrating, in its substance, how human beings are driven to connect because of, and notwithstanding, the fragility of the self.

As with the material from earlier periods explored in this book, the sometimes radically different adaptations analysed in this chapter reflect the inherently unfixed nature of the text. Gill's employment of the spinning, cast-determining wheel makes the point eloquently. *Reigen*, perhaps more than any other work in Schnitzler's corpus, demonstrates the capacity of texts to evolve and mutate endlessly as they are re-interpreted in new places and new times. If we recall the manifold British variations produced since 2002, especially those seemingly based on Hare's *The Blue Room*, as well as the re-translation of that text into German, translation itself starts to look like a distinctly contagious process and *Reigen* like the exemplary contaminated (and contaminating) text. Like the minimal selves portrayed in each scene, plays do not obviously have sealed borders or a constant core. Rather they behave as vehicles of intercultural exchange and textual movement, actively infecting the target culture, or mutating in order to find accommodation in a new language. It is tempting to draw lines between modern conceptions of the minimal self in Schnitzler and postmodern ideas about the autonomy of the text, given their shared concerns with sameness, identity and continuity through time. However, these questions demand answers falling outside the scope of this book.

The particular approaches of DiPietro, De Angelis and Gill can be seen to have been informed by their respective ontological narratives, hinted at above in the writers' personal biographies (as far as they are known), as well as by contemporary public debates around AIDS, gender performativity, capitalism and feminist theory. The myth of 'Gay Vienna', the conceptual narrative historically influencing Schnitzler reception, has been well and truly left behind. These are unapologetically confrontational interpretations, wholly permissible according to the norms of a theatre culture that had witnessed the provocative and explicit works of Sarah Kane and Mark Ravenhill two decades earlier. In the absence of control from Schnitzler or his son, power now indisputably lies within the target culture: with its agents and within its institutions, exercised in line with its audiences' expectations and driven by its narratives.

CONCLUSION

The research carried out for the purposes of this book provides substantial evidence of the complex labyrinths of power affecting the translation and dissemination of Arthur Schnitzler's dramas in English. Through an analysis of that research it has been possible to pin down individual manifestations of power, identifying where and with whom power lies at specific moments on the journey which Schnitzler's texts take from German print to English performance. It has also been possible to assess the role of individual agents and their means of manipulating textual production, as well as that of larger, institutional players in the overlapping systems which determine how meaning is generated or restricted. Methods and theories derived from a range of disciplines, as well as from a number of interdisciplinary thinkers, have allowed a response to the archive material and the translated play texts as they are found, rather than imposing upon them a ready-made, strict framework. The result of that tactic, at the conclusion of the project, is that by abstracting from the particulars of Schnitzler's case this book presents new cross-disciplinary reflections on the nature of power in intercultural exchange.

Historical Overview

By examining translations written and produced over the course of 115 years, this study has provided a unique perspective on Schnitzler's international reception. It has been possible to isolate three distinct periods within that long century for the purposes of assessing power over the translated text: first, the years during which Schnitzler was alive and actively engaged with the dissemination of his works outside German-speaking lands (1896–1931); second, the fifty years following the writer's death, when Heinrich Schnitzler managed the literary estate (1931–81); and, third, the post-copyright era (1982–). In drawing conclusions from these research findings, value can be gained from addressing each period in turn, as each has generated its own patterns of production.

Schnitzler's own attempts to promote and then regulate the spread of his works beyond Vienna were thwarted by numerous factors lying outside his control. The situation in Britain was unlike any other, insofar as Schnitzler had members of his family in situ and keen to assist. Detailed inspection of the correspondence with Julie and Felix Markbreiter reveals, however, that the competing wishes of a number of agents and translators, together with Julie Markbreiter's inevitably amateur management, meant that Schnitzler arguably suffered more than he gained from the familial link. Whereas his affairs in Scandinavia benefitted from a relatively consistent approach lasting many decades,[1] matters in Britain remained confused throughout Schnitzler's lifetime, with frequent changes in the interested parties. Far from controlling the translations of his works in any substantive sense, Arthur Schnitzler was left struggling even to ensure he was appropriately remunerated for those of his works which were performed.

The consistency missing from the early years was finally achieved through Heinrich Schnitzler and his extended professional relationship with Eric Glass. By contrast to his father, Heinrich Schnitzler had the linguistic capacity and the will to assess proposed translations in detail before giving the requisite permission on behalf of the literary estate. Perhaps because of his competence in English, Heinrich Schnitzler took a keen interest in the anglophone reception of his father's works, but that interest quickly evolved into a desire to re-direct perceptions of Arthur Schnitzler in Britain, a desire which resulted in permission being withheld on numerous occasions. By promoting the claims of authorial succession by the legatee, international copyright legislation might be said in this instance to have frustrated dissemination as well as to have protected Arthur Schnitzler's literary property. Notwithstanding the constraints imposed by the estate, the combined efforts of Heinrich Schnitzler and Eric Glass eventually contributed to the National Theatre's decision to produce a translation of *Das weite Land*. The equal billing of Schnitzler alongside Tom Stoppard in 1979 represents the moment of canonization for the Austrian writer in Britain. It had taken eighty-four years from domestic appreciation of Schnitzler as a major playwright when *Liebelei* was performed at the Burgtheater in 1895 to recognition of his status by the British theatrical institution.

The post-copyright reception has been assessed in this book by focusing on two narrower periods in which Schnitzler's plays were translated for London stages. *Dalliance* (1986) provides a basis for comparison with Stoppard's previous adaptation (*Undiscovered Country*). Clearly evident in the later 'version' is a freedom not seen seven years earlier. Stoppard's ownership of this second Schnitzler play is found to have been reflected in the altered view of authorship legible in critical reviews. Three adaptations of *Reigen* from the last

1 Pinkert, 'Skandinavien', p. 373.

fifteen years complete the analysis. They appear on first reading far removed from Schnitzler's play, but closer inspection reveals that common to each is the drawing out of themes intimated in the source text: each queries (and often queers) the identity of Schnitzler's characters, highlighting their insecurities, their vulnerability to the influences of their environment and their shared need for intimacy.

Methodological Conclusions

By assessing Schnitzler reception in Britain through the translations themselves as well as paratextual documents such as reviews and correspondence, and by reading the translations across more than a century, this study provides evidence of the shifting degrees of power exercised by individual translators over the texts they translate. More particularly, the genetic material examined shows that the study of translation, and especially translation for theatre, requires a nuanced framework which can accommodate the multitude of agents involved, and the multitude of texts generated, when a dramatic work is translated from one language into another. Were this research to be extended to incorporate the translation of Schnitzler's prose works, for example, or by including comparison with the translations of other writers' works, that framework could be developed further.

As a preliminary to any later consideration of methodological extensions, the following general conclusions are worth drawing from the preceding analysis of the Schnitzler material. First, there are clear advantages in carrying out translation studies which cover several decades, if not centuries. By subjecting more extended periods of cultural transfer to analysis we are able to assess the patterns of dissemination which appear over time. More significantly, we can also treat any patterns identified with greater confidence when comparative periods of transfer are available for analysis on either side of the decade(s) in question. Second, it is often possible to discern where (or with whom) control over the text lies at any given moment: control does not lie with one person from creative inception to ultimate dissemination. Any useful conceptualization of authorship or translatorship should accordingly accommodate the constant flux evident in the power exercised over the text. It should recognize that such power can be shared, is often challenged and is frequently legible in unexpected places. This book has thus argued for an approach to translation studies which spreads the research net widely in order to uncover the variously collaborative and combative mechanics of translation work.

This study builds on and expands methods advocated by Mona Baker, Jeremy Munday, Anthony Cordingley, Chiara Montini and Céline Frigau

Manning. Theirs is a shared ambition to reveal how individual, state and corporate agents influence textual production through the detailed unpicking of historical material. The work of this book shows how these theories can be applied specifically to theatre translation and how they can be employed in conjunction, one with another, to expose the intricacies of power as it is exercised in processes of commission, translation, production and dissemination.

Future Directions

The findings presented here represent only a careful selection of the vast array of archived documents at the researcher's disposal. The analysis in this study could therefore fruitfully be supplemented, extended and developed in a number of ways. An investigation of Heinrich Schnitzler's activities as trustee of the estate in Germany and Austria, for example, would reveal how he influenced his father's standing within that region, not least through his involvement in the publication of the *Gesammelte Werke* (1961–62) and various volumes of correspondence.[2] It would also open up for consideration how a Jewish writer is re-established in the post-Holocaust German canon. Mona Baker's conceptualization of 'narratives' in translation would possibly assist once more in understanding how power is asserted in such a politically sensitive context.

The relationship between the BBC and German-language writers, both during and after the Second World War, is another little-explored field which would benefit from a multi-sided micro-historical investigation of Heinrich Schnitzler's papers in Vienna and those held by the BBC Written Archives Centre. An otherwise redundant snippet from this project's findings hints at the potential results of such a search: according to a letter from Heinrich Schnitzler to Eric Glass dated 22 June 1945, the BBC chose one of Arthur Schnitzler's plays for 'immediate post-war broadcasting to Germany'.[3] Time unfortunately did not allow further enquiry to establish which of the plays had been deemed an appropriate post-war prescription for the defeated. German-language broadcasting has not been entirely ignored by academia (see, for example, the edited volume *'Stimme der Wahrheit': German-Language Broadcasting by the BBC* (2003)),[4] but much could be gained from more extensive research in this area. Further consideration of Heinrich Schnitzler's papers could also shed more light on the role of German and Austrian exiles

2 Urbach, 'Heinrich Schnitzler', pp. 5–6 and 17–18.

3 Heinrich Schnitzler to Eric Glass, 22.6.1945 (Schn 21/4/52).

4 *'Stimme der Wahrheit': German-Language Broadcasting by the BBC*, ed. by Charmian Brinson and Richard Dove (Amsterdam; New York: Rodopi, 2003).

at the BBC: his correspondents included Martin Esslin, for example, who had fled Vienna in 1938 and was head of BBC Radio Drama from 1963 to 1977; and the material concerning *Vienna 1900: Games with Love and Death* (1973–74), the BBC serial adaptation of five Schnitzler stories dramatized by Robert Muller, a Jewish refugee from Hamburg, could also prove informative.

A number of other English-language translations would reward proper analysis alongside the findings in this book. David Harrower's *Sweet Nothings* (directed by Luc Bondy at The Old Vic in 2010) might be read alongside *Dalliance* and its reception in the press compared with that given to Stoppard's version. *The Lonely Road* (directed by Christopher Fettes at The Old Vic in 1984 to 1985) provides a rare example of one of the less popular Schnitzler plays being produced on a major London stage and hence deserves attention. The aforementioned television series *Vienna 1900* also warrants detailed consideration simply by virtue of the size of the project (six episodes, each fifty minutes long) and its reach.[5] In 2019 yet another production 'in the style of' *Reigen* was heard on BBC Radio 4: a five-part documentary, *Full Circle*, using real stories and voices, could be interpreted in the light of Chapter 4.

A new approach is required if the questions of power asked in respect of the earlier interpretations are going to be extended properly to the most recent productions in Britain, for which the archive does not yet offer any assistance. The most obvious candidate is a methodology which incorporates interviews with active translators, directors, actors, agents and theatre managers; a combination of techniques from ethnography and Theatre Studies would provide a good starting point. Finally, as touched on earlier, there is a need for the English translations of Arthur Schnitzler's prose works to be surveyed more extensively. Such an enterprise would admittedly be substantial in terms of the number of texts to be identified and examined and the paratextual material to be collated, but only through this sort of engagement can the project begun by this study approach completion.

5 One of the stories, 'A Confirmed Bachelor', was broadcast in two parts, so there were six rather than five episodes.

APPENDIX 1

Published Translations of Dramatic Works 1903–2018

Included in this table are North American publications catalogued in the British Library. Dates in square brackets represent the first publication date when it does not coincide with the date recorded in the British Library. Where a translator's name appears in square brackets, acknowledgment for that translator's work does not appear in the publication.

Year Published	Title	Journal / Anthology / Publisher	Translator
1903	*Questioning the Irrevocable*	*The Drama: Its History, Literature and Influence on Civilization*, ed. by Alfred Bates, 22 vols (London: The Athenian Society)	W. H. H. Chambers
1911	*Anatol: A Sequence of Dialogues by Arthur Schnitzler, Paraphrased for the English Stage*	London: Sidgwick and Jackson; New York: McKennerley	Harley Granville Barker
1913	*The Green Cockatoo and Other Plays* [*Paracelsus*; *The Mate*]	London: Gay and Hancock; Chicago: McClurg	Horace Samuel [and P. Morton Shand]
1914	*Gallant Cassian. A Puppet Play in One Act*	London: Gowans and Gray	Adam L. Gowans
1914	*Playing with Love*	London: Gay and Hancock; Chicago: McClurg	P. Morton Shand

(*continued*)

Year Published	Title	Journal / Anthology / Publisher	Translator
1923 [1917]	*Comedies of Words, and Other Plays* [*Literature*; *His Helpmate*]	Cincinnati: Stewart Kidd	Pierre Loving
1927	*Professor Bernhardi*	London: Faber and Gwyer	Hetty Landstone
1929	*Hands Around* (with illustrations by Rene Gockinga)	Newark, NJ: Julian Press	Keene Wallis
1934	*A Farewell Supper*	*Fifty One-Act Plays*, ed. by Constance M. Martin (London: Gollancz)	Harley Granville Barker
1936	*Professor Bernhardi*	*Famous Plays of 1936* (London: Gollancz)	Ronald Adam and Louis Borell
1940	*Gallant Cassian*	*Fifty One-Act Plays: Second Series*, ed. by Constance M. Martin (London: Gollancz)	Adam L. Gowans
1953	*Merry-Go-Round* (with an introduction by Ilse Barea and illustrations by Philip Gough)	London: Weidenfeld and Nicolson	Frank and Jacqueline Marcus
1960s			
1977 [1917]	*Anatol*; *Living Hours*; *The Green Cockatoo*	Great Neck, NY: Core Collection Books	Grace Colbron
1980	*Undiscovered Country*	London: Faber & Faber	Tom Stoppard
1982	*The Round Dance and Other Plays* [*Anatol*; *Love Games*]	Manchester: Carcanet	Charles Osborne
1982	*Anatol*	London: Methuen	Frank Marcus
1982	*La Ronde* (with an introduction by Frank Marcus)	London: Methuen	Frank and Jacqueline Marcus

Year Published	Title	Journal / Anthology / Publisher	Translator
1982	*La Ronde* (*Reigen*)	London: Penguin	John Barton and Sue Davies
1982	*Flirtations*	Arthur Schnitzler, *Plays and Stories*, ed. by Egon Schwarz (New York: Continuum)	Arthur S. Wensinger, Clinton J. Atkinson and Susanne Mrozik
	La Ronde		Eric Bentley
	Countess Mitzi or The Family Reunion		Edwin Bjorkman and Caroline Wellbery
1986	*Illusion and Reality: Plays and Stories of Arthur Schnitzler* [Three Anatol playlets: *Anatol's Delusions of Grandeur*; *The High-Strung Woman*; *One-Thirty; New Year's Eve*; *At the Green Cockatoo*]	New York: Lang	Paul F. Dvorak
1986	*Dalliance* with *Undiscovered Country*	London: Faber & Faber	Tom Stoppard
1989	*Anatol*	Bath: Absolute Classics	Michael Robinson
1992	*Three Late Plays* [*The Sisters, or Casanova in Spa*; *Seduction Comedy*; *The Way to the Pond*]	Riverside, CA: Ariadne Press	G. J. Weinberger
1998	*The Blue Room*	London: Faber & Faber	David Hare
1998	*Sleeping Around*	London: Methuen	Hilary Fannin, Stephen Greenhorn, Abi Morgan and Mark Ravenhill

(*continued*)

Year Published	Title	Journal / Anthology / Publisher	Translator
2002	*Ten Rounds*	Belfast: Lagan Press	Carlo Gébler
2004	*Round Dance and Other Plays* [*Flirtations*; *The Last Masks*; *Countess Mizzie*; *Professor Bernhardi*; *The Vast Domain*; *The Green Cockatoo*] (with an introduction by Ritchie Robertson)	Oxford: Oxford University Press	J. M. Q. Davies
2005	*Professor Bernhardi*	London: Oberon	Samuel Adamson
2007	*La Ronde*	London: Nick Hern	Stephen Unwin and Peter Zombory-Moldovan
2009	*Unbroken*	London: Nick Hern	Alexandra Wood
2009	*Foreplay*	London: Oberon	Mpumelelo Paul Grootboom
2009	*Anatol*	*Still Laughing: Three Adaptations* (Vancouver: Talonbooks)	Morris Panych
2010	*Sweet Nothings*	London: Faber & Faber	David Harrower
2017	*La Ronde*	London: Oberon	Max Gill

APPENDIX 2

Theatre Productions 1900–2018

Records are collated from: J. P. Wearing's six volumes on *The London Stage [...]: A Calendar of Productions, Performers and Personnel* (Lanham: Rowman & Littlefield / Scarecrow Press, 2014), which covers the years between 1900 and 1959; the Lord Chamberlain's Archive, British Library; the Papers of Heinrich Schnitzler in the Theatermuseum, Wien; published translations; and online reviews. Where a translator's name appears in square brackets, acknowledgment of that translator's work has not been published.

Year performed	Title	Theatre / Company	Number of Performances	Translator / Adaptor
1900	*Liebelei*	Great Queen Street	2	N/A – performed in German
1905	*In the Hospital*	Court	9	'Christopher Horne' [Charles Wheeler and Harley Granville Barker]
1908	*Literature* and *The Farewell Supper*	Bijou / New Stage Club	1	Edith A. Browne and Alix Grein
1909	*Light o' Love*	His Majesty's	3	Valentine G. Williams
1911	*Anatol* (6 playlets)	Little	15	Harley Granville Barker
1912	*Das Märchen*	Little / Adelphi Play Society	1	C. E. Wheeler and Granville-Barker

(*continued*)

Year performed	Title	Theatre / Company	Number of Performances	Translator / Adaptor
1913	*Comtesse Mizzi* (double bill with *The Green Cockatoo*)	Aldwych / Incorporated Stage Society	2	H. A. Hertz
1913	*The Green Cockatoo* (double bill with *Comtesse Mizzi*)	Aldwych / Incorporated Stage Society	2	Penelope Wheeler
1913	*The Green Cockatoo*	Vaudeville	27	Penelope Wheeler
1920	*Gallant Cassian*	Old Vic	1	Adam Gowans
1921	*A Farewell Supper* (part of *The Pedlar's Basket* presented by Norman MacDermott)	Everyman	14	Harley Granville Barker
1921	*A Farewell Supper* (presented with Shaw's *The Dark Lady of the Sonnets*)	Queen's / Everyman Theatre Company	29	Harley Granville Barker
1925	*Light o' Love*	Kingsway / in aid of the Royal Free Hospital	1	Wearing: "([trans G. Valentine Williams] of *Liebelei*, 1895; revised by Moreton Shand)"
1927	*Professor Bernhardi* (a dramatic reading by the Jewish Drama League)	Little	1	? in German?

Year performed	Title	Theatre / Company	Number of Performances	Translator / Adaptor
1927	*The Farewell Supper* (in aid of the Save the Children Fund)	New	1	Harley Granville Barker
1928	*Gallant Cassian* (in quadruple bill with *Ask No Questions*, *Anatol's Wedding Morning*; and *The Proposal* by Chekhov)	Arts / International Theatre Society	1	Adam Gowans Harley Granville Barker Harley Granville Barker Constance Garnett
1931	*Professor Bernhardi*	Phoenix / Jewish Drama League	1	Hetty Landstone
1932	*Fräulein Elsa*	Kingsway / Independent Theatre Club	approx. 17	Adapted by Theodore Komisarjevsky
1933	*La Ronde*	Arts	7	Suzanne Clauser and M. Remon and W. Bauer – performed in French
1935	*Anatol*	Gate Theatre Studio		Harley Granville Barker
1936	*Professor Bernhardi*	Phoenix	30	Louis Borell and Ronald Adam. Directed by Heinrich Schnitzler
1939	*A Farewell Supper*	Westminster / London Mask Theatre	24	Harley Granville Barker

(*continued*)

Year performed	Title	Theatre / Company	Number of Performances	Translator / Adaptor
1948	*The Green Cockatoo*	Lyric Hammersmith		Horace B. Samuel [and P. Morton Shand]
1949	*Anatol?*	Highbury Players		
1950	*Christmas Presents*	Watergate		
1956	*Anatol*	Birmingham Repertory		Fay and Michael Kanin
1960s				
1976	*Anatol*	The Open Space		Frank Marcus
1979	*Anatol*	Cambridge Theatre Company		Frank Marcus
1979	*Undiscovered Country*	Olivier Theatre, National	67	Tom Stoppard
1982	*La Ronde*	Aldwych Theatre / Royal Shakespeare Company		John Barton and Sue Davies
1982	*La Ronde*	Crucible, Sheffield / Central School of Art and Design / Shared Experience Group, then Drill Hall, London		Mike Alfreds
1982	*Round Dance*	Royal Exchange, Manchester		Charles Osborne

Year performed	Title	Theatre / Company	Number of Performances	Translator / Adaptor
1985	*The Lonely Road*	Yvonne Arnaud, Guildford, then Old Vic		Ronald Adam and Christopher Fettes
1985	*Intermezzo*	Greenwich		
1986	*Dalliance*	Lyttelton Theatre, National	54	Tom Stoppard
1989	*Summer Breeze*	Gate Theatre Club		Michael Robinson
1993	*Literature*	Two Way Mirror Theatre Club		Daniel Meyer-Dinkgräfe
1994	*Escapade*	Drama Centre		
1994	*Comforting Myths* *The Hysterical Woman* *Literary Matters* *Half Past One*	Greenwich Studio		Margaret Forsyth
1994	*The Green Parakeet*	Greenwich Studio		Julian Forsyth
1996	*Fairgame*	New End		Michael Robinson (edited by Jonathan Banatvala)
1998	*Sleeping Around*	Salisbury Playhouse, then Donmar Warehouse, then on tour	approx. 50	Hilary Fannin, Stephen Greenhorn, Abi Morgan, Mark Ravenhill
1998	*The Blue Room*	Donmar Warehouse		David Hare
2000	*The Blue Room*	Haymarket		David Hare

(*continued*)

Year performed	Title	Theatre / Company	Number of Performances	Translator / Adaptor
2001	*Anatol*	Gate, then Nottingham Playhouse		Michael Robinson
2002	*Ten Rounds*	Tricycle		Carlo Gébler
2002	*Modern Dance for Beginners*	Soho		Sarah Phelps
2005	*Professor Bernhardi*	Arcola		Samuel Adamson
2006	*Anatol*	Arcola		Carl Mueller
2006	*La Ronde*	The Brockley Jack		Simon Beyer
2009	*Fucking Men*	King's Head		Joe DiPietro
2009	*La Ronde*	Riverside Studios		Directed by Neil Sheppeck
2009	*Unbroken*	Gate		Alexandra Wood
2009	*Foreplay*	Theatre Royal Stratford East / South African State Theatre		Mpumelelo Paul Grootboom
2010	*Sweet Nothings*	Young Vic		David Harrower
2011	*Dream Story*	Gate		Adapted by Anna Ledwich
2011	*La Ronde*	Rose Branch		Peter Scott-Presland and David Harrod
2011	*La Ronde*	White Bear		Lukas Raphael
2014	*Swings and Roundabouts*	White Bear		Richard Listor
2014	*Love to Love to Love You*	The Library (private members' club)		Florence Keith-Roach

Year performed	Title	Theatre / Company	Number of Performances	Translator / Adaptor
2015–17	*Professor Bernhardi*	Barts Pathology Museum / Anatomy Lecture Theatre, Cambridge / Barnfield Theatre, Exeter	5	Judith Beniston with Nicole Robertson
2017	*La Ronde*	The Bunker		Max Gill
2017	*Fucking Men*	The Vault		Joe DiPietro
2017	*La Ronde*	Theatro Technis / The Acting Gymnasium		Gavin McAlinden
2017	*Roundelay*	Southwark Playhouse / Visible Ensemble		Sonja Linden
2018	*The Affairs of Anatol*	Pentameters		Harley Granville Barker

APPENDIX 3

BBC Broadcasts 1923–2008

The purpose of the table below is to show the spread of radio and television broadcasts across the years. For this reason repeats within the same year have been excluded. Except where noted as 'a reading', all prose works listed involved some element of dramatization and featured at least two actors playing different parts. Records are collated from the *Radio Times* Archive (BBC Genome Project) and Audience Research Reports at the BBC Written Archives Centre.

Year Broadcast	Channel	Title	Acknowledged Translator
1927	5WA Cardiff	*Ask No Questions and You'll Hear No Stories*	Harley Granville Barker
1927	5GB (Experimental)	*The Triple Warning* (a reading)	
1932	National Programme	*A Farewell Supper*	Granville Barker
1935	Regional Programme and National Programme	*Liebelei*	P. Morton Shand. Adapted for broadcasting by Marianne Helweg
1935	National Programme	*A Farewell Supper*	[character called 'Mimi' suggests it is Granville Barker]
1936	Regional Programme and National Programme	*Liebelei*	P. Morton Shand. Adapted for broadcasting by Marianne Helweg
1937	National Programme	*Christmas Presents*	

Year Broadcast	Channel	Title	Acknowledged Translator
1938	Regional Programme	*Liebelei*	P. Morton Shand. Adapted for broadcasting by Marianne Helweg
1940	Home Service	*Liebelei*	P. Morton Shand. Adapted for broadcasting by Marianne Helweg
1945	Home Service	*The Man Who Pulls Strings*	Alec Macdonald
1946	Home Service	*Anatol*	Granville Barker
1947	Home Service	*Anatol*	Granville Barker
1950	BBC TV	An Episode from *The Anatol Dialogues*	Granville Barker
1953	Home Service	*Professor Bernhardi*	Louis Borell and Ronald Adam. Adapted for radio by Mollie Greenhalgh
1954	BBC TV	*Liebelei*	Frank and Jacqueline Marcus
1955	Home Service	*An Episode* and *A Farewell Supper*	Granville Barker
	Light Programme	*Playing with Love*	P. Morton Shand
1956	Home Service	*Anatol*	Adapted by Fay and Michael Kanin. Adapted for radio by Peter Dews
1960	BBC TV	*Parasol* (based on the *Anatol Dialogues*)	Caryl Brahms and Ned Sherrin
1962	Third Programme	*Lieutenant Gustl*	Sheila Stern

(*continued*)

Year Broadcast	Channel	Title	Acknowledged Translator
1962	Light Programme	*Playing with Love*	P. Morton Shand. Adapted by Marianne Helweg
1963	Third Programme	*Lieutenant Gustl*	Sheila Stern
1963	Third Programme	*Fraulein Else*	F. H. Lyon with Hilda Schroder
1964	Third Programme	*Merry-Go-Round*	Frank and Jaqueline Marcus
1965	BBC Two (television)	*Anatol*	Granville Barker
1965	Network Three	*Fraulein Else*	F. H. Lyon with Hilda Schroder
1966	BBC Two (television)	*Anatol*	Granville Barker
1971	BBC Radio 4	*The Lonely Road*	Ronald Adam
1971	BBC Radio 4	*Professor Bernhardi*	Louis Borell and Ronald Adam. Adapted for radio by Mollie [Greenhalgh] Hardwick
1971	BBC Radio 4	*Lieutenant Gustl*	Sheila Stern
1972	BBC Radio 4	*Daybreak*	Thomas Schwalm and Howard Thompson
1972	BBC Radio 4	*The Uncharted Sea*	Ronald Adam
1973	BBC Radio 4	*Anatol*	Granville Barker
	BBC Radio 4	*The Lonely Road*	Ronald Adam
1973–74	BBC Two (television)	*Vienna 1900: Games with Love and Death* (six-part series adapting five 'stories' by Schnitzler)	Dramatized by Robert Muller

Year Broadcast	Channel	Title	Acknowledged Translator
1974	BBC Radio 3	*Dead Gabriel* (a reading)	Eric Sutton. Adapted by Patricia Brent
1974	BBC Radio 3	*Redegonda's Diary* (a reading)	H. Steinhauer and Helen Jessiman
1974	BBC Radio 3	*What a Hysterical Girl*	
1975	BBC Radio 3	*Redegonda's Diary* (a reading)	H. Steinhauer and Helen Jessiman
1975	BBC Two (television)	*Vienna 1900: Games with Love and Death* (six-part series adapting five 'stories' by Schnitzler)	Dramatized by Robert Muller
1976	BBC Radio 3	*Dead Gabriel* (a reading)	Eric Sutton
1976	BBC Radio 3	*What a Hysterical Girl*	
1978	BBC Radio 3	*The Prince is in the Audience* (a reading)	David Heald
1979	BBC Radio 3	*The Prince is in the Audience* (a reading)	David Heald
1979	BBC Radio 4	*Daybreak*	Thomas Schwalm and Howard Thompson
1980	BBC Radio 4	*The Festival of Bacchus*	Basil Ashmore
1982	BBC One (television)	*La Ronde*	Frank and Jacqueline Marcus
1982	BBC Two (television)	*Fraulein Else*	Dramatized by Thomas Ellice
1986	BBC Radio 3	*Il ritorno di Casanova* (opera)	Libretto by Giuseppe de Leva
1987	BBC Radio 3	*Intermezzo*	Robert David MacDonald
1987	BBC Radio 3	*Anatol*	Michael Robinson
1988	BBC Two (television)	*Liebelei* (in German)	Directed by Max Ophüls

(*continued*)

Year Broadcast	Channel	Title	Acknowledged Translator
1989	BBC Radio 4	*Lieutenant Gustl*	George Roubicek
1989	BBC Radio 3	*Anatol*	Michael Robinson
1991	BBC Radio 3	*Undiscovered Country*	Tom Stoppard, adapted by Gerry Jones
1992	BBC Two (television)	*La Ronde* (in French)	Directed by Max Ophüls
1993	BBC Radio 3	*Undiscovered Country*	Tom Stoppard, adapted by Gerry Jones
	BBC Radio 3	*Dalliance*	Tom Stoppard
1995	BBC Two (television)	*La Ronde* (in French)	Directed by Max Ophüls
2000	BBC Radio 4	*A Confirmed Bachelor*	Dramatized by Vanessa Rosenthal
2003	BBC Radio 4	*The Spring Sonata*	Dramatized by Vanessa Rosenthal
2005	BBC Radio 4	*Cashcows* (5 parts)	April de Angelis
2006	BBC Radio 3	*Flowers* (a reading)	
2007	BBC Radio 3	*Professor Bernhardi*	Samuel Adamson
2008	BBC Radio 7	*Dream Story* (a reading; 8 parts)	
2008	BBC Radio 3	*Professor Bernhardi*	

BIBLIOGRAPHY

Archive Materials

The Papers of Arthur Schnitzler are held by the Cambridge University Library and the Deutsches Literaturarchiv, Marbach. The following letters and manuscripts were consulted.

Deutsches Literaturarchiv, Marbach

Barker, H. Granville to Robert Vansittart, HS.NZ85.0001.05250
Hertz, Fanny to Arthur Schnitzler, HS.NZ85.0001.03427
Horowitz, Johannes to Arthur Schnitzler, HS.NZ85.0001.03519a
Macdonell, Helen to Arthur Schnitzler, HS.NZ85.0001.03960
Markbreiter, Felix and Julie, Correspondence, HS.NZ85.0001.03999, 04000, 04001, 01377
Pogson, Bertha, Correspondence, HS.NZ85.0001.04209 and 01611
Schnitzler, Arthur to H. Granville Barker, HS.NZ85.0001.00881
Schnitzler, Arthur to E. A. Browne, HS.NZ85.0001.00469
Schnitzler, Arthur to J. T. Grein, HS.NZ85.0001.00889
Schnitzler, Arthur to Ernst Meyer, HS.NZ85.0001.01419
Schnitzler, Arthur to G. Valentine Williams, HS.NZ85.0001.02224
Shand, P. Morton, Correspondence, HS.NZ85.0001.01919, 01920, 04586
St. John, Christopher, Correspondence, HS.NZ85.0001.02694 and 01744
Trebitsch, Siegfried to Arthur Schnitzler, HS.NZ85.0001.04810
Vansittart, Robert to Arthur Schnitzler, HS.NZ85.0001.04822

Cambridge University Library

Fischer, Samuel to Arthur Schnitzler, B121a, B121b, B121c
Schnitzler, Arthur to Ashley Dukes, A20,5
Schnitzler, Arthur, 'Verzeichnis der Einnahmen aus fremdsprachigen Drucken', A237,5
Schrumpf, Beatrice M., 'The Reception of Arthur Schnitzler in the United States', A239,2
Wheeler, C. E. to Arthur Schnitzler, B550
Whelen, Frederick to Arthur Schnitzler, B1030
Williams, G. Valentine to Arthur Schnitzler, B1038

Theatermuseum, Vienna

The Papers of Heinrich Schnitzler are held by the Theatermuseum in Vienna. The following letters were consulted:

BBC, Correspondence, Schn 7/7
Dyer, Charles to Heinrich Schnitzler, Schn 12/25/1
Glass, Eric, Correspondence, Schn 21/8, 21/9, 21/10, 21/11, 21/12, 21/13
Hands, Terry, Correspondence, Schn 23/35
Marcus, Frank, Correspondence, Schn 34/18
Marowitz, Charles, Correspondence, Schn 34/29
National Theatre, Correspondence, Schn 38/50
Schnitzler, Heinrich to Ronald Adam, Schn 5/10
Schnitzler, Heinrich to Ilsa Barea, Schn 6/24
Schnitzler, Heinrichto Eric Glass, Schn 21/4, 21/5, 21/6, 21/7
Schnitzler, Heinrich to Gerda Niedieck, Schn 40/5
Schnitzler, Heinrich to Ned Sherrin, Schn 55/42

Lord Chamberlain's Archive, British Library

The following playscripts were consulted:

Light o' Love, trans. by G. Valentine Williams, LCP 1909/11
Anatol – A Sequence of Dialogues, trans. by H. Granville Barker, LCP 1911/7
In the Hospital, trans. by 'Christopher Horne', LCP 1905/5

Harry Ransom Center, The University of Texas at Austin

Harley Granville-Barker Collection 1895–1959
David Hare Papers 1968–1993
Tom Stoppard Papers 1939–2000

BBC Written Archives Centre, Reading

BBC playscripts, Audience Research Reports and further correspondence concerning BBC broadcasts of Arthur Schnitzler's works are held by the BBC Written Archives Centre, Reading.

Theatre and Performance Archives, Victoria and Albert Museum

Materials relating to Frank Marcus's translation of *Anatol*, including a playscript and programme, are held at the Theatre and Performance Archives, Victoria and Albert Museum, London: THM/271.

National Theatre Archive, London

Prompt scripts for *Undiscovered Country* and *Dalliance* are held by the National Theatre Archive, London: RNT/ SM/1/152 and RNT/SM/1/265.

Most newspaper articles concerning British reception of Arthur Schnitzler's works during the writer's lifetime stem from his collection, the Schnitzler Press-Cuttings Archive, now held in Special Collections at the University of Exeter (EUL MS 214). The newspaper articles concerning Tom Stoppard's adaptations *Undiscovered Country* and *Dalliance* were found in the National Theatre Archive, London. Newspaper articles concerning the performance of *Anatol* at the Open Space Theatre are held in the Theatre and Performance Archives, Victoria and Albert Museum, London. Often the archived articles fail to include the full details of title, page number and author. It has, therefore, not always been possible to give complete references but as much information as was available is given below, ordered (where appropriate) chronologically and by reference to the production reviewed.

General Reception of German-Language Plays

'Notes', *The Outlook*, 21 April 1900, pp. 357–59
'In Passing', *The Outlook*, 22 December 1901, p. 660–01
'Great Queen Street Theatre. "Rosmersholm"', *The Times*, 14 May 1906, p. 15

Light o' Love (1909)

'The Afternoon Theatre', *Daily Telegraph*, 15 May 1909, p. 6
A.H., 'Light O' Love', *Daily Mail*, 15 May 1909, p. 3
'The Afternoon Theatre', *The Times*, 15 May 1909, p. 12
'Drama. The Week', *Athenaeum*, 22 May 1909, pp. 627–28

Anatol (1911)

'The Little Theatre', *The Times*, 13 March 1911, p. 10
'The Little Theatre', *The Times*, 20 March 1911, p. 12
[Review of *Anatol*], *Daily Chronicle*, 20 March 1911

Anatol (1976)

Billington, Michael, 'Anatol', *Guardian*, 12 February 1976, p. 8
Cushman, Robert, 'Austrian Attitudes', *Observer*, 15 February 1976, p. 26

Hobson, Harold, 'Recipe for a Revolution', *Sunday Times*, 15 February 1976, p. 37
Nurse, Keith, 'Six into One', *Sunday Telegraph*, 15 February 1976, p. 18.
Shulman, Milton, 'A Wry Look at Love', *Evening Standard*, 12 February 1976
Wardle, Irving, 'Anatol', *The Times*, 12 February 1976, p. 13
Young, B. A., 'Anatol', *Financial Times*, 12 February 1976, p. 3

Undiscovered Country (1979)

Anon., *Mid Sussex Times*, 24 August 1979
Barber, John, 'Tragi-comical Study of a Philanderer', *Daily Telegraph*, 21 June 1979
Bennett, Peter, 'Upstage', *Gay News*, 12–25 July 1979, p. 34
Billington, Michael, 'Vintage Wiener Schnitzler', *Guardian*, 21 June 1979, p. 12
Billington, Michael, 'A Penchant for Foreign Affairs', *Guardian*, 23 June 1979, p. 11
Cushman, Robert, 'Wenching in Old Austria', *Observer*, 24 June 1979, p. 14
Grant, Steve, *Time Out*, 28 June 1979
Hurren, Kenneth, *What's On IN LONDON*, 29 June 1979
Jaggi, Maya, 'You can't help being what you write', *Guardian*, 6 September 2008
Jenkins, Peter, 'Theatre', *Spectator*, 7 July 1979
Rank, Hugh, '"My distrust in matters of love was universal. Faithfulness in lovers, to say nothing of married couples, was at best a lucky coincidence" – Schnitzler', *Guardian*, 19 June 1979, p. 8
Stewart, Ian, *Country Life*, 19 July 1979
Taylor, John Russell, *Plays & Players*, July 1979
Tinker, Jack, 'Grand National!', *Daily Mail*, 22 June 1979, p. 26
Walker, Michael, 'Mesmerising Discovery', *Chelsea News* and *Chelsea Post*, 6 July 1979

La Ronde (various productions) (1982)

Appleyard, Bryan, 'The Race to Stage a Liberated *La Ronde*', *The Times*, 7 September 1981, p. 11
Banks-Smith, Nancy, 'Vienna's Bitter-Sweet Taste', *Guardian*, 20 April 1982, p. 9
Coveney, Michael, 'La Ronde', *Financial Times*, 5 April 1982, p. 17
Ensor, Patrick, 'La Ronde', *Guardian*, 3 April 1982, p. 10
French, Philip, 'Returning to Eboli: Philip French on a Film by Francesco Rosl and the Revival of Ophuls's [*sic*] 'La Ronde', *Observer*, 2 May 1982, p. 32
Mackenzie, Suzie, *Time Out*

Murray, James, 'So naughty – but it's in the best possible taste', *Daily Express*, 19 April 1982, p. 19

'Pit', 'La Ronde', *Variety*, 27 January 1982, p. 90

Radin, Victoria, 'Nudge-nudge, wink-wink', *Observer*, 10 January 1982, p. 27

Rank, Hugh, 'Der *Reigen* begann sich zu drehen', *Wiener Zeitung*, 28 January 1982

Dalliance (1986)

Anon., *Midweek*, 12 June 1986

'Curtain Up', *Today*, 8 June 1986, p. 34

'DSC.', *London Weekly Diary*, 15 June 1986

Barber, John, 'Stoppard worth the wait', *Daily Telegraph*, 19 May 1986, p. 13

Billington, Michael, 'Fiddling with a Game of Love: Michael Billington Doubts the Wisdom of Tom Stoppard's Transposition of Schnitzler's play', *Guardian*, 29 May 1986, p. 10

Harron, Mary, 'Vanessa's Calculating Cleopatra', *Observer*, 1 June 1986, p. 21

Hirschorn, Clive, 'Theatre', *Sunday Express*, 1 June 86

King, Francis, 'Playing by the Rules', *Sunday Telegraph*, 1 June 1986, p. 16

Nathan, David, 'Too Much Dalliance for the National', *Jewish Chronicle*, 6 June 1986

Peter, John, 'For Disservices Rendered', *Sunday Times*, 1 June 1986, p. 49.

Shannon, David, 'Don't lock up your daughters', *Today*, 2 June 1986

Shulman, Milton, 'That Fritz is a Cad', *London Evening Standard*, 26 May 1986, p. 30

Theobold, Megan, 'Left High and Dry', *West Herts & Watford Observer*, 6 June 1986

Tinker, Jack, 'Here's a girl to break your heart', *Daily Mail*, 28 May 1986, p. 3

Trewin, J. C., 'The Tragic Dangers of Dalliance', *Illustrated London News*, July 1986

Cashcows (2005)

Petty, Moira, 'Fine start to lifting curse of Austen's Abbey', *Stage*, 22 September 2005, p. 15

Fucking Men (2008)

Gardner, Lyn, 'Fucking Men', *Guardian*, 10 January 2009, https://www.theguardian.com/stage/2009/jan/10/review-fucking-men [accessed 27 October 2018]

Hofler, Robert, 'The L.A. Side of DiPietro', https://variety.com/2009/legit/news/the-l-a-side-of-dipietro-1118010074/ [accessed 17 July 2018]

Obituaries (1931)

'Death of Arthur Schnitzler: The Creator of "Anatol"', *Manchester Guardian*, 22 October 1931, p. 4

'Austrian Doctor Who Created "Anatol"', *Scotsman*, 22 October 1931

Works by Arthur Schnitzler

Anatol; Anatols Größenwahn; Der grüne Kakadu (Stuttgart: Reclam, 2008)

Anatol. Historisch-kritische Ausgabe, ed. by Evelyne Polt-Heinzl and Isabella Schwentner, in *Werke in historisch-kritischen Ausgaben*, 12 vols (Berlin and Boston, MA: de Gruyter, 2011–), II (2012)

Aphorismen und Betrachtungen (Frankfurt a. M.: Fischer, 1967)

Arthur Schnitzler digital. Historisch-kritische Edition (Werke 1905–1931) (2018–), https://www.arthur-schnitzler.org [accessed 22 March 2021]

Briefe, 2 vols, I: *1875–1912*, ed. by Therese Nickl and Heinrich Schnitzler (Frankfurt a. M.: Fischer, 1981)

Briefe, 2 vols, II: *1913–1931*, ed. by Peter Michael Braunwarth and others (Frankfurt a. M.: Fischer, 1984)

Das weite Land, in *Gesammelte Werke. Die Dramatischen Werke*, 2 vols (Frankfurt a. M.: Fischer, 1962), II, 217–320

Jugend in Wien. Eine Autobiographie, ed. by Therese Nickl and Heinrich Schnitzler (Vienna: Molden, 1968)

Liebelei. Historisch-kritische Ausgabe, ed. by Peter Michael Braunwarth, Gerhard Hubmann and Isabella Schwentner, 2 vols, in *Werke in historisch-kritischen Ausgaben*, 12 vols (Berlin and Boston, MA: de Gruyter, 2011–), IV (2014)

Medizinische Schriften, ed. by Horst Thomé (Vienna: Zsolnay, 1988)

Reigen. Historisch-kritische Ausgabe, ed. by Marina Rauchenbacher and Konstanze Fliedl, in *Werke in historisch-kritischen Ausgaben*, 12 vols (Berlin and Boston, MA: de Gruyter, 2011–), XII (2019)

Tagebuch, ed. by Peter Michael Braunwarth and others, 10 vols (Vienna: Verlag der Österreichischen Akademie der Wissenschaften, 1981)

Werke in historisch-kritischen Ausgaben, ed. by Konstanze Fliedl, 12 vols (Berlin and Boston, MA: de Gruyter, 2011–)

Published English-Language Translations of Works by Arthur Schnitzler

Barton, John, and Sue Davies, *La Ronde (Reigen)* (London: Penguin, 1982)

Caro, Alexander, and Edward Woticky, 'The Vast Domain', *Poet Lore*, 34 (1923), 317–407

Chambers, W. H. H., 'Questioning the Irrevocable', in *The Drama: Its History, Literature and Influence on Civilization*, ed. by Alfred Bates, 22 vols (London: The Athenian Society, 1903), XII, 329–44

Colbron, Grace Isabel, *Anatol; Living Hours; The Green Cockatoo* (New York: Boni & Liveright, 1917)

Davies, J. M. Q., *Round Dance and Other Plays* (Oxford: Oxford University Press, 2004)

DiPietro, Joe, *Fucking Men* (New York: Dramatists Play Service, 2014)

Fannin, Hilary, Stephen Greenhorn, Abi Morgan and Mark Ravenhill, *Sleeping Around* (London: Methuen, 1998)

Gill, Max, *La Ronde* (London: Oberon, 2017)

Granville Barker, Harley, *Anatol: A Sequence of Dialogues* (London: Sidgwick & Jackson, 1911)

Hare, David, *The Blue Room* (London: Faber & Faber, 1998)

Harrower, David, *Sweet Nothings* (London: Faber & Faber, 2010)

Marcus, Frank, *Anatol* (London: Methuen, 1982)

Marcus, Frank, and Jacqueline Marcus, *Merry-Go-Round* (London: Weidenfeld and Nicholson, 1953)

Osborne, Charles, *The Round Dance and Other Plays* (Manchester: Carcanet New Press, 1982)

Shand, P. Morton, *Playing with Love* (London: Hancock & Gay, 1914)

Stoppard, Tom, *Dalliance*, in *Dalliance and Undiscovered Country* (London: Faber & Faber, 1986), pp. 1–53

— *Undiscovered Country*, in *Dalliance and Undiscovered Country* (London: Faber & Faber, 1986), pp. 55–147

Wood, Alexandra, *Unbroken* (London: Gate, 2009)

Other Primary Sources

Bahr, Hermann, and Arthur Schnitzler, *Briefwechsel, Aufzeichnungen, Dokumente 1891–1931*, ed. by Kurt Ifkovits and Martin Anton Müller (Göttingen: Wallstein, 2018)

Fontane, Theodor, *Effi Briest*, 3rd edn (Munich: Deutscher Taschenbuch, 1987)

Forster, E. M., *Howard's End* (London: Penguin, 2000)

Hofmannsthal, Hugo von, 'Vienna Letter, July 1922', *The Dial*, August 1922, pp. 206–14

James, Henry, *The Complete Letters of Henry James, 1878–1880*, ed. by Pierre A. Walker and Greg W. Zacharias, 2 vols (Lincoln, NE and London: University of Nebraska Press, 2014), I

McKenna, Stephen, *The Undiscovered Country* (London: Hutchinson, 1932)

Mitchell, Julian, *The Undiscovered Country* (London: Constable, 1968)

Orwell, George, *Animal Farm: A Fairy Story*, First Cheap Edition (London: Secker & Warburg, 1949 [1945])

Seidlin, Oskar (ed.), *Der Briefwechsel Arthur Schnitzler – Otto Brahm* (Tübingen: Niemeyer, 1975)

Shakespeare, William, *Hamlet*, ed. by Harold Jenkins, The Arden Shakespeare (London: Methuen, 1982)

— *Julius Caesar*, ed. by David Daniell, The Arden Shakespeare (London: Thomas Nelson, 1998)

Secondary Literature

Aaltonen, Sirkku, 'Translating Plays or Baking Apple Pies: A Functional Approach to the Study of Drama Translation', in *Translation as Intercultural Communication*, ed. by Mary Snell-Hornby, Zuzana Jettmarová and Klaus Kaindl (Amsterdam: Benjamins, 1997), pp. 135–46

— *Time-Sharing on Stage: Drama Translation in Theatre and Society* (Clevedon: Multilingual Matters, 2000)

Adam, Ronald, *Overture and Beginners* (London: Gollancz, 1938)

Agate, James, *A Short View of the English Stage, 1900–1926* (London: Jenkins, 1926)

Alewyn, Richard, *Probleme und Gestalten* (Frankfurt a. M.: Insel, 1974)

Alexander, Michael, *The Poetic Achievement of Ezra Pound* (Berkeley, CA and Los Angeles, CA: University of California Press, 1981)

Allardyce Nicoll, John Ramsay, *English Drama 1900–1930: The Beginnings of the Modern Period* (Cambridge: Cambridge University Press, 1973)

Alth, Minna von, *Burgtheater von 1776–1976. Aufführungen und Besetzungen von zweihundert Jahren*, 2 vols (Vienna: Ueberreuter, 1979)

Alvarez, Roman, and M. Carmen-Africa Vidal (eds), *Translation, Power, Subversion* (Clevedon: Multilingual Matters, 1996)

Anderman, Gunilla, *Europe on Stage* (London: Oberon, 2005)

Appiah, Kwame Anthony, 'Thick Translation', in *The Translation Studies Reader*, ed. by Lawrence Venuti (New York: Routledge, 2002), pp. 389–401

Apter, Emily, *Against World Literature: On the Politics of Untranslatability* (London and New York: Verso, 2013)

Archer, William, and Harley Granville Barker, *Scheme & Estimates for a National Theatre* (London: Duckworth, 1907)

Arrojo, Rosemary, 'The "Death" of the Author and the Limits of the Translator's Visibility', in *Translation as Intercultural Communication*, ed. by Mary Snell-Hornby, Zuzana Jettmarová and Klaus Kaindl (Amsterdam: Benjamins, 1997), pp. 21–32

Ashton, Rosemary, *The German Idea: Four English Writers and the Reception of German Thought, 1800–1860* (Cambridge: Cambridge University Press, 1980)

Bahr, Hermann, 'Die Moderne', *Moderne Dichtung*, 1 (1890), 13–15

— 'Das unrettbare ich', *Neues Wiener Tagblatt*, 10 April 1903, pp. 1–4; repr. in Hermann Bahr, *Dialog vom Tragischen* (Berlin: Fischer, 1904), pp. 79–101

— 'Philosophie des Impressionismus', in Hermann Bahr, *Dialog vom Tragischen* (Berlin: Fischer, 1904), pp. 102–44

— *Dialog vom Tragischen* (Berlin: Fischer, 1904)

— *Tagebuch* (Berlin: Cassirer, 1909)

Baker, Mona, 'Narratives in and of Translation', *SKASE Journal of Translation and Interpretation*, 1 (2005), 4–13

— *Translation and Conflict: A Narrative Account* (London & New York: Routledge, 2006)

Baldwin, Peter, *Contagion and the State in Europe 1830–1930* (Cambridge: Cambridge University Press, 1999)

Balme, Christopher B., *The Cambridge Introduction to Theatre Studies* (Cambridge: Cambridge University Press, 2008)

Barea, Ilsa, *Vienna: Legend and Reality* (London: Secker and Warburg: 1966)

Barker, Andrew W., '"Der Grosse Überwinder": Hermann Bahr and the Rejection of Naturalism', *Modern Language Review*, 78 (1983), 617–30

Barthes, Roland, 'The Death of the Author', in Roland Barthes, *Image Music Text*, ed. and trans. by Stephen Heath (London: Fontana, 1977), pp. 142–48; orig.: 'La mort de l'auteur', *Manteia*, 5 (1968), 12–17

— 'From Work to Text', in *Image Music Text*, ed. and trans. by Stephen Heath (London: Fontana, 1977), pp. 155–64; orig.: 'De l'oeuvre au texte', *Revue d'esthetique*, 3 (1971) 225–32

Bartholomew, Kevin, and Katja Krebs, 'Arthur Schnitzler 1862–1931: Austrian Dramatist, Novelist and Short-Story Writer', in *Encyclopaedia of Literary Translation into English*, ed. by Olive Class, 2 vols (London: Fitzroy Dearborn, 2000), II, 1241–43

Bassnett, Susan, 'Ways through the Labyrinth: Strategies and Methods for Translating Theatre Texts', in *The Manipulation of Literature: Studies in Literary Translation*, ed. by Theo Hermans (London: Croom Helm, 1985), pp. 87–102

— 'Translating for the Theatre: The Case Against Performability', *TTR*, 4 (1991), 99–111

— 'Still Trapped in the Labyrinth: Further Reflections on Translation and Theatre', in *Constructing Cultures: Essays on Literary Translation*, ed. by Susan Bassnett and André Lefevere (Clevedon and Philadelphia, PA: Multilingual Matters, 1998), pp. 90–108

— 'Theatre and Opera', in *The Oxford Guide to Literature in English Translation*, ed. by Peter France (Oxford: Oxford University Press, 2000), pp. 96–103

— 'Culture and Translation', in *A Companion to Translation Studies*, ed. by Piotr Kuhiwczak and Karin Littau (Clevedon: Multilingual Matters, 2007), pp. 13–23

Bassnett, Susan, and André Lefevere, 'Introduction. Proust's Grandmother and the Thousand and One Nights: The Cultural Turn in Cultural Studies', in *Translation, History and Culture*, ed. by Susan Bassnett and André Lefevere (London: Pinter, 1990), pp. 1–13

Baumann, Gerhart, 'Nachwort', in Arthur Schnitzler, *Anatol; Anatols Größenwahn; Der grüne Kakadu* (Stuttgart: Reclam, 2008), pp. 158–74

Bayerdörfer, Hans-Peter, 'Weitere Rezeption und Wirkung', in *Schnitzler-Handbuch. Leben – Werk – Wirkung*, ed. by Christoph Jürgensen, Wolfgang Lukas and Michael Scheffel (Stuttgart and Weimar: Metzler, 2014), pp. 380–87

Beardsley, M. C., and W. K. Wimsatt, 'The Intentional Fallacy', *The Sewanee Review*, 54 (1946), 468–88

Beharriell, Frederick J., 'Schnitzler's Vienna, 1966', *Journal of the International Arthur Schnitzler Research Association*, 6 (1967), 4–13

Bell, Anthea, 'Translation as Illusion', *Shelving Translation* conference proceedings (2004), https://www.brunel.ac.uk/creative-writing/research/entertext/documents/entertext0431-supplement/Anthea-Bell-pdf-Translation-as-Illusion.pdf [accessed 8 June 2021]

Beller, Steven (ed.), *Rethinking Vienna 1900* (Oxford: Berghahn, 2001)

Bellettini, Lorenzo, and Christian Staufenbiel, 'The Schnitzler Nachlass. Saved by a Cambridge Student', in *Schnitzler's Hidden Manuscripts*, ed. by Lorenzo Bellettini and Peter Hutchinson (London: Lang, 2010), pp. 11–22

Belobratow, Alexander, 'Russland und Osteuropa', in *Schnitzler-Handbuch. Leben – Werk – Wirkung*, ed. by Christoph Jürgensen, Wolfgang Lukas and Michael Scheffel (Stuttgart and Weimar: Metzler, 2014), pp. 358–63

Beniston, Judith, 'Drama in Austria, 1918–1945', in *A History of Austrian Literature 1918–2000*, ed. by Kathrin Kohl and Ritchie Robertson (Rochester, NY: Camden House, 2006), pp. 21–50

— 'Doctors Talking to Doctors in Arthur Schnitzler's *Professor Bernhardi*', in *Adapting Translation for the Stage*, ed. by Geraldine Brodie and Emma Cole (London: Routledge, 2017), pp. 39–55

— 'Schnitzler und die "Uebersetzungs-Miseren"', in *Textschicksale. Das Werk Arthur Schnitzlers im Kontext der Moderne*, ed. by Wolfgang Lukas and Michael Scheffel (Berlin and Boston, MA: de Gruyter, 2017), pp. 251–66

Benjamin, Walter, 'Die Aufgabe des Übersetzers', in Walter Benjamin, *Gesammelte Schriften*, ed. by Rolf Tiedemann and Hermann Schweppenhäuser, 7 vols (Frankfurt a. M.: Suhrkamp, 1985), IV.I, 9–21

Bergel, Kurt, 'The Recent Reception of Arthur Schnitzler's "Das weite Land" on Two American Stages', *Modern Austrian Literature*, 9.3 (1986), 90–96

Berlin, Jeffrey B., 'Arthur Schnitzler's views on intellectual property, illustrated by the trials and tribulations of *Casanova's Homecoming*', in *Arthur Schnitzler: Zeitgenossenschaften / Contemporaneities*, ed. by Ian Foster and Florian Krobb (Bern: Lang, 2002), pp. 89–111

Bloom, Harold, *Dramatists and Dramas* (Philadelphia, PA: Chelsea House, 2005)

Bourdieu, Pierre, 'Censorship and the Imposition of Form', in *Language and Symbolic Power*, ed. by John B. Thompson, trans. by Gino Raymond and Matthew Adamson (Cambridge: Polity Press, 1991), pp. 137–62; orig.: 'Censure et mise en forme', in Pierre Bourdieu, *Ce que parler veut dire: l'économie des échanges linguistiques* (Paris: Librairie Arthème Fayard, 1982), pp. 167–205

Brandreth, Gyles, *Camilla and Charles. Portrait of a Love Affair* (London: Random House, 2006)

Brater, Enoch, 'Tom Stoppard's Brit/lit/crit', in *The Cambridge Companion to Tom Stoppard*, ed. by Katherine E. Kelly (Cambridge: Cambridge University Press, 2006), pp. 203–12

Brinson, Charmian, and Marian Malet, '"Die sonderbarste Stadt, die man sich denken kann"? Arthur Schnitzler in London', in *Arthur Schnitzler: Zeitgenossenschaften / Contemporaneities*, ed. by Ian Foster and Florian Krobb (Bern: Lang, 2002), pp. 71–87

Brinson, Charmian, and Richard Dove (eds.), *'Stimme der Wahrheit': German-Language Broadcasting by the BBC* (Amsterdam; New York: Rodopi, 2003)

Brociner, Marco, 'Professor Bernhardi', *Neues Wiener Tagblatt*, 22 December 1918, p. 10

Brodie, Geraldine, 'Translation in Performance: Theatrical Shift and the Transmission of Meaning in Tony Harrison's Translation of Euripides' "Hecuba"', *Contemporary Theatre Review*, 24 (2014), 53–65

— 'Indirect Translation on the London Stage: Terminology and (In)visibility', *Translation Studies*, 11 (2018), 333–48

— *The Translator on Stage* (London: Bloomsbury, 2018)

Brodie, Geraldine, and Emma Cole, 'Introduction', in *Adapting Translation for the Stage*, ed. by Geraldine Brodie and Emma Cole (London: Routledge, 2017), pp. 1–18

Bryant, John, *The Fluid Text: A Theory of Revision and Editing for Book and Screen* (Ann Arbor, MI: University of Michigan Press, 2002)

Cagneau, Irène, '*Anatol* (Einakterfolge, 1889–1893; inkl. *Anatols* Größenwahn, aus dem Nachlass 1955)', in *Schnitzler-Handbuch. Leben – Werk – Wirkung*, ed. by Christoph Jürgensen, Wolfgang Lukas and Michael Scheffel (Stuttgart and Weimar: Metzler, 2014), pp. 111–15

Carlson, Marvin, 'Theatrical Performance: Illustration, Translation, Fulfillment, or Supplement?', *Theatre Journal*, 37 (1985), 5–11

— *The Haunted Stage: The Theatre as Memory Machine* (Ann Arbor, MI: University of Michigan Press, 2003)

Carson, L. (ed.), *'The Stage' Year Book 1913* (London: Carson & Comerford, 1913)

Chamberlain, Lori, 'Gender and the Metaphorics of Translation', *Signs*, 13 (1988), 454–72

Chisholm, Anne, *Frances Partridge: The Biography* (London: Weidenfeld & Nicholson, 2009)

Colvin, Clare, 'The Real Tom Stoppard', *Drama*, 3 (1986), 9–10

Conolly, L. W., 'The Abolition of Theatre Censorship', *Queen's Quarterly*, 75 (1968), 569–84

Corballis, Richard, *Stoppard: The Mystery and the Clockwork* (Oxford: Amber Lane Press; New York: Methuen, 1984)

Cordingley, Anthony, and Chiara Montini, 'Genetic Translation Studies: An Emerging Discipline', *Linguistica Antverpiensia*, 14 (2015), 1–18

Cordingley, Anthony, and Céline Frigau Manning, 'What Is Collaborative Translation?', in *Collaborative Translation: From the Renaissance to the Digital Age*, ed. by Anthony Cordingley and Céline Frigau Manning (London: Bloomsbury Academic, 2017), pp. 1–30

Cronin, Michael, *Translation and Globalization* (London: Routledge, 2003)

Crook, Tim, *Radio Drama: Theory and Practice* (London & New York: Routledge, 1999)

Cutchins, Dennis, and Kathryn Meeks, 'Adaptation, Fidelity and Reception', in *The Routledge Companion to Adaptation*, ed. by Dennis Cutchins, Katja Krebs and Eckhart Voigts (London & New York: Routledge, 2018), pp. 301–13

Daviau, Donald G., 'The Reception of Arthur Schnitzler in the United States', in *The Fortunes of German Writers in America: Studies in Literary Reception*, ed. by Wolfgang Elfe, James Hardin and Gunther Holst (Columbia, SC: University of South Carolina Press, 1992), pp. 145–65

Davis, Todd F., and Kenneth Womack, 'Reading (and Writing) the Ethics of Authorship: "Shakespeare in Love" as Postmodern Metanarrative', *Literature/Film Quarterly*, 32 (2004), 153–62

Davis, Tracy C., 'The Independent Theatre Society's Revolutionary Scheme for an Uncommercial Theater', *Theatre Journal*, 42 (1990), 447–54

Decloedt, Leopold R. G., 'Eine mühsame Reise ins Unbekannte. Arthur Schnitzler und Belgien', in *Arthur Schnitzler: Zeitgenossenschaften / Contemporaneities*, ed. by Ian Foster and Florian Krobb (Bern: Lang, 2002), pp. 55–70

Dekker, John Nicholas, 'The Modern Catalyst: German Influences on the British Stage, 1890–1918' (unpublished doctoral dissertation, Ohio State Universtiy, 2007)

Delaney, Paul (ed.), *Tom Stoppard in Conversation* (Ann Arbor, MI: University of Michigan Press, 1995)

Demastes, William W., *The Cambridge Introduction to Tom Stoppard* (Cambridge: Cambridge University Press, 2012)

Denk, Rudolf, 'Arthur Schnitzlers *Das weite Land.* Theater und Film im Medienvergleich', in *Arthur Schnitzler und der Film*, ed. by Achim Aurnhammer, Barbara Beßlich and Rudolf Denk (Würzburg: Ergon, 2010), pp. 271–95

— '*Das weite Land. Tragikomödie in fünf Akten* (1911)', in *Schnitzler-Handbuch. Leben – Werk – Wirkung*, ed. by Christoph Jürgensen, Wolfgang Lukas and Michael Scheffel (Stuttgart and Weimar: Metzler, 2014), pp. 87–92

Denneler, Iris, *Von Namen und Dingen: Erkundungen zur Rolle des Ich in der Literatur am Beispiel von Ingeborg Bachmann, Peter Bichsel, Max Frisch, Gottfried Keller, Heinrich von Kleist, Arthur Schnitzler, Frank Wedekind, Vladimir Nabokov und W.G. Sebald* (Würzburg: Königshausen & Neumann, 2001)

Derré, Françoise, 'Schnitzler und Frankreich', *Modern Austrian Literature*, 19 (1986), 27–48

Derrida, Jacques, *Spectres de Marx: l'état de la dette, le travail du deuil et la nouvelle Internationale* (Paris: Galilée, 1993)

— 'Archive Fever: A Freudian Impression', trans. by Eric Prenowitz, *Diacritics*, 25.2 (1995), 9–63; orig.: *Mal d'archive: une impression freudienne* (Paris: Galilée, 1995)

Dirscherl, Margit, 'England', in *Schnitzler-Handbuch. Leben - Werk - Wirkung*, ed. by Christoph Jürgensen, Wolfgang Lukas and Michael Scheffel (Stuttgart and Weimar: Metzler, 2014), pp. 369–71

D'Monté, Rebecca, 'April de Angelis', in *Methuen Drama Guide to Contemporary British Playwrights*, ed. by Martin Middeke, Peter Paul Schnierer and Aleks Sierz (London: Methuen Drama, 2011), pp. 123–43

Doppler, Alfred, 'Die Frauengestalten in Arthur Schnitzlers Schauspiel "Der einsame Weg" und in der Tragikomödie "Das weite Land"', in *Arthur Schnitzler im zwanzigsten Jahrhundert*, ed. by Konstanze Fliedl (Vienna: Picus, 2003), pp. 92–104

Eltis, Sos, 'The Court Theatre', in *George Bernard Shaw in Context*, ed. by Brad Kent (Cambridge: Cambridge University Press, 2015), pp. 68–75

Evans, Richard J., 'A New Vision of Germany', *The New York Review of Books*, 14 January 2016, https://www.nybooks.com/articles/2016/01/14/new-vision-of-germany/ [accessed 5 February 2016]

Fernández-Capparrós Turina, Ana, '"A swirling, brilliant, cloudy mass of blues": David Hare's Adaptation of Arthur Schnitzler's *La Ronde*', in *Adaptations, Versions and Perversions in Modern British Drama*, ed. by Iganacio Ramos Gay (Newcastle: Cambridge Scholars, 2013), pp. 57–70

Field, Frank, *The Last Days of Mankind: Karl Kraus and his Vienna* (London: MacMillan, 1967)

Fischer, Beatrice, and Matilde Nisbeth Jensen (eds), *Translation and the Reconfiguration of Power Relations. Revisiting Role and Context of Translation and Interpreting* (Münster: Lit, 2012)

Fliedl, Konstanze, 'Love's Labour's Lost: Translations of Schnitzler's Reigen', in *Theatre and Performance in Austria. From Mozart to Jelinek*, ed. by Ritchie Robertson and Edward Timms (= *Austrian Studies*, 4 (1993)), pp. 61–72

— *Arthur Schnitzler: Poetik der Erinnerung* (Vienna: Böhlau, 1997)

— *Arthur Schnitzler* (Stuttgart: Reclam, 2005)

— 'Arthur Schnitzler und Italien', in *Ferne Heimat - Nahe Fremde. Bei Dichtern und Nachdenkern*, ed. by Eduard Beutner und Karlheinz Rossbacher (Würzburg: Königshausen & Neumann, 2008), pp. 132–47

Flood, John L., 'John G. Robertson', in *Oxford Dictionary of National Biography*, 61 vols (Oxford: Oxford University Press, 2004), XLVII: *Rippon–Rowe*, pp. 247–48

Foss, Rachel, 'Collecting Translators' Papers', *In Other Words*, 38 (2011), 30–32

Foucault, Michel, *The Archaeology of Knowledge*, trans. by A. M. Sheridan Smith (London & New York: Routledge Classics, 2002); orig.: *L'archéologie du savoir* (Paris: Gallimard, 1969)

— 'What Is an Author?', in *Language, Counter-Memory, Practice*, ed. by Donald F. Bouchard, trans. by Donald E. Bouchard and Sherry Simon (Oxford: Blackwell, 1977), pp. 113–38; orig.: 'Qu'est-ce qu'un auteur?', *Bulletin de la Société française de philosophie*, 3 (1969), 73–104

Friedrich, Vivien, '*Liebelei. Schauspiel in drei Akten* (1895)', in *Schnitzler-Handbuch. Leben – Werk – Wirkung*, ed. by Christoph Jürgensen, Wolfgang Lukas and Michael Scheffel (Stuttgart and Weimar: Metzler, 2014), pp. 60–64

Gabler, Hans Walter, 'Note on the Second Impression', in James Joyce, *Ulysses: A Critical and Synoptic Edition*, ed. by Hans Walter Gabler, Wolfhard Steppe and Claus Melchior (New York: Garland, 1986), pp. vii–ix

Gay, Frances, and Janet Bray, 'The Mind as a Theatre: Radio Drama since 1971', *New Theatre Quarterly*, 1 (1985), 292–300

Gay, Peter, *Schnitzler's Century: The Making of Middle-Class Culture, 1815–1914* (London: Norton, 2002)

Genette, Gérard, *Paratexts: Thresholds of Interpretation*, trans. by Jane E. Lewin (Cambridge: Cambridge University Press, 1997); orig.: *Seuils* (Paris: Seuil, 1987)

Gentzler, Edwin, 'Translation, Poststructuralism, and Power', in *Translation and Power*, ed. by Maria Tymoczko and Edwin Gentzler (Amherst, MA and Boston, MA: University of Massachusetts Press, 2002), pp. 195–218

Gentzler, Edwin, and Maria Tymoczko, 'Introduction', in *Translation and Power*, ed. by Maria Tymoczko and Edwin Gentzler (Amherst, MA and Boston, MA: University of Massachusetts Press, 2002), pp. xi–xxviii

— (eds), *Translation and Power* (Amherst, MA and Boston, MA: University of Massachusetts Press, 2002)

Gillman, Abigail, '"Ich suche ein Asyl für meine Vergangenheit". Schnitzler's Poetics of Memory', in *Arthur Schnitzler: Zeitgenossenschaften / Contemporaneities*, ed. by Ian Foster and Florian Krobb (Bern: Lang, 2002), pp. 141–56

Glancey, Jonathan, 'Townscape and the AR: Humane Urbanism and the 20th Century', *The Architectural Review*, 7 June 2013, http://www.architectural-review.com/rethink/viewpoints/townscape-and-the-ar-humane-urbanism-in-the-20th-century/8648215.fullarticle [accessed 10 December 2015]

Göbels, Bettina, 'The German Classics on the British Stage' (unpublished PhD thesis, University of Cambridge, 2008)

Gomersall, Meg, 'Fanny Hertz', in *Oxford Dictionary of National Biography*, 61 vols (Oxford: Oxford University Press, 2004), XXVI: *Haycock–Hichens*, pp. 843–44

Goodwin, John (ed.), *Peter Hall's Diaries: The Story of a Dramatic Battle* (London: Hamish Hamilton, 1983)

Grimstad, Kari, 'The Institution of Marriage in Schnitzler's *Komtesse Mizzi oder der Familientage* and *Das weite Land*', *Modern Austrian Literature*, 25 (1992), 141–56

Guppy, Shusha, 'Tom Stoppard: The Art of Theater VII', in *Tom Stoppard in Conversation*, ed. by Paul Delaney (Ann Arbor, MI: University of Michigan Press, 1995), pp. 177–92; first publ. *Paris Review*, 109 (Winter 1988), 26–51

Gussow, Mel, 'Stoppard's Intellectual Cartwheels Now With Music', in *Tom Stoppard in Conversation*, ed. by Paul Delaney (Ann Arbor, MI: University of Michigan Press, 1995), pp. 129–34; first publ. *New York Times*, 29 July 1979, sec. 2, pp. 1 and 22

Gutt, Barbara, *Emanzipation bei Arthur Schnitzler* (Berlin: Spiess, 1978)

Hand, Richard J., 'Radio Adaptation', in *The Oxford Handbook of Adaptation Studies*, ed. by Thomas Leitch (Oxford: Oxford University Press, 2017), pp. 340–55

Hannum, Hunter G., '"Killing Time": Aspects of Schnitzler's "Reigen"', *Germanic Review*, 37 (1962), 190–207

Hardin, Nancy Shields, 'An Interview with Tom Stoppard', *Contemporary Literature*, 22 (1981), 153–66

Hayles, N. Katherine, 'Translating Media: Why We Should Rethink Textuality', *The Yale Journal of Criticism*, 16 (2003), 263–90

Heilborn, Ernst, 'Germany', *Athenaeum*, 6 July 1901, pp. 16–19; 5 July 1902, pp. 13–18

Hemecker, Wilhelm, and David Österle, '"... so grundfalsch war alles Weitere". Zur Geschichte des Nachlasses von Arthur Schnitzler', *Jahrbuch der deutschen Schillergesellschaft*, 58 (2018), 3–40

Heresch, Elisabeth, *Schnitzler und Russland. Aufnahme – Wirkung – Kritik* (Vienna: Braumüller, 1982)

Hermans, Theo, 'Metaphor and Image in the Discourse on Translation: A Historical Survey', in *Übersetzung. Translation. Traduction. Ein internationales Handbuch zur Übersetzungsforschung. An International Encyclopedia of Translation Studies. Encyclopédie Internationale de la recherche sur la traduction*, ed. by Harald Kittel and others, 3 vols (Berlin; New York: de Gruyter, 2004), I, 118–28

— (ed.), *The Manipulation of Literature: Studies in Literary Translation* (London: Croom Helm, 1985)

Hesse, Beatrix, 'Rediscovered Country – Tom Stoppard's Austrian Plays', in *Austria and Austrians: Images in World Literature*, ed. by Wolfgang Görtschacher and Holger Klein (Tübingen: Stauffenberg, 2003), pp. 171–82

Hetzel, Florence, 'The Reception of Arthur Schnitzler on the French Stage: Contemporary Adaptations of "Reigen"', *Austrian Studies*, 13 (2005), 191–210

'History of the BBC: The Radio Times', https://www.bbc.co.uk/historyofthebbc/research/general/radio-times [accessed 17 July 2018]

Howe, Susan, *Spontaneous Particulars: The Telepathy of Archives* (New York: Christine Burgin/New Directions, 2014)

Hutcheon, Linda, *A Theory of Adaptation*, 2nd edn, with an epilogue by Siobhan O'Flynn (London & New York: Routledge, 2012 [2006])

Inghilleri, Moira, 'The Sociology of Bourdieu and the Construction of the "Object" in Translation and Interpreting Studies', *The Translator: Studies in Intercultural Communication*, 11 (2005), 125–45

'Interview: Max Gill, La Ronde', *Theatre Things* (14 January 2017), https://theblogoftheatrethings.com/2017/01/14/interview-max-gill-la-ronde/ [accessed 15 November 2018]

Jakobson, Roman, 'On Linguistic Aspects of Translation', in *The Translation Studies Reader*, ed. by Lawrence Venuti, 3rd edn (Abingdon: Routledge, 2012), pp. 126–31

James, Clive, 'Count Zero Splits the Infinite: Tom Stoppard's Plays', *Encounter*, 45.5 (November 1975), 68–75

Janz, Rolf-Peter, and Klaus Laermann, *Arthur Schnitzler. Zur Diagnose des Wiener Bürgertums im Fin de Siècle* (Stuttgart: Metzler, 1977)

Jenkins, Anthony, *The Theatre of Tom Stoppard* (Cambridge: Cambridge University Press, 1989)

Johnston, David, 'Historical Theatre: The Task of the Translator', *Trans*, 13 (2009), 57–70

— 'Sister Act: Reflection, Refraction, and Performance in the Translation of *La Dama Boba*', *Bulletin of the Comediantes*, 67 (2015), 79–98

Johnston, John, *The Lord Chamberlain's Blue Pencil* (London: Hodder & Stoughton, 1990)

Johnston, William, *The Austrian Mind: An Intellectual and Social History, 1848–1938* (Berkeley, CA and Los Angeles, CA: University of California Press, 1972)

Jolles, Michael A., Hilary L. Rubinstein and William D. Rubinstein (eds), *The Palgrave Dictionary of Anglo-Jewish History* (Basingstoke: Macmillan, 2011)

Jürgensen, Christoph, Wolfgang Lukas and Michael Scheffel (eds), *Schnitzler-Handbuch. Leben – Werk – Wirkung* (Stuttgart and Weimar: Metzler, 2014)

Kelly, Katherine E., 'Introduction: Tom Stoppard in Transformation', in *The Cambridge Companion to Tom Stoppard*, ed. by Katherine E. Kelly (Cambridge: Cambridge University Press, 2006), pp. 10–22

Kennedy, Dennis, *Granville Barker and the Dream of the Theatre* (Cambridge: Cambridge University Press, 1985)

Kenney, Joseph M., 'The Playboy's Progress: Schnitzler's Ordering of Scenes in *Anatol*', *Modern Austrian Literature*, 27 (1994), 1–24

Kierkegaard, Søren, *A Kierkegaard Anthology*, ed. by Robert Bretall (Princeton, NJ: Princeton University Press, 1946)

King, Martina, 'Anarchist and Aphrodite: On the Literary History of Germs', in *Contagionism and Contagious Diseases: Medicine and Literature 1880–1933*, ed. by Martina King and Thomas Rütten (Berlin: de Gruyter, 2013), pp. 101–29

Koebner, Thomas, *Arthur Schnitzler: Reigen: Erläuterungen und Dokumente* (Stuttgart: Reclam, 2012)

Kolkenbrock, Marie, 'Gothic Infections: Arthur Schnitzler and the Haunted Culture of Modernism', *Modern Language Review*, 113 (2018), 147–67

Kosofsky Sedgwick, Eve, *Between Men: English Literature and Male Homosocial Desire* (New York: Columbia University Press, 1992)

Krebs, Katja, 'Anticipating Blue Lines: Translational Choices as Sites of (Self)-Censorship', in *Modes of Censorship and Translation: National Contexts and Diverse Media*, ed. by Francesca Billiani (Manchester: St Jerome, 2007), pp. 167–86

— *Cultural Dissemination and Translational Communities: German Drama in English Translation, 1900–1914* (Manchester: St Jerome, 2007)

— 'Theatre, Translation and the Formation of a Field of Cultural Production', in *Betwixt and Between: Place and Cultural Translation*, ed. by Stephen Kelly and David Johnston (Newcastle: Cambridge Scholars, 2007), pp. 69–82

— 'A Portrait of a European Cultural Exchange: The Deutsches Theater in London at the Turn of the Twentieth Century', *Angermion*, 5 (2012), 119–34

— 'Translation and Adaptation – Two Sides of an Ideological Coin', in *Translation, Adaptation and Transformation*, ed. by Lawrence Raw (London & New York: Bloomsbury, 2012), pp. 42–53

Kühnelt, Harro H., 'Harley Granville-Barker und Arthur Schnitzlers "Anatol"', in *Studien zur Literatur des 19. und 20. Jahrhunderts in Österreich. Festschrift fürAlfred Doppler zum 60. Geburtstag*, ed. by Johann Holzner, Michael

Klein and Wolfgang Wiesmüller (Innsbruck: Institut für Germanistik der Universität Innsbruck, 1981), pp. 69–77

Lacher, Rolf-Peter, *'Der Mensch ist eine Bestie': Anna Heeger, Maria Chlum, Maria Reinhard und Arthur Schnitzler* (Würzburg: Königshausen & Neumann, 2014)

Laera, Margherita, 'Theatre Translation as Collaboration: Aleks Sierz, Martin Crimp, Nathalie Abrahami, Colin Teevan, Zoë Svendsen and Michael Walton Discuss Translation for the Stage', *Contemporary Theatre Review*, 21 (2011), 213–25

— 'Introduction', in *Theatre and Adaptation: Return, Rewrite, Repeat*, ed. by Margherita Laera (London and New York: Bloomsbury, 2014), pp. 1–18

Landy, Joshua, 'The Most Overrated Article of All Time?', *Philosophy and Literature*, 41 (2017), 465–70

Lăzărescu, Mariana Virginia, 'Zur Rezeption Schnitzlers in Rumänien. Schnitzlers Beziehungen zur rumänischen Literatur', in *Arthur Schnitzler: Zeitgenossenschaften / Contemporaneities*, ed. by Ian Foster and Florian Krobb (Bern: Lang, 2002), pp. 43–53

Leask, Margaret, *Lena Ashwell: Actress, Patriot, Pioneer* (Hatfield: University of Hertfordshire Press, 2012)

Lee, Hermione, *Tom Stoppard: A Life* (London: Faber & Faber, 2020)

Leeds, Ryan, 'Clever and Eclectic: An Interview with Playwright Joe DiPietro', *Manhatten Digest*, 16 January 2016, https://www.manhattandigest.com/2016/01/16/clever-and-eclectic-an-interview-with-playwright-joe-dipietro/ [accessed 14 July 2018]

Lefevere, André, *Translation, Rewriting and the Manipulation of Literary Fame* (London & New York: Routledge, 1992)

Le Rider, Jacques, 'Warum *Professor Bernhardi* von der Wiener Zensur verboten wurde', in *Textschicksale. Das Werk Arthur Schnitzlers im Kontext der Moderne*, ed. by Wolfgang Lukas and Michael Scheffel (Berlin and Boston, MA: de Gruyter, 2017), pp. 231–50

Linden, Sonja, 'Roundelay by Sonja Linden: Note from the Author', *Visible Theatre Ensemble*, http://www.visible.org.uk/2017/05/22/roundelay-by-sonja-linden/ [accessed 30 July 2018]

Liptzin, Sol, 'The Genesis of Schnitzler's *Das Weite Land*', *PMLA*, 46 (1931), 860–66

London Theatre Record, 10 vols (London: Herbert, 1981–1990), II (1982)

Lorenz, Dagmar C. G., 'Introduction', in *A Companion to the Works of Arthur Schnitzler*, ed. by Dagmar C. G. Lorenz (Rochester, NY: Camden House, 2003), pp. 1–24

Lukas, Wolfgang, and others, 'Editorischer Bericht', in *Arthur Schnitzler digital. Historisch-kritische Edition (Werke 1905–1931)* (2018–), https://www.schnitzler-edition.net/edb [accessed 23.6.21]

MacCarthy, Desmond, *The Court Theatre, 1904–1907: A Commentary and Criticism* (London: Bullen, 1907)

MacDonald, Jan, 'Shaw and the Court Theatre', in *The Cambridge Companion to George Bernard Shaw*, ed. by Christopher Innes (Cambridge: Cambridge University Press, 1998), pp. 261–82

Mach, Ernst, *Die Analyse der Empfindungen und das Verhältnis des Physischen zum Psychischen*, 9th edn (Jena: Fischer, 1922 [1886])

Maier, Julia-Stefanie, 'Cannibalizing Cultures: Schnitzler in London, Stoppard in Vienna. The Influence of Socio-Cultural, Literary, and Power-Related Norms on Drama Translation' (unpublished Master's thesis, University of Vienna, 2010)

Marcuse, Ludwig, *Obscene: The History of an Indignation*, trans. by Karen Gershon (London: Macgibbon & Kee, 1965); orig.: *Obszön: Geschichte einer Entrüstung* (Munich: List, 1962)

Marowitz, Charles, *Burnt Bridges* (London: Hodder & Stoughton, 1990)

Mateo, Marta, 'Translation Strategies and the Reception of Drama Performances: A Mutual Influence', in *Translation as Intercultural Communication*, ed. by Mary Snell-Hornby, Zuzana Jettmarová and Klaus Kaindl (Amsterdam and Philadelphia, PA: John Benjamins, 1995), pp. 99–110

May, Arthur J., *Vienna in the Age of Franz Joseph* (Norman, OK: University of Oklahoma Press, 1966)

Mazer, Cary M., 'New Theatres for a New Drama', in *The Cambridge Companion to Victorian and Edwardian Theatre*, ed. by Kerry Powell (Cambridge: Cambridge University Press, 2004), pp. 207–21

Meyer, Kinereth, '"It Is Written": Tom Stoppard and the Drama of the Intertext', *Comparative Drama*, 22 (1989), 105–22

Minic, Danica, 'What Makes an Issue a Woman's Hour Issue? The Politics of Recognition and Media Coverage of Women's Issues and Perspectives', *Feminist Media Studies*, 8 (2008), 301–15

Munday, Jeremy, 'Using Primary Sources to Produce a Microhistory of Translation and Translators: Theoretical and Methodological Concerns', *The Translator*, 20 (2014), 64–80

Neumann, Annja, 'Entstehungsgeschichte von "Zum großen Wurstel"', in Arthur Schnitzler, *Marionetten*, ed. by Annja Neumann and others, in *Arthur Schnitzler digital. Historisch-kritische Edition (Werke 1905–1931)*

(2018–), <https://www.schnitzler-edition.net/entstehungsgeschichtetext/10118 [accessed 23.6.21]

Neuse, Erna, 'Die Funktion von Motiven und stereotypen Wendungen in Schntizlers *Reigen*', *Monatshefte*, 64 (1972), 359–70

Nicholson, Steve, 'Charles Marowitz', in *Oxford Dictionary of National Biography*, https://doi.org/10.1093/odnb/9780198614128.013.108751 [accessed 7 February 2019]

North, John S. (ed.), 'Cosmopolis', *Waterloo Directory of English Newspapers and Periodicals 1800–1900*, 10 vols (Waterloo: North Waterloo Academic Press, 1997), II: *C-D*, p. 1274

Offermanns, Ernst L., 'Materialien zum Verständnis der Texte', in Arthur Schnitzler, *Anatol: Anatol-Zyklus, Anatols Größenwahn, Das Abenteuer seines Lebens*, ed. by Ernst L. Offermanns, Komedia, 6 (Berlin: de Gruyter, 1964)

— *Arthur Schnitzler. Das Komödienwerk als Kritik des Impressionismus* (Munich: Fink, 1973)

Orme, Michael, *J. T. Grein: The Story of a Pioneer 1862–1935* (London: Murray, 1936)

Otis, Laura, 'The Language of Infection: Disease and Identity in Schnitzler's "Reigen"', *The Germanic Review*, 70 (1995), 65–75

— *Membranes: Metaphors of Invasion in Nineteenth-Century Literature, Science, and Politics* (Baltimore, MD: Johns Hopkins Press, 1999)

Ozawa, Yukio, *Japanisches bei Arthur Schnitzler. Japanische Einflüsse auf Schnitzler und die Rezeption Schnitzlers in Japan* (Frankfurt a. M.: Lang, 1995)

Pearl, Monica B., *AIDS Literature and Gay Identity: The Literature of Loss* (New York & London: Routledge, 2012)

Perteghella, Manuela, 'Adaptation: "Bastard Child" or Critique? Putting Terminology Centre Stage', *Journal of Romance Studies*, 8.3 (2008), 51–65

Pfoser, Alfred, 'Wer hat Angst vor Arthur Schnitzler? Der Wiener *Reigen*-Skandal 1921 - ein unerledigtes Drama', *Die Presse. Literaricum* (2/3 May 1981), p. v

Pfoser, Alfred, Kristina Pfoser-Schewig and Gerhard Renner (eds), *Schnitzlers 'Reigen'. Zehn Dialoge und ihre Skandalgeschichte. Analysen und Dokumente*, 2 vols (Frankfurt a. M.: Fischer, 1993)

Pietrzak-Franger, Monika, *Syphilis in Victorian Literature and Culture: Medicine, Knowledge and the Spectacle of Victorian Invisibility* (Basingstoke and New York: Palgrave Macmillan, 2017)

Pinkert, Ernst-Ullrich, 'Skandinavien', in *Schnitzler-Handbuch. Leben – Werk – Wirkung*, ed. by Christoph Jürgensen, Wolfgang Lukas and Michael Scheffel (Stuttgart and Weimar: Metzler, 2014), pp. 372–74

Plant, Richard, 'Notes on Arthur Schnitzler's Literary Technique', *The Germanic Review*, 25 (1950), 13–25

Pokorn, Nike K., 'In Defence of Fuzziness', in *The Metalanguage of Translation*, ed. by Luc van Doorslaer and Yves Gambier (Amsterdam: Benjamins, 2009), pp. 135–44

Polt-Heinzl, Evelyne, 'Der Genia Effekt oder Schnitzlers Umgang mit den strukturellen Lücken im Verhältnis der Geschlechter', *Internationales Archiv für Sozialgeschichte der deutschen Literatur*, 33 (2008), 101–12

Postlewait, Thomas, 'The London Stage, 1895–1918', in *The Cambridge History of British Theatre*, ed. by Joseph Donohue and others, 3 vols (Cambridge: Cambridge University Press, 2004), III: *Since 1895*, ed. by Baz Kershaw, pp. 34–59

Prescott, Paul, 'Inheriting the Globe: The Reception of Shakespearean Space and Audience in Contemporary Reviewing', in *A Companion to Shakespeare and Performance*, ed. by Barbara Hodgdon and W. B. Worthen (Oxford: Blackwell, 2005), pp. 359–75

Reik, Theodor, *Arthur Schnitzler als Psycholog* (Minden: Bruns, 1913)

Report from the Joint Select Committee of the House of Lords and the House of Commons on the Stage Plays (Censorship) (London: H.M. Stationery Office, 1909)

Richards, Jeffrey, 'Henry Irving: The Actor-Manager as Auteur', *Nineteenth Century Theatre and Film*, 32 (2005), 20–35

Ritzheimer, Kara L., *'Trash', Censorship and National Identity in Early Twentieth-Century Germany* (Cambridge: Cambridge University Press, 2016)

Robertson, John G., 'Current German Literature', *Cosmopolis* (August 1896), pp. 357–73

Robertson, Ritchie, 'Modernism and the Self 1890–1924', in *Philosophy and German Literature, 1700–1990*, ed. by Nicholas Saul (Cambridge, Cambridge University Press, 2002), pp. 150–96

Robinson, Douglas, *Translation and Empire: Postcolonial Theories Explained* (Manchester: St Jerome, 1997)

Roche, Mark W., 'Schnitzler's "Anatol" as a Philosophical Comedy', *Modern Austrian Literature*, 22.3 (1989), 51–63

Roe, Ian F., 'The Comedy of Schnitzler's "Reigen"', *Modern Language Review*, 89 (1994), 674–88

Roelofs, Hans, *'Man weiss eigentlich wenig von einander'. Arthur Schnitzler und die Niederlande, 1895–1940* (Amsterdam: Rodopi, 1989)

Rüger, Jan, 'Revisiting the Anglo-German Antagonism', *The Journal of Modern History*, 83 (2011), 579–617

Rühle, Günther, 'Der ewige Reigen', in Arthur Schnitzler, *Reigen / Liebelei* (Frankfurt a. M.: Fischer, 1996), pp. 7–21

Ryan, Judith, *The Vanishing Subject: Early Psychology and Literary Modernism* (Chicago, IL and London: University of Chicago Press, 1991)

Sabler, Wolfgang, 'Heinrich Schnitzler, passeur entre les cultures et les héritages', *Études Germaniques*, 252 (2008), 737–48

Said, Edward, *Orientalism* (New York: Vintage Books, 1979)

Sanders, Julie, *Adaptation and Appropriation* (London & New York: Routledge, 2006)

Schiffer, Helga, 'Arthur Schnitzlers *Reigen*', *Text & Kontext*, 11 (1983), 7–34

Schinnerer, Otto P., 'The History of Schnitzler's Reigen', *PMLA*, 46 (1931), 839–59

Schippers, J. G., 'Stoppard's Nestroy, Schnitzler's Stoppard or Humpty Dumpty im Wiener Wald', *Linguistics and the Study of Literature*, 53 (1986), 245–67

Schlein, Rena R., 'Das Duellmotiv in Schnitzlers Dramen "Ritterlichkeit," "Das weite Land" und "Das Wort"', *Modern Austrian Literature*, 8 (1975), 222–35

Schneider, Gerd K., *Die Rezeption von Arthur Schnitzlers Reigen. 1897–1994. Text, Aufführungen, Verfilmungen. Pressespiegel und andere zeitgenössische Kommentare* (Riverside, CA: Ariadne Press, 1995)

— 'Zur künstlerischen Umsetzung von Arthur Schnitzlers REIGEN in Europa und den Vereinigten Staaten', in *Internet-Zeitschrift für Kulturwissenschaften*, 3 (March 1998), http://www.inst.at/trans/3Nr/schneider.htm [accessed 14 November 2018]

Schnitzler, Henry, 'Some Remarks on Austrian Literature', *Books Abroad*, 17 (1943), 215–21

— '"Gay Vienna" - Myth and Reality', *Journal of the History of Ideas*, 15 (1954), 94–118

Schnitzler, Olga, *Spiegelbild der Freundschaft* (Salzburg: Residenz-Verlag, 1962)

Schober, Johannes, 'Zensur. Eine aktuelle Betrachtung', *Neue Freie Presse*, 4 April 1926, 10–11

Schonlau, Anja, *Syphilis in der Literatur. Über Ästhetik, Moral, Genie und Medizin* (Würzburg: Königshausen & Neumann, 2005)

Schorske, Carl E., *Fin-de-Siècle Vienna: Politics and Culture* (London: Weidenfeld and Nicholson, 1980)

Schrumpf, Beatrice, 'The Perception of Arthur Schnitzler in the United States' (unpublished Master's thesis, Columbia University, 1931)

Schwartz, Joan M., and Terry Cook, 'Archives, Records, and Power: The Making of Modern Memory', *Archival Science*, 2 (2002), 1–19

Seville, Catherine, *The Internationalisation of Copyright Law: Books, Buccaneers and the Black Flag in the Nineteenth Century* (Cambridge: Cambridge University Press, 2006)

Shingler, Martin, and Cindy Wieringa, *On Air: Methods and Meanings of Radio* (London: Arnold, 1998)

Shuttleworth, Mark, *Studying Scientific Metaphor in Translation* (New York & London: Routledge, 2017)

Sichel, Walter, 'The "Time-Spirit" in German Literature', *Quarterly Review* (October 1903), 404–35

Sierz, Aleks, *In-Yer-Face Theatre: British Drama Today* (London: Faber & Faber, 2001)

Simon, Sherry, 'Germaine de Staël and Gayatri Spivak: Culture Brokers', in *Translation and Power*, ed. by Maria Tymoczko and Edwin Gentzler (Amherst, MA and Boston, MA: University of Massachusetts Press, 2002), pp. 122–40

Somers, Margaret R., and Gloria D. Gibson, 'Reclaiming the Epistemological "Other": Narrative and the Social Constitution of Identity', in *Social Theory and the Politics of Identity*, ed. by Craig Calhoun (Oxford and Cambridge, MA: Blackwell, 1994), pp. 37–99

Sontag, Susan, *Illness as Metaphor and AIDS and its Metaphors* (London: Penguin Classics, 2002 [1979/1989])

Spencer, Catherine, 'Translating Schnitzler for the Stage: Losing *Liebelei*?', in *Arthur Schnitzler: Zeitgenossenschaften / Contemporaneities*, ed. by Ian Foster and Florian Krobb (Bern: Lang, 2002), pp. 273–90

Spiel, Hilde, 'Die geselligen Eigenbrötler', in *Wien – Spektrum einer Stadt*, ed. by Hilde Spiel (Munich: Biederstein, 1971), pp. 110–23

Spoo, Robert, *Modernism and the Law* (London: Bloomsbury, 2018)

Stark, Susanne, *'Behind Inverted Commas': Translation and Anglo-German Cultural Relations in the Nineteenth Century* (Clevedon: Multilingual Matters, 1999)

Stern, Guy, 'From Austria to America via London: Tom Stoppard's Adaptations of Nestroy and Schnitzler', in *The Fortunes of German Writers in America: Studies in Literary Reception*, ed. by Wolfgang Elfe, James Hardin and Gunther Holst (Columbia, SC: University of South Carolina Press, 1992), pp. 167–83

Stern, J. P., 'Anyone for Tennis, Anyone for Death? The Schnitzler/Stoppard "Undiscovered Country"', *Encounter*, 53/54 (October 1979), 26–31

Stewart, Janet, 'Raum und Raumwahrnehmung in den dramatischen Werken Schnitzlers', in *Arthur Schnitzler im zwanzigsten Jahrhundert*, ed. by Konstanze Fliedl (Vienna: Picus, 2003), pp. 105–19

Stoppard, Tom, 'Introduction', in *Dalliance and Undiscovered Country* (London: Faber & Faber, 1986), pp. ix–x

— 'The Event and the Text', from The Whidden Lectures, McMaster University in Hamilton, Ontario, 24 October 1988, transcribed and edited by Doreen DelVecchio for *Ta Panta* (McMaster University Faculty Association), 6.1 (1988), in *Tom Stoppard in Conversation*, ed. by Paul Delaney (Ann Arbor, MI: University of Michigan Press, 1995), pp. 199–211

Sullivan, Hannah, *The Work of Revision* (Cambridge, MA and London: Harvard University Press, 2013)

Swales, Martin, *Arthur Schnitzler: A Critical Study* (Oxford: Clarendon Press, 1971)

— 'Schnitzler's Tragi-comedy: A Reading of "Das weite Land"', *Modern Austrian Literature*, 10 (1977), 233–45

Thomé, Horst, 'Kernlosigkeit und Pose. Zur Rekonstruktion von Schnitzlers Psychologie', in *Fin de Siécle. Zu Naturwissenschaft und Literatur der Jahrhundertwende im deutsch-skandinavischen Kontext / Vorträge des Kolloquiums am 3. und 4. Mai 1984*, ed. by Klaus Bohnen, Uffe Hansen and Friedrich Schmöe, *Text & Kontext*, Sonderreihe, 20 (Copenhagen/Munich: Fink, 1984), pp. 62–87

— 'Vorwort. Arthur Schnitzlers Anfänge und die Grundlagenkrise der Medizin. Walter Müller-Seidel zum siebzigsten Geburtstag', in Arthur Schnitzler, *Medizinische Schriften*, ed. by Horst Thomé (Vienna: Zsolnay, 1988), pp. 11–59

Thompson, Bruce, *Schnitzler's Vienna: Image of a Society* (New York & London: Routledge, 1990)

Thum, Reinhard H., 'Symbol, Motif and Leitmotif in Fontane's Effi Briest', *The Germanic Review*, 54 (1979), 115–24

Timms, Edward, *Karl Kraus: Apocalyptic Satirist*, 2 vols (New Haven, CT and London: Yale University Press, 1986–2005), II: *The Post-War Crisis and the Rise of the Swastika* (2005)

Toury, Gideon, *Descriptive Translation Studies – and Beyond* (Amsterdam & Philadelphia, PA: Benjamins, 1995)

Treaty of St. Germain-en-Laye (1919), in *The Treaties of Peace, 1919–1923*, 2 vols (New York: Carnegie Endowment for International Peace, 1924), I: *Containing the Treaty of Versailles, the Treaty of St. Germain-en-Laye and the Treaty of Trianon*, pp. 267–456

Trebitsch, Siegfried, *Chronik eines Lebens* (Zurich: Artemis, 1951)

Trewin, J. C., *The Edwardian Theatre* (Oxford: Blackwell, 1976)

Trussler, Simon, 'Charles Marowitz in London: Twenty-Five Years Hard: Marowitz in the Sixties', *New Theatre Quarterly*, 30 (2014), 203–06

Tymoczko, Maria, and Edwin Gentzler (eds), *Translation and Power* (Amherst, MA and Boston, MA: University of Massachusetts Press, 2002)

Tynan, Kenneth, 'Some Plays: A List Compiled for the National Theatre by Kenneth Tynan', https://www.nationaltheatre.org.uk/sites/default/files/kenneth-tynan_list-of-plays.pdf [accessed 16 January 2019]

Ubersfeld, Anne, *Reading Theatre*, trans. by Frank Collins (Toronto: University of Toronto Press, 1999); orig.: *Lire le théâtre* (Paris: Éditions sociales, 1977)

Urbach, Reinhard, 'Heinrich Schnitzler – 75 Jahre', *Modern Austrian Literature*, 10 (1977), 1–18

— 'Arthur Schnitzler. *Das weite Land.* Genia. Lesarten und Sichtweisen. Anmerkungen zu einer spekulativen Dramaturgie', in *Überschreitungen. Dialoge zwischen Literatur- und Theaterwissenschaft, Architektur und Bildender Kunst. Festschrift für Leonhard M. Fiedler zum 60. Geburtstage*, ed. by Jörg Sader and Anette Wörner (Würzburg: Königshausen und Neumann, 2002), pp. 127–37

— 'Schnitzlers Anfänge: Was Anatol wollen soll', *Internationales Archiv für Sozialgeschichte der deutschen Literatur*, 33 (2008), 113–54

Venn, John, *Biographical History of Gonville and Caius College 1349–1897*, 2 vols (Cambridge: Cambridge University Press, 1897–98), I (1898)

Venuti, Lawrence, *The Translator's Invisibility: A History of Translation*, 2nd edn (London and New York: Routledge, 2008 [1995])

— (ed.), *The Translation Studies Reader*, 3rd edn (London: Routledge, 2012 [2000])

Vermeer, Hans J., 'Skopos and Commission in Translational Action', in *The Translation Studies Reader*, ed. by Lawrence Venuti, 3rd edn (London: Routledge, 2012 [2000]), pp. 191–202

Vogel, Margot Elfving, *Schnitzler in Schweden. Zur Rezeption seiner Werke* (Uppsala and Stockholm: Almqvist & Wiksell International, 1979)

Walton, Sarah Luverne, '*Anatol* on the New York Stage', *Modern Austrian Literature*, 2.2 (1969), 30–44

Waterloo Directory of English Newspapers and Periodicals 1800–1900, 10 vols (Waterloo: North Waterloo Academic Press, 1997)

Wearing, J. P., *The London Stage 1900–1909: A Calendar of Productions, Performers and Personnel*, 6 vols, 2nd edn (Lanham, MD: Scarecrow Press, 2014 [1976])

— *The London Stage 1910–1919: A Calendar of Productions, Performers, and Personnel*, 2nd edn (Lanham, MD: Scarecrow Press, 2013 [1982])

— *The London Stage 1920–1929: A Calendar of Productions, Performers, and Personnel*, 2nd edn (Lanham, MD: Rowman & Littlefield, 2014 [1984])

Webber, Andrew J., 'Namens- oder Familienähnlichkeiten. Fallgeschichte und Falldrama bei Schnitzler und Freud', in *Textschicksale. Das Werk Arthur Schnitzlers im Kontext der Moderne*, ed. by Wolfgang Lukas and Michael Scheffel (Berlin and Boston, MA: de Gruyter, 2017), pp. 72–92

Weininger, Otto, *Geschlecht und Charakter* (Vienna and Leipzig: Wilhelm Braumüller, 1903)

Weiss, Samuel A. (ed.), *Bernard Shaw's Letters to Siegfried Trebitsch* (Stanford, CA: Stanford University Press, 1986)

Welsch, Wolfgang, 'Transculturality – the Puzzling Form of Cultures Today', in *Spaces of Culture: City, Nation World*, ed. by Mike Featherstone and Scott Lash (London: Sage, 1999), pp. 194–213

Williams, G. Valentine, *The World of Action* (London: Hamish Hamilton, 1938)

Windsor, Alan, 'Letters from Peter Behrens to P. Morton Shand, 1932–1938', *Architectural History*, 37 (1994), 165–87

Wisely, Andrew C., *Arthur Schnitzler and Twentieth-Century Criticism* (Rochester, NY: Camden House, 2004)

Woodfield, James, *English Theatre in Transition: 1881–1914* (London and Sydney: Croom Helm; Totowa, NJ: Barnes & Noble, 1984)

Woodsworth, Judith, 'Bernard Shaw On and In Translation', in *Translation, Translation*, ed. by Susan Petrelli (Amsterdam; New York: Rodopi, 2003), pp. 531–52

Wu, Xiaoqiao, 'Die Rezeption Arthur Schnitzlers in China', in *Textschicksale. Das Werk Arthur Schnitzlers im Kontext der Moderne*, ed. by Wolfgang Lukas and Michael Scheffel (Berlin and Boston, MA: de Gruyter, 2017), pp. 267–80

Yates, W. E., 'The Tendentious Reception of Professor Bernhardi: Documentation in Schnitzler's Collection of Press-Cuttings', in *Vienna 1900: From Altenberg to Wittgenstein*, ed. by Edward Timms and Ritchie Robertson (= *Austrian Studies*, 1 (1990)), pp. 108–25

— *Schnitzler, Hofmannsthal, and the Austrian Theatre* (New Haven, CT and London: Yale University Press, 1992)

— *Theatre in Vienna: A Critical History 1776–1995* (Cambridge: Cambridge University Press, 1996)

— 'Internationalization of European Theatre: French Influence in Vienna between 1830 and 1860', *Austrian Studies*, 13 (2005), 37–54

— 'Continuity and Discontinuity in Viennese Theatrical Life from the 1860s to the Turn of the Century', *Austrian Studies*, 16 (2008), 51–68

Zeifman, Hersh, 'The Comedy of Eros: Stoppard in Love', in *The Cambridge Companion to Tom Stoppard*, ed. by Katherine E. Kelly (Cambridge: Cambridge University Press, 2006), pp. 185–200

Zieger, Karl, *Arthur Schnitzler et la France, 1894–1938. Enquête sur une réception* (Villeneuve d'Ascq: Presses Universitaires du Septentrion, 2012)

Ziolkowski, Theodore, *Scandal on Stage: European Theater as Moral Trial* (Cambridge: Cambridge University Press, 2009)

Zojer, Heidi, *Kulturelle Dimensionen in der literarischen Übersetzung. Eine übersetzungstheoretische Untersuchung mit exemplarischer Analyse von Arthur Schnitzlers 'Reigen'* (Stuttgart: Hans-Dieter Heinz, 2000)

— 'Vienna-London-Belfast: Schnitzler's *Reigen* on the Translation Roundabout', *New Theatre Quarterly*, 25 (2009), 88–98

INDEX

CPSIA information can be obtained
at www.ICGtesting.com
Printed in the USA
JSHW041302290522
26078JS00001B/1

9 780854 572816